NEW ROMANTICISMS

THEORY / CULTURE

General Editors: Linda Hutcheon, Gary Leonard,
Janet Paterson, and Paul Perron

EDITED BY DAVID L. CLARK AND
DONALD C. GOELLNICHT

New Romanticisms:
Theory and Critical Practice

UNIVERSITY OF TORONTO PRESS
Toronto Buffalo London

© University of Toronto Press Incorporated 1994
Toronto Buffalo London

Printed in Canada

ISBN 0-8020-2890-X

Printed on acid-free paper

Canadian Cataloguing in Publication Data

Main entry under title:

New romanticisms : theory and critical practice

(Theory/culture)
Based on a conference held at McMaster University in Oct. 1990 under the auspices of the English Association's annual seminar.
Includes bibliographical references and index.
ISBN 0-8020-2890-X

1. English literature – 19th century – History and criticism – Congresses. 2. Romanticism – Great Britain – Congresses.
I. Clark, David L., 1955–   . II. Goellnicht, Donald C., 1953–
III. Series.

PR457.N48 1994   820.9'145'09034   C94-930890-0

For
Tracy Wynne
        D.L.C.

For my parents,
Elsie and John Goellnicht
                D.C.G.

Contents

ILLUSTRATIONS ix

ACKNOWLEDGMENTS xi

Introduction

DAVID L. CLARK AND DONALD C. GOELLNICHT
Discriminations: Romanticism in the Wake of Deconstruction 3

I Narrating the Subject

TILOTTAMA RAJAN
'The Web of Human Things': Narrative and Identity in *Alastor* 27

SHELLEY WALL
Baffled Narrative in *Julian and Maddalo* 52

II The World, the Text, the Reader

ALAN BEWELL
Keats's 'Realm of Flora' 71

DONALD C. GOELLNICHT
The Politics of Reading and Writing: Periodical Reviews of Keats's *Poems* (1817) 101

III The Scene of Displacement

J. DOUGLAS KNEALE
Symptom and Scene in Freud and Wordsworth 135

DAVID L. CLARK
Against Theological Technology: Blake's 'Equivocal Worlds' 164

IV Gender, Language, Power

IAN BALFOUR
Promises, Promises: Social and Other Contracts in the English Jacobins (Godwin/Inchbald) 225

JEAN WILSON
Romanticism's Real Women 251

Coda

ASHA VARADHARAJAN
Romanticism Unbound 275

NOTES ON CONTRIBUTORS 289

INDEX 293

Illustrations

1. *Glad Day, Albion Rose,* or *The Dance of Albion*, by William Blake. Colour-printed line engraving finished in pen and watercolour, c. 1794. Trustees of the British Museum   167

2. *'Europe,' Plate i; Frontispiece: The Ancient of Days*, by William Blake. Relief etching finished in colour-printing and watercolour, c. 1795. Lessing J. Rosenwald Collection, Rare Book and Special Collections Division, Library of Congress, Washington, D.C.   173

3. *When the Morning Stars Sang Together,* illustration to the Book of Job, no. 14, by William Blake. Line engraving, c. 1823–6. Tate Gallery, London / Art Resource, New York   191

4. *Behemoth and Leviathan,* illustration to the Book of Job, no. 15, by William Blake. Line engraving, c. 1823–6. Tate Gallery, London / Art Resource, New York   194

5. *When the Morning Stars Sang Together,* illustration to the Book of Job, no. 14, by William Blake. Pen and watercolour, c. 1805–6. Pierpont Morgan Library, New York. III, 45   202

Acknowledgments

A collaborative and pluralistic effort from its inception, the *New Romanticisms* project has been made possible only because of the keen support of numerous individuals and academic units at McMaster University and at several neighbouring universities. The origins of this book lie in a lively conference held at McMaster University in October 1990 under the auspices of the English Association's Annual Seminar. For their support of that conference, we are grateful to the Department of English (Brian John, Chair), the Office of the Vice-President, Academic (Art Heidebrecht, Provost), the Faculty of Humanities (David Gagan, then Dean), the School of Graduate Studies (Chauncey Wood, Dean), and the Women's Studies Programme (Joan Coldwell, Director). Many people helped organize and run the conference: we would especially like to thank Clover Nixon, Administrative Assistant, the Department of English, as well as Robert Alexander, Carolyn Brendon, Anne Garton, Douglas Gessell, Kathleen Hall, Tomo Hattori, Lorraine Kooistra, Edward Parkinson, Mark Rozahegy, and Tracy Wynne.

A general scarcity of money, familiar to all of us who work in the human sciences, made it necessary for us to seek creative funding solutions for the publication of this book, and we are very pleased to be able to express our appreciation here to those who generously helped us find them. First we wish to thank Marnie Spears, former Director of the McMaster Development Office, and Alexander McKay (Emeritus Professor) for their helpful advice. Publication of this book was made possible by the financial support of the McMaster University Patent and Intellectual Property Board (Mark R. McDermott, Chair). We are grateful to Ronald Childs, Vice-President (Research), who, in consultation with Evan Simpson, Dean of the Faculty of Humanities, and Emmi Morwald,

Director of the Arts Research Board, initially recommended our project to the Board. C. Barber Mueller (Emeritus Professor) and Jean Mueller each made generous bequests in support of the project, for which we are also grateful. At a crucial turning point, Alvin Lee, Emeritus Professor and former President of McMaster, took a personal interest in seeing the book completed. Because of his timely intervention, additional funding for the project was received from the following: the Offices of the Presidents of the University of Toronto (J.R.S. Prichard, President), the University of Western Ontario (K.G. Pederson, President), and York University (S. Mann, President), and the Office of the Principal of Queen's University (D.C. Smith, Principal). We are grateful to all of these offices and individuals for their financial support.

Two of the essays in this volume have been published elsewhere. We are grateful to the respective editors and publishers for their permission to reprint the following: Alan Bewell, 'Keats's "Realm of Flora,"' *Studies in Romanticism* 32 (1992): 71–99, copyright © by the Graduate School, Boston University; and Tilottama Rajan, '"The Web of Human Things": Narrative and Identity in *Alastor*,' from *The New Shelley: Later Twentieth-Century Views*, 67–80, ed. Kim Blank, copyright © 1992 Macmillan Press (U.K.) and St Martin's Press (U.S.).

For permission to reproduce five illustrations by William Blake, we are grateful to the following: Trustees of the British Museum, for *Glad Day*; Pierpont Morgan Library, New York, for *When the Morning Stars Sang Together*; National Gallery of Art (Lessing J. Rosenwald Collection), Washington, D.C., for *The Ancient of Days*; Tate Gallery, London, for *When the Morning Stars Sang Together* and *Behemoth and Leviathan*.

At University of Toronto Press, we would like to express our thanks to Linda Hutcheon and Paul Perron, General Editors of the Theory/Culture series, in which this book appears. It was Linda Hutcheon who generously invited us to submit the book for this series. We very much appreciate the detailed and critically precise assessments made by our anonymous readers, whose suggestions no doubt helped make this a better book. Warm thanks too go to our editors, Laura Macleod and Suzanne Rancourt, and to our copy-editor, Ken Lewis, who expertly shepherded this project into print.

Introduction

DAVID L. CLARK AND
DONALD C. GOELLNICHT

Discriminations: Romanticism in the Wake of Deconstruction

I

> Dangerous distinction between 'theoretical' and 'practical,' e.g., in the case of Kant, but also in the case of the ancients: – they act as if pure spirituality presented them with the problems of knowledge and metaphysics; – they act as if practice must be judged by its own measure, whatever the answer of theory might be.
>
> Friedrich Nietzsche, *The Will to Power*

About the notion of a plurality of 'Romantic*s*,' there is in fact nothing 'new.' Indeed, the argument that the term 'Romantic' names a multiplicity of conceptual positions, critical questions, and literary styles can be traced back to Arthur O. Lovejoy's largely polemical address to the History of Ideas Club at Johns Hopkins University in 1923, in which he argued 'that we should learn to use the word "romanticism" in the plural' and 'begin with a recognition of a *prima-facie* plurality of Romanticisms, of possibly quite distinct thought-complexes' (68). By insisting upon 'the discrimination of Romanticisms,' as he put it, Lovejoy urged a philosopher's exactness upon what was then an insufficiently and imprecisely theorized area of literary history. To say therefore that Lovejoy simply rescued Romanticism from the Victorian clichés and confused generalizations with which it had long-since become encumbered is probably not enough; it should also be pointed out that modern Romantic criticism emerged as such at the precise moment that 'Romanticism' was seen to be irreducibly complex, divided from itself. Moreover, in calling attention to the almost insurmountable difficulties facing modern readers attempting to fix the nature of their shifty subject, and in summoning these readers to ever stricter standards of intellectual precision, Lovejoy paradoxically also opened the door to the recognition, fundamental to the essays collected in this volume, that Romanticism does not exist apart from the discriminating practices that represent it, theorize it, and respond to it.

From the beginning Romanticism was understood to contain multitudes, even if subsequent characterizations of the period have powerfully suggested otherwise. Inasmuch as this volume has an organizing theoretical agenda, it is vigorously to return the terms of critical discussion to a renewed sense of that original difference, although admittedly in ways that Lovejoy probably could not have foreseen. In so doing, our contributors either implicitly or explicitly engage an intervening generation of Romantic critics whose work – though made possible by Lovejoy – signalled the waning of the 'history of ideas' criticism which he championed and which he had hoped to see used properly to discern Romanticism's multiple faces. When in 1949 René Wellek confidently announced that 'we can then go on speaking of the future of romanticism as one European movement' (205), he effectively registered the intellectual distance which criticism had put between itself and Lovejoy's insights, and accurately predicted the path that thinking about Romanticism would more or less take until the advent of the next French revolution – this one emanating from the Ecole Normale Supérieure.[1] At its deepest level, Lovejoy's work calls into question not only the usefulness of a totalizing term like 'Romanticism,' but also the efficacy of any systematic attempt to name a given moment in cultural and intellectual history through the unsparing suppression of its immanent differences. One of the ironies of the history of criticism, however, is that notwithstanding the troublesome implications of Lovejoy's work, Romantic literature and theory went on to form the dialectical ground for totalizing approaches which would have a broad impact on the critical scene precisely through their remarkable ability to sublate these differences into higher unities. As Tilottama Rajan has pointed out, these approaches included, primarily, 'the New Criticism, which developed its notions of ambiguity and paradox from a Coleridgean aesthetic of unity in multeity, and the archetypal criticism of Frye, which sought unity on a more global level by making individual texts, myths and modes episodes in a phenomenology of spirit' ('The Future of Deconstruction' 131). The fact that the New Critics treated the Romantics with ambivalence, despite having their theoretical origins in Coleridge's philosophy of art, indicates just how complex the negotiation between criticism and Romanticism has been in the twentieth century. Critical approaches that gathered Romantic writers – or, at least, a certain, relatively small group of apparently like-minded writers – into 'the visionary company' succeeded brilliantly in overcoming Eliot's and Leavis's rejection of the Romantics, although, significantly, at the cost of subsuming the distinctions which Lovejoy had originally urged upon critical readers. The powerful residual effects of defining Romanticism in terms of the work of a restricted circle of male poets are evident even in the essays collected here, which were written after a decade of debates over the make-up of the literary canon. In what might be described as a calculated interpretive risk in the light of these debates, six of the eight essays deal with canonical figures, their authors frankly choosing to remain within a more or less familiar Romantic canon precisely in order to read its texts otherwise (i.e., in a non-canonical fashion).

For reasons which have yet to be fully explored, the Canadian academic scene has in the past proven extraordinarily responsive to the unifying imperatives of Romantic criticism, and has been home to some of the field's most powerful and articulate exponents. For example, in addition to Frye's seminal contribution, we have witnessed Hans Eichner's and Cyrus Hamlin's work on the Germans, the work on Shelley by Milton Wilson and Ross Woodman, as well as the large critical-editorial projects on Wordsworth and Coleridge by W.J.B. Owen and by Kathleen Coburn, Barbara Rooke, and George Walley. Without question our contributors write their essays in the critical light cast by these luminaries; in several cases, they were once their graduate students. We make this point not to suggest the existence of some unified and uniquely Canadian approach to the problem of Romanticism, but to register a shared element in the intellectual history of our contributors. What distinguishes them from their strong precursors, however, are the ways in which they read *for the difference*, that is, how they discriminate between a number of Romanticisms by focusing on the conflicting pressures at work within and among the texts of Romantic writers. It is therefore no accident that all but one of the contributors to this volume completed their doctoral studies in the last twenty years, a charged period of critical *perestroika* in which post-structuralism made its complex impact on the human sciences in general and on literary criticism in particular. To the extent that they attend to what de Man calls the 'hidden fragmentations and articulations' (*Allegories of Reading* 249) that unsettle the Romantic text, our contributors bear witness to the initial influx of post-structuralism into the academic scene during the 1970s: in effect, and with varying degrees of resistance and collaboration, they write in its wake. Romantic studies have continued to function as a flashpoint for a wide range of theories and critical practices, some of which either have brought out the self-differences inhabiting post-structuralism or have sought to develop the connections between deconstruction and cultural criticism in a far more explicitly materialist fashion.[2]

The essays collected here constitute a reflection on this unfolding interpretive drama. The initial impact of post-structuralism and deconstruction on the work of Romantic critics was characterized at the most general level by a 'shift from historical definition to the problems of reading' (de Man, *Allegories* ix). This brought with it a sharpened resistance to falling into the trap of what Fredric Jameson has described as 'the vacuousness of the narratives of manuals of literary history, which ... [were] constitutively unable to confront the texts themselves except as examples' (221). These changes are crucial to understanding how a specifically post-structuralist discourse of Romanticism was set, even if Romantic studies *today* – of which this volume is intended to be a selected cross-section – can proceed in quite different ways. The decade before 'deconstruction' became a familiar word in Romantic studies saw the first signs of important change. In a seminal essay published in 1964, Earl Wasserman sublated the problem of defining the term 'Romantic' by redirecting – and narrowing – the discussion to the subject-object dialectic in Shelley, Keats, Coleridge, and Wordsworth. Wasserman's focus on 'the grounds of knowledge' (335), as he put it, inaugurated an epistemological emphasis in Romantic criticism that continues to be felt in the field. According to this view, Romanticism is ideally a project of the symbolic imagination which resolves the fission of the universe into thought and things. During the same decade, however, de Man had published two ground-breaking essays – in several senses of the word 'ground' – which decisively turned thinking about Romanticism to much less happily resolvable questions about language, rhetoric, temporality, and human finitude, questions whose Heideggerian and Sartrean impetus disrupted the philosophical idealism underwriting the work of Wasserman and like-minded readers.[3] In 1970, the same year that saw the publication of the English translation of de Man's 'Intentional Structure of the Romantic Image,' M.H. Abrams, a persuasively synthetic thinker and historian of ideas in the manner of

Lovejoy, responded defensively to these Continental influences, and to the larger implications that they had not only for Romantic studies but also for literary criticism as a whole: 'some critics,' he complains, 'looking back at earlier literature through the gloomy contemporary perspective ... [suggest] that Romantic writers could not really have meant what they claimed, hence that they must have been self-divided, or even unconsciously committed to the negations of the positives they so confidently asserted' (*Natural Supernaturalism* 446). Abrams's evaluative rhetoric is revealing, registering as it does a critical anxiety that is less about the specific problem of determining the meaningfulness of 'unconscious' authorial intentions, and much more about the generally threatening prospect of a proliferation of Romanticisms once it is conceded that neither the text nor its author coincides seamlessly with itself. Here the 'gloomy perspective' provided by what amounts to a psychoanalysis of Romanticism stands metonymically for all those theories which find the historical, cultural, and literary text to be irreducibly in excess of itself. Notwithstanding Abrams's warnings (which he has continued to make in the face of more recent developments in Romantic theory),[4] the field has only seen a marked proliferation of these self-divisions, negativities, silences, and unconsciousnesses (political, rhetorical, and psychic), as well as a more searching interrogation of what, precisely, Romanticism could be said 'positively' to 'assert.' After de Man, as it were, what was unhappy exorbitancy for Abrams is revalued as an opening for productive dissent and the sign of a certain resistance to (organicist) theory. What has changed and continues to change are the varied ways in which Romanticism's differences (and thus, necessarily, its continuities) are theorized in criticism. If de Man and 'deconstructive' reading strategies can be said to have opened the way to a de-idealized view of Romanticism, it needs also to be said that subsequent interpretations, while implicitly or explicitly using this view as their dialectical ground, have raised – and are raising – questions about the number and nature of Romanticisms that de Man was unwilling or unable to engage.

Post-post-structuralism, then, could be said (awkwardly) to describe the self-conscious historical-theoretical situation of this book. Each of its contributors resists making facile declarations about the 'end' of 'deconstruction,' as well as the temptation *either* to negate the significance of de Man (which at the very least would be to deny his impact in the history of criticism, not to say his on-going importance, among certain critics, in the field today) *or* unreflectively to reproduce the findings and interpretive strategies that are identified, not always accurately, with his name. Arguably the most significant recent development within Romanticism in the wake of deconstruction has been the new historicism, led by such critics as Marjorie Levinson, Marilyn Butler, David Simpson, and, more problematically, Jerome McGann, whose work is broadly cultural and richly contextualized. These critics generate readings that attend as much to the socio-political as to the literary text because they see the two as inextricably bound up together. Without question, as many if not all of the essays which follow attest, 'history' – especially in the form of an expanded conception of political culture and social 'energies' – has come to play an increasingly larger role in how Romanticists teach, think, and write about their subject. Whether this relatively recent shift in interpretive emphasis marks a 'return' to history, as some suggest, or simply the reconfiguration, by different forms of discourse, of concerns that were always already present in the critical community is far from clear. Historically situated as we are, it naturally remains difficult to see and understand precisely what place history occupies in our own writings. Foucault would say that this is the result of our constitutive inability to 'describe our own archive' (*Archaeology of Knowledge* 130),[5] and one sign of that blindness might be the fact that it seems impossible to determine conclusively whether or to what extent the new historicism is a complex outgrowth of post-structuralism or its determinate negation.[6] At the very least, we might heed Frances Ferguson's recent warning against being too easily satisfied with the 'narrative most readily available' to Romanticists seeking to totalize the history of their field – namely, 'one that trace[s] the rise of a deconstructive, language-oriented, and rhetorical account of literature and its recent *replacement* by a more historically and politically oriented model' (100; emphasis ours). As one of the contributors to this volume remarks in another context, the only way that such a narrative can be constructed, in which the former reading strategy is forced to yield to the latter on the grounds that it 'necessarily bypass[es] issues of history, ethics, and politics,' is if 'one has an impoverished conception of language to begin with' (Balfour 10). In different ways, the essays collected here resist the palliative attractions of the literary historiographical fiction that Ferguson describes, and do so by neither idealizing the evidences of history (or what Alan Liu calls 'romanticiz[ing] the particular' ['Review' 179] – this, from *within* the historicist camp), nor by reducing Romanticism merely to a Nietzschean army of metaphors and metonymies. Not language *or* history, then, but language *and* history. 'Between the Scylla

Introduction: Discriminations 9

of de Manian skepticism and the Charbydis of positivist self-assurance (still common enough to make one suspicious of any mere "return" to "literary history" ...),' David Simpson has recently written, 'there is enormous space calling for careful redescription' (723). And *discrimination*, we might add. The space of the in-between is necessarily one of dialogue, like the public conversation out of which this book arose.[7] By writing in precisely the critical-theoretical interval that Simpson describes, these essays demonstrate how contemporary theory has not only complicated our conception of the Romantic text, but, perhaps more important, how theory has in turn been complicated by Romanticism, so much so that the task of the redescription of Romanticisms has now become indistinguishable from that of the discrimination of (post-) post-structuralisms.

For each of the contributors, the life of the text lies not in its identity with itself, still less with the degree to which it uncritically embodies the 'Spirit of the Age.' The criteria for distinguishing between Romanticisms lies not even in discerning distinct 'thought-complexes,' as Lovejoy would have had it, but in tracing the lines of difference and displacement inscribed by class, gender, and language itself. In this volume Romantic writers are thus not simply read through contemporary theory; theory is instead employed in a critical practice which brings out the distinct ways in which Romanticism theorizes and examines itself from within. To the extent that the contributors register these self-critical energies in their own writing, they also resist falling prey to what Jerome McGann calls '*the* Romantic ideology' (emphasis ours). To denounce 'Romantic' readings of Romanticism – as McGann does – presupposes that Romantic authors are unwilling or unable to read the figures of their own understanding, and thus to write against as well as within the ideological closure of their self-representations. Moreover, as the definite article of the title of McGann's book indicates, it is to suggest Romanticism is synonymous with a single, master ideology.[8] But the essays in this volume suggest that Romantic texts do not unreflectively or univocally reproduce a politics of de-politicization that McGann sees capturing like-minded modern readers. The plurality of methodological positions and reading tactics represented in the following essays alone registers a measure of resistance to the hegemonic claims of that ideology, reproducing as it does a concomitant plurality about Romanticism, now reconsidered as expressing a complex incredulity towards the very credal positions that have in the past been identified with being 'Romantic' (and with which many readers have, as

McGann rightly points out, themselves too often identified). These positions include: the resolution of historical, political, social, and psychic difference through the 'esemplastic' power of the imagination; the sense of the 'one life' that transcends divisions between subject and object, and that unites nature with humankind; the valuation of a masculinist, Promethean ideology of questing self-sufficiency; the unequivocal affirmation of an autonomous, inward, and unmediated vision. In these essays, the targets of Romanticism's self-critical energies extend, as it were, from top to bottom: from nineteenth-century metaphysics and epistemology to the configurations of the world's body; from the field of social and institutional structures to the structure of language; and from the question of authorial identity to the make-up of intended and actual audiences. (And, as J. Douglas Kneale's paper demonstrates, even the metaphor of surface and depth at work here is subject to analysis and critique.) In this volume the Romantic text is therefore characterized by multiple strands of significance which entwine but do not build towards a synthesis. In bringing out these details, the critical practice of the following essays would thus seem to respond to the spirit – though not necessarily the theoretical substance – of a prediction that de Man made in 1979 about the generation of students of Romanticism that were then just coming of critical age, which is to say more or less the generation represented in this book: as he wrote, these critics would be the ones to show 'by reading the close readings more closely that they were not nearly close enough' ('Introduction: The Rhetoric of Romanticism' 497).

II

> ... perhaps one is a philologist still, that is to say, *a teacher of slow reading* [ein Lehrer des langsamen Lesens].
>
> Friedrich Nietzsche, 'Preface' to *Daybreak*

Jean Wilson's paper forms part of what Anne K. Mellor has recently described as 'the coming of age of feminism in Romantic criticism' (3). The fact that this maturation has occurred so recently attests not only to the general belatedness of criticism's engagement with the question of gender, but also to certain resistances within Romanticism itself. Citing the case of Lotte in Goethe's *The Sorrows of Young Werther*, and, more spectacularly, of Olimpia in E.T.A. Hoffmann's 'The Sandman,' Wilson points out that the representation of women in Romantic texts is conventionally one of a 'lovely, ideal image of unaffected simplicity, the creation of the male hero's imagination.' But Wilson also discerns an important counter-image in Romantic texts written by men, in which women, far from being excluded from 'speaking subjectivity,' play the role of ironic demystifier, exploding the male Romantic hero's narcissistic pretensions with the calm voice of rationality. Yet as Wilson also argues, the attribution of a certain ironic power to women brings with it a subtler disempowerment: '... if woman as "the other and the object" is excluded from speaking subjectivity, woman as the "reasonable" voice of disillusionment risks becoming equally silent – risks never being allowed to say more than is commonsensical, realistic, "probable."' For Wilson, *women's* Romantic writing partly circumvents this trap, rereading the ironic 'feminism' of its male counterparts precisely by resisting both 'the silence imposed by male figuration and the merely reasonable voice habitually called forth to challenge that silence.'

Significantly, Wilson finds evidence of this 'other' feminism, which unsettles rather than replicates the established polarities of reason and unreason, sense and sensibility, not in any single (male or female) voice but in the dialogical relationship between voices: De Lacey's invitation to the creature to share his unhappy story in Mary Shelley's *Frankenstein* offers one suggestive instance, as does the postmodernist conversation making up an important part of Christa Wolf's parodically Romantic *No Place on Earth*, written in what was until recently East Germany. In both cases the mutually qualifying processes of intersubjectivity put into question the efficacy of the monological, whether that truth finds expression in the voice of reason or un-reason, feminine or masculine. Wolf looks back to her Romantic predecessors not simply to parody their sexism but also to adapt their incipient ideological critique to a contemporary context: that the postmodernist present shares this kind of double relationship with its nineteenth-century past suggests that one of the tasks awaiting critical readers beyond Wilson's essay is that of discerning the presence of the 'Romantic' within the contemporary.

Although Wilson's is the only paper to take what could be called a primarily feminist approach, feminist theory and critical practice powerfully inform several of the volume's other essays. In her discussion of embedded narrative in *Julian and Maddalo*, for example, Shelley Wall argues that reason's other is not Faustian imagination, as is the case in the Romantic prose which Wilson examines, but madness: like the opposition of reason and imagination, however, that of reason and madness functions in a thoroughly sexualized manner. Taking as her point of departure Elaine Showalter's observation that 'the symbolic gender of the insane person shifted from male to female at the end of the eighteenth century,' Wall analyses Shelley's poem from the perspective of the figure of the Maniac, whose irrationality, objectification, and confinement identify him with a 'feminine' subject position. Wall argues that interpreting the poem as a debate between idealism and scepticism, as has often been done in the past, amounts to a recapitulation of the masculinist, rationalist perspective of the poem's titular characters. In focusing instead on the position and condition of the Maniac under the 'scopic mastery' of those characters, she emphasizes 'the *use* that ratiocentrism and androcentrism make of their professed others, madness and the feminine.' Julian and Maddalo come ostensibly to observe the Maniac but in fact reduce him to the status of an objectified exhibit: yet the mere presence of his 'scandalously open' speech, embedded in the host discourse of Julian and Maddalo, points up how that discourse 'defines itself by the exclusion of [the Maniac's] "incoherent" alterity.' Moreover, insofar as the Maniac is feminized, he shares a covert connection with Maddalo's daughter, who is similarly unnamed and whose confinement at home bears a discomforting resemblance to the 'domesticated' existence of the Maniac. The uncanny similarity between the situations of the Maniac and of Maddalo's daughter thus constitutes an example of what Jean Baudrillard calls the 'simulacrum' or 'hyperreal' (12) in social structures: while the Maniac's incarceration appears to mark the safe isolation of madness from reason, in reality it serves to distract the critical eye from the *generally* 'carceral' nature – both inside and outside the asylum walls – of society in which power is articulated in gendered terms.

The subject position of the 'feminine' within a predominantly 'masculine' discourse is an issue that Alan Bewell takes up and gives a rhetorical focus in his prize-winning essay on Keats's floral imagery.[9] Bewell asks: why did Keats continue to draw upon the traditional connection between flowers and the pastoral long after floral imagery had come to be seen as the primary poetic discourse of women? According to the logic of a literary biographical model that is not without its own sexism, Romantic criticism has often assumed that the highly stylized, 'effeminate' floral imagery of Keats's earlier poetry gave way to the later, and, as it were, more 'manly' visionary verse. But, as Bewell suggests, this model fails to register the complexity of the imagistic texture of Keats's poetry in at least two ways. On the one hand, Keats does not so much abandon floral imagery in his maturely 'masculine' verse as alter the way in which it is used. On the other hand, the difficulty in detecting this shift reflects the fact that 'we do not understand, with any historical accuracy, what it meant for a male poet, during the Regency period, to write poetry in which floral imagery functions as the main discursive component.' By recognizing the intertwined forces of class and gender that are inscribed in Keats's poems, Bewell argues, we begin the task of filling in this revealing lacuna in understanding literary history. Rather than simply reflecting a personal obsession, Bewell reminds us, Keats's recasting of human desire in terms of flowers presupposes the presence of a sophisticated, leisured audience that is 'conversant with botany and willing to enter into the play upon the analogy between the sexuality of plants and people.' More problematically, as a male writer who self-consciously chooses to develop the floral metaphor, Keats at once mimics and subverts the ideological agenda of popular botanical literature – literature which was written mostly by women for women and which served in its own way to enforce conventional ideas about their 'proper' place in society. At a certain level, Keats's poems represent a case of linguistic cross-dressing that brings out the relationship of gender and figure, power and language, within the culture of urbane Regency London.

Bewell's reading is thus formalist in its relatively tight focus on the poet's figural language, but hermeneutical and (new) historical in its attempt to account for the material circumstances of the poems and the kinds of audiences which they envisioned. Donald C. Goellnicht is similarly concerned with Keats's readership, but in his essay the issue is not so much the poet's struggle to find a language with which to address his audience as with that audience's highly partisan response to Keats. Goellnicht has elsewhere argued that Keats conceived of literature 'as a stimulant, "a starting post" for the reader's own "voyage of conception," which is based on his or her own creative energies' (195). In the essay contributed to this volume, Goellnicht extends and complicates his earlier discussion of Keats's *theory* of reading by analysing in detail the discursive *practice* of Keats's first readers, namely those writing the reviews of his 1817 volume, *Poems*. Keats wrote during the height of periodical reviewing in England; and, as Goellnicht points out, the journals in which his poetry received its initial written reception represented the whole literary and political spectrum of the period. Generally speaking, however, the response to Keats reflects the precariousness of the poet's position as a liberal, middle-class poet striving to belong to a distinguished line of predecessors while writing before a conservative, capitalist, class-conscious audience. Analysing these reviews, Goellnicht shows how the contemporary response to the poetry can be discussed in terms of interpretive communities that constructed a 'Keats' around questions of class and gender, race and nationality, a practice still much in evidence in today's criticism. What seems certain is that the poet's place cannot be confined to that of a political naïf caught in the cross-fire of the intensely partisan politics of the periodical press. As Goellnicht argues, Keats's writings reflect a sophisticated engagement with the contemporary social context, whose outlines can be traced in his ongoing engagement with the ideological positions, political prejudices, and aesthetic values of his reviewers.

The triangulation of rhetoric, interpretation, and historical circumstance characterizing the papers by Bewell and Goellnicht finds a pointedly different articulation in the essay by J. Douglas Kneale. Kneale's essay is as much about Wordsworth as it is about recent readings of Wordsworth which seek to stabilize critical discussion of his poetry by returning it to its ostensibly historical 'grounds.' For Kneale, Alan Liu's monumental *Wordsworth and the Sense of History* is the primary example of this kind of reading, a book which has done for Wordsworth criticism roughly what Stephen Greenblatt's *Renaissance Self-Fashioning* did for sixteenth- and seventeenth-century studies: integrate a poststructuralist sensitivity to the text's conflicting strata of awareness with a renewed emphasis on the political and economic conditions of the text's production. Kneale nowhere disputes the particularities of Liu's argument, which he justifiedly characterizes as 'one of the strongest readings of Wordsworth in the last decade.' In a way that reflects recent theory's emphasis on the *rhetoric* of criticism, he instead reads for the controlling metaphors of Liu's discussion, using Wordsworth and Freud to discuss its unexamined assumptions about the nature of the interpretive task.

Briefly put, Liu reconceives the conventional Romantic dialectic of 'nature' and the 'self,' arguing instead that these terms function in Wordsworth as figural displacements or symptoms of a third term, the literal ground of 'history.' As the repressed other of the Wordsworthian text, history represents the pretextual 'scene' to which the poem and the reader are alike ultimately answerable. Liu's rhetoric of symptomatology recalls Freud's earliest interpretive model in privileging scene over symptom and depth over surface. But, as Kneale argues, Liu also represses Freud, or at least Freud's subsequent doubt that symptoms could be traced back to a single, historical 'moment.' Freud was compelled to conclude, in the final analysis, that no 'scene' existed that was not already 'symptomatic,' no history free from an interminably tangled web of signification. What is remarkable for Kneale is that Liu's assumption about history as the stable ground of reading takes for granted what Wordsworth's poetry – long before Freud – in fact consistently poses as a question: whether there are histories, scenes, or personal experiences, much less natures, that are not already interpreted and textualized through and through. As Kneale demonstrates through close readings of paradigmatic passages from *The Prelude*, Wordsworth's poetry is most evocative when the distinctions between literal and figural levels of meaning collapse and when the desire to *see* into the life of things is understood to be irreducibly one of *reading* and of interpretation.

The metacritical emphasis of Kneale's paper reflects how Wordsworth, perhaps more than any other Romantic writer, has been the subject of theoretical discussion and controversy in the last fifteen years. The same cannot be said for Blake, who until recently has remained relatively untouched by the influx of new theory and critical practice. M.H. Abrams is typical of a certain strain in Blakean criticism when he states that it is 'very dubious indeed that Blake, for all his controverting standard usages of language, can be read by a deconstructor as paradigmatic; beyond most poets, he is an essentialist who claims that his fundamental assertions disclose presence' ('Construing and Deconstructing' 169). As David L. Clark argues, however, Blake never makes such 'claims' unequivocally. His visual and verbal texts instead embody a theoretical tension between the claims of *logos* and *dialogos*, essentialism and a deep incredulity towards essence understood as univocal in nature. Blake's later accounts of what he calls 'Fourfold Humanity' suggest that he viewed the Absolute not as a stable substance but as a conflictual condition which ceaselessly undoes itself, creatively deferring rather than obsessively seeking the stability of final form.

Clark's paper moves from these general principles of Blake's conception of truth-as-difference to discuss the language – both verbal and visual – that he uses to affirm multiplicity over self-sameness, the equivocality of dialogue over the commanding power of the Word, and the 'mutual interchange' of the Many over the mute inertia of the One. Blake's insistence upon what Foucault calls 'horizontal' rather than 'vertical' principles of human relations (*Discipline and Punish* 219–20) finds its most vivid embodiment in the artist's late illustrations to the Book of Job. In these illustrations, Clark argues, Blake interrogates the regulatory and disciplinary mechanisms (or 'technology,' as Foucault would say) by which the 'theological' subject is at once produced and maintained under the aegis of the Judeo-Christian tradition, a tradition in which being-human is indistinguishable from being-visible to a cruelly panoptic creator. In painting and engraving what amount to spectacles of *assujettissement*, Blake's illustrations, crowded with multiple frames and bounding gestures, do not thereby simply oppose Urizen's closural imperatives to a 'postmodernist' notion of infinitized free-play. For the artist, frames and framings paradoxically remain necessary *and* provisional: necessary for articulating the difference of one entity from another, provisional for exposing each entity's irreducible relation to the other. Frames are thus not the site of a prohibitive violence, but radically equivocal boundaries where what is inside and what is outside endlessly complicate and transgress each other. Beyond destabilizing the totalitarian imperatives of identity thinking, the boundary's sheer excess with respect to the understanding circumscribes human finitude, pointing to what Manfred Frank calls, after Heidegger, consciousness's 'not-Being-the-basis-for-itself' (88): that which makes consciousness (or 'imagination') possible also makes it *absolutely* impossible since it is unavoidably dependent upon the 'prior' principle of its articulation. In this way, Blake's illustrative practice suggests that 'a boundary is not that at which something stops but ... is that from which something begins its presencing' (Heidegger 154).

The fact that Blake does not reduce the human subject to a depthless play of surfaces, and that truth is not so much dissolved into an army of metaphors as reconceived as dialogical in nature, suggests that he cannot be translated into Nietzsche and one post-structuralist law applied to both. In her essay on *Alastor* Tilottama Rajan similarly argues that Shelley's deconstruction of lyric consciousness is not to be confused with the destruction of the knowing subject. Drawing from Schiller's *Naïve and Sentimental Poetry* and Hegel's *Aesthetics*, Rajan argues that the Romantics treat genres as representations of modes of consciousness rather than classifications of forms of literature. In this 'phenomenology of genres,' lyrics such as Wordsworth's Lucy poems embody the Romantic ideal of a purely subjective, autonomous imagination, whereas the choice of the narrative genre signals the Romantic writer's parallel and often conflicting awareness that no consciousness can be entirely alone, but must always be understood as part of a network of differences: like the nodes or intersecting points in a *web*, to cite Shelley's own metaphor for dialogism. In other words, language as a structure of differences disarticulates the Romantic desire for an autotelic or lyric mode of consciousness; yet, as Rajan is careful to point out, the opposition between narrative and lyric does not simply function to the detriment of the latter. In *writing* out the lyric voice in narrative, Shelley also provides visionary intent with a dimension of being-in-the-world: as Rajan puts it, narrative thus possesses a double structure of 'promise and risk,' both embodying lyric desire and exposing it to a discursive space 'no longer defined purely by the subject.'

Shelley's *Alastor* embodies the subtle displacement of lyricism by narrative in several ways, most evidently in the difference between the Narrator's idealistic desire to identify with the Poet and the irreducibly self-displacing means by which that desire is expressed: although the Narrator characterizes himself as emerging from the temporalizing and deferral of identity that is endemic to narrative, he ends up telling a tale in which the Poet's failure to find his epipsyche reproduces the Narrator's failure to cast his own story in the form of lyric. This structure of repetition and difference extends down to the poem's syntax and rhetoric, where the translation of conception into expression produces shifts in meanings which are non-synthetically incorporated into the fabric of *Alastor*'s narrative. Like Wall's paper on *Julian and Maddalo*, then, Rajan reads Shelley's text both mimetically, as referring to events and characters, and diegetically, that is, as self-consciously exploring the nature and limitations of representation at the level of language. Yet in another way Rajan's paper would seem a mirror image of Wall's discussion. For Wall narrative functions as the discourse of subjection, attempting to frame and contain the disarticulated speech of the Maniac in a prison-house – or insane asylum – of language. For Rajan, by contrast, narrative serves a dis-illusioning function analogous to the feminist plain-speakers of Wilson's paper because it compels the autonomously lyrical subject to enter into a temporal and historical world – a world peopled by *others*.

Rajan has elsewhere characterized her critical model as one of 'phenomenological deconstruction,' a model whose theoretical provenance can be traced to the Romantics' own willingness to explore 'the hiatuses in textual identity without renouncing the notion of a consciousness enmeshed in its representation' ('The Future of Deconstruction' 131). Ian Balfour, however, occupies a more radically post-structuralist position in which Romantic writing proves to be the site where language, and a certain 'law of language,' exceeds and precedes rather than merely complicates subjectivity. Balfour's focus on the deeply problematic status of speech-acts in the work of Elizabeth Inchbald and William Godwin is informed by de Man's later essays, especially those collected in *Allegories of Reading*. Because these essays have not played as large a role in shaping Romantic criticism as the earlier work, it may be useful at this juncture briefly to rehearse the relevant features of de Man's argument. In the formidable concluding chapters on 'Promises' and 'Excuses,' de Man radicalizes J.L. Austin's distinction between the performative and constative aspects of language, using it to theorize what he elsewhere calls the 'senseless power of positional language' ('Shelley Disfigured' 117), the opening 'act' or taking-place of signification, blankly insignificant and radically undecidable as such, whose effacement constitutes the condition of the possibility of readable signs. 'Innocently lacking sense,' as de Man provocatively describes it in the context of a discussion of Rousseau, this originary 'performance' 'gets at once misinterpreted into a determination which is, *ipso facto*, overdetermined. Yet without this moment, never allowed to exist as such, no such thing as a text is conceivable' (*Allegories of Reading* 293). Simply put, in de Man's formulation, language is at root a necessarily displaced allegorization of its hidden origins, and all theories, histories, sciences, and narratives but allegories of that allegory. Hence the threat to thinking that comes increasingly to preoccupy de Man's work after *Allegories of Reading*: language's taking-place in effect promises meaning, but *as* a promise, strictly speaking, it 'stands entirely out of the system of truth, virtue, and understanding' (289). This 'system,' it scarcely needs to be said, coincides with what it is to be human. As the subversion of all meaningful (or constative) language, its radical senselessness everywhere imperils cognition with the disconcerting prospect that 'the fact of something's having been said is no proof of anything other than the existence of the linguistic material' (Ferguson, 'Romantic Studies' 119).

As Balfour demonstrates, it is precisely around the question of the difficulty and excess of the promise that Godwin and Inchbald come closest to theorizing this special form of jeopardy to the understanding. As a speech-act that carries out the action to which it refers, the promise is an exemplary case of the performative, a linguistic positing rather than a description of reality. Balfour argues that Godwin and Inchbald are revealingly anxious about vows and oaths of all kinds despite or perhaps because of the fact that they appear to form a constitutive feature of social intercourse and social structures, from marriages to government. The narrative of Inchbald's *A Simple Story* (1791), for example, revolves almost obsessively around the making and breaking of promises, and is centred upon marriage vows which are prohibited, rehearsed, made, and unmade by turns. Inchbald finds these speech-acts to be untrustworthy and wildly unpredictable in their consequences, yet the characters of her novel are compelled to move in a social framework that is incapable of performing without them. In other words, the performance of Inchbald's novel, the motor driving the vicissitudes of its complex plot, relies practically upon the very speech-act that it has renounced theoretically. Balfour goes on to suggest that Inchbald's distrust of the promise at the domestic level informs Godwin's political critique, whether in the fictional or the philosophical mode. As in *A Simple Story*, the central characters of Godwin's *Caleb Williams* are victims of the oaths they have made or made others swear to, captives of the speech-acts whose aberrant consequences interrupt the free and natural progress of truth. As such, the promise can only be 'evil,' anathema to Godwin's abiding Enlightenment faith in the perfectibility of human understanding. For Godwin, the stakes cannot be any higher because, as the linguistic structure of the law, the promise is the fundamental speech-act of government. Balfour shows how Godwin's *Enquiry Concerning Political Justice* unerringly brings out the enigmatic operation of the promise at the heart of the social contract itself. Like declarations of any sort – including declarations of 'independence,' to name but one that Derrida has recently explored[10] – the social contract presupposes the very thing that it is contracted to construct: namely, 'society.' In this sense, society is perpetually in arrears vis-à-vis the linguistic event of its inauguration, constitutively unable to catch itself in its own (speech-)act. From the stand-point of the contracted parties, as it were, this originary promise has always already receded out of mind, and can therefore only be narrativized, after the fact, in fictions – for example, in highly improbable stories (or allegories) about humankind instantaneously transforming itself 'politically' from a state of uncontracted, animalistic asociality to contracted sociality, and linguistically from a condition of primitive performative utterances to one of the apprehension and communication of constative knowledge. But it is upon the unsteady premise of these kinds of fictions about the history of social institutions and the history of language that social structures are formed and political injustices perpetrated. Godwin attempts to contain the destabilizing force of the speech-act by insisting that language is *essentially* constative, yet the very fact that his history of language returns insistently to the performative suggests that it functions as something more than a dangerous supplement to the advance of reason. For Balfour, however, Godwin's denunciation of the promise amounts to more than what Roland Barthes would call *semioclasm* (7), a radical political critique rooted in questions about the use and abuse of sign systems – although it is undoubtedly that too. The promise also represents a point of maximum resistance to the Enlightenment assumption that language can be put fully into the service of rational critique: language is reason's crisis, not its perfectible instrumentality, a realization that could be said to mark the fitful emergence of Romantic 'theory' out of 'philosophy.'[11] As in the work of Austin, de Man, and Derrida, the promise provides Godwin with a means by which to think the being-language of language, and to see the 'absolute theoretical independence' of its senseless positing power from the law. Balfour economically describes the problem thus: 'If the discourse of politics, for Godwin, is essentially a language of meaning and of truth, one nonetheless has to recognize that before language means, language promises meaning.' Rather than simply reflecting an awareness of the relationship among language, power, and knowledge, then, the distrust of the performative that underwrites Jacobin fiction and philosophy amounts to a negative knowledge of the 'before' or 'already' of language whose traces it reveals.

NOTES

1 The significance of the positions adopted by Lovejoy and Wellek for Romantic criticism is discussed in helpful detail by Jerome McGann and Frances Ferguson.
2 For example, see, respectively, Rajan ('Displacing Post-Structuralism') and Marjorie Levinson (*Wordsworth's Great Period Poems*).
3 See de Man's 'Intentional Structure of the Romantic Image' (first published in French in 1960) and 'The Rhetoric of Temporality' (1969).
4 Alan Liu describes a revealing exchange at a conference which one of the editors of this volume also attended:

> In his 'On Reading Wordsworth's *Lyrical Ballads*' paper presented at the conference on 'Wordsworth and the Borders of Romanticism,' Yale University, November 14, 1987, Abrams made a memorably strong attack on the New Historicism in Romanticism (particularly in its materialist expressions). The core of the attack was that the New Historicism is at once too deterministic in its insistence that texts are

'necessarily' grounded in history and too *in*determinate in its dependence on purely negative or silent evidence (i.e., the history that the poem displaces or refuses to talk about). ('Wordsworth and Subversion' 94 n31)

Abrams's criticism of the new historicist emphasis on 'purely negative or silent evidence' is strikingly similar to his misgivings, almost twenty years earlier, about reading Romanticism for the 'negations of the positives.' For a fuller articulation of his position vis-à-vis the new historicism, see 'On Political Readings of *Lyrical Ballads*.'

5 Foucault's entire statement in *The Archaeology of Knowledge* reads: 'It is obvious that the archive of a society, a culture, or a civilization cannot be described exhaustively; or even, no doubt, the archive of a whole period. On the other hand, it is not possible for us to describe our own archive, since it is from within these rules we speak, since it is that which gives to what we can say – and to itself, the object of our discourse – its modes of appearance, its forms of existence and coexistence, its system of accumulation, historicity, and disappearance'(130).
6 On this question, see especially Alan Liu, 'The Power of Formalism.' Although arguing from a quite different theoretical perspective, Tilottama Rajan similarly concludes that 'the Yale school ... is by no means the only form of post-structuralism, for the New Historicist challenge to its hermetic exclusion of the "outside" world claims as its father another post-structuralist: namely Michel Foucault' ('The Future of Deconstruction' 132).
7 This volume grew out of a conference held at McMaster University in October 1990, called 'New Romanticisms: Recent Developments in Theory and Critical Practice,' under the auspices of the English Association.
8 Peter Thorslev also makes this point in 'German Romantic Idealism' (84).
9 Alan Bewell's essay won the Keats-Shelley Association Prize for 1992.
10 See, for example, 'The Laws of Reflection: Nelson Mandela, in Admiration' (17ff).
11 For a discussion of the distinction between 'theory' and 'philosophy,' see David L. Clark and Tilottama Rajan, 'Speculations: Idealism and Its Rem(a)inders.' Briefly, post-Kantian philosophers like Schelling and Hegel proceed by appropriating areas as diverse as history, mythology, and aesthetics, as well as early versions of psychoanalysis and semiotics. But the inclusion of these various discourses means that this philosophy is constantly 'reframing' itself, resisting its encyclopaedic claims to truth.

The strange and estranging insistence of the speech-act in Godwin's philosophy would then be a case in point. By venturing into a form of linguistics, Godwin circumscribes and complicates his rationalist project by exposing it to other-than-rational elements which that project can neither evade nor comprehend: political philosophy becomes *theory*.

WORKS CITED

Abrams, M.H. 'Construing and Deconstructing.' *Romanticism and Contemporary Criticism*. Ed. Morris Eaves and Michael Fischer. Ithaca: Cornell UP, 1986. 127–82.
– *Natural Supernaturalism: Tradition and Revolution in Romantic Literature*. New York: Norton, 1973.
– 'On Political Readings of *Lyrical Ballads*.' *Doing Things with Texts*. Ed. Michael Fischer. New York: Norton, 1991. 364–91.
Balfour, Ian. '"Difficult Reading": De Man's Itineraries.' *Responses: On Paul de Man's Wartime Journalism*. Ed. Werner Hamacher, Neil Hertz, and Thomas Keenan. Lincoln: U of Nebraska P, 1989. 6–20.
Barthes, Roland. *Mythologies*. Trans. Annette Lavers. London: Granada, 1973.
Baudrillard, Jean. *Simulations*. Trans. Paul Foss, Paul Patton, and Philip Beitchman. New York: Semiotext(e), 1983.
Clark, David L., and Tilottama Rajan. 'Speculations: Idealism and Its Rem(a)inders.' *Intersections: Nineteenth-Century Philosophy and Contemporary Theory*. Ed. David L. Clark and Tilottama Rajan. State University of New York P, 1994.
de Man, Paul. *Allegories of Reading: Figural Language in Rousseau, Nietzsche, Rilke, and Proust*. New Haven: Yale UP, 1979.
– 'Intentional Structure of the Romantic Image.' *The Rhetoric of Romanticism*. New York: Columbia UP, 1984. 1–17.
– 'Introduction: The Rhetoric of Romanticism.' *Studies in Romanticism* 18 (1979): 495–9.
– 'The Rhetoric of Temporality.' *Blindness and Insight: Essays in the Rhetoric of Contemporary Criticism*. 2d rev. ed. Minneapolis: Minnesota UP, 1983. 187–228.
– 'Shelley Disfigured.' *The Rhetoric of Romanticism*. New York: Columbia UP, 1984. 93–123.
Derrida, Jacques. 'The Laws of Reflection: Nelson Mandela, in Admiration.' Trans. Mary Ann Caws and Isabelle Lorenz. *For Nelson Mandela*. New York: Seaver Books, 1987. 13–42.

Ferguson, Frances. 'Romantic Studies.' *Redrawing the Boundaries: The Transformation of English and American Literary Studies*. Ed. Stephen Greenblatt and Giles Gunn. New York: MLA, 1992. 100–29.

Foucault, Michel. *Discipline and Punish: The Birth of the Prison*. Trans. Alan Sheridan. New York: Vintage, 1979.

– *The Archaeology of Knowledge / The Discourse on Language*. Trans. A.M. Sheridan Smith. New York: Pantheon, 1972.

Goellnicht, Donald C. 'Keats on Reading: "Delicious Diligent Indolence."' *Journal of English and Germanic Philology* 88 (1989): 190–210.

Greenblatt, Stephen. *Renaissance Self-Fashioning*. Chicago: U of Chicago P, 1980.

Heidegger, Martin. *Poetry, Language, Thought*. Trans. Albert Hofstadter. New York: Harper and Row, 1971.

Jameson, Fredric. *Postmodernism, or, The Cultural Logic of Late Capitalism*. Durham: Duke UP, 1991.

Levinson, Marjorie. *Wordsworth's Great Period Poems*. Cambridge: Cambridge UP, 1986.

Liu, Alan. 'The Power of Formalism: The New Historicism.' *ELH* 56 (1989): 721–71.

– Review of David Simpson's *Wordsworth's Historical Imagination: The Poetry of Displacement*. *The Wordsworth Circle* 19 (1988): 172–81.

– 'Wordsworth and Subversion, 1793–1805: Trying Cultural Criticism.' *Yale Journal of Criticism* 2 (1989): 55–100.

– *Wordsworth and the Sense of History*. Stanford: Stanford UP, 1989.

Lovejoy, Arthur. 'On the Discrimination of Romanticisms.' *Romanticism: Points of View*. Ed. Robert F. Gleckner and Gerald E. Enscoe. Englewood Cliffs: Prentice Hall, 1970. 66–81.

McGann, Jerome. *The Romantic Ideology*. Chicago: U of Chicago P, 1983.

Mellor, Anne K. 'On Romanticism and Feminism.' *Romanticism and Feminism*. Ed. Anne K. Mellor. Bloomington: Indiana UP, 1988. 3–9.

Rajan, Tilottama. 'Displacing Post-Structuralism: Romantic Studies after Paul de Man.' *Studies in Romanticism* 24 (1985): 451–75.

– 'The Future of Deconstruction in Romantic Studies.' *Nineteenth-Century Contexts* 11 (1987): 131–47.

Simpson, David. 'Literary Criticism and the Return to "History."' *Critical Inquiry* 14 (1988): 721–47.

Thorslev, Peter. 'German Romantic Idealism.' *The Cambridge Companion to British Romanticism*. Ed. Stuart Curran. Cambridge: Cambridge UP, 1993. 74–94.

Wasserman, Earl. 'The English Romantics: The Grounds of Knowledge.' *Romanticism: Points of View*. Ed. Robert F. Gleckner and Gerald E. Enscoe. Englewood Cliffs: Prentice-Hall, 1970. 331–46.

Wellek, René. 'The Concept of Romanticism in Literary History.' *Romanticism: Points of View*. Ed. Robert F. Gleckner and Gerald E. Enscoe. Englewood Cliffs: Prentice-Hall, 1970. 181–205.

PART ONE

Narrating the Subject

TILOTTAMA RAJAN

'The Web of Human Things': Narrative and Identity in *Alastor*

I

Labyrinths, weavings and related figures are ubiquitous in Shelley's texts, whether they are used to characterize language or other ways of grasping the world, such as thought, vision, or emotion. Thus in *Prometheus Unbound* language rules with 'Daedal harmony a throng / Of thoughts and forms' whose complexity it does not so much eliminate as contain within its own labyrinthine structure (4.416–17). In an essay on imagery the mind is described as 'a wilderness of intricate paths ... a world within a world' (Shelley 1911, 2:102). Perhaps the most famous of such images occurs in *The Revolt of Islam* where Cythna describes the tracing of signs on the sand to range

> These woofs, as they were woven of my thought:
> Clear elemental shapes, whose smallest change
> A subtler language within language wrought (7.32)

Like the epipsyche, which is 'a soul within our soul' (Shelley 1977, 474), language in this account seems implicated in intricacies and involutions that promise not difference but a grasping of identity. But on closer inspection we can see that the passage describes reference as displacement rather than *epoche*. For it seems that the process of articulation generates a secondary discourse by which the clear elemental shapes with which we begin are subtly shifted, and that representation is a recursive activity, a turning inwards which is not so much the finding of a centre as an act of self-reflection. Taken together these images suggest that Shelley senses in language a disseminative potential, and that the representation of desire, its embodiment in language, will prove to be a mirror stage that discloses hidden articulations and fragmentations within the elemental shapes projected on the plane of the imaginary.

That there is this potential in language is registered from the beginning in Shelley's poetic practice, which manifests in its syntax as well as its imagery that tendency, condemned by Leavis, to 'forget the status' of the initiating metaphor or proposition and 'to assume an autonomy and a right to propagate' (Leavis 206). Shelley himself describes this tendency more positively when he defines imagination as a non-synthetic productivity that composes from its initiating thoughts 'as from elements, other thoughts, each containing within itself the principle of its own integrity' (Shelley 1977, 480). But the way Shelley's language works is frequently at odds with what he seems to desire for the creative process in metafictional texts like *Alastor*, and the history of his poems is thus the history of their gradual alignment with the mode of functioning of their discourse. This alignment takes form as an increasing acceptance of lyric as (dis)placed within more extensive structures like narrative. For insofar as genre can be considered phenomenologically as representing the desire, though not necessarily the possibility, for a certain kind of language, lyric resists those differences that emerge in more dialogical forms of utterance like narrative and drama. Traditionally Romanticism has been associated with the lyric and with the 'lyricization' of various other forms such as epic, drama, and quest-narrative (Rajan, 'Romanticism and the Death of Lyric Consciousness' 194–207). Lyricization, in turn, has been a metaphor for 'internalization,' for a retreat away from history or temporality and into the visionary or the transcendental. Emulating the inscription of lyric as transcendence that he associated with Wordsworth, Shelley in *Alastor* also thematizes lyric by bringing it into an uneasy dialogue with narrative, so as to make both modes an object of reflection within the text.

In dealing with *Alastor*, I shall approach it, not at the mimetic level, as a poem about a visionary who seeks for his ideal in nature and then defers it to an afterlife, but at the level of the signifier, as a text which presents the process by which the Narrator tries to represent the Poet and discloses to himself the inevitable functioning of language as difference. Through the Poet, Shelley presents a thematic nexus he had inherited from Wordsworth and which he was to elaborate in *Adonais*: that of a vocation that is visionary rather than ordinary, invested in a special being whose life and death are understood only by nature, and whose memory becomes for his or her survivors the site of a bitter separation between the public and private realms. The Narrator tries to idealize the Poet and present him as an epipsyche who stands in relation to him as the veiled woman does to the Poet himself. But as has been widely recognized, his sentimentalization of the Poet is haunted by doubts he is barely able to repress about the value of the visionary life (Rajan, *Dark Interpreter* 75–82). We can attribute this ambivalent attitude to a 'Wordsworth' who is himself a construction of Shelley's desire to the latter's re-visionary position in relation to his precursor. Inheriting the Wordsworthian myth in the second generation,[1] Shelley inherits it as a set of symbols. Moreover, he departs from the Wordsworth of the Lucy poems by conveying the myth through elegiac narrative rather than lyric. Representing himself as a narrator, Shelley encounters in the process of representation, and specifically in the problematic of genre, a kind of mirror stage in which the search for a unified self-representation is enacted and called into question. As the Narrator, who represents himself in the form of a lyric poet, finds his lyricism subtly displaced by the pressures of narrative, so too 'Shelley' finds a language within his language. He discovers that narrative is not simply a more ambitious version of lyric, an extensive rather than intensive totality in Lukács's terms,[2] but a deconstruction of lyric totality. *Alastor*, in short, is more about the process of its production than about the product of that process: the figure of the Poet. For one of the curious things about the poem is that its main figure never comes alive, speaking only once and reverting at the end to an 'image, silent, cold, and motionless' (661). Summoned up from a realm of 'incommunicable dream, / And twilight phantasms' (39–40), the Poet seems an archetype or more properly a semiotype in the Narrator's consciousness. He is less a person than a textual figure: a sign that has no objective referent, being rather the sign of a desire, a desire for a Romantic ideology of vision that remains still (to be) born. And the poem of which he is the nominal subject is thus a poem about itself: about the process of making figures true, and about whether it is possible to find a mode of language that will confer identity on the Poet and thus on his author, the Narrator.

As narcissistic narrative, *Alastor* thus defers its referent from the mimetic to the discursive level so as to make its subject the signification of a visionary ideology. This movement from the sublime to the hermeneutic brought about through a displacement of interest from the signified to the signifier is connected to another phenomenon: the unwilling transposition of the visionary theme from the lyric to the narrative mode. The pre-text for Alastor is the Wordsworthian motif of the visionary self: the sensitive soul who, like Lucy or the Boy of Winander (or, somewhat differently, Margaret), dies young. Thus the Narrator's initial 'There was a Poet' (50) recalls Wordsworth's 'There was a boy.' The depiction of the Poet as unrecognized except by nature recalls Lucy, who dwelt by the untrodden ways and whose death made a difference only to Wordsworth. And the final reabsorption of the Poet by nature resembles, though more nihilistically, Lucy 'Rolled round in earth's diurnal course / With rocks and stones and trees' ('A slumber did my spirit seal,' 7–8). The figure of the sensitive soul is by no means uncomplicated in Wordsworth. For even in its simplest inscription as the visionary child it is rendered ambiguous by the child's death, which seals it in an identity with its essence yet denies it any being in the world, as though in some sense it has not been, and yet as though by not having been it has not *yet* been. But in those pre-texts which comprise for Shelley's Narrator an ideal limit, the figure of the beautiful soul is sealed against any probing of its liminality by being re-called in the mode of lyric rather than narrative. Lyric thus becomes for the Narrator the mode in which he can best approximate a discourse that will make the figure of the poet identical with itself. For the autonomous (as opposed to the intertextual) lyric comes as close as is possible in language to the forgetting of difference. Lyric concentrates on a single spot of time: on someone like Lucy seen in a single moment, and not in a series of situations in which she might appear differently. In reducing time to a moment, it also selects the moment that most expresses the essence of the subject's life: the moment that is, like the epipsyche, a 'soul within our soul.' Unfolding as voice rather than narrative, lyric does not posit a narrator different from the subject of his story or caught in relationships of (non)-identity with characters who displace him from his desire. Finally lyric, as Frye points out, is overheard rather than heard (Frye 249). By forgetting its reader, or at least by eliding its reader as someone different from the author, it simulates a hermeneutics of identity that confirms the oneness of the speaker with his subject.

The lyricization of the beautiful soul is thus part of the Romantic attempt to embody it in a language that will not displace it. By and large the Romantics conceive of the lyrical consciousness as one that is present to itself, able to bypass the reflective and therefore reflexive mode of language in song, or at least to make language the true voice of feeling. There are later deconstructions of lyric and music, such as those of Schopenhauer and Nietzsche, who see feeling as itself a mobile army of metaphors and 'mood,' that quintessentially lyric attunement, as a conflictual site.[3] But representations of lyric in terms of nightingales and Aeolian harps largely ignore this association of music with the subconscious and the will, and thus with the trace of non-identity. Instead they make art identical with nature, while conceiving of nature immediately as song and not reflexively as the book of nature. If lyric functions in terms of a semiotics of presence, it also involves a suppression of temporality. Lyric compression, as Sharon Cameron points out, produces an abridgement of time: a concentration on the moment rather than the sequence which has the effect of exempting the self from action, from involvement in the complex intertexture of events (Cameron 204, 250), and thus from a reading that would situate its values. Often focusing on experiences of loss or death that seem to confirm the triumph of a life that thwarts the desires of the subject, lyric protects the subject's interiority from what is merely exterior through an idealism that sublates material circumstance into its rhetorical figuration. For lyrics, as Cameron suggests, 'oppose speech to the action from which it exempts itself, oppose voice as it rises momentarily from the enthusiasms of temporal advance to the flow of time that ultimately rushes over and drowns it' (Cameron 23). Or as Adorno puts it, lyric is a 'self-forgetting in which the subject submerges in language' (Adorno 62).

Narrative by contrast is the insertion of the subject into a temporal and historical world: into a space populated by other people and no longer defined purely by the subject. If *Alastor*, which is concerned with only one character, is in this respect an ellipsis of the mode, the pressure of narrative is still felt in the presence of figures like the Arab maiden and the veiled woman, whose unreality renders interiority symptomatically as an effacement of, rather than an exemption from, being-in-the-world. The chronotope of narrative, its configuration of space as something inhabited by others and of time as something that continues beyond the moment of speech, necessarily generates a more complex hermeneutic than that of lyric. The fact that the narrator is telling the story *of* someone other than himself reminds us that he is telling it *to* someone other than himself, a fact emphasised in more complex narratives by the presence of characters telling each other things. But as importantly in *Alastor*, as in most narratives, the time of the poem is not identical with the time of the Poet's story, still less with a moment of that story expressive of a single mood. 'There was a boy' in its form as an autonomous lyric ends with the epiphanic absorption of the boy in nature. The time of the poem is the time of the poet's memory, and the poem ceases when he stops speaking.[4] In *Alastor* the Narrator survives the Poet, reflecting on his death not for two lines but at length, and thus breaking whatever mood he has created. Inserting the past into the present, the format of narrative as a story told *to* someone necessarily implicates it in a future in which the story may be retold, re-visioned. The time of narrative is a space that others will come to inhabit, as the text recognizes in the gesture of a preface: a preface, moreover, whose uncertainty as to whether it should idealize or didactically dismiss the Poet uneasily anticipates a division in the poem's audience.

The vulnerability of narrative to a hermeneutics of difference is corroborated by other features of the mode. Narrative is both psychoanalytically and structurally a mode of difference at odds with unmediated vision. That texts like *Alastor* are not narratives in the way that novels are, and seem closer to the lyric in making the main character a version of the speaker, is not crucial. For if they interiorize narrative so as to conserve lyric identity, that identity is now articulated in terms of a splitting of the subject. Subjective narratives of the sort the Romantics write project the self in the form of an *alter ego* who is then inside and outside the narrative voice. Where the lyric poet is undivided and speaks in *propria persona*, the Narrator of *Alastor* projects himself as the Poet, seeking to identify with a visionary ideology that he also constructs through someone he is not. Endemic to such narrative is a structure of repetition, a doubling of the subject into narrator and character, author and narrator, by which the self is repeated as something outside itself and displaced from itself. Or put differently, narrative is also the displacement of the self into an objective world that will disclose it as other than itself. The events of the Poet's life, the path followed by the Narrator's (poetic) desire in the actual world, divide him from this desire and force him to know (however reluctantly) its gaps and inadequacies. Narrative is, in this sense, the mirror stage of lyric. Even as it promises the subject an identity in the objective world, it also marks the unsettling insertion of the imaginary ego both into what Lacan calls the symbolic and into what Kristeva calls the semiotic order.[5]

If from a psychological point of view narrative is a process in which the self discloses its difference from itself, on a structural level its very length creates in it complications elided by the brevity of the lyric and by the hermeneutics of the lyric mode, which elicits unreflective reading. For narratives contain characters and episodes which are linked to each other in relations of connection and difference. The intratextual complexity of narrative is inevitably the source of hermeneutic difference. For the various characters provide more than one perspective from which the reader can view the project of the protagonist. Moreover, the elements of a narrative are interimplicated, present within each other, in such a way that no element exists in and of itself. A narrative thus forms an intratextual network of differences much like that of language or the text as Derrida describes it:

The play of differences supposes, in effect, syntheses and referrals which forbid at any moment, or in any sense, that a simple element be *present* in and of itself, referring only to itself, ... no element can function like a sign without referring to another element which itself is not simply present. This interweaving results in each 'element' ... being constituted on the basis of the trace within it of other elements of the chain or system. (Derrida 26)

To put it differently, the syntagmatic arrangement of events in a plot is suspended by paradigmatic relations between these events that render the reading of plot recursive rather than progressive. Thus the Poet in his wanderings through lands whose foreignness registers his self-estrangement seems to proceed from the Middle East to India, cradle of the human race, in a Hegelian journey towards greater inwardness that should bring him closer to cultural identity. But the vacancy that follows his vision of the veiled maid recalls the similar vacancy of his mind in Ethiopia, and makes us wonder whether the second episode does not contain traces of the first, where inspiration is asserted but not described, so that it seems to reproduce the vacancy it replaces (106–28).

Shelley himself speaks of difference in representation in *A Defence of Poetry* when he contrasts the semiotics of language with that of other artistic media:

... language is arbitrarily produced by the Imagination and has relation to thoughts alone; but all other materials, instruments and conditions of art, have relations among each other, which limit and interpose between conception and expression. The former is as a mirror which reflects, the latter as a cloud which enfeebles, the light of which both are mediums of communication. (Shelley 1977, 483)

A word directly evokes its referent, whereas a painting distracts us from using it mimetically by allowing us to be caught up in the interplay between its parts, between its forms and its colours. But if Shelley at this point allows words to exist in and of themselves, he later complicates the opposition between language and other forms of art by conceding that 'Sounds as well as thoughts have relation both between each other and towards that which they represent' (Shelley 1977, 484). His hesitations about narrative in the *Defence* may be due, among other things, to a distrust of forms that fail to abstract the poetical 'parts of a composition' from the 'intertexture' produced when the hermeneutic whole conceived by inspiration is executed in parts that develop relations among each other as well as towards the whole they are supposed to create (Shelley 1977, 485, 504).

That intertexture is troubling on grounds that are semantic as well as syntactic. Distinguishing narrative from poetry (presumably lyric), Shelley criticizes the 'story of particular facts' for failing to idealize that 'which is distorted' (Shelley 1977, 485), for failing to omit those elements of chronology and circumstance whose interference prevents the text from being 'a mirror whose surface reflects only the forms of purity and brightness' (Shelley 1977, 474). Moreover, as a 'catalogue of detached facts' (Shelley 1977, 485), narrative strikes Shelley as episodic rather than epipsychic. It introduces scenes, and thus considerations, at odds with a causality that would make plot into the text's self-explanation, and it thus inhibits the closure that allows narrative to refer directly to what it represents. Telling the story of the Poet chronologically rather than according to principles of retrospective selection that would make each episode a stage in an argument, the Narrator includes in it an encounter with an Arab maid who plays no further part in the poem. The episodic character of her appearance is visually marked by her insertion into an unusually short verse-paragraph that is simply dropped into the poem, unintegrated with anything else. We can read her as constellating a phase in the phenomenology of the Poet's mind, and can thus absorb her into the poem's causal structure as a shadowy material type of the more spiritual veiled maid. But some of the questions she raises – about the Poet's meta-physical quest as an evasion of his existence in the material world – challenge the phenomenology she is supposed to subserve. Moreover these questions (repeated in the preface) do not recur in the poem, which raises epistemological but not ethical doubts about the Poet's quest. Rather they are symptomatic of the narrative's tendency to generate complications that it is not always able to integrate into a more complex unity: subplots that contain within themselves the principle of their own integrity.

From the invocation where the Narrator describes himself as a 'long-forgotten lyre' (42) and asks nature to favour his 'solemn song' (18), to the end where the dead Poet is described as a 'lute' and the Narrator refers to his own poem as a 'simple strain' (667, 706), lyric and not narrative is the desired mode of *Alastor*. But curiously the Narrator describes his own previous history as given over to narration, though he tries to view this stage as merely a prelude to vision:

> I have made my bed
> In charnels and on coffins where black death
> Keeps record of the trophies won from thee.
> Hoping to still these obstinate questionings
> Of thee and thine, by forcing some lone ghost,
> Thy messenger, to render up the tale
> Of what we are. (23–9)

Narrative is pictured psychoanalytically as a search for identity in language, but one that yields only inadequate self-representations: as a mirror stage that discloses the specular structure of any identity between Narrator and text. Proclaiming that he has had enough of 'twilight phantasms' (39–40), the Narrator sees himself as about to emerge from the temporalizing and deferral of identity endemic to narrative through a resumption of his long-forgotten lyre. But what he constructs is another narrative in which the Poet's failure to find his ideal reproduces the Narrator's failure to create a figure that will render up the tale of what he is. The poem, in other words, is the story of the Narrator's failure to write his text as lyric. Moreover, if lyric ideally is a transcendence of narrative, its belatedness in the Narrator's career suggests that it has no more than a liminal status, as a desire produced by what it seeks to forget. It is interesting that the Narrator describes the music produced by his Aeolian lyre as a 'woven' hymn (48), suggesting that he cannot really conceive of a form of expression which points single-mindedly outwards to a referent or source or affective state, rather than inwards to its own intratextual complications. Images of weaving are the site of a crossing in Shelley's aesthetics from an essentialist to a differential concept of language. In *The Revolt of Islam* it is arguable that the subtler language within language produced by the woof of thought is meant to be like that soul within a soul defined as the epipsyche, more identical with itself as it becomes more refined and complex. But increasingly weaving becomes a figure for the autonomous complexity of language and other forms of mediation as something that displaces and produces rather than simply signifies thought.

The (un)weaving of lyric desire is thematized in the poem's most important episode: the scene of his own creative origination in which the Poet sees the veiled maid in the vale of Cashmire. It is well known that she develops from simple to complex as she is unveiled, that her ideality turns out to contain a darker subtext, and that the attempt to articulate concretely what begins as a dreamy abstraction discloses what seems spiritual and pure as purely material. The intense physicality of what the Poet projects as a Platonic form, so troubling that he swoons rather than consummate his love, enacts the embodiment of vision: the linguistic process by which the Idea is given a body in words that do not exist by themselves but inevitably refer to other elements in the chain or system. To begin with, the veiled woman is characterized in terms of allegorical abstractions that allow her song (or that of the Poet who projects her as muse) to bear a direct relation to transcendental referents:

> Knowledge and truth and virtue were her theme,
> And lofty hopes of divine liberty,
> Thoughts the most dear to him, and poesy,
> Herself a poet. (158–61)

Yet the multiplication of these referents makes us wonder if she is indeed simple in essence: whether knowledge, truth, and virtue are the same thing, and whether there lies beneath these simple terms what Nietzsche calls a philosophic mythology, which makes these concepts into figures in a series of stories and family romances. This diffusion of reference is linked to the presence of the woman's body, or rather to the body of her emotions: her 'tremulous sobs,' 'beating heart,' and her 'pure mind,' which is confusingly experienced only through her body, kindling 'through all her frame / A permeating fire' (161–72). For the body has been linked by Nietzsche and more recently by Kristeva to the problem of representation. The female body is for Kristeva the site of pulsions that disturb the order of both the symbolic and the imaginary: of what cannot be said or imagined and thus of something felt in language only in terms of gaps and absences.[6] Resisting logical representation, the body of the veiled woman disrupts the Poet's attempt to link her to a transcendental signified or to make the music she sings the vehicle of a disembodied and simple lyricism.

The multivocality of the veiled woman corresponds to her profound ambiguity as a figure for poetry and for a lyricism linked not just to the feelings but de-idealized and complicated by the association of feeling itself with the female body. The veiled woman is both epipsyche and Muse, 'Herself a poet' who plays upon a harp. As lyric poet, she produces a Wagnerian music strangely lacking in lyric serenity: 'wild numbers then / She raised, with voice stifled in tremulous sobs' (163–4). Her music, moreover, tells an 'ineffable tale' (168), a tale curiously like the poem itself in that it cannot be interpreted so as to render up the tale of what we are. Describing it as ineffable rather than obscure, the Narrator tries to etherealize its disruptiveness. Yet even as he transforms narrative into music by figuring its silences as unheard melodies, the song he creates in his mind is 'intermitted' (172), full of gaps and absences, as if there is more to be told about this woman who never becomes present in the song she sings and must be pursued beyond the 'realms of dream' (206) if the Poet is to discover to what the song refers. As a *mise-en-abime* of the larger poem, the vision of the veiled woman thus deconstructs lyric as the epipsyche of narrative. Lyric is not so much the antitype of narrative as a sublimation maintained only by the absence of narrative. As the withholding of narrative, the woman's song is present only as the absence of something which the Poet must recover if the song is to be fully self-present, but which paradoxically might deconstruct its identity as song.

That lyric is no more than the absence of narrative, constituted on the trace of what it does not tell, is suggested by the fact that the woman's song is associated with weaving. We shall return again to this image, which is Shelley's image for the differential texture of language. At the end of the poem 'the web of human things' becomes an image for everything that the Poet, in imagining the epipsyche, seeks to forget: for 'Nature's vast frame ... / Birth and the grave' (719–20), and thus for the complex intertexture of existence in which nothing is present without its opposite. As a mode which tells of life from birth to the grave, narrative inevitably recreates this intertexture. By contrast lyric, as the attempt to abstract a single moment and thus a single referent from life, brackets the interconnections between this and other moments so as to reduce existence to some simple essence. But it is precisely this simplicity that the Poet fails to find through the veiled woman, who seems a natural rather than transcendental muse (associated with 'streams and breezes' [155]), and whose voice thus creates no single mood:

> Her voice was like the voice of his own soul
> Heard in the calm of thought; its music long,
> Like woven sounds of streams and breezes, held
> His inmost sense suspended in its web
> Of many-coloured woof and shifting hues.   (153–7)

As already observed, images of weaving are the site of an unfolding complication in Shelley's aesthetics, in which the very notion of lyric as an *epoche* achieved through interiorization is here implicated. Associated with interiority and thus with the promise of a deep truth, they reveal the Poet's inmost sense not as a centre but as a place of dissemination. As used in *The Triumph of Life*, where the place in which the Shape all Light appears is filled with 'many sounds woven into one / Oblivious melody' (340–1), weaving is explicitly presented as the creation of an illusory unity: of something which seems a single fabric only because we are oblivious to how it is woven of multiple strands. As weaving, lyric is thus no more than the illusory unification of that web of differences which unravels in more extensive structures like narrative.

II

The development of the poem as a web of differences is everywhere apparent, most obviously in the fact that the Narrator tells the story of the Poet's journey towards death twice, but also in the syntax and texture of the poem. This unravelling of the poem's identity may be ascribed to the tendency of extended structures to organize themselves in terms of repetition. It is in the nature of language to repeat along different axes: to illustrate concepts through figures or fables, or conversely to reduce symbols or narratives to conceptual paraphrases. These textual repetitions combine in larger forms of utterance with doublings of characters and repetitions of similar episodes. While repetition may be intended to confirm and emphasize, it also produces differences and functions as part of the economy of the supplement. We do not repeat something in different words if we mean to say exactly the same thing. And if we repeat something, it is because what we said is not sufficient: because there is also something else to say.

Let us consider the passage which follows the Poet's futile attempt to pursue the veiled woman beyond the 'realms of dream.' What exactly this passage says is crucial to determining the Poet's choice of death, and whether it is legitimized by the existence of a transcendent realm:

> Does the dark gate of death
> Conduct to thy mysterious paradise,
> O Sleep? Does the bright arch of rainbow clouds,
> And pendent mountains seen in the calm lake,
> Lead only to a black and watery depth,
> While death's blue vault, with loathliest vapours hung,
> Where every shade which the foul grave exhales
> Hides its dead eye from the detested day,
> Conducts, O Sleep, to thy delightful realms? (211–19)

Logic tells us to interpret the second question as a gloss on the first. In that case the speaker begins with the paradox of something apparently negative yielding its opposite: the dark gate of death leading to the paradise of sleep. He then expands on this view of life as operating through a system of paradoxes by asking if the apparently negative paradox of appearance and reality does not conceal its own reversal into a positive paradox. Does the possibility that the promise of the rainbow clouds seen in the lake may hide the reality of death by drowning, yield in turn to the possibility that this ugly and dark appearance may hide the more positive reality of sleep? Logic tells us also that the expansion of the first question is designed to valorize the transcendent over the natural realm. For it is nature which tricks us with the appearance of beauty only to reveal the clouds in the lake as an atmospheric illusion, while the reality of ugliness ceases to be a reality as soon as we move beyond the merely material world. But this reading is far from easy to extract from the passage, for its syntax blocks or at least retards our attempts at paraphrase. The problem is the labyrinthine complexity of the second question, which introduces a long and not clearly subordinate clause between the subject, 'death's blue vault,' and the main verb, 'Conducts.' This syntactic detour allows various other grammatical possibilities to come into play, and while they may not finally prevail, the paraphrase suggested is destabilized by the presence within it of these other alternatives. Initially it seems that the first three lines of the second question provide an alternative to the first question, and that the Narrator, having suggested that death may lead to the positive condition of sleep, raises the possibility that what seems beneficent may hide something threatening. The very next line makes it clear that this is not his intention, and that the Narrator means to overturn the negative alternative with a further positive paradox. But the positive alternative is a long time in coming, and the depressing description of death's blue vault seems to take over the sentence. This is all the more true because the subordinate clause on death contains two further subordinate clauses ('Where every shade ... / Hides it dead eye from the detested day' and 'which the foul grave exhales'). The effect is to convert the larger subordinate clause into a main clause in relation to the subordinate clauses which it contains, and thus to give it a certain autonomy in relation to the main sentence in which it is contained. It is not immediately clear where the second question ends and whether the verb 'Hides' or the verb 'Conducts' is the main verb of the sentence. Or to put it differently, if the aim of the text is to subordinate the negative concessions in this second question to an affirmative suggestion, the subordination is disrupted, and we are made aware of how each suggestion is diacritically constituted on the trace of what it does not say. Syntax is not the only source of complications in this sentence. The second question is organized around an opposition between the deceptive paradoxes of nature and the saving paradoxes of transcendence. But the image of death's blue vault uneasily recalls the earlier sky image of rainbow clouds in the lake. It reminds us, even as we hope death's vault will prove an exit to something better, that all constructions of hope may lead 'only to a black and watery depth,' and that the Poet's deferral of his ideal to the afterlife may also be futile.

This microscopic analysis has been directed to a larger point about the way extended systems of representation function. Their very extensiveness brings into play the differential potential of language. For the more elaborate the structure, the more our attention becomes riveted on the interrelations of its parts, and the more parts there are to generate such interrelations. Such relations often disrupt on the connotative axis the relationship of individual signifiers to their referents on the denotative axis. We saw, for instance, how the subtextual resonance of the earlier sky image in 'death's blue vault' unsettled the ability of those lines to convey the superiority of death to life, how the intratextual relations between images interposed between conception and expression. The 'intertexture' of an elaborate structure, to borrow Shelley's word, creates detours in the movement of a narrative to its conclusion. Though the passage in question is not a narrative, as the lengthening out of what begins as a simple question it functions as a paradigm for the process of extension and repetition at the heart of narrative. It does not simply pose a philosophic question using concepts like sleep and death. It goes on to narrate the relation of sleep and death, by replacing them with figures which not only embody their relation but also unfold its complexities and create a subtler language within language.

The differential repetition which pervades the texture of the poem is similarly present in its macrostructure. One of the curious things about this poem is the doubling of the narration, whether because the Narrator actually tells the Poet's story twice, or because he has him go through a similar sequence of events twice in a vain attempt to construct his life as a history with a beginning, a middle, and an end.[7] It is as though in the course of the initial narration the Narrator has discovered gaps and possibilities that make it necessary to weave the strands differently, so as to achieve a closure that will again be impossible because the re-enactment of the Poet's life simply displaces the gaps in the first version. The doubling of the narration makes it clear that the poem is involved in a kind of auto-signification. It does not so much give us a finished product in the form of the Poet's story as manifest the process of narrative as (dis)articulation. Very briefly the Poet sees the veiled woman (140ff) and, having failed to find her again, is seized by a daemonic passion that rouses him from his couch 'As an eagle grasped / In folds of the green serpent' (227ff). The futility of his quest leads him to waste away (245ff), until at the end of his journey he arrives in a nook, nature's 'cradle, and his sepulchre' (430). But now, when we expect him to die, he again sees a feminine spirit (469ff), is roused from his couch by a 'joyous madness' (517), ages in a ghastly way (531ff), and again arrives in a cove where he expires (571ff). The repetition of the story undoes the Narrator's attempt at mimesis, giving the Poet's life a phantasmatic quality. For, as Hillis Miller has pointed out, repetition can function in a Nietzschean way, creating a world of 'simulacra' or 'phantasms,' a series of 'ungrounded doublings which arise from differential interrelations among elements which are all on the same plane' (Miller 6).

It is impossible to separate neatly the different figurative intentions behind the two versions of the Poet's life, since these intentions are largely swallowed up in the intratextual complications of the poem. But the crucial problem in the text is clearly the significance of the Poet's life and death, and one of the more awkward aspects of the text is thus the repetition and deferral of a climax that would retrospectively confer value on the Poet's life. Although the Narrator, in the conventionalized opening and closing of the poem, seems to idealize the Poet, his postponement of the latter's death some two hundred and fifty lines beyond its announcement, and his seemingly endless protraction of the narrative, manifest an emergent doubt as to whether the death is indeed a climactic event. This doubt is augmented by the fact that narrative proves to be a hermeneutic rather than a mimetic process. For the Narrator has no clear view of what the Poet's story 'means,' and thus he produces accounts which try to determine this meaning as they work themselves out, and which tacitly re-read themselves as they proceed. Thus one way of viewing the first account is to say that in it the Narrator sees the Poet's vision as having some external sanction which legitimizes his pursuit of it beyond the realm of life. Correspondingly he tries to see the Poet's life as having come full circle, bringing him to a sepulchre that is also the cradle of his mother nature, an end which is an origin. But in this positive figuration of the Poet there are numerous gaps. For one thing it is never clear whether he is in sympathy with nature or at odds with her, and thus whether the benediction of circularity that the Narrator has her confer on the Poet's death is an empty formula. Even at the beginning of the poem, where there are no 'human hands' to build the Poet's 'untimely tomb,' the pyramid of mouldering leaves that shelters his remains seems assembled more by the random movements of the wind than by design (50–4). Then at the end, although the Poet's blood is described as having beaten in 'mystic sympathy / With nature's ebb and flow,' heaven remains 'Utterly black' at the moment of his death (651–60). Moreover, it is unclear whether there is any reality beyond death where the mirage of the veiled woman can be found again. Nor is it clear that she is anything but a narcissistic projection. Her voice is, after all, like the voice 'of his own soul / Heard in the calm of thought' (153–4).

Because of the many questions that the first narration raises, we can speculate that the Narrator recasts the Poet's death as the conscious pursuit of an interior ideal. This time the scene of his encounter with the female spirit is overtly narcissistic. She appears immediately after he has seen his reflection in a well and is without links to the transcendent or to nature:

>   ... clothed in no bright robes
> Of shadowy silver or enshrining light,
> Borrowed from aught the visible world affords   (480–2)

When he follows her, it is in obedience to 'the light / That shone within his soul' (492–3), and thereafter he consciously interiorizes the landscape by seeing it as an image of his life (502–8), exploring whether meaning can be found in the landscape of the self, when it cannot be found outside or above the self. Finally, according to this version, he dies at peace with himself, having made the mind its own place: 'Yet the grey precipice and solemn pine / And torrent, were not all; – one silent nook / Was there' (571–3). But this account, while it resolves some of the contradictions in the previous one, is not without its complications. For it does not follow that the landscape of the self is any less labyrinthine than that of nature. Nor do we ever make contact with the Poet's self except as displaced from itself into some specular image, reflected in the water in the form of a 'treacherous likeness' (474). Even the closing description of the nook in which the Poet peacefully dies begins, on closer inspection, to unravel:

>   Even on the edge of that vast mountain,
> Upheld by knotty roots and fallen rocks,
> It overlooked in its serenity
> The dark earth, and the bending vault of stars.
> It was a tranquil spot, that seemed to smile
> Even in the lap of horror.   (571–8)

The spatial position of the nook is ambiguous. It is described, on the one hand, as overlooking the dark earth, as though its serenity comes from its having transcended the complications of life; and, on the other hand, it is described as being in the *'lap* of horror,' as though it is surrounded by what it seeks to forget, to overlook. What the repetition of the story makes clear is that narrative is a potentially endless process: not a closed structure, but a proliferating web of complexities.

This is not, however, the way that the Narrator would like to conceive of narrative. At least at the level of desire, narrative is for him a supplement to lyric. For in deferring lyric as a way of achieving identity with his text, he casts his poem as quest narrative: the quest of the Poet for the epipsyche and of the Narrator for the essential meaning of the Poet's life. In troping narrative as quest, he assumes that he can fulfil the goals of lyric by a more circuitous path, like the one modelled in Hegelian phenomenology, where the subject must become alienated from himself in order to achieve an identity that is not simply unreflective. Through the self-repetition of himself as the Poet, the Narrator thus tries to gain access to himself, to construct himself to himself, so as to find an *alter ego* who will no longer make a ghost of the self but will render up the tale of what we are. This *alter ego* must be a unity; it must not be different from itself if it is to tell its tale clearly. But from the beginning the attempt to achieve such identity is accompanied by difficulties. For no representation of the Poet succeeds in making him present to us, or making the Narrator's conception fully present to him. Since the Poet is rarely represented as speaking, we know him only from the outside, like the pyramids among which he wanders in search of meaning, which similarly present an exterior that baffles penetration and perhaps conceals an absence. His mind is repeatedly described as 'vacant' (126, 191), and though we are once told that 'meaning' flashed on it 'like strong inspiration' (126–8), we have no sense of what that meaning is and infer from the parenthetical way in which the claim is made that it may be simply a trick of light. Onto this empty schema the Narrator projects different and contradictory interpretations that constantly unravel each other.

In *Alastor* Shelley for the first time faced the sense that there might be no ground behind language, a possibility to which he returns very differently in Asia's visit to the Cave of Demogorgon. At a structural level the doubled narration can seem to evaporate the poem as a vicarious achievement of identity for the Narrator, because it shows him assembling and disassembling an identity for the Poet. But even at the textural level the vanishing ground of the poem is constantly felt in its blurred and tangled descriptions. There is, for instance, the passage in which the Poet embarks in the death-boat:

> Following his eager soul, the wanderer
> Leaped in the boat, he spread his cloak aloft
> On the bare mast, and took his lonely seat
> And felt the boat speed o'er the tranquil sea
> Like a torn cloud before the hurricane.
>
> As one that in a silver vision floats
> Obedient to the sweep of odorous winds
> Upon resplendent clouds, so rapidly
> Upon the dark and ruffled waters fled
> The straining boat. (311–20)

Here it is unclear whether the weather – both physical and emotional – is calm or stormy. The sea is tranquil, yet the boat proceeds as if driven by a hurricane. The Poet floats in a silver dream, yet he moves rapidly along the dark waters. On the one hand, he seems at peace with himself, masterfully in control of his destiny as he stands at the steady helm (333), having chosen freely to embrace death in the pursuit of his ideal. On the other hand, he appears a harried figure, a victim of forces without and within which push him helplessly towards destruction. The radical contradictions that occur in the space of a few lines make it seem that his identity is an arbitrary linguistic construct, so that the Narrator is left with the failure of his attempt to make figures true, to make the Poet more than a textual figure.

III

The Narrator's failure can be seen as a failure of narrative as well as lyric. Unable to make the Poet credible as a character, the Narrator is also unable to give his life the status of fact, of something that has happened. But it is just as possible to say that the contradictions that haunt the figure of the Poet arise precisely from his being the subject of a narrative, and that the narrative process generates a series of differences: differences between the narrator and a character who is other than him, differences between the narrator and a reader whose presence dialogizes the narrator's relationship to his protagonist. Insofar as he is committed to a model of narrative as *mimesis* and interpretive closure, in other words as plot, the Narrator resists those elements in its structure and reception that make it a dialogical mode. This resistance manifests itself in a nostalgia for lyric and in a concluding attempt to bring back lyric as elegy. Yet the opposition between lyric and narrative does not simply function to the detriment of the latter. In writing the beautiful soul into the form of narrative, Shelley seeks to give it what it lacks in Wordsworth: namely the dimension of being-in-the-world. *Adonais* and *Alastor* are longer than Wordsworth's 'She dwelt among the untrodden ways' because Shelley wants to claim for his visionaries a status that Wordsworth does not claim for the reclusive, almost invisible Lucy. Given no voice and scarcely spoken of in a poem whose brevity feels language to be a profanation, Lucy exists only as an unheard melody. The figure of genius in *Alastor* is similarly silent, but his Narrator is not. In describing the life of the Poet at such great length, the poem presses beyond the modesty of the Lucy poems, with their concession that Lucy's death makes no difference except to Wordsworth. Similarly, in describing his displaced wanderings through various foreign cultures, the Narrator pleads – albeit by negation – for the Poet's place in his own culture. In speaking about the Poet and trying to create a cultural context for him, the Narrator inevitably opens the figure of the Poet to an ideological contestation that is symptomatically present in his own inability to sustain a uniformly idealized portrayal of the Poet. Narrative, in other words, is not simply a deconstruction but also an expansion of lyric, a mode that embodies desire in the world. At the same time it removes this desire from the protection of a self-contained subject and requires us to view it from more than one perspective. We wonder whether the Poet's life is to be deemed a success according to his own criteria or a failure according to the standards of others. We wonder whether his ideal is an illusion and whether or not that matters. We also ask whether his wanderings through cultures associated with the infancy of the world mark the visionary ideology he (dis)embodies as outdated, though this response is divided by our sense of him as closer to lost origins than we are. The diacritical structure of narrative, in other words, makes it profoundly self-critical.

As a moment in the history of Romantic attitudes towards narrative, Shelley's poem is thus something much more complex than an elegy for the death of lyric consciousness. The Narrator can no more abstract lyric from narrative than the Poet can achieve an *epoche* that will bracket the body of the veiled maid and give him access only to her soul. Narrative, as a form that gives vision a history, is precisely the (re)visionary Narrator's means of access to history: to the readers to whom he tells his story and to a future that may see beyond the death of the Poet. Writing the Poet into a narrative, he enables him to survive, if only as a sign of something still (to be) born. The Narrator, in other words, does not simply fail to be a lyric poet. He also chooses to write his text as narrative. The double structure of narrative as promise and risk, as an embodiment of visionary intention that also complicates it, is something that Shelley accepts in *Prometheus Unbound*. In writing a lyrical drama, he transposes a relatively private vision of the Promethean age into the public domain, recognizing at the same time that the emplotment of this vision in terms of characters who enact it and events that bring it about inevitably discloses aporias in the Promethean ideology (Rajan, 'Deconstraction or Reconstruction' 317–38). The Narrator of *Alastor*, however, never really resolves his discomfort with the web of narrative, which prevents us from reducing the text to a single strand without recognizing how one possibility is interwoven with others. At the end he abandons narrative for elegy. Through elegy he appeals to his readers to re-member the Poet, and yet seals his subject against further reading by leaving us with the reproach of the Poet's death, which would make any questioning of his life a profanation. Mourning the departure of a 'Spirit' whose death leaves the world empty, the Narrator renounces 'Art and eloquence' as inadequate (711ff). As a silencing of the reader, elegy attempts to restore the hermeneutics of lyric, but in a form whose assumption of a public voice conflicts with the enforced privacy of its grief, and which is thus infiltrated by the very dialogism it resists. A similar avoidance of ambivalence is evident in the preface, where the writer seeks to simplify narrative by suggesting that the Poet's life is a picture 'not barren of instruction to actual men' and that it is 'allegorical of one of the most interesting situations of the human mind' (Shelley 1977, 69). Replacing lyric sympathy with allegorical didacticism, the preface-writer tries to restore the direct relation between language and referent disrupted by the narrative process, which through the introduction of multiple characters generates different perspectives from which to view the protagonist. But paradoxically he supports his allegory by providing an account of the Poet's career: a narrative which divides his attempt to assume a position outside the Poet's life, by requiring him also to see that life from the perspective of the Poet.

This uneasiness with a mode to which he keeps returning has its roots in a more fundamental ambivalence on the part of the Narrator towards the functioning of language as difference. It may be apparent that I have said two somewhat different things here, perhaps because Shelley at this stage does not clearly distinguish between the two. On the one hand, I have described narrative as an intertexture in which the process of representation does not simply translate conception into expression, but also produces autonomous and destabilizing meanings which are non-synthetically incorporated into the pattern of the fabric and displaced further. These displacements do not call into question the value of telling stories; they comprise the conditions under which narratives are transmitted and survive. By disclosing gaps within the telling of a story, they open narrative to what Ricoeur calls 'refiguration' (Ricoeur 160): a concept which means that the 'work of narrative does not conclude with the closure of emplotment but continues into the reception of the work by the reader' (Harpham 84–5). On the other hand, I have suggested, in descriptions of how the Narrator assembles and disassembles the character of the Poet, that language produces figures upon a vacant ground. The web of language is not quite the same thing as the abyss of language, though some contemporary theory tacitly identifies the two. These two images, drawn from

Shelley himself, define the parameters within which his perception of the disarticulating potential of language moves. The web or tissue is a favourite image among current theorists for what Barthes calls a 'text' as opposed to a 'work' (Barthes 155–64), because unlike other forms of aesthetic construction it can be unravelled. And indeed a weaving is potentially endless, its apparent centres functioning also as points of dissemination, its individual strands more confusingly woven into and underneath each other than appears to the superficial eye. But for all this the process of weaving creates something, though it is complicated and problematic. Moreover, the web expresses not only the differential relations between elements of a text, but also their connectedness. Because it is the image with which *Alastor* concludes, it is not unfair to see it as a de-idealized version of the image with which the poem begins: that of the 'brotherhood' of the elements (1). In this poem the complications of (self)-representation produce a fear that what underlies language may be an abyss of meaning. As the poem veers philosophically between faith in a transcendental realm and a nihilistic materialism, so too it oscillates between positing a transcendental signified accessible through lyric or allegory and seeing language as subtended only by a vacancy. This sense that the intertexture of language conceals something destructive is apparent in the way the Narrator associates it with a spider's web. The music of the veiled woman's voice, we are told, holds the Poet 'suspended in its web / Of many-coloured woof and shifting hues' (156–7). The Poet cannot live in what at the end is described as 'the web of human things, / Birth and the grave.' That perhaps is why he rarely speaks. The Narrator, though he speaks at length and lives in a world where everything is constituted on the trace of its opposite, cannot reconcile himself to it. Whether one can find meaning in the web of differences and displacements that constitutes speech, life, and all systems of representation is a question that preoccupies Shelley for the remainder of his career.

NOTES

Unless otherwise indicated all references are to *Shelley's Poetry and Prose*, ed. Donald Reiman and Sharon Powers (New York: Norton, 1977). The edition used for *The Revolt of Islam* is Thomas Hutchinson, ed., *Poetical Works* (Oxford: Clarendon, 1905).

1 For a thorough discussion of the Wordsworth-Shelley relationship as it pertains to this poem, see Blank 50–4, 98ff. Blank links *Alastor* to *The Excursion*; I have followed a somewhat different path in linking the poem to Wordsworth's figurations of the visionary child.
2 Georg Lukács uses the terms 'extensive' and 'intensive' totality to describe epic and drama respectively, with the latter term indicating a completeness that is more inward and solitary than the social plenitude of the epic. The novel, by contrast, is extensive but lacks totality (46).
3 Schopenhauer 1:248–51; Nietzsche, *The Birth of Tragedy* 49–56. For a discussion of Nietzsche's concept of 'mood' see Stanley Corngold's 'Nietzsche's Moods.'
4 I refer to the first version of the poem from MS JJ, which lacks the lines about the boy's death. This early draft can be found in Wordsworth 1979, 492.
5 The 'symbolic' in contrast to the 'imaginary' is, according to Lacan, the order of language and the law in which the subject finds himself inscribed, displaced. To this dyad Kristeva adds a third category, the 'semiotic,' associated with physiological drives and pulsions whose residual presence disrupts language, being felt in terms of absence, contradiction, silence. Whereas the symbolic is patriarchal, the semiotic is associated with the mother's body, so that the feminine resistance to male *logos* is not pleasure (as in Cixous's valorization of the imaginary) but rather a de-idealized difference (Kristeva, *Desire in Language* 133–4).
6 For Nietzsche's discussion of the body see Nietzsche, *The Will to Power* 271, 281. On the relation between the semiotic and the body in Kristeva, see Kristeva, *Desire in Language* 6, and *Revolution in Poetic Language* 25–30.
7 Thomas Weiskel suggests that the Poet's journey falls into 'two phases, an upward, regressive journey to origins (ll.222–468), and a downward course, following a river that is meant to image the progress of his life' (Weiskel 146).
8 The two exceptions are 280–90 and 366–9.

WORKS CITED

Adorno, Theodor. 'Lyric Poetry and Society.' *Telos* 20 (1974): 56–71.
Barthes, Roland. *Image, Music, Text.* Trans. Richard Howard. New York: Hill and Wang, 1977.
Blank, G. Kim. *Wordsworth's Influence on Shelley: A Study of Poetic Authority.* London: Macmillan, 1988.

Cameron, Sharon. *Lyric Time: Dickinson and the Limits of Genre*. Baltimore: Johns Hopkins UP, 1976.
Corngold, Stanley. 'Nietzsche's Moods.' *Studies in Romanticism* 29 (1990): 67–90.
Derrida, Jacques. *Positions*. Trans. Alan Bass. Chicago: U of Chicago P, 1981.
Frye, Northrop. *Anatomy of Criticism: Four Essays*. Princeton: Princeton UP, 1957.
Harpham, Geoffrey Galt. *The Ascetic Imperative in Culture and Criticism*. Chicago: U of Chicago P, 1987.
Kristeva, Julia. *Desire in Language: A Semiotic Approach to Literature and Art*. Trans. Thomas Gora, Alice Jardine, and Leon S. Roudiez. New York: Columbia UP, 1980.
– *Revolution in Poetic Language*. Trans. Margaret Waller. New York: Columbia UP, 1984.
Leavis, F.R. *Revaluation: Tradition and Development in English Poetry*. London: Chatto and Windus, 1936.
Lukács, Georg. *The Theory of the Novel*. Trans. Anna Bostock. Cambridge: MIT P, 1971.
Miller, J. Hillis. *Fiction and Repetition: Seven English Novels*. Cambridge: Harvard UP, 1982.
Nietzsche, Friedrich. *The Birth of Tragedy and the Case of Wagner*. Trans. Walter Kaufmann. New York: Vintage, 1967.
– *The Will to Power*. Trans. Walter Kaufmann and R. J. Hollingdale. New York: Vintage, 1967.
Rajan, Tilottama. *Dark Interpreter: The Discourse of Romanticism*. Ithaca: Cornell UP, 1980.
– 'Deconstruction or Reconstruction: Reading Shelley's *Prometheus Unbound*.' *Studies in Romanticism* 28 (1984): 317–38.
– 'Romanticism and the Death of Lyric Consciousness.' *Lyric Poetry: Beyond New Criticism*. Ed. Chaviva Hosek and Patricia Parker. Ithaca: Cornell UP, 1985. 194–207.
Ricoeur, Paul. *Time and Narrative*. Trans. Kathleen McLaughlin and David Pellaver. Chicago: University of Chicago P, 1985.
Schopenhauer, Arthur. *The World as Will and Representation*. 2 vols. Trans. E.F.J. Payne. New York: Dover, 1966.
Shelley, Percy Bysshe. *Note Books of Percy Bysshe Shelley*. 3 vols. Ed. H.B. Forman. Boston: Bibliophile Society, 1911.
– *Poetical Works*. Ed. Thomas Hutchinson. Oxford: Clarendon, 1905.
– *Shelley's Poetry and Prose*. Ed. Donald Reiman and Sharon Powers. New York: Norton, 1977.

Weiskel, Thomas. *The Romantic Sublime: Studies in the Structure and Psychology of Transcendence.* Baltimore: Johns Hopkins UP, 1976.

Wordsworth, William. *The Prelude 1799, 1805, 1850.* Ed. Jonathan Wordsworth, M.H. Abrams, and Stephen Gill. New York: W.W. Norton, 1979.

SHELLEY WALL

Baffled Narrative in *Julian and Maddalo*

I

I rode one evening with Count Maddalo
Upon the bank of land which breaks the flow
Of Adria towards Venice: a bare strand
Of hillocks, heaped from ever-shifting sand
...
Is this ...   (ll. 1–4, 7)

Thus begins Shelley's *Julian and Maddalo*. The dichotomy between Julian's simultaneous freedom of movement – on horseback with his powerful Byronic friend the count – and his situation at a point of interruption – on 'the bank of land which *breaks the flow* / Of Adria towards Venice' – prefigures the poem's shifting narrative sands.

The poem's subtitle, 'A Conversation,' appears to refer to that held between Maddalo and Julian as they ride on the Lido. The ride and the conversation share a certain freedom of movement: 'So, as we rode, we talked; and the swift thought, / Winging itself with laughter, lingered not, / But flew from brain to brain' (ll. 28–30). The men speak 'Of all that earth has been or yet may be, / All that vain men imagine or believe, / Or hope can paint or suffering may achieve' (ll. 43–5). Julian, the narrator, argues for the boundless potential of the human spirit, finding evidence in the sublime expanses of the landscape and the sky. In this mood, he sings the Lido, yet his words contain within themselves a counter-argument, a suggestion that desire projects infinity onto what is in fact a narrow, abandoned space of wreckage and stunted growth; the Lido is

> ... an uninhabited sea-side,
> Which the lone fisher, when his nets are dried,
> Abandons; and no other object breaks
> The waste, but one dwarf tree and some few stakes
> Broken and unrepaired, and the tide makes
> A narrow space of level sand thereon
> ...
>   I love all waste
> And solitary places; where we taste
> The pleasure of believing what we see
> Is boundless, as we wish our souls to be.   (ll. 7–12, 14–17)

The sunset sends Julian into further raptures, for in it he witnesses the apocalyptic marriage of heaven and earth 'dissolved into one lake of fire' (l. 81). At this point, Maddalo, countering Julian's Shelleyan idealism with Byronic gloom,[1] points out a madhouse – 'a windowless, deformed and dreary pile' (l. 101) – silhouetted against the setting sun. Human thoughts and desires, argues Maddalo, are like madmen clustering in mindless prayer around a 'rent heart,' and the soul is like a madhouse vesper-bell. Next morning, Julian renews the debate by pointing to Maddalo's daughter, an untrammelled infant, not self-enchained by 'sick thoughts' (l. 169). Their debate still undecided, they travel to the madhouse to observe one final exhibit, a maniac whom Maddalo is lodging there at his own expense. They enter the apartment of the Maniac (who never becomes aware of their presence) and eavesdrop as he launches into a possessed monologue.

Thus far, the narrative is structured as a series of gazes. Maddalo and Julian objectify and transform the world around them into a series of exempla in the service of a debate whose terms – idealism versus cynicism – appear to represent the poem's conceptual poles. This kind of scopic mastery – the mastery of the gaze – is of course an issue in feminist theory. Maddalo and Julian occupy the 'masculine' position of masterful subject – a stance duplicated in Julian's first-person narrative control[2] – while the daughter and the madhouse inmates (Maddalo's protégé specifically) are allotted the 'feminine' position of object. The infant daughter does not speak,[3] and the Maniac, although he speaks, cannot return the gaze, being unaware of his visitors' presence; neither daughter nor Maniac has any name beyond the generic one.

The style of this opening section is of a piece with the masterful stance of the protagonists: it is controlled, though informal, and marked by class affiliations. Shelley claimed to be attempting in this poem something 'in a different style ... a *sermo pedestris* way of treating human nature,' employing 'a certain familiar style of language to express the actual way in which people talk with each other whom education and a certain refinement of sentiment have placed above the use of vulgar idioms' (*Letters* 2:196; 2:108). It is marked by 'the easy familiarity of two articulate and literary men of aristocratic families' (Brewer 128), with all the 'gentlemanly' virtues of politeness and urbanity that this implies. Kelvin Everest observes that 'the style is interestingly problematic for a radical poet, for it involves the danger of acceding to the ideological implications of that familiar idiom. And there is a strong possibility that Shelley was fully alert to this problem in *Julian and Maddalo*, where the single most striking rhetorical effect of the poem is the violently contrasting idiom of the maniac's soliloquy, which is set against the gentlemanly discourse of Maddalo and Julian' (79).

The Maniac's monologue is reproduced in the centre of the narrative. It retains the rhyming couplets of Julian's narrative but lapses completely from the 'urbane' style, consisting instead of short, broken paragraphs in which thought succeeds thought according to no clear logic.[4] The Maniac is reputed to have gone mad after being abandoned by his lover; in the monologue he appears to address a number of absent women, or a number of aspects of the woman who has betrayed him. His manner shifts from moment to moment: he spoke, recalls Julian,

> ... – sometimes as one who wrote, and thought
> His words might move some heart that heeded not,
> If sent to distant lands: and then as one
> Reproaching deeds never to be undone
> With wondering self-compassion; then his speech
> Was lost in grief, and then his words came each
> Unmodulated, cold, expressionless, –
> But that from one jarred accent you might guess
> It was despair made them so uniform.   (ll. 286–94)

When the Maniac's monologue ends, his unannounced 'guests' return to Maddalo's palace, their debate forgotten; Julian soon leaves for London, and the Maniac appears no more.

A brief epilogue concludes the poem: Julian returns to Venice years later; and Maddalo is in Armenia, so that Julian is received by Maddalo's daughter, now grown up. Julian questions her about the Maniac; he learns that the lover returned, and the Maniac grew better, but that then the lover left again; the daughter is reluctant to tell more than that of his subsequent history. The conclusion of their interview, and of the poem, is this:

> 'Ask me no more [says the daughter], but let the silent years
> Be closed and cered over their memory
> As yon mute marble where their corpses lie.'
> I urged and questioned still [resumes Julian], she told me how
> All happened – but the cold world shall not know.   (ll. 613–17)

So the narrative culminates in a suppression of narrative. In his act of withholding, Julian aims, apparently, to protect the Maniac – the gossip will go no further; and yet there is something unsettling in the gesture, both in the violence of its rejection of the reader, and in the suggestion of hypocrisy in Julian's discretion, given that he has coerced the daughter, the original reticent narrator, into revealing the Maniac's history in the first place. It has been suggested that the poem's conclusion de- emphasizes the Maniac's story, chastening the over- curious reader.[5] Yet the epilogue explicitly foregrounds the Maniac's story as an object of gossip. If the particulars of the Maniac's subsequent life and death are unimportant, the fact of his persistence as an object of scandal, rumour, and inquiry is not. By suppressing the Maniac's history, Julian in fact impresses the Maniac's curious power all the more firmly on the reader's awareness; his act of closure leaves the poem, at its 'conclusion,' radically open.

This gesture which doubles back upon itself, and the unsettling nature of the narrative's abrupt suspension, point to larger divisions opened up in the course of the poem's unfolding. *Julian and Maddalo* consists of two separate discourses inhabiting the same title: Julian's narrative, and the Maniac's monologue. By various strategies (including the co-optive power of first-person narration and the machinations of the Preface, to be described below), the poem invites the reader to accept Julian's as the primary discourse and to regard the Maniac's monologue as a kind of exemplary accessory, embedded in the host discourse simply to help the narrative along. By the same token, Maddalo and Julian – the titular, and the only *named*, characters – become the poem's protagonists, and the Maniac, even when he emerges as more than one of the legion of the emblematic mad, is officially granted no more than a supporting role.

And yet he exceeds this role, both within the represented world where Maddalo and Julian converse and at the level of narrative. Before their visit to the madhouse, the friends' talk is full of the semi-scientific language of demonstration and proof: the Maniac's 'wild talk will show / How vain are [Julian's] aspiring theories,' claims Maddalo, while Julian 'hope[s] to prove the induction otherwise' (ll. 200–1, 202). When the mad monologue draws to a close, however, the friends 'we[ep] without shame,' their argument 'quite forgot' (ll. 516, 520). And just as the spectacle of the Maniac disarms the debate and renders meaningless the language of logical argument, so the reproduction of his disconnected monologue within the poem breaks the urbane narrative's trajectory and seems to hasten the poem to its end. The narrated conversation leading up to the visit is protracted: 299 lines cover one evening and one day; after the visit, 106 lines cover a span of 'many years'; the poem speeds to its truncated conclusion with a sort of desperation. Two distinct but corresponding 'moments' inform the poem: the fictional past in which the conversation and monologue take place, and the fictional present in which an older Julian recalls past events and reproduces the Maniac's words. If Julian finds it impossible, in his first encounter with the Maniac, to fit him to his own argument, he finds it equally impossible to assimilate the Maniac upon 'revisiting' him in recollection to write down his words. The Maniac consistently baffles attempts to 'contain' him, to reduce him to the status of objectified exhibit or reified speech.

The issue that concerns me in this paper is not Maddalo and Julian's debate between idealism and cynicism, but, rather, the subject position that this debate allots the Maniac, and the issues raised thereby of objectification, and of the use that ratiocentrism and androcentrism make of their professed others, madness and the feminine.[6] In other words, what are the implications of Julian's masterful narrative stance, and what is it about the Maniac that seems to baffle this mastery?

II

Maddalo and Julian inhabit a world of *connections*. Shelley's Preface alerts us to their irreproachable family connections: 'Count Maddalo is a Venetian nobleman of ancient family and of great fortune'; 'Julian is an Englishman of good family' (Preface, pp. 189, 190). They never fail to make their travel connections, either; they move freely from sight to sight assisted by inconspicuous attendants, and the sheer frequency of these instances is worth noting. Here are just a few:

> Just where we had dismounted, the Count's men
> Were waiting for us with the gondola
>
>   As thus I spoke
> Servants announced the gondola, and we
> Through the fast-falling rain and high-wrought sea
> Sailed to the island where the madhouse stands
>
>   Having said
> These words we called the keeper, and he led
> To an apartment opening on the sea
>
>   ... then we lingered not,
> Although our argument was quite forgot,
> But calling the attendants, went to dine
> At Maddalo's ...   (ll. 61–2, 211–14, 270–2, 519–22)

Temporal progression is signalled just as obsessively as spatial progression: the progress from the first evening, through sunset, to the next morning is meticulously marked, and of course there are temporal markers in the lines quoted above, in the referencing of movement to moments in the conversation.

The poem's Preface, too, is important in connecting the reader to the world of the poem: it is presented as the utterance of a fictional persona, corresponding neither to Shelley nor to Julian but bearing a class resemblance to both. The Preface consists of three paragraphs describing the poem's *dramatis personae*; these paragraphs decrease in length and specificity from Maddalo, to Julian, to the Maniac. The Preface-writer addresses the reader as a member of his own 'relatively small class of the refined and educated' capable of understanding Maddalo and Julian and their philosophical concerns (Brewer 129); he provides a quantity of physical and psychological information about the title characters and invites the reader to participate in his mild ironies. From the start, by means of the Preface, Maddalo and Julian's section of the poem appears to be a fairly 'closed' text, to adopt a term from reader-response theory; our understanding of their world and their debate operates within the defined set of social and philosophical meanings laid out by this initial guide.

The Maniac, by contrast, presents a scandalously open text; he inhabits a country for which no maps exist. Whereas the Preface-writer is acquainted with information about Maddalo and Julian beyond that available in Julian's narrative, concerning the Maniac he is as dependent as the reader on the information given in the poem – by Julian (on the basis of observation) and by Maddalo (on the basis of rumour). The Preface releases the Maniac to the reader's care with no guarantees. This is all it says:

Of the Maniac I can give no information. He seems, by his own account, to have been disappointed in love. He was evidently a very cultivated and amiable person when in his right senses. His story, told at length, might be like many other stories of the same kind: the unconnected exclamations of his agony will perhaps be found a sufficient comment for the text of every heart. (Preface, p. 190)

Thus, even before the poem begins, we have an intimation of the Maniac's potency. That he is cast as unconscious 'commentator' relegates him to a literally marginal role; at the same time, however, commentary's power to transform the text it glosses can be immense.

The Maniac's is a world of missed connections, disconnections. The madhouse stands on an island, its physical isolation emblematic of the segregation of madness beyond the mainland of reason. The Maniac is singing in an upper cell as Maddalo and Julian enter the madhouse courtyard; 'fragments of most touching melody' float down to them (l. 221). He occupies a present disconnected from the past; to Julian's inquiries about the Maniac's origins, Maddalo replies:

>   Of his sad history
> I know but this: ... he came
> To Venice a dejected man, and fame
> Said he was wealthy, or he had been so.
>   ...
> ... he was always talking in such sort
> As you do – far more sadly – he seemed hurt,
> Even as a man with his peculiar wrong,
> To hear but of the oppression of the strong
>   ...

> A lady came with him from France, and when
> She left him and returned, he wandered then
> About yon lonely isles of desert sand
> Till he grew wild – he had no cash or land
> Remaining ...   (ll. 231–4, 236–9, 246–50)

Discussing their impressions of him later, the friends decide that 'he had store / Of friends and fortune once ... These were now lost' (ll. 534–5, 537).

The Maniac's speech, too, is divorced from the familiar connectives of sequential utterance. Published versions of the poem, following Shelley's instructions,[7] break the text of the monologue into sections separated by rows of dots – indicating breaks in the train of thought, and perhaps suggesting temporal pauses in the monologue's delivery. The community of speakers implied in conversation is also gone: the Maniac's interlocutors are absent phantoms, at times even the dead (ll. 384, 395, 445–6). Finally, the monologue is self-consuming; the Maniac complains of both an uncontrollable urge to expression and an equally powerful drive towards the silence and oblivion of death; his discourse seeks a point of self-annihilation:

>   How vain
> Are words! [he exclaims] I thought never to speak again,
> Not even in secret, – not to my own heart –
> But from my lips the unwilling accents start,
> And from my pen the words flow as I write,
> Dazzling my eyes with scalding tears ... my sight
> Is dim to see that charactered in vain
> On this unfeeling leaf which burns the brain
> And eats into it ... blotting all things fair
> And wise and good which time had written there.   (ll. 473–81)

In the overdetermined language of this passage, speech and writing are one; breath and ink become scalding tears; tears in turn become the acid in a corrosive writing that engraves itself on the brain – a destructive script that overwrites the benevolent inscriptions of memory. Commentators have seen the Maniac as representing 'the poet';[8] Maddalo suggests that 'Most wretched men / Are cradled into poetry by wrong, / They learn in suffering what they teach in song' (ll. 544–6); and the monologue's radical mode of presentation--overheard by an unseen audience – is that conventionally associated with lyric. But if the Maniac represents a poet, he is a poet in whom the self-unbuilding properties of language come to the fore. If he resembles Prometheus – and this has also been suggested[9] – then he is a Beckettian Prometheus, subverting the structure of narrative authority only by virtue of the unspeakable impossibility of his situation. We might conceive of the Maniac's utterance in terms of a negative series of imbricated Chinese boxes – a sequence of negation within negation, as in his concluding words:

> I do but hide
> Under these words, like embers, every spark
> Of that which has consumed me – quick and dark
> The grave is yawning ... as its roof shall cover
> My limbs with dust and worms under and over
> So let Oblivion hide this grief ... the air
> Closes upon my accents, as despair
> Upon my heart – let death upon despair! (ll. 503–10)

Thus words function as instruments of obliteration and concealment, rather than providing the illumination Maddalo and Julian sought in first proposing to visit the madhouse. The conversational ideal confronts, in the speech of the Maniac, its demonic other. Rather than resembling dialogue, in which idea kindles idea in an intersubjective act of creative exchange, the Maniac's speech implodes upon itself. The Maniac feels the air 'close ... upon [his] accents,' as if air *baffled* speech, rather than being the very breath and medium in which it lives.

It is no wonder, then, that curious disjunctions and elisions occur at the points where these worlds of 'connection' and 'disconnection' intersect, or, rather, approach each other and then fail to intersect. The Maniac's implosive world does not open out towards his observers; Maddalo and Julian's world defines itself by the exclusion of this 'incoherent' alterity. Julian, for example, claims to dream of 'reclaiming' the Maniac –

> ... I imagined that if day by day
> I watched him, and but seldom went away,
> And studied all the beatings of his heart
> With zeal, as men study some stubborn art
> For their own good, and could by patience find

> An entrance to the caverns of his mind,
> I might reclaim him from his dark estate (ll. 568–74)

– yet this vaguely imperialistic dream of penetration remains curiously self-seeking – the study is for the *student's* 'own good'; it maintains the Maniac in the position of object; it retains the dynamics of the gaze. Julian's plans, moreover, carry this proviso: 'If I had been an *unconnected* man,' he writes, 'I, from this moment, should have formed some plan / Never to leave sweet Venice' (ll. 547–9); 'urged by [his] affairs,' however, he returns to London (l. 582). Thus it is Julian's very *connectedness* that *prevents* his 'connecting' with the Maniac.

An interesting figure of connection arises in Maddalo and Julian's suggestion, quoted above, that the madman had *'had store* / Of friends and fortune once' (ll. 534–5). The phrase 'had store' is significant in that it indicates the negative economy of madness: connectedness is a commodity; the onset of the Maniac's madness coincides with the disappearance, not only of his lover and of his store of relatives, but also of his 'cash [and] land' (l. 249). Maddalo and Julian commodify the destitute Maniac in making a literal 'conversation piece' out of his situation and his utterance. Although Maddalo might be said to have given something in exchange in providing for the Maniac's maintenance, nevertheless his and Julian's activity in listening to the monologue is described in terms of theft: 'we stood behind / Stealing his accents from the envious wind / Unseen' (ll. 296–8). Their eavesdropping, their voyeurism, are figured, moreover, as *tangible* theft – a physicality suggested also in the likening of the Maniac's speech to letter-writing, in Julian's observation that he speaks 'sometimes as one who wrote, and thought / his words might move some heart that heeded not, / If sent to distant lands' (ll. 286–9). In eavesdropping as they do, Maddalo and Julian effectively intercept and open the Maniac's mail, an epistolary discourse which, like Poe's purloined letter, has black-market value. In purveying the Maniac's speech as part of his own narrative, Julian packages and sells the reader something that is not really his to give.

III

The poem raises this question: how to deal with such a disconnected person, severed from lover, family, property, and, above all, bankrupt in the economy of reason? It is impossible that the scandal of his madness should be left at large. Maddalo recounts the story of the Maniac's incarceration: when his lover left him

> ... he wandered then
> About yon lonely isles of desert sand
> Till he grew wild – he had no cash or land
> Remaining, – the police had brought him here –
> Some fancy took him and he would not bear
> Removal; so I fitted up for him
> Those rooms beside the sea, to please his whim,
> And sent him busts and books and urns for flowers,
> Which had adorned his life in happier hours,
> And instruments of music.　　　　　　　(ll. 247–56)

Note the rapid elision, in this account, of the role of 'the police.'[10] The Maniac immediately learns to love his captivity; then Maddalo domesticates the situation by providing aesthetic amenities, and thus what begins as an episode of police discipline concludes in a genteel household scene. This movement towards domestication reflects a movement within the poem to align the Maniac – and his threatening irrationality – with the feminine. As Alice Jardine notes, 'The space "outside of" the conscious subject has always connoted the feminine in the history of Western thought – and any movement into alterity is a movement into that female space' (114–15). The Maniac in Shelley's poem is male yet occupies a number of subject positions coded as female. Maddalo implies that an overly acute sense of political injustice initially made the Maniac 'a dejected man' poised on the verge of insanity; in this way, he fits the type of male melancholia; but his madness has sexual origins as well – an attribute of female hysteria. Like the knight in Keats's 'La Belle Dame Sans Merci,' the Maniac is placed in a traditionally female subject position by being seduced, betrayed, and then abandoned. In adopting epistolary strategies ('sp[eaking] as one who wr[ites]' [l. 286]), the Maniac joins a line of letter-writing heroines – from those of Ovid's *Heroides* to Abelard's Eloisa – who have been, in the words of a theorist of epistolary genres, 'literally exiled or imprisoned or metaphorically "shut up" – confined, cloistered, silenced,' their 'discourses of desire ... repressed' (Kauffman 20). He is further feminized when Maddalo 'espouses' his cause and turns his madhouse cell into a pleasant home which, nevertheless, he cannot leave. Thus the Maniac's confinement by police is quickly assimilated to culturally acceptable images of female domestication and confinement. In this way his incarceration is 'naturalized' – that is, its strangeness is made to seem unremarkable, and therefore escapes questioning.[11]

Given the Maniac's feminized subject position, it is surprising that similarities between the Maniac and Maddalo's model daughter have not been more often remarked. At least three separate moments of speech are represented in the poem subtitled 'A Conversation': the initial 'urbane' conversation; the anti-conversation, in which the Maniac addresses phantom interlocutors and the invisible Maddalo and Julian 'steal' his words from the sidelines; and Julian's conversation with Maddalo's daughter in the epilogue. In this last conversation, both parties speak – Julian truly 'visits' with the daughter, as he did not in his so-called 'visit' to the Maniac; and yet this conversation does not replicate the free exchange represented in the initial scene between Maddalo and Julian, where 'swift thought[s]' fly 'from brain to brain' (ll. 28, 30). Julian's final visit, like his visit to the Maniac, devolves into a one-way flow of goods, replicating the economy of voyeurism. The daughter gives up the secret she has in keeping from the Maniac and his lover, and Julian absorbs it like an unreflective surface.

The Maniac and the daughter are initially introduced to the reader as competing examples, the ridiculous and the sublime; while the Maniac lives in a state of bondage and blindness, the daughter is 'a wonder of this earth, / Where there is little of transcendent worth, – / Like one of Shakespeare's women' (ll. 590–2). Yet Maniac and daughter become allies, even doubles; they share at first the role of nameless object; later, the daughter becomes custodian of the Maniac's story. Her plea to 'let the silent years / Be closed and cered over their memory / As yon mute marble where their corpses lie' (ll. 613–15) seems to imply, in her curious use of the word 'yon,' that she lives within view of the lovers' tombs. Hers is figured as a world separate from the 'real' world of her father and his acquaintance – it is the world of literary representations, as Julian's reference to Shakespeare implies. As the woman who remains constant and stationary in the home while men like her father and Julian travel the globe, she represents the ideal of female confinement which the Maniac's domestication mimics.

IV

Julian's is the 'host' discourse, in which the Maniac's discourse is embedded as an exemplary object. In becoming 'guests' of the Maniac, however – in making *him* their unwitting 'host' – Maddalo and Julian perform an act of reversal that lays them open to subversion. In attempting to consume madness (as a conversation piece) without becoming infected by a kind of madness themselves – in attempting to represent the alterity of mad discourse without altering the terms of rational narrative – Maddalo and Julian manifest what Foucault calls 'that other form of madness, by which men, in an act of sovereign reason, confine their neighbours, and communicate and recognize each other through the merciless language of non-madness ... that "other form" which relegates Reason and Madness to one side or the other of its action as things henceforth external, deaf to all exchange, and as though dead to one another' (ix).

The madhouse visit is supposed to answer the questions raised in Maddalo and Julian's conversation; instead, it puts into question the very terms on which the initial argument is erected.[12] Even before the friends enter the madhouse, we *know* that they will not find what they are looking for. Here is Maddalo's initial 'reading' of the madhouse when it appears against the sunset:

'... such ... is our mortality,
And this must be the emblem and the sign
Of what should be eternal and divine! –
And like that black and dreary bell, the soul,
Hung in a heaven-illumined tower, must toll
Our thoughts and our desires to meet below
Round the rent heart and pray – as madmen do
For what? they know not, – till the night of death
As sunset that strange vision, severeth
Our memory from itself, and us from all
We sought and yet were baffled.' (ll. 120–9)

In a perverse way, the failure of Maddalo and Julian's quest attests to the success of Maddalo's interpretation. In his emblematic reading, the madhouse they appeal to stands at the point where searches are defeated, the very sign of bafflement. The Maniac literally inhabits this sign; he signals the fragmented self, self-unseeing; what illumination, then, can be hoped for from him?

Julian and Maddalo can be, and has been, read as a critique of Julian as narrator, with the implication that he represents certain aspects of Shelley himself. This critique is focused at one level on Julian as a dramatic character who lacks self-awareness, who does not learn anything in the course of the poem, whose theories fail to coincide with his actions. At another level, as Kelvin Everest has noted, the critique is directed at Julian, not only as an individual, but as a member of Shelley's own social class – a class whose hegemony Shelley repudiated, and yet certain of whose values had formed him, and inform his poetry.[13]

This aspect of Shelley's critique extends, I would suggest, to the very ideology of framing that has seen the Maniac's soliloquy embedded in the urbane frame of Maddalo and Julian's gentlemanly conversation. Julian's narrative re-enacts, at the level of discourse, the confinement of the Maniac. Just as the police arrest the wandering Maniac and place him within walls, so Julian attempts to contain the Maniac's 'unconnected exclamations' within the reasonable limits of his own narrative. Conversely, the Maniac's speech enacts, at the level of discourse, a thwarting of narrative that corresponds to the emotional and intellectual confusion he evokes in Maddalo and Julian; this mock-lyric, mock-epistolary monologue, that is, refuses assimilation into the genre of urbane conversation in which it appears.

The Maniac represents the disenfranchised 'others' who inhabit Maddalo and Julian's world. He is to them as unreason is to reason, as feminine is to masculine, as vagrancy is to established institutions – the first term subjected to definition by the second term, yet exercising a dangerous power of subversion. The Maniac and his utterance represent the negation of the terms on which Maddalo and Julian's conversation depends for its very existence; Julian's ultimate suppression of the Maniac's history, although represented as both a protective and a tedium-saving gesture, is at the same time a second narrative attempt to 'confine' the Maniac, he and his discourse having once already exceeded the container that was prepared to receive them. And yet this act of closure merely opens the poem up more radically than ever; the Maniac and his story are consigned to the oblivion and silence of the tomb, to use one of the daughter's final figures, but they are also, by the same gesture, all the more deeply engraved.

NOTES

All references are to Percy Bysshe Shelley, *Poetical Works*, ed. Thomas Hutchinson, corrected by G.M. Matthews (1970; London: Oxford UP, 1975), and to *The Letters of Percy Bysshe Shelley*, ed. Frederick L. Jones, 2 vols. (Oxford: Clarendon, 1964).

1 For a discussion of biographical explications of the poem prior to 1963, see G.M. Matthews 57–61.
2 That is, Julian's is the primary 'point of view.' Beth Newman notes the pervasive presence of 'visual metaphors' in narratology. She writes: 'Such terms implicitly invoke a gaze: a look that the subject(s) whose perceptions organize the story direct at the characters and acts represented.' Newman cites E. Ann Kaplan's statement that 'the gaze is not necessarily male (literally), but to own and activate the gaze, given our language and the structure of the unconscious, is to be in the "masculine" position,' and notes that 'this gaze in turn raises issues important for feminist criticism' (1029).
3 She does, however, have eyes full of 'deep meaning' (l. 149) – a gaze of her own, prefiguring her emergence in the epilogue as a narrator in her own right (a right granted and then denied).
4 Which is not to say that the Maniac's monologue is 'incoherent,' but, rather, that it deviates from standards of 'coherence' implied in the narrative that frames it.
5 For example, James L. Hill reads the poem's conclusion as 'an admonition to make us consider the poem as more than a mere story'; 'a clue to direct the attention of the serious reader toward finding the conceptual kernel embodied in the narrative' (84).
6 For 'post-biographical' readings of the poem, see: G.M. Matthews, '"Julian and Maddalo": The Draft and the Meaning'; James L. Hill, 'Dramatic Structure in Shelley's "Julian and Maddalo"'; Earl R. Wasserman, *Shelley: A Critical Reading*; Bernard A. Hirsch, '"A Want of That True Theory": "Julian and Maddalo" as Dramatic Monologue'; Vincent Newey, 'The Shelleyan Psycho-Drama: "Julian and Maddalo"'; Kelvin Everest, 'Shelley's Doubles: An Approach to *Julian and Maddalo*'; Ronald Tetrault, *The Poetry of Life: Shelley and Literary Form*; Tracy Ware, 'Problems of Interpretation and Humanism in "Julian and Maddalo"'; William D. Brewer, 'Questions without Answers: The Conversational Style of "Julian and Maddalo."'
7 Shelley writes to Charles Ollier, 14 May 1820: 'If you print "Julian and Maddalo," I wish it to be printed in some unostentatious form ... and exactly in the manner in which I send it' (*Letters* 2:196).
8 For example, G.M. Matthews asserts that the Maniac 'must typify the situation *of the poet*' (75). Bernard A. Hirsch, too, sees the Maniac as consistent with a conception of the poet expressed throughout Shelley's work (24). Kelvin Everest relates the issue of the poet to social critique, suggesting that the poem presents 'Julian's creative, "poetic" potential as

frozen within his quiescent commitment to the manner of a repressive and repressed dominant social group. The figure of the maniac may then emerge in the poem as the externalized representation of this buried poetic potential in Julian, a potential tragically unmediated for any audience and thus possessing the aspect of a tragic incoherence' (80). Tracy Ware has seen the Maniac more recently as representing a misguided conception of poetry 'obviously at odds with Shelley's own theory, as expressed in *A Defense of Poetry* and elsewhere' (120).

9 '[T]he Maniac is a *sermo pedestris* kind of Prometheus, written down to the domestic level' (Matthews 74).
10 'In the draft of lines 249–50, the Maniac is brought to the madhouse first by "soldiers," next by "watchmen," and ultimately by "the police"' (Matthews 82).
11 His speech is naturalized as well. Julian not only frames it as an element in his own narrative; he also fits it to the rhyme and metre of the host discourse, although he claims that the Maniac's words were *not* 'in measure' (l. 542), and that he has reproduced the monologue verbatim (ll. 298–9).
12 We might refer here to Julia Kristeva's assertion that 'in a culture where the speaking subjects are conceived of as masters of their speech, they have what is called a "phallic" position. The fragmentation of language in a text calls into question the very posture of this mastery' (165).
13 Julian is one of 'Shelley's poetic doubles' who 'characteristically represent conditions of limited or misdirected social awareness' (Everest 68).

WORKS CITED

Brewer, William D. 'Questions without Answers: The Conversational Style of "Julian and Maddalo."' *Keats-Shelley Journal* 38 (1989): 127–44.

Everest, Kelvin. 'Shelley's Doubles: An Approach to *Julian and Maddalo*.' *Shelley Revalued: Essays from the Gregynog Conference*. Ed. Kelvin Everest. Leicester: Leicester UP, 1983. 63–88.

Foucault, Michel. *Madness and Civilization: A History of Insanity in the Age of Reason*. Trans. Richard Howard. New York: Random House, 1965.

Hill, James L. 'Dramatic Structure in Shelley's "Julian and Maddalo."' *ELH* 35 (1968): 84–93.

Hirsch, Bernard A. '"A Want of That True Theory": "Julian and Maddalo" as Dramatic Monologue.' *Studies in Romanticism* 17 (1978): 13–34.

Jardine, Alice A. *Gynesis: Configurations of Woman and Modernity*. Ithaca and London: Cornell UP, 1985.

Kauffman, Linda S. *Discourses of Desire: Gender, Genre, and Epistolary Fictions.* Ithaca: Cornell UP, 1986.

Kristeva, Julia. 'Oscillation between Power and Denial.' *New French Feminisms.* Ed. Elaine Marks and Isabelle de Courtivron. New York: Schocken, 1981. 165–7.

Matthews, G.M. '"Julian and Maddalo": The Draft and the Meaning.' *Studia Neophilologica* 35 (1963): 57–84.

Newey, Vincent. 'The Shelleyan Psycho-Drama: "Julian and Maddalo."' *Essays on Shelley.* Ed. Miriam Allott. Totowa: Barnes and Noble, 1982. 71–104.

Newman, Beth. '"The Situation of the Looker-On": Gender, Narration, and Gaze in *Wuthering Heights*.' *PMLA* 105 (1990): 1029–41.

Shelley, Percy Bysshe. *The Letters of Percy Bysshe Shelley.* Ed. Frederick L. Jones. 2 vols. Oxford: Clarendon, 1964.

– *Poetical Works.* Ed. Thomas Hutchinson, corrected by G. M. Matthews. 1970. London: Oxford UP, 1975.

Tetrault, Ronald. *The Poetry of Life: Shelley and Literary Form.* Toronto: U of Toronto P, 1987.

Ware, Tracy. 'Problems of Interpretation and Humanism in "Julian and Maddalo."' *Philological Quarterly* 66.1 (1987): 109–25.

Wasserman, Earl R. *Shelley: A Critical Reading.* Baltimore: Johns Hopkins UP, 1971.

PART TWO

The World, the Text, the Reader

ALAN BEWELL

Keats's 'Realm of Flora'

An obvious feature of Keats's poetry that has often been noted, both by his contemporaries and modern critics, but has not been adequately studied, is his extensive use of floral imagery. It is hard to miss in the early poetry, the *Poems* of 1817 and *Endymion*, where poetry is likened to a luxurious bower where the poet can feed at leisure on floral pleasure. In 'Sleep and Poetry,' Keats's early poetic manifesto, the 'realm of Flora' is depicted as a space of poetic beginnings, one that must be passed if he is to write a greater poetry that deals with 'the agonies, the strife / Of human hearts' (124–5). This description has often been used as a template for understanding Keats's progress as a poet. We speak of the unrestrained floral imagery run riot in *Endymion* and of the Spenserean 'budding' ephebe giving way to the 'more naked and grecian Manner' of *Hyperion* and the controlled ambiguities of the Odes.[1] And with this shift, a poetry of flowers gives way to a verse influenced by Milton, Shakespeare, and Dante. We speak of a passive, weak, poetry of sensual excess – viewed as 'effeminate' by Keats's contemporaries – as being displaced by a more serious, more masculine, philosophical poetry that seeks to master literary traditions. As adolescent sexual fantasy gives way to mature poetic desire, the decorative and ephemeral floral imagery of pastoral is superseded by the authority of monumental verse.

This perspective on the role of flowers in Keats's poetry has two major related weaknesses. The first is that Keats's later poetry does not so much move beyond floral symbolism as use it differently. Keats shows a deepening, more ambivalent, understanding of how the 'realm of Flora' can be used to speak about human suffering, division, and loss. In *The Eve of St. Agnes*, Porphyro's strategem for escaping the dangerous ascetic fictions of medieval romance and, at the same time, gaining access to Madeline, appears 'suddenly ... like a full-blown rose / Flushing his brow' (136–7). In 'Ode to Psyche,' the poet is portrayed as a horticulturalist, building with 'gardener Fancy,' a 'rosy sanctuary' in 'some untrodden region' of his mind. And even in this poem, in the copy Keats sent to his brother and sister-in-law, he falls back upon the floral style of *Endymion*, apostrophizing Psyche, '*O Bloomiest!* though too late for antique vows' (*Letters* 2:107, my italics). In the abandoned bower of *The Fall of Hyperion*, the floral Underworld of 'Ode to a Nightingale,' the pastoral scenes of *Lamia*, or the 'mellow fruitfulness' of 'To Autumn,' Keats continues to use floral imagery almost as frequently as in his earlier poetry. Yet what he says through flowers changes. Our lack of an understanding of the nature of this change leads me to my second point: we do not understand this change because we do not understand, with any historical accuracy, what it meant for a male poet, during the Regency period, to write poetry in which floral imagery functions as the main discursive component. Most critics vaguely recognize the traditional association between flowers, poetry, sex, and women. What has not been adequately understood, however, are the specific ways in which Keats's poetry draws upon these analogues and the ways in which his floral style reflects his changing conception of his sexual and poetic identity.

As many of his contemporaries recognized, Keats's use of floral imagery is quite different in its sources and character from Wordsworth's. There can be little doubt that he wished to be regarded as a 'poet of nature,' in the tradition of Wordsworth. His close friend J.H. Reynolds, in a review of the *Poems* of 1817, attempts to establish this link when, after extolling the verse, he argues that 'this youthful poet appears to have tuned his voice in solitudes – to have sung from the pure inspiration of nature.'[2] Keats may have wished to 'tune his voice in solitudes,' but he did not live in the Lake District. And, except for the Northern England and Scotland excursion with Charles Brown from June to August 1818, Keats's poetry was written either in London and Hampstead or at various popular holiday resorts, such as Margate, the Isle of Wight, Burford Bridge, and Winchester. Keats was quite different from the first-generation Romantic poets because he was a poet of the suburbs, a member, as Byron deprecatingly remarked, of the 'Suburban School' of poets. 'He took the wrong line as a poet,' writes Byron in another letter, 'and was spoilt by Cockneyfying and Surburbing [*sic*].'[3] Whereas Wordsworth's plant imagery reflects a daily contact with nature and natural forces, Keats's arises from an urban middle-class context. Furthermore, Keats very much belongs to an incipient Victorian culture. Keats and his circle, like their Victorian counterparts, saw botany and gardening as hobbies, as being intrinsically linked to pleasure and the leisure-time escape from the demands of city life. Charles Cowden Clarke, his childhood friend, later wrote a children's book entitled *Adam, the Gardener* (1834), and Clarke's brother-in-law, John Towers, whom Keats knew, wrote *The Domestic Gardener's Manual* (1830).[4] Leigh Hunt was also interested in botany. His sister-in-law, the botanist Elizabeth Kent, lived with him in Hampstead. Her *Flora Domestica; or, The Portable Flower Garden* (1823) and *Sylvan Sketches; or, A Companion to the Park and Shrubbery* (1825) were both published by Taylor and Hessey, who were also Keats's and John Clare's publishers.[5] In Keats's poetry, one can see the beginning of what was to become, in Lynn Barber's words, the 'heyday of natural history,' as middle-class Victorians combed the English countryside looking for plants. In *The Victorian Fern Craze* (1969), David Elliston Allen describes how, at the height of this plant mania, the popular craze for plants literally transformed the English landscape (along with many colonial landscapes, one might add) as whole species of plants disappeared under the onslaught of weekend botanists and gardeners.[6] Whereas the eighteenth century was the great age of nature produced, the nineteenth century was the great age of nature commercialized. It saw the emergence of an enormous project of textualizing nature, as the urban middle class bought anything – from books, to dishes, to wallpaper – that had a flower on it, a flower in it, or a flower pressed between its leaves.[7] Like his contemporaries, Keats linked excursions into nature with collecting. At the end of *Endymion*, the hero, who has frequently been identified with Keats, calls himself 'a lord / Of flowers, garlands, love-knots, silly posies, / Groves, meadows, melodies, and arbour roses,' thus linking poetry, in the anagrammatic pun on 'poesis' in 'posies,' not only to botany, but also to the kind of use made of flowers – that is, 'garlands, love-knots, silly posies' – that we have come to associate with the Victorian period.[8] But instead of pressing real plants physically between the pages of books, Keats was concerned with gathering textual flowers and poetically reproducing them in his poems. As Donald Goellnicht has insightfully shown, Keats displays an extensive knowledge of botany in his poetry, derived from his education as an apothecary at Guy's Hospital.[9] An equally important force shaping his floral rhetoric is his participation in the production of a nascent Victorian culture of flowers, in which floral imagery was produced for an urban public, who saw flowers as eminently aesthetic and decorative objects, linked to leisure, recreation, wealth, and a nature that was no longer a part of everyday life. Flowers had become pre-eminently marketable and collectable – they were produced to be consumed.

Keats directly links poetry to flowers when he argues that 'the Lovers of Poetry like to have a little Region to wander in where they may pick and choose, and in which the images are so numerous that many are forgotten and found new in a second Reading' (*Letters* 1:170). Two points are worth making here. The first is that Keats understands a poem as being a textual equivalent to a garden, as it offers its readers a luxurious abundance of images from which to 'pick and choose' and to which they can return repeatedly, finding new images on each return. The second is that Keats is here describing not only how readers should read his poetry, but how he himself read other poets. The early Keats, especially, read poetry with the eye of a poet-nurseryman, someone who makes it his business to find, produce, and sell flowers – the flowers found either in nature or in literary texts.

Here we see a quite radical difference between Keats's and Wordsworth's understanding of a poem. Whereas Wordsworth viewed it as a representation of human beings and their relationship to their environments, Keats sees nature as something that is purposefully gathered, planted, and arranged for display and pleasure. It is a social product. From this perspective, Keats's poetry is actually much closer to Erasmus Darwin's botanical verse in *The Loves of the Plants* than it is to Wordsworth's *Michael*. In the 'Ode to Psyche,' Keats provides an allegory of the genesis of 'nature' in his poems. There he celebrates not only love but also the power of 'the gardener Fancy' (62) – the poet as horticulturalist – to build a garden 'in some untrodden region of my mind' (51). Starting with Wordsworth's nature – 'Far, far around shall those dark-cluster'd trees / Fledge the wild-ridged mountains steep by steep' (54–5) – Keats landscapes it, populating this wild setting with the familiar figures of Keatsean imagination, with 'zephyrs, streams, and birds, ... bees' and 'moss-lain Dryads' (56–7). Having turned Wordsworth's nature into a garden or park, Keats then constructs, 'in the midst of this wide quietness' – that is, the textual space opened within his own revisioning psyche – a 'rosy sanctuary' with 'the wreath'd trellis of a working brain' (58–60). To underscore the fact that this garden is a textual product, rather than a representation of nature, Keats insists that the flowers to be found there are not like those in common gardens because they are all botanical hybrids: they 'never breed the same.' Where Wordsworth would have emphasized 'common nature,' Keats is concerned with nature as a product of art and labour.

The garden, as a place where nature meets culture and is socially transformed, is an appropriate symbol for Keats's understanding of poetry. Gardens are also expressions of power, of 'nature controlled to human satisfaction,' whether it be the power to dominate and transform nature (as in the formal gardens of Europe) or to utilize nature by working out relationships of cooperation and accommodation (as in the landscape gardens of the English gentry or cottage gardens).[10] Equally importantly, gardens have always served as the insignia of social class and status. In 'Ode to Psyche' and the previously cited 'little region' passage, Keats represents the poem as being analogous to a pleasure garden, a landscape garden, or botanic garden, the terms, at this time, not being mutually exclusive. One of the more obvious features of these gardens is that they were produced by and for the leisured classes; they were embodiments of social status and power. Janet Browne, in her excellent discussion of Erasmus Darwin's *The Loves of the Plants*, notes that

> for Darwin, as for other members of the intellectual leisured classes, reference to a botanic garden evoked a constellation of ideas and emotions that combined scientific purpose with recreational pleasure. Gardens glorified both the practical expertise of horticulturalists and the serious activities of taxonomists and medical personnel. National pride was reflected in the breadth and variety of such collections, each plant representing geographical explorations in the past and the nation's political allegiances and commercial intentions. Gardens were also obvious repositories of 'nature,' a display of plants outside their usual geographic boundaries conjuring up notions of an untrammeled, fecund world.[11]

Over the course of the eighteenth and nineteenth centuries, a powerful association was thus forged between gardens, leisure, geographical exploration, and commerce. In fact, especially in the case of Cook's first voyage, exploration was as much driven by the search for plants as for gold.[12] That Keats conceives of his poetry as a textualized version of such gardens suggests, then, a form of social aspiration. To Keats, the long poem was equivalent to a landscape garden: it was the embodiment of wealth, power, leisure, and the authority associated with them.

But such gardens were quite removed from Keats's own world. Though he would have been familiar with botanic gardens from his medical training, and though he may have visited some of the many private botanic gardens in the London area, Keats probably had little immediate familiarity with the landscape gardens maintained by the gentry, which were difficult to gain entry into. What Keats did know a good deal about was 'town gardening,' the gardens that had become popular with the rising urban middle class. Such gardening was done on a small scale because land in urban areas had become quite expensive over the course of the eighteenth century. On 12 April 1819, when Keats was living at Wentworth Place, he wrote to his sister Fanny, declaring that 'I ordered some bulbous roots for you at the Gardeners, and they sent me some, but they were all in bud – and could not be sent, so I put them in our Garden There are some beautiful heaths now in bloom in Pots – either heaths or some seasonable plants I will send you instead – perhaps some that are not yet in bloom that you may see them come out' (*Letters* 2:51). Here we see a poet who frequents local nurseries, businesses that had become increasingly prominent over the previous fifty years and were about to become a familiar part of the urban landscape.[13] Three weeks later, Keats writes to Fanny that he plans to 'call in passing at the tottenham nursery and see if I can find some seasonable plants for you,' ending with the query, is there not 'a twig-manufacturer in Walthamstow?' (*Letters* 2:56). Keats's mention of 'some beautiful heaths now in bloom in Pots' should remind us that the early nineteenth century saw the full-scale emergence of container gardening. One of the best-known authorities on this subject was, in fact, Elizabeth Kent, whose *Flora Domestica; or, The Portable Flower Garden* (1823) set out to supply 'such information as should be requisite for the rearing and preserving a portable garden in pots.'[14] In her preface, Kent observes that people 'condemned to a town life' frequently lack a portion of ground in which to cultivate a garden, so that a 'portable garden' can serve as a substitute. She quotes *The Task*, where Cowper observes that these gardens indicate that man

> ... still retains
> His inborn, inextinguishable thirst
> Of rural scenes, compensating his loss
> By supplemental shifts, the best he may.[15]

A problem that emerges when one recognizes that flowers in Keats's poetry are primarily cultural products or 'supplemental shifts,' part of the burgeoning Victorian commerce in flowers, rather than, as in Wordsworth, elements drawn from nature, is that it is often difficult to know whether Keats's floral imagery derives from natural observation or from textual sources, such as book illustrations, botanical prints and engravings, literary sources (notably Spenser, Drayton, Milton, Wordsworth, and Hunt), botany manuals, or the increasing use of plants in the textile and decorative arts. As Geoffrey Hartman has noted, rarely do we look on a Keatsean landscape without feeling that, to some degree, we are seeing it artistically framed.[16] Even when, for instance, Keats does speak of observing nature, he generally does so with a view to reproducing it in textual form. Writing from Dean Street to Joseph Severn, Keats declares that 'all the Week' he has been particularly looking forward to Saturday because he 'want[s] to look into some beautiful Scenery – for poetical purposes' (*Letters* 1:115). The phrasing 'look into' makes this weekend outing in nature sound much more akin to finding nature in a book with good engravings. And the language of 'poetical purposes' is that of the poet/nurseryman, who reads a text not only for pleasure, but also for gain. When, in 'Sleep and Poetry', Keats imagines himself being enticed by a young woman to journey

> Through almond blossoms and rich cinnamon;
> Till in the bosom of a leafy world
> We rest in silence, like two gems upcurl'd
> In the recesses of a pearly shell   (118–21)

one senses that this 'leafy world' is not natural, but textual, its floral elements, like the 'spiced dainties' (269) that Porphyro offers Madeline in *The Eve of St. Agnes*, are sights, drawn from exotic bookish regions, to be seen more than eaten.

John Gibson Lockhart, in his attack upon the poetry of the 'Cockney School of Poetry,' indicates the manner in which the suburbanism of Keats's poetry was perceived by his contemporaries. Though few are likely to agree with Lockhart's biases, his criticism does provide us with ingress into some of the more distinctive contemporary features of Keats's poetry. He complains that despite the fact that Leigh Hunt and Keats raved about nature, 'about "green fields," "jaunty streams," and "o'er-arching leafiness,"' they do so 'exactly as a Cheapside shop-keeper does about the beauties of his box on Camberwell road.' 'Mr Hunt,' he writes, 'is altogether unacquainted with the face of nature in her magnificent scenes; he has never seen any mountain higher than Highgate-hill, nor reclined by any stream more pastoral than the Serpentine River. But he is determined to be a poet eminently rural, and he rings the changes – till one is sick of him, on the beauties of the different "high views" which he has taken of God and nature, in the course of some Sunday dinner parties, at which he has assisted in the neighbourhood of London.'[17] The 'Cockney School of Poetry,' it seems, had produced a 'Cockney nature,' a floral diction that Lockhart associates with middle-class, urban commercial culture, the language of the 'Cheapside shop-keeper' in speaking of 'the beauties of his box on Camberwell road.' Cockney poets are small-minded, it would seem, because nature in the suburbs is small. In an article written a year later, Lockhart applies the same criticism to Keats, arguing that he is a little-minded poet who engages in 'laborious affected descriptions of flowers seen in window-pots, or cascades heard at Vauxhall.'[18] For Lockhart, if poetry is to be likened to gardening, Keats is not the Capability Brown of Romantic verse, but instead a suburban pot-gardener whose knowledge of landscapes is limited to Vauxhall Gardens.

We need not fully agree with Lockhart's claim that there is no nature in Keats's poetry, that it is no more than an urban commodity, to recognize that Keats's poetry characteristically produces a sophisticated and often disturbing dioptric play between nature, culture, and social class. His floral imagery points in two directions: even as flowers embody social aspiration in their metaphoric link to values implicit in the idea of the landscape garden (those of leisure, wealth, and, as will become clear, eroticism), they equally draw attention to themselves as signs or substitutes – 'supplemental shifts' – for that world. Flowers never lose their textual and ornamental status, as cultural artefacts on display. But they are inherently contradictory in meaning, as they point both to their origin in worlds that are removed from the aspiring poet and to the suburban, commercial world of the poet, who values them particularly because they give him entry into those worlds.[19] A passage from 'I stood tip-toe upon a little hill' provides a good example of these stylistic dualisms:

> For what has made the sage or poet write
> But the fair paradise of Nature's light?
> In the calm grandeur of a sober line,
> We see the waving of the mountain pine;
> And when a tale is beautifully staid,
> We feel the safety of a hawthorn glade:
> When it is moving on luxurious wings,

> The soul is lost in pleasant smotherings:
> Fair dewy roses brush against our faces,
> And flowering laurels spring from diamond vases;
> O'er head we see the jasmine and sweet briar,
> And bloomy grapes laughing from green attire;
> While at our feet, the voice of crystal bubbles
> Charms us at once away from all our troubles:
> So that we feel uplifted from the world,
> Walking upon the white clouds wreath'd and curl'd.   (125–40)

Initially, Keats seems to assert the priority of nature as the source of poetic inspiration; it makes 'the sage or poet write.' With the mention of a 'sober line,' however, the priority is reversed, as it seems that the 'line' produces, almost by the necessities of rhyme, the need for a 'mountain pine.'[20] In the 'tale' that is 'staid,' we see a 'hawthorn glade'; the tale 'moving on luxurious wings' produces the 'pleasant smotherings' of 'dewy roses.' With the mention of 'luxury,' flowering laurels 'spring from diamond vases.' Here, the dioptric qualities of this verse are clear, for this is a nature that offers us cut flowers. This superimposition of the natural and the artificial carries over from the 'diamond' (that is, the 'cut glass') vases, to the 'voice of crystal bubbles.' Again, one wonders whether Keats is finding nature epitomized in crystal glass, or whether his luxury-driven imagination is not attempting to find something approaching 'crystal' in nature. The echo, in these lines, of the valentine written earlier that year, 'Hadst thou liv'd in days of old,' confirms that these floral images are less representations of nature than substitutes for social and erotic desires. Keats describes Mary Frogley's hair as resting in a casque

> O'er which bend four milky plumes
> Like the gentle lilly's blooms
> Springing from a costly vase.   (53–5)

Poetry, nature, gardens, wealth, women: since each, in Keats's poetry, is analogically related to and superimposed upon the others, metaphors drawn from one usually carry the traces of their associative link to the others. The special semantic effects of Keats's verse lie in this carry-over of meaning, not as a symbolic accumulation, but instead in the slight disjunction, dislocation, or skewing of the image that such carry-overs produce. Looking at nature or flowers through Keats's eyes, we begin to see a woman; the desire for nature and to be a 'poet of nature' fuses with erotic desire and masculine authority: his bees 'wrestle' with flowers, his heroes sleep with nature, his eye ranges among flowers in a desire to possess them. 'A dimpled hand' hangs from Calidore's shoulder like 'the drooping flowers / Of whitest cassia' and is 'fondled' by his 'happy cheek' ('Calidore' 95–7); nature becomes a 'swelling leafiness' ('Calidore' 34); a woman's 'honied voice' ('Hadst thou liv'd' 24) is implicitly likened to the nectar in the 'throat' of a flower, a throat of 'bubbling honey' (*Lamia* 1.65); the 'graceful bends' of a woman's 'dark hair' become 'leaves of hellebore' ('Hadst thou liv'd' 13–15); a bee 'buzz[es] round two swelling peaches' ('Calidore' 66); and Zephyr, 'ere Phoebus mounts the firmament, / *Fondles* the flower amid the sobbing rain' (*Endymion* 1.330–1, my italics). Yet desire stems from want or absence, so even as Keats seeks to fuse an analogical link between poetry, nature, gardens, and women, in a poetry equivalent to a 'store / Of luxuries' ('Sleep and Poetry' 346–7), his poetry also points to the fact that he stands outside of or distant from these idealizations. Each can be mutually substitutable because each is but a sign of aspiration and desire.

Once one recognizes the play of dioptric, anamorphic transformations within Keats's verse, one is in a position to recognize, as did Shelley when he urged Keats to avoid 'system and mannerism,' that though Keats draws extensively from Wordsworth, he does so as a literary mannerist, his style being much more attuned to the work of Robert Herrick or Andrew Marvell than to other English Romantics.[21] Keats, in fact, is probably best understood as constituting, with Hunt, the School, not of Cockney Poetry, but of Romantic Mannerism. Reading Keats is an exercise in image collation: as images slide beneath each other, they do not fuse but instead produce a slight disorder. Natural images are distorted as they are recast as products of urbane Regency London culture, while poetic ornament attempts, disturbingly, to become nature: 'Vermilion-spotted' and 'crimson-barr'd' (1.48–50) the snake Lamia smiles, but with 'a woman's mouth with all its pearls complete' (1.60).

This dioptric quality is especially clear in the ways in which Keats juxtaposes sex and botany. Probably the best instance of this is in 'Sleep and Poetry':

> First the realm I'll pass
> Of Flora, and old Pan: sleep in the grass,
> Feed upon apples red, and strawberries,

> And choose each pleasure that my fancy sees;
> Catch the white-handed nymphs in shady places,
> To woo sweet kisses from averted faces, –
> Play with their fingers, touch their shoulders white
> Into a pretty shrinking with a bite
> As hard as lips can make it. (101–9)

As Ian Jack has noted, this reflection is occasioned, not by nature, but instead by Poussin's painting *The Realm of Flora*, which Keats saw in Leigh Hunt's study.[22] The passage, then, is not describing a poet's perception of a natural scene, but instead his response to an engraving of a mythical world into which he desperately wants entry. Unlike Poussin, and writers such as Erasmus Darwin and Blake, who saw the 'realm of Flora' as a state, not a gender, as a world ruled by a goddess and the pleasures she provided, Keats renews its traditional identification with women. In Rousseau, Erasmus Darwin, or Blake, flowers can be either male or female: in Keats, they are almost exclusively female. Entrance into the realm of flora thus constitutes both a poetic and a sexual act, a point that is allegorized in this passage. Beginning with a blurred distinction between human culture and the world of plants, as the poet enters the scene to sleep in the grass or feed on apples or strawberries, Keats speaks of catching 'the white-handed nymphs in shady places.' The slight dioptric skewing that I have been suggesting as being characteristic of Keats's mannerist style occurs with 'shady places,' because we are not sure whether the location that is being referred to is geographical or bodily. And matters are not simplified by the recognition that the word 'nymphs,' at this time, was also an anatomical term, which Keats would have known from his medical studies, referring to female genital labia. Similarly, when he then imagines himself biting into 'their shoulders white,' he reinvokes the previous botanical imagery of feeding on apples and strawberries, so that a semantic or metaphoric overlay occurs. Hungry for pleasure, having intensely imagined himself into an erotic world where plants and women are the same – all being daughters of Flora – Keats is not fussy where his next meal comes from.

Ovid's idea of myth as a poetic means of linking the human and natural spheres plays a major role in Keats's poetry, especially as metamorphosis provides an interpretive framework for understanding the identity underlying the dioptric skewing of images. 'I stood tip-toe ...,' which is Keats's Ovidean manifesto, provides an extended reflection on the poetic possibilities in the mythological interplay between the floral and the human spheres. The poem opens in the following manner:

> I stood tip-toe upon a little hill,
> The air was cooling, and so very still,
> That the sweet buds which with a modest pride
> Pull droopingly, in slanting curve aside,
> Their scantly leaved, and finely tapering stems,
> Had not yet lost those starry diadems
> Caught from the early sobbing of the morn. (1–7)

A striking feature of this passage is its fusion of an uncommonly decorative or ornamental style with overt erotic intent. Though superficially, the passage has affinities with the floral personification that one associates with Albert Grandville's *Les Fleurs Animées*,[23] it is actually much closer to being a verbal equivalent of *The Temple of Flora*, a lavishly illustrated coffee-table style of book produced by the botanist Robert Thornton, who taught at the United Hospitals just before Keats began courses there. Even as Thornton's flowers retain their autonomous beauty – and are not personified – they nevertheless serve as idealized figures of erotic desire.[24] In 'I stood tip-toe …,' Keats emphasizes the sexuality of flowers, their 'modest pride,' which powerfully links the traditional association of female modesty, innocence, and chastity with 'sweet buds' even as it employs the language of sexual freedom (perhaps, too, there is a sense of the Elizabethan meaning of 'pride' as sexual desire, especially female heat).[25] Keats is interested here less in the scientific understanding of the sexuality of flowers than in the erotic possibilities of overt anthropomorphization; we are asked to project a powerfully amatory image onto these 'scantly leaved' sweet buds with their 'finely tapering stems.' Keats focuses on the ways that plants provide him with an opportunity for sexual myth-making and for talking about aspects of human life that would not, otherwise, be easily addressed. If the landscape of 'I stood tip-toe …' is charged with eroticism, it is not by accident; it is the poetry of a speaker who knows that he is deliberately seeing human sexual life in flowers.[26]

A less successful example of this process can be seen in Keats's description of sexual defloration. Having heard how 'a spring-head of clear waters' babbles 'wildly of its lovely daughters / The spreading blue bells,' we are told that this same spring

> ... may haply mourn
> That such fair clusters should be rudely torn
> From their fresh beds, and scattered thoughtlessly
> By infant hands, left on the path to die. (41–6)

The passage is a parody of the kind of moralized reflection on flowers that became popular among women writers during the early part of the nineteenth century. Yet the moral of this tale is not at all clear. Given the homonymic play on 'belles,' the word 'spreading' is vulgar, while the addition of 'fresh' to the obvious pun on 'beds' is all too graphic. Thus, the analogy between the sexuality of plants and of human beings, basic to this popular form of moralistic tale, provides the generic underpinnings of this passage, culminating as it does in the image of the fallen flowers 'left on the path to die,' even as Keats self-consciously subverts this genre.

Other examples of the anthropomorphic sexualization of flowers might be noted, for instance, the poet's appeal to 'ardent marigolds' to 'open afresh your round of starry folds' (47–8). One further example, however, will help clarify the ways in which Keats's 'realm of flora' represents a mannerist reworking of botanical analogy:

> Here are sweet peas, on tip-toe for a flight:
> With wings of gentle flush o'er delicate white,
> And taper fingers catching at all things,
> To bind them all about with tiny rings. (57–60)

Here again one is given an image of an animated nature, as the flowers of the sweet pea, with their lateral petals or 'wings,' to use the botanical term, seem as if they are about to take flight. The tendrils of the plant, evoking the idealized tapering of women's fingers, are actively sexual and totally impartial in their embraces – they catch 'at all things' – yet, like the 'modest pride' of the 'sweet buds' (3), they are also marriage-minded, bent on binding 'all about with tiny rings.' The 'gentle flush o'er delicate white,' at once a colour and a feeling, suggests the passion that motivates their embrace. As John Barnard has noted, the passage 'means to overleap any concern for conventional verbal decorum in its eager excitement to catch a physical sense of the flower world.'[27] Donald Goellnicht has observed that the scientific source of the metaphor derives from the fact that the sweet pea belongs to the class of flowers termed 'papillionacious,' because their 'four petals,' as Robert Thornton noted, 'resemble a butterfly on the wing.'[28] The passage, then, constitutes a metaphoric cultivation of the analogy between the flowers of the sweet pea and butterflies 'on tip-toe for a flight.'

Two quite interesting things emerge from this recognition. The first is that what is being described here is truly a sexual embrace, an embrace so close that we cannot distinguish the wings and 'taper fingers' of the butterflies from the wing petals and taper tendrils of the sweet pea. The idea of the mutual sexual pleasure of butterfly and flower was a favourite of Keats. In 'Sleep and Poetry,' he describes 'A butterfly, with golden wings broad parted, / Nestling a rose, convuls'd as though it smarted / With over pleasure –' (343–5). Here one cannot tell grammatically whether it is the insect or the rose that is in the state of sexual ecstasy. In a letter, Keats again uses the relationship between insect and flower to develop, in ways similar to eighteenth-century radical botanical writing, both an idealized vision of what human sexual pleasure can be and a theoretical argument for what constitutes true poetic inspiration:

It has been an old Comparison for our urging on – the Bee hive – however it seems to me that we should rather be the flower than the Bee – for it is a false notion that more is gained by receiving than giving – no the receiver and the giver are equal in their benefits – The f[l]ower I doubt not receives a fair guerdon from the Bee – its leaves blush deeper in the next spring – and who shall say between Man and Woman which is the most delighted? Now it is more noble to sit like Jove that [sic] to fly like Mercury – let us not therefore go hurrying about and collecting honey-bee like, buzzing here and there impatiently from a knowledge of what is to be arrived at: but let us open our leaves like a flower and be passive and receptive – budding patiently under the eye of Apollo and taking hints from every noble insect that favours us with a visit – sap will be given us for Meat and dew for drink – I was led into these thoughts, my dear Reynolds, by the beauty of the morning operating on a sense of Idleness. (*Letters* 1:232)

Here, flowers provide Keats with a language for talking about a world where love is freely enjoyed by both sexes--and, by women, perhaps even more than by men. Claiming that poetic authority would be wiser to model itself upon female passion, Keats suggests that Wordsworth's 'wise passiveness' should actually be understood as wise receptiveness.[29]

Keats's willingness to maintain male-female gender distinctions – the male is a bee, the female, a flower – while simultaneously associating 'negative capability' with a feminized poetic is a complex issue to which I will return. For now, it is enough to recognize that the image of the sweet peas, standing 'on tip-toe for a flight,' constitutes a metapoetic figure for the poet's own pleasure in the text, his relationship to the 'flowers of rhetoric' that constitute the poem, for he too is described, at the beginning of the poem, as being 'tip-toe upon a little hill.' This figural repetition serves an important purpose, which critics have failed to recognize. It suggests that the poem has an overt mannerist intention in that it is implicitly structured from the point of view of a poet/butterfly, surveying a vast field of flowers, intending before nightfall to visit them all. Whereas Milton represents the poet's inspired flight using the spiritual symbol of the dove, Keats, in a much earthier fashion, consistently portrays the poet's imaginings in terms of the flight of a butterfly/bee, whose honeyed song is the product of his sensual, wrestling play with flowers – that is, with poetic metaphors and metaphorized women.[30] Having, in truly mannerist fashion, shrunk the world to microscopic proportions, to the world as it appears through the eyes of an insect, Keats delights in the possibility of enjoying a sexual/poetic fantasy acted out on an epic scale. 'There was wide wand'ring,' he says, 'for the greediest eye, / To peer about upon variety; / Far round the horizon's crystal air to skim' (16–18). Likening himself to the winged Mercury, his 'thought a pair of little wings' (cancelled lines, draft, following line 122), he tells us that

> ... many pleasures to my vision started;
> So I straightway began to pluck a posey
> Of luxuries bright, milky, soft, and rosy.   (26–8)

In the play on 'posey' and 'poesy,' and Keats's almost complete inability to see flowers in any way other than in a sexualized manner – as dimorphic figures of women – we see how closely poetry, sex, and botany are linked in this poem. The poet's 'honied lines' ('This pleasant tale is like a little copse'), in fact, are the product of such visionary pleasures: 'O for three words of honey, that I might / Tell but one wonder of thy bridal night!' (209–10).

It is difficult to know what kind of audience Keats envisioned for 'I stood tip-toe ...' Like Erasmus Darwin's *The Loves of the Plants*, published as part of his *Botanic Garden*, the poem would seem to require a sophisticated and urbane audience, conversant with botany and willing to enter into the play upon the analogy between the sexuality of plants and people. Also like Darwin, Keats is interested in transgressing accepted sexual mores, in pointing to the sexual desire that underlies and shapes the conventions of social life. The poem also has affinities with eighteenth-century 'botanical pornography,' a popular form of writing, the most notable of these being James Perry's *Mimosa; or, The Sensitive Plant* (1779), which drew upon the analogy between plants and sexual organs. Most of these works are satires, however, and usually are little more than catalogues of overworked metaphors and puns about bodily parts. In Keats's early poetry, the engagement with flowers is much more intimate, as flowers have become the very language of pleasure: most of the intensity, in fact, in Keats's portrayal of sexuality, derives from the description not of human lovemaking but of the floral bowers within which this activity takes place. At times, for instance in the vegetable striptease of the opening lines of 'I stood tip-toe ...,' the poetry even verges on what might be called 'botanical voyeurism.' The bower of Adonis in *Endymion*, or the 'cool-rooted flowers' and 'bedded grass' of the bower in 'To Psyche,' are typical in this regard, as is the bower that Keats describes in his epistle 'To George Felton Mathew,' where

> ... intertwined the cassia's arms unite,
> With its own drooping buds, but very white;
> Where on one side are covert branches hung,
> 'Mong which the nightingales have always sung
> In leafy quiet: where to pry, aloof,
> Atween the pillars of the sylvan roof,
> Would be to find where violet beds were nestling,
> And where the bee with cowslip bells was wrestling.
> There must be too a ruin dark, and gloomy,
> To say 'joy not too much in all that's bloomy.' (43–52)

In this poem, the universal sexuality of nature has not yet been mythologized, made into an idealized mirror of human life through Ovidean metamorphosis, yet one nevertheless can recognize the ground from which such sexualized metaphor grows.[31]

It would be relatively easy to argue that in his early poetry Keats was writing floral erotica for himself and other men, using flowers as substitute textual pleasures. However, this view misses the important fact that, during the opening decades of the nineteenth century, popular botanical literature was primarily the domain of women, a literature being written by women for a female audience.[32] One of the reasons why many of Keats's contemporaries, among them Hazlitt, considered his poetry as being effeminate, was that floral language had become increasingly associated with women's writing over the course of the previous forty years.[33] A brief glance at Mrs Montolieu's poem *The Enchanted Plants*, written in 1803, can serve as a basis of comparison.[34] Like Frances Arabella Rowden's *Poetical Introduction to the Study of Botany* (1801), Montolieu's *The Enchanted Plants* belongs to a literature that made the teaching of botany (and natural history in general) an essential part of a woman's role as domestic educator of her children. In her introduction, we are given the basic fiction of the book, drawn, like Keats's early poetry, from Ovid and Darwin:

> Oft, to beguile the sultry hours,
> In thought I've animated flowers,
>   Enlivening every walk;
> And though no botanist professed,
> Their reasoning powers have shrewdly guessed,
>   And longed to hear them talk. (p. 1)

She tells us how one day in June she pronounced this wish aloud only to be surprised by a female fairy emerging from a pansy. The pixie flies to her ear and in a language previously unknown speaks the following words:

> 'Flora,' it murmured, 'grants thy prayer,
> Long have her treasures been thy care,
>   Receive thy recompense.'
>
> This said, she vanished from my sight,
> And since, with ever new delight,
> I tend my fragrant hoards;
> No solitude exists for me,
> Since every flower and shrub and tree,
> Society affords. (p. 2)

The book consists of a series of poems written on various moral subjects, such as ambition, prejudice, envy, love, and so on, which arise when the author listens in on the conversation of flowers. The poem entitled 'Scandal; or the Painted Lady Sweet-Pea' is representative of the book as a whole. It seems that two botanical luxuriants, 'Gay Anemone, daughter of Art' and Ranunculus, have been gossiping about the sweet pea:

> 'Look there!' said the fanciful flower,
>   (By whimsical botanists dressed)
> 'How yon vain youthful plant of an hour,
>   Smiles and flaunts like a beauty professed.
>
> Though with us in the garden displayed,
>   Unimproved her corollas remain,
> Still blushing, unformed, unarrayed,
>   Like cousins who bask on the plain.'   (pp. 22–3)

As a luxuriant, Anemone is a product of botanical 'fancy,' a horticultural 'whimsy,' and she demeans the 'unimproved' features of Sweet Pea. Ranunculus responds by suggesting that this plainness is itself a form of art; he has heard Daffodil assert that the Sweet Pea only pretends to blush:

> 'And you know on those subjects she's wise,
> That this innocent paints red and white.'
>
> While her exquisite honeyed perfume,
>   For which the bees tease her to death,
> They found too, and so I presume,
>   Is fictitious ... to cover her breath.   (p. 23)

Lucky for Sweet Pea, Sweet William is nearby, and he defends her in knightly fashion, attacking the other two flowers by calling them gossiping spinsters, who have been made sterile and deformed by the cultivation of petals at the expense of the organs of generation:

> Doomed malicious old virgins to fade,
>   Whom multiplied petals deform,
> While she her soft banner displayed,
>   Soon will shelter her fruit from the storm.
>
> The ladies felt something like shame,
>   And indignant, were ready to cry,

>They e'en vowed no more beauties to blame ...
>   That is ... when Sweet William is by. (p. 25)

Moralistic and stylized, the poem is hardly equivalent to some of the more complex uses of botanical imagery, such as in Charlotte Smith's *Beachy Head*. Here the botanical analogy is being used, as increasingly came to be the case, not in order to call into question gender roles, but instead to reaffirm conventional ideas about the proper role of women in society.

Keats, in writing 'I stood tip-toe ...,' was clearly aware of this kind of moralistic writing. At one point, describing the blades of grass carried slowly on the surface of the stream, he alludes to this literature:

>Why, you might read two sonnets, ere they reach
>To where the hurrying freshnesses aye preach
>A natural sermon o'er their pebbly beds. (69–71)

Here, rather than simply alluding to William Paley, Keats is ironically citing those moralistic sonnets on natural history that had been the eminent domain of women for almost thirty years. Other poems in the 1817 collection exhibit what amounts to a form of genre 'cross-dressing.' There is a sonnet entitled 'To a Friend Who Sent Me Some Roses.' In 'To Some Ladies,' written to Caroline and Ann Matthews, Keats reworks Coleridge's 'This Lime-Tree Bower My Prison,' arguing that though he cannot join them on their natural history outing, 'the wonders of nature exploring' (1), he nevertheless can be with them imaginatively. He even envisions that moment when they stooped 'to pick up the keep-sake intended for me,' a curious shell. No other present, he argues, would create 'a warmer emotion' (a phrase particularly resonant of the female literature of sensibility), not even if a cherub had brought a gem from heaven along with the blessings of Mary Tighe, the author of *Psyche*. The subsequent poem in the collection, part of a poetic dialogue between Keats and the Matthew sisters, is entitled 'On Receiving a Curious Shell, and a Copy of Verses, from the Same Ladies.'

'To Some Ladies,' with its mention of Mary Tighe, suggests that Keats was acquainted with the concerns characterizing early nineteenth-century 'ladies verse,' and it appears, at least in this poem, that he adopted it, as did many women during the time, in order to talk discreetly about sexuality.[35] At one point, he imagines Caroline and Ann 'mark[ing] the clear tumbling crystal, its passionate gushes, / In spray that the wild flower kindly bedews' (7–8). The same idea is reworked in more explicit terms in 'I stood tip-toe ...,' where Keats speaks of the 'interchange of favours' between the cresses and the brook:

> The ripples seem right glad to reach those cresses,
> And cool themselves among the em'rald tresses;
> The while they cool themselves, they freshness give,
> And moisture, that the bowery green may live:
> So keeping up an interchange of favours,
> Like good men in the truth of their behaviours. (81–6)

Keats is, as he suggests, following the contemporary practice of using analogies drawn from nature to instil moral values, to 'preach a natural sermon o'er their pebbly beds.' However, it is not at all clear that the brook actually serves as an exemplum of male fidelity – 'good men in the truth of their behaviours.' Keats draws our attention to 'the swarms of minnows' that 'ever wrestle / With their own sweet delight, and ever nestle / Their silver bellies on the pebbly sand' (72–7). The fact that the image is explicitly sexual (the sand is a 'pebbly bed') makes it clear that the lesson being taught in 'I stood tip-toe ...' is that life is universally engaged in seeking 'sweet delight.'

In a letter to J.H. Reynolds, Keats explicitly has recourse to botany, as a kind of insider language, which he and women share: 'Will you have the goodness to do this? Borrow a Botanical Dictionary – turn to the words Laurel and Prunus show the explanations to your sisters and Mrs Dilk and without more ado let them send me the Cups Basket and Books they trifled and put off and off while I was in Town' (*Letters* 1:133). Anticipating the Victorians, Keats adopted the 'language of flowers,' assuming that some things could be said through them that could not be said otherwise. It is worth noting, in this connection, that it appears that homosexual males, during the Regency period, when prosecutions for homosexuality had increased, equally had recourse to botany as an encoded sexual language. Byron, while travelling to the East, writes to his Cambridge friend Charles Skinner Matthews that 'we are surrounded by Hyacinths & other flowers of the most fragrant [na]ture, & I have some intention of culling a handsome Bouquet to compare with the exotics I hope to meet in Asia. One specimen [whom he later refers to as "Abbé Hyacinth"] I shall surely carry off, but of this hereafter.'[36] That Matthews understood Byron's meaning is clear from his own letter, where he declares that 'as to your Botanical pursuits, I take it that the flowers you will be most desirous of culling will be of the class polyandria and not monogynia but nogynia.' He thus encourages Byron to collect polyandrous flowers, those with an indefinite number of 'males' or stamens, to collect flowers with 'no females' (i.e., 'nogynia'), while avoiding flowers that are monogynous, having a single female. He goes on to add: 'However so as you do not cut them it will all do very well. A word or two about hyacinths. Hyacinth, you may remember was killed by a Coit [punning on quoit and coit(ion)], but not that "full and to-be-wished-for-Coit." Have a care your Abbey Hyacinth be not injured by either sort of coit. If you should find anything remarkable in the botanical line, pray send me word of it, who take an extreme interest in your anthology; and specify the class and if possible the name of each production.'[37] I do not want to claim that either Matthews or Byron – or, for that matter, Keats – are particularly original in using botany as an encoded language of sexuality. Shelley, for instance, uses it equally successfully in 'The Sensitive Plant.' The fact that these metaphors emerge so easily in an epistolary context suggests that, at least during the Regency period, they were ready to hand. The frequent claim by Regency critics that Keats's poetry was 'effeminate' points out the degree to which Keats's contemporaries saw in his floral style an appeal to an audience that was not obviously male and heterosexual.

It should be stressed, then, that the chameleon poet Keats found his own style not only by adopting the language of Spenser, Hunt, Shakespeare, Milton, Dryden, and Wordsworth, but also by drawing largely on the language of contemporary women's poetry.[38] Though social class certainly played a role in the antagonism of the contemporary reviewers towards Keats's early poetry, an even greater source of antagonism lay in Keats's stylistic cross-dressing. A reviewer of the 1817 *Poems*, though willing to concede that Keats was a 'poet of promise,' was highly critical of certain phrasings, which he considered to be both affected and feminine. '"Leafy luxury,"' '"jaunty streams,"' '"lawny slope,"' '"the moon-beamy air,"' '"a sun-beamy tale,"' he argues, 'these, if not namby-pamby, are, at least, the "holiday and lady terms" of those poor affected creatures who write verses "in spite of nature and their stars" ... This is worthy only of the Rosa Matildas whom the strong-handed Gifford put down.'[39] Lockhart, in suggesting that Keats suffered from 'metromanie,' not only placed his poetry in the class of 'farm-servants ... unmarried ladies ... and superannuated governesses,' but also adopted a term that had traditionally been used as an alternative name for female hysteria, that is, mania caused by the matrix.[40]

One effect of the antagonism expressed in the 1817 and 1818 reviews of Keats's poetry is that it split the poetry along gender lines. The fundamental unresolved conflict of Keats's later verse lies in his struggle, often against his own better poetic instincts, to distance himself from the intimacy with women and women's floral style that he sought in his earlier poems. Keats's remark, reported by Richard Woodhouse, that 'he does not want ladies to read his poetry: that he writes for men' should not, therefore, be taken simply at face value, for it is less a statement about his poetry as a whole, than about his intentions in reaction to the reviews (*Letters* 2:163). Keats set out to write like a man, to pass beyond the feminine style, which he associated with the 'Chamber of Maiden Thought.'

Keats's answer to this gender conflict is to enact it within the later poems themselves as a matter for revision. In these poems, Keats consistently rewrites the conflict between women's literature and the male visionary tradition as a conflict between his earlier and later self. The floral poet of the 1817 *Poems* and *Endymion* is continually conjured in these poems, but as a ghost to be exorcised. 'Ode to Psyche' is typical of this revisionary strategy as it summons up the early Keatsean poet, wandering through a forest 'thoughtlessly' and 'fainting with surprise' to find two lovers embracing 'beneath the whisp'ring roof / Of leaves and trembled blossoms' (10–11), only to replace naive pleasure with a poetry that embodies the work ethic and a new emphasis on the priority of mind over body. In *Isabella*, the floral language of the early poetry reappears as Keats describes the love of Isabella and Lorenzo growing 'like a lusty flower in June's caress' (72). The remainder of the poem represents a grisly parody of urban horticulture and of poetic creation reduced to pot gardening, as both the poet and the heroine Isabella seek to recreate a 'green world' out of 'wormy circumstance' (385). In 'To a Nightingale,' Keats returns to the poetic bower, but the bower is now linked to death, situated in the Underworld. He can no longer 'see what flowers are at my feet,' but in this 'embalmed darkness,' he can guess 'each sweet' (41–3):

> White hawthorn, and the pastoral eglantine;
>   Fast fading violets cover'd up in leaves;
>   And mid-May's eldest child,
> The coming musk-rose, full of dewy wine,
>   The murmurous haunt of flies on summer eves. (46–50)

The bower is still redolent with sexuality, as it is presided over by the 'coming musk-rose.' The sexual symbolism of the 'musk-rose,' with its 'dewy wine,' is reinforced by the word *coming*, which, as Eric Partridge indicates in his *Dictionary of Slang and Unconventional English*, would have meant 'wanton' or 'forward' when applied to a woman. Traces of the early Keatsean figure of the desiring poet as a 'butterfly/bee' also appear in the figure of the rose as 'the murmurous haunt of flies on summer eves.' However, the sexual symbolism of these scents has given way to the more powerful language of death, as the musk-rose womb becomes a tomb, a place of decaying flesh. And the figure of the poet, embodied in the poetic song of the 'butterflies' or moths, is literally displaced, in ways that anticipate the gnats of 'To Autumn,' by a song integrally bound up with death, the haunting murmurs of flies, which traditionally were understood as embodying the souls of the dead. This shift from eros to thanatos is further emphasized by the dominating presence of the Virgilian symbol of the 'bird' as the poet's guide to the Underworld.

The haunting presence of Keats's early floral rhetoric in the later poetry, as a dead language that it actively incorporates in order to revise, could be discussed in other poems: in the desolate bower at the beginning of *The Fall of Hyperion*, in the poisonous catalogue of plants in 'Ode on Melancholy,' or in the lillied brow and 'fading rose' (11) cheek of the knight in 'La Belle Dame Sans Merci.' In these poems, floral language is linked to death, as Keats talks directly, often through the figure of sacrifice, of the need to produce and the cost of producing a more 'manly,' less smokable, style. Another way in which this revisionary activity is manifested is in the figural association between sexuality and defloration. In many of the later poems, poetic maturity is to be achieved only through a masculine *deflowering* of the self. The seduction narrative thus becomes, for Keats, a narrative that speaks of the cost of a new style. Though *The Eve of St. Agnes*, for instance, is explicitly about the physical deflowering of Madeline, it is, even more importantly, a poem about the defloration of Madeline's and Porphyro's dreams. At the beginning of the poem, the idea of sex blossoms in Porphyro's mind 'like a full-blown rose, / Flushing his brow' (136–7). By the end of the poem, however, the early Keatsean fantasy that sexual bliss might be embodied by botanical metaphor, as a 'solution sweet,' the 'rose' blending 'its odour with the violet' (320–2), has been relegated to the sphere of Romance. It is under constant threat of destruction. In

'La Belle Dame Sans Merci,' seduction is similarly linked to poetic defloration: 'the sedge has wither'd from the lake, / And no birds sing' (3–4). *Lamia* begins by invoking the mythological link between flowers and sexuality. And it culminates in sexuality and metamorphosis. At the touch of Hermes, Keats writes, the 'bland' eyelids of the Cretan nymph

> ... like new flowers at morning song of bees,
> Bloom'd, and gave up her honey to the lees.
> Into the green-recessed woods they flew;
> Nor grew they pale, as mortal lovers do. (1.141–5)

But this world passes out of existence and is 'heard no more' (1.170), to be replaced by the commercial urbanism of Corinth. There, love is inseparably linked to jealously, rivalry, money, and power. Lycius resorts to floral language in speaking of his love for Lamia:

> 'My silver planet, both of eve and morn!
> Why will you plead yourself so sad forlorn,
> While I am striving how to fill my heart
> With deeper crimson, and a double smart?
> How to entangle, trammel up and snare
> Your soul in mine, and labyrinth you there
> Like the hid scent in an unbudded rose? (2.48–54)

Here floral metaphor is permeated with violence – the 'deeper crimson,' the 'double smart' – as love is transformed into a sado-masochistic struggle, a 'striving' for power over another person. Having lost his virginity, Lycius longs to recover his 'maidenhood' through possessing Lamia, 'your soul in mine,' labyrinthed 'like the hid scent in an unbudded rose.' In *Lamia*, poetry is viewed as a commercial substitute for lost floral pleasures. At the banquet, each guest is provided with the object of his desire:

> Soon was God Bacchus at meridian height;
> Flush'd were their cheeks, and bright eyes double bright:
> Garlands of every green, and every scent
> From vales deflower'd, or forest-trees branch-rent,
> In baskets of bright osier'd gold were brought
> High as the handles heap'd, to suit the thought
> Of every guest. (2.213–19)

Keats points to the cost and conditions of this art: it exists because of 'vales deflower'd' (Lycius' and Lamia's defloration being an expression on a private level of a cultural event), and it continues to destroy these vales in its effort to recover those lost pleasures.

Keats's most pessimistic expression of the conflict he felt between the floral, feminized ideal of his earlier poetry and the demands of a masculine tradition is to be found in the sonnet 'On Fame.' Poetry and sexuality are once more fused in this poem, as Keats draws on the language of sexual perversion in order to call into question such demands. Poetic maturation is again symbolized by defloration; here, however, the focus is upon self-seduction, the poet's fevered rape of his maidenhood:

> How fever'd is the man who cannot look
>   Upon his mortal days with temperate blood,
> Who vexes all the leaves of his life's book,
> And robs his fair name of its maidenhood. (1–4)

In the first quatrain, Keats deliberately emphasizes maleness – 'the man,' 'his ... days,' 'his ... book,' 'his ... name' – in order to foreground what male conceptions of fame deny: the female component of a 'fair name.' In seeking fame, men rob their names of their 'maidenhood.' It is a sterile form of narcissism, a perversion of sexual love into self-love, an onanistic pleasure or 'vex[ing]' of 'the leaves of life's ... book.' In the next quatrain, Keats provides analogies of what such striving would be like in the realm of flora:

> It is as if the rose should pluck herself,
>   Or the ripe plum finger its misty bloom,
> As if a Naiad, like a meddling elf,
>   Should darken her pure grot with muddy gloom. (5–8)

The vulgarity of this passage is part of its message: nature does not 'meddle' with itself; female masturbation, for Keats, is not only unnatural, but unnecessary. In this regard, it is worth noting that Keats is just as antagonistic towards 'male' readers, as females, and in describing his poetry, he characteristically views it as feminine. He writes in a letter that he would prefer 'to avoid publishing – I admire Human Nature but I do not like Men – I should like to compose things honourable to Man – but not fingerable over by Men' (*Letters* 1:415).

In the sestet, as an alternative to the masculine conception of fame as 'fierce' rivalry, a 'miscreed,' punning on the meaning of screed as a long, monotonous harangue, Keats reaffirms the ideal of floral sexuality, of a world of mutual satisfaction:

> But the rose leaves herself upon the briar,
>   For winds to kiss and grateful bees to feed,
> And the ripe plum still wears its dim attire,
>   The undisturbed lake has crystal space;
>   Why then should man, teasing the world for grace,
> Spoil his salvation for a fierce miscreed? (9–14)

Keats is a unique male poet because he continued to draw upon the traditional link between flowers and pastoral poetry long after floral imagery had come to be seen as primarily the poetic discourse of women. At a time when women were both adopting and attempting to escape the constraints imposed upon them by the notion that they were flowers, at a time when floral imagery of all kinds was the appropriate medium of female communication and the epitome of feminine beauty, at a time when botany had become the most popular of female scientific occupations, Keats's wholesale adoption of a highly decorous floral imagery in order to talk about sexual desire and to communicate it to others raises problems concerning gender and its boundaries that are less frequently raised by other male Romantic poets. Keats was pressured by the reviews to regret the voice he had adopted in his early poetry, and in the later poetry one can discern his attempt to adopt alternate, more overtly masculine voices, distancing himself from a feminized poetic without disowning it. Floral imagery, in the later poetry, is thus very much a register of the poet's increasing recognition of and discomfort with contemporary attitudes towards gender and the ways in which the age demanded that an author's gender be expressed in a specific style.

NOTES

1 John Keats, *The Letters*, ed. Hyder Edward Rollins, 2 vols (Cambridge: Harvard UP, 1958), 1:207. References are to *The Poems of John Keats*, ed. Jack Stillinger (Cambridge: Harvard UP, 1978).
2 John Hamilton Reynolds, *Champion* 9 March 1817: 73

3 *Byron's Letters and Journals*, ed. Leslie A. Marchand, 12 vols (London: John Murray, 1973–82), 8:166; 8:102
4 See Stuart M. Sperry, 'Isabella Jane Towers, John Towers, and Keats,' *Keats-Shelley Journal* 28 (1979): 42–8.
5 See Donald C. Goellnicht, *The Poet-Physician: Keats and Medical Science* (Pittsburgh: U of Pittsburgh P, 1984), 85–6. I am grateful to Anne B. Shteir for allowing me to read a chapter, in manuscript, which details the importance of Elizabeth Kent's botanical writings to contemporary Romantic poets. See also Molly Tatchell, 'Elizabeth Kent and Flora Domestica,' *Keats-Shelley Memorial Bulletin* 27 (1976): 15–18.
6 David E. Allen, *The Victorian Fern Craze* (London: Hutchinson, 1969)
7 Lynn Barber, *The Heyday of Natural History: 1820–1870* (Garden City, N.Y.: Doubleday, 1980)
8 Some of Keats's early poetry was copied by thirteen-year-old Mary Strange Mathew into an album of poetic effusions entitled *The Garland* (Robert Gittings, *John Keats* [1968; Harmondsworth: Penguin, 1971], 76).
9 See Goellnicht, *Poet-Physician* 84–119.
10 Robert B. Riley, 'Flowers, Power, and Sex,' in *The Meaning of Gardens: Idea, Place, and Action*, ed. Mark Francis and Randolph T. Hester, Jr (Cambridge: MIT P, 1990), 5
11 Janet Browne, 'Botany for Gentlemen: Erasmus Darwin and *The Loves of the Plants*,' *ISIS* 80 (1989): 593–621
12 On the relationship between exploration and plants during the eighteenth century, see Marguerite Duval, *The King's Garden*, trans. Annette Romarken and Claudine Cowen (Charlottesville: UP of Virginia, 1982). See also D.D.C. Chambers, *The Planters of the English Landscape Garden: Botany, Trees, and 'The Georgics'* (New Haven: Yale UP, 1993).
13 For a discussion of London nurserymen during the eighteenth century, see Dawn MacLeod, 'Market Gardeners and Nurserymen of the 16th, 17th and 18th Centuries,' in *The Gardener's London: Four Centuries of Gardening, Gardeners and Garden Usage* (London: Duckworth, 1972), 189–201.
14 Elizabeth Kent, *Flora Domestica; or, The Portable Garden; with Directions for the Treatment of Plants in Pots* (London: Taylor & Hessey, 1823), xiii, xxxii. John Claudius Loudon's frequently reprinted *The Suburban Gardener and Villa Companion* was published in 1838.
15 Kent, *Flora Domestica*, xiii, xxxii–xxxiii
16 See Geoffrey H. Hartman, 'Poem and Ideology: A Study of Keats's "To Autumn,"' in *The Fate of Reading* (New Haven: Yale UP, 1975), 124–46.
17 *Blackwood's Edinburgh Magazine* October 1817: 39

18 John Gibson Lockhart, 'Cockney School of Poetry, no. IV,' *Blackwood's Edinburgh Magazine* August 1818: 521
19 The dioptric quality of Keats's verse – its ability to point to the erotic elements it is concealing – is central to Christopher Ricks's excellent study *Keats and Embarrassment* (Oxford: Clarendon, 1974). For a study of the social forces voiced by the contradictory qualities of Keats's verse, see Marjorie Levinson, *Keats's Life of Allegory: The Origins of a Style* (Oxford: Blackwell, 1988).
20 John Wilson Croker, in his criticism of *Endymion*, went so far as to claim that Keats was 'amusing himself and wearying his readers with an immeasurable game at Bouts-rimés' (*Quarterly Review* 19 [1818]: 205–6).
21 *The Letters of Percy Bysshe Shelley*, ed. Frederick L. Jones, 2 vols (Oxford: Clarendon, 1964), 2:221
22 Ian Jack, *Keats and the Mirror of Art* (Oxford: Clarendon, 1967), 136–40
23 J.J. Grandville, *The Court of Flora: Les Fleurs Animées*, introd. Peter A. Wick (New York: Brazillier, 1981)
24 Robert Thornton, *The Temple of Flora* (London: Weidenfeld and Nicolson, 1981)
25 For a discussion of the idea of modesty during the period, see Ruth Bernard Yeazell's *Fictions of Modesty: Women and Courtship in the English Novel* (U of Chicago P, 1991).
26 In the valentine written to Mary Frogley, Keats draws on the same analogy, only rather than transforming flowers into women, with 'finely tapering stems,' he turns Ms. Frogley's legs into 'twin water lillies, born / In the coolness of the morn' ('Hadst thou liv'd in days of old' 26–34).
27 John Barnard, *John Keats* (Cambridge: Cambridge UP, 1987), 16
28 Robert Thornton, *New Illustration of the Sexual System of Carolus von Linnaeus*, cited by Goellnicht, *Poet-Physician*, 90
29 For an alternative reading of this passage, see Margaret Homans, 'Keats Reading Women, Women Reading Keats,' *SiR* 29 (1990): 341–70.
30 Keats's mannerist revision of Milton, replacing the dove with the butterfly, is indicated in his choice of a passage from Spenser's 'Fate of the Butterfly' as an epigraph for the 1817 *Poems*: 'What more felicity can fall to creature, / Than to enjoy delight with liberty.' In a letter to Fanny Brawne, dated 1 July 1819, Keats writes, 'I almost wish we were butterflies' (*Letters*, 2:123). Many other examples of Keats's identification of the poet with a bee or butterfly might be noted. For instance, in *Endymion*, the seasonal progress of the poet's song is linked to the floral activities of bees: 'ere yet the bees / Hum about globes of clover and sweet peas, / I must be near the middle of my story' (1.51–3). In *The Fall*

Keats's 'Realm of Flora' 99

of *Hyperion*, the poet enters the realm of Saturn after drinking 'a cool vessel of transparent juice, / Sipp'd by the wander'd bee' (1.42–3). In the 'Ode on Melancholy,' pleasure turns 'to poison while the bee-mouth sips' (24). And the song of 'To Autumn' emerges from the poet's recognition that the songs of summer, like the honey that 'o'er-brim[s]' the bees' 'clammy cells' (11), must give way to a new music, that of the 'small gnats' mourning 'among the river sallows' (27–8). The centrality of the language of flowers in Keats's understanding of his relationship with Fanny Brawne is equally explicit, as in the letter where he declares, 'I kiss'd your writing over in the hope you had indulg'd me by leaving a trace of honey' (*Letters*, 2:127).

31 Marilyn Butler places Keats's interest in love and pagan mythology within a context of radical speculation, by people such as Erasmus Darwin, Richard Payne Knight, Shelley, and Peacock, in primitive myth as an expression of early mankind's perception 'that the natural world was driven by sex' (*Romantics, Revels, and Reactionaries: English Literature and Its Background, 1760–1830* [Oxford: Oxford UP, 1981], 130).

32 For a discussion of the extensive role that women played in the sphere of botanical publications, see the work of Anne B. Shteir, notably, 'Botanical Dialogues: Maria Jacson and Women's Popular Science Writing in England,' *Eighteenth-Century Studies* 23 (1990): 301–17; 'Botany in the Breakfast Room: Women and Early Nineteenth-Century British Plant Study,' in *Uneasy Careers and Intimate Lives: Women in Science, 1789–1979*, ed. Pnina G. Abir-Am and Dorinda Outram (New Brunswick, N.J.: Rutgers UP, 1987), 31–43; and 'Linnaeus's Daughters: Women and British Botany,' in *Women and the Structure of Society: Selected Research from the Fifth Berkshire Conference on the History of Women*, ed. Barbara J. Harris and JoAnn K. McNamara (Durham, N.C.: Duke UP, 1984), 67–73.

33 In the conclusion of his essay 'On Effeminacy of Character,' Hazlitt cites Keats's poetry as an example of 'effeminate style,' a style that is 'all florid, all fine.' Such poetry, he argues, is deficient 'in masculine energy of style,' for 'all is soft and fleshy, without bone or muscle' (*The Complete Works of William Hazlitt*, ed. P.P. Howe, 21 vols [London, 1930–4], 8: 254–5).

34 Mrs Montolieu, *The Enchanted Plants: Fables in Verse*, (New York: David Longworth, 1803)

35 For a study of the ways in which nineteenth-century female writers confronted ideas of female propriety, see Mary Poovey, *The Proper Lady and the Woman Writer: Ideology as Style in the Works of Mary Wollstonecraft, Mary Shelley, and Jane Austen* (Chicago: U of Chicago P, 1984).

36 *Byron's Letters and Journals*, 1:206–7

37 Quoted in Louis Crompton, *Byron and Greek Love: Homophobia in Nineteenth-Century England* (Berkeley: U of California P, 1985), 128–9
38 Marlon B. Ross makes a similar claim in *The Contours of Masculine Desire: Romanticism and the Rise of Women's Poetry* (Oxford: Oxford UP, 1989), 155–72.
39 *Scots Magazine* October 1817: 257
40 'Cockney School of Poetry, no. IV,' 519

DONALD C. GOELLNICHT

The Politics of Reading and Writing: Periodical Reviews of Keats's *Poems* (1817)

> Because Keats's social relations were so much more primitive than that of the other Romantics, one learns very little through inquiries into mimetic manners and objects (present, distorted, or unaccounted for), and not too much from research into reception, actual and anticipated.
>
> Marjorie Levinson, *Keats's Life of Allegory* 37–8

Given that Marjorie Levinson's *Keats's Life of Allegory* has been the most celebrated and controversial study of Keats in the last decade, and given its entirely unwitting attempt – as indicated in the epigraph – to undermine the validity of my current project before it was even begun, I must agonize over this text at the outset. Such agonistic encounter will, I hope, assist in representing our situation as readers of Keats, for 'Keats' remains today as much a construction of his critics and their ideological projects as he was when he first published his poetry.

For all her Marxist stress on dialectic, Levinson's representation of Keats and the evidence concerning him remains myopic in its brilliance: she focuses only on Keats's desire to transcend his lower-middle-class status in order to belong to the Literary Tradition; as her use of the adjective 'primitive' to describe his social relations indicates, she casts Keats as a man on the margins who longs to live at the urbane and sophisticated centre, who envies the freedom granted Byron by birth and Wordsworth by claim.[1] She fails to entertain the possibility of Keats's harbouring genuinely revolutionary ambitions, of his holding an oppositional social perspective from within the historical structure, of his desiring to destroy the very Tradition to which he wishes to belong. She reads any such movement as envy, a perverse and perverting desire. This is apparent in her valorizing of Byron, that 'mad bad man' who is, for her, always astutely accurate in his readings of Keats, even though she admits that Byron may be a threatened poet defensively lashing out at the new breed of middle-class poet who promises eventually to displace him. Ironically, of course, Byron was the one who thrived on the capitalist book exchange that he felt himself above.

Levinson's perspective on Keats is intricately entangled with what I suspect are her own desires to belong to a certain critical tradition, desires she projects onto her subject and which emerge initially in a negative fashion. From the outset she rejects the Harvard Keatsians, the ivy-league establishment from which she seems to feel alienated in America. Apart from attacking their criticism, she refuses to use the Hyder Rollins edition of the letters, and she banishes the Stillinger edition of the poems to the purgatory of parentheses, where its deviance – in the form of 'variants preferred by Jack Stillinger' (iv) – is recorded. Instead, she attempts to incorporate herself into an apparently purer, more originary British critical centre, using Allott's Longman edition of the poems and Gitttings's Oxford selection of the letters, thanking Marilyn Butler and Terry Eagleton, and publishing with Basil Blackwell. Levinson almost admits to such attitudes when she states: 'We want [i.e., need] to approximate the style of [John] Bayley and [Christopher] Ricks: to become easy enough with our subjects to forget ourselves and, more important, to have the bad taste to *represent* that lapse' (30). She spends three pages of her introduction (29–31) demonstrating the superiority of the Bayley-Ricks (Oxford-Cambridge) criticism, which emphasizes the vulgar, sensuous, and erotic Keats, over the 'Vendler' (a metonym for the Harvard school of Bate, Bush, Perkins, Vendler, and Wasserman) criticism, with its valorization of the serious, visionary, and intellectual Keats, which has dominated the American market since the mid-1950s.[2]

At the close of her introduction, Levinson reveals, unselfconsciously I believe, what appears to be a large part of her motivation in this project: the justification of her own method (from the 'marginal' position of Pennsylvania) against the critical norm of the Harvard Keatsians: 'in that we have so deeply and for so long identified with Keats – so taken his subject-form for our own – it would seem that we can only start seeing him *clearly in the idea of him* by an act of self-estrangement' (37). I would suggest that in rejecting the Harvard norm, Levinson substitutes her own form of identification, which amounts to self-projection masquerading as self-estrangement: she uses Keats as a vehicle for her own assault on the critical establishment, thus projecting him as a mirror of her own timidity and defensiveness about this project – a stance that turns out to be ironically unnecessary given the frequently positive reception of her book, unlike the one Keats's books received. Keats's reception reveals a great deal more about the poet and his work than Levinson is willing to admit: it enables us, as far as is possible based on entirely textual evidence, to reconstruct the material conditions of Keats's career, first by mapping his contemporary readerly context, and then by locating his tangled position in that context. It also reveals the attenuated nature of Levinson's supposed identification with Keats, pointing up the blindness – productive as it is – implicit in her contradictory attempt to see through Keats's eyes while writing in a theoretically sophisticated style clearly designed to establish her as superior to her subject, whom she describes as 'not ... a middle-class poet but a young man who aspired to the condition of the legitimate middle class, and to the profession of poetry' (89). Levinson's style itself reminds us of the privileged and elite position of reviewers in both the Romantic period and the present day. As professional academics paid to re-view literature from positions of relative security and comfort, we share a great deal in common with the class of nineteenth-century reviewers. An examination of early reviews of Keats has the potential of bringing into focus, then, the fact that our class-based perspectives to some degree reproduce those of Keats's first readers.[3]

I

> Since the interesting era of the French Revolution, the people of these Kingdoms have been an inquisitive, prying, doubting and reading people.
>
> Anonymous, *The Periodical Press of Great Britain and Ireland* [1824] 24

The most extensive public response to Keats's poetry by contemporary readers is to be found in the reviews of the three volumes of poetry he published. Apart from periodical reviews, sustained commentary on Keats, which might be said to constitute a reading, is 'scattered and sketchy' (Redpath 439). I wish to examine the reviews of Keats's first volume, *Poems* (1817), in some detail, not because they necessarily represent rigorous and informed literary criticism – though many of them are highly perceptive, focusing on issues that still concern us today – but because these readings are the ones that Keats was aware of. As we know, Keats reacted, often keenly, to critical response, so that the reviews of each volume of poems helped to shape the creation of the subsequent volume. Hans Robert Jauss points out that 'the historicity of literature as well as its communicative character presupposes a dialogical and at once processlike relationship between work, audience, and new work that can be conceived in the relations between message and receiver as well as between question and answer, problem and solution' (19). Poetic composition is almost always bound up with the conditions of publication and the demands of critical reception; it is this reciprocal relationship between poetic creation, the responses it evokes from readers, and new creation that I wish to trace as a way of placing Keats in a particular historical, social, political, and ideological context, and of demonstrating the complex and intricate connections between art and material life, of seeing art, in fact, as part of material culture. Keats's social relations are not so much primitive as they are overdetermined – by birth, education, friendships, and so on. This becomes abundantly clear in the reception granted his work, a reception that demonstrates how tightly literary 'merit' is entangled in the web of issues like class and gender.

The highly charged political and ideological nature of book reviewing at the start of the nineteenth century needs to be understood in order to grasp the context into which Keats's productions were being written and published. Rather than rehearse in the limited space available here the periodical scene at the opening of the nineteenth century, however, I will instead draw attention to valuable earlier studies. Edmund Blunden examined this subject in the 1920s, G.L. Marsh and N.I. White in the 1930s, and Harold E. Briggs and W.S. Ward in the 1940s; the early 1970s witnessed an explosive revival of interest in Romantic reviewing (see John O. Hayden, Theodore Redpath, Donald Reiman, Tsokan Huang, G.M. Matthews, and Lewis M. Schwartz). All of these studies, however valuable in themselves, reflect the critical context of their own time, so that while the work of the early 1970s consciously attempts to place Keats in a historical context, in contradiction to New Criticism's primarily ahistorical stance, it still suffers from a number of New Critical assumptions about Keats; for example, it attempts to recuperate him as an apolitical poet who was caught in the cross-fire of intensely partisan literary politics, a victim of, rather than a participant in, the internecine warfare of the periodical press. This is a view of Keats that has been strongly challenged – and, I believe, corrected – in the 1980s by such critics as Morris Dickstein, William Keach, David Bromwich, Paul

Fry, and Alan Bewell (whose essays appear in a special *Studies in Romanticism* forum on 'Keats and Politics'), as well as Clifford Siskin, Jerome McGann, Thomas A. Reed, Theresa M. Kelley, Kurt Heinzelman, Daniel P. Watkins, Susan Wolfson, Terence Allan Hoagwood, and Marjorie Levinson herself, all of whom work, in their various ways, to historicize and materialize Keats. I wish to push this argument further with reference to contemporary reviewer responses in an attempt to complement and flesh out my own earlier work on Keats's 'theory' of reading.[4]

II

> I hope sincerely I shall be able to put a Mite of help to the Liberal side of the Question before I die.
>
> Keats to Dilke, 22 September 1819

On 3 March 1817 Keats's first volume of poetry was published, by the Ollier brothers, in a small edition of probably five hundred, at a price of six shillings apiece. In the inflated market of the early nineteenth century – prices were pushed up by the financial uncertainty of the postwar period, by the artificial inflation of conservative publishers, and by the high cost of material and labour in a labour-intensive industry (Altick 260–2) – this was the average price for a 12mo / foolscap 8mo. In the Keats circle and family, expectations for the success of this volume ran high (Bate 145–50), although in retrospect such hopes seem naïve given the rather blatant political nature of some of these poems and the latent political implications of many others. In a country attuned to subtle political messages after years of ingrained siege mentality resulting from the war with France, which had ended two years earlier, and from its aftermath of unemployment, inflation, and labour unrest, Keats must have been aware that his poetry would be read in the glare of political light.

Many of the poems, of course, are apparently apolitical in their youthful praise of beautiful women, their retrospective gaze at the Elizabethan era of chivalry, and their warm celebration of friendship. (Even here, though, sexual politics and an implicit damning of the present via nostalgia for the past are at play.) Some of the poems, however, express open political ambitions. 'Written on the Day That

Mr. Leigh Hunt Left Prison,' 'Great spirits ...' 'To Kosciusko,' and 'To Leigh Hunt, Esq.,' while composed in the highly conservative form of the Petrarchan sonnet, make bold statements on the contemporary scene. The first aggressively confronts the reader as a member of the 'wretched crew'[5] that supports the 'flatter'd state' and thus has been complicitous in securing Hunt's incarceration for slandering the Prince Regent; the second, addressed to Haydon, talks of the great artistic spirits of the time – Wordsworth, Hunt, and Haydon – as wielding political and moral influence in the world ('These, these will give the world another heart, / And other pulses. Hear ye not the hum / Of mighty workings – / Listen awhile ye nations, and be dumb'); the third, first published in Hunt's reformist journal the *Examiner* in February 1817,[6] celebrates the Polish republican hero and forecasts 'a happy day, / When some good spirit walks upon the earth'; and the fourth, addressed to one of the most famous reformers in the realm, serves as the dedicatory verses to the whole volume. The language of these sonnets is resonant with apocalyptic echoes of the promise of the French Revolution – 'Upon the forehead of the age to come' – even though the Napoleonic wars had come to an end in 1815 with England victorious. Keats seems to believe that art will achieve what military action could not: the new age of freedom. He still thinks of Wordsworth as a revolutionary poet at this stage; certainly Hunt was, and for Keats to identify with such a radical was an openly political act. Moreover, in addition to claiming that poetry can have a political effect on the reader, Keats does not seem bothered yet by the potential for didacticism and propaganda in art, a subject upon which he would later expound at length when his opinion on Wordsworth shifted considerably (see *Letters* 1:223–4).[7]

The epistle 'To My Brother George,' which appears earlier in the volume, is equally full of political fire. Keats imagines for George the bard's death-bed speech, in which the bard predicts:

> The patriot shall feel
> My stern alarum, and unsheath his steel;
> Or, in the senate thunder out my numbers
> To startle princes from their easy slumbers.
> The sage will mingle with each moral theme
> My happy thoughts sententious; he will teem
> With lofty periods when my verses fire him,
> And then I'll stoop from heaven to inspire him.   (73–80)

As a political instrument that will influence the reader, poetry has the power to inspire and persuade, although Keats in (mock) humility does not consider his verses as yet worthy of accomplishing these tasks: 'As to my sonnets, though none else should heed them, / I feel delighted, still, that you will read them. / Of late, too, I have had much calm enjoyment, / Stretch'd on the grass at my best lov'd employment / Of scribbling lines for you' (117–21). Keats conceives his audience as small, intimate, sympathetic, but he has much larger ambitions for his verse, which he is not afraid to share with his brother. Once he publishes these poems, that ambition is translated into action in the political sphere. Still, the volume contained enough 'apolitical' poetry for the conservative Haydon, who had become alarmed at Keats's being drawn into the Hunt-Shelley-Hazlitt nexus of radical activity in January and February of 1817 (see his warning in a letter of 17 March [*Letters* 1:124–5]), to feel relieved and to be optimistic in his praise of 'Sleep and Poetry.'

III

> The early nineteenth century was in fact the heyday of periodical reviewing; never before or since has it been so energetic and widespread. The *Edinburgh Review* and the *Quarterly Review* were the two most important periodicals concerned, but there were at least sixty other periodicals between 1802 and 1824.
>
> John O. Hayden, *The Romantic Reviewers* 1

On 9 March, within a week of publication, the first review of *Poems*, by Keats's close friend John Hamilton Reynolds, appeared in the *Champion*, to be followed over the next seven months by five more reviews: in the *Monthly Magazine* in April (a brief notice rather than a full review); in the *European Magazine* in May (by his former friend George Felton Mathew); in the *Examiner* in June and July (Leigh Hunt did a three-part review); in the *Eclectic Review* in September (by Josiah Conder, the editor); and in the *Edinburgh Magazine* (formerly the *Scots Magazine*) in October. (A joint review of the 1817 *Poems* and *Endymion* appeared in *Blackwood's Edinburgh Magazine* in August 1818, as the fourth instalment in the series 'On the Cockney School of Poetry'; that [in]famous review appeared too late, of course, to influence Keats's preparation of *Endymion* for publication and so will not be dealt with here.)[8]

The reviews of this first volume were highly predictable, given the political stripe of the particular journal in which each appeared and the nature of Keats's relationship with a number of the reviewers. Reynolds produced ecstatic praise for Keats's abilities in his *Champion* review, an approach explained in part by their close personal friendship and by the weekly newspaper's progressive, liberal politics, which reflected the opinions of the new owner-editor, John Thelwall, radical friend of Godwin and Coleridge.[9] The *Champion* was thus sympathetic to Hunt and his circle. Still, Reynolds – as if anticipating the negative impact of a too close association between Hunt and Keats – seems determined to distance Keats from all possible influences, from the aristocratic to the radical:

At a time when nothing is talked of but the power and the passion of Lord Byron, and the playful and elegant fancy of Moore, and the correctness of Rogers, and the sublimity and pathos of Campbell ... a young man starts suddenly before us, with a genius that is likely to eclipse them all. He comes fresh from nature, – and the originals of his images are to be found in her keeping. Young writers are in general in their early productions imitators of their favourite poet; like young birds that in their first songs, mock the notes of those warblers, they hear the most, and love the best: but this youthful poet appears to have tuned his voice in solitude, – to have sprung from the pure inspiration of nature. (Reiman C260)

With canny prescience, Reynolds seeks at the outset to shield Keats against the very accusations that would soon be levelled at him. By presenting nature as Keats's muse, the origin of his images, Reynolds attempts to establish the purity of Keats's verse and to forestall the charges that Keats is an urban, Cockney poet unfamiliar with nature. More important, however, is the implicit claim that Keats does *not* imitate the poet he hears the most and loves the best: Hunt, who is conspicuous in his absence from this list of named poets. Instead, Keats's poetry emerges as *sui generis*, independent of all schools or parties; yet the fact that Reynolds thinks it necessary to go to such lengths to erase the influence of Hunt indicates how close the connection was. This strategy of distancing did not prevent Reynolds, however, from faulting the poetry for the 'Huntian' weaknesses (looseness of versification, excessive use of compound epithets, and overwrought descriptions) others would later emphasize, although again these faults are blamed solely on youth, with Hunt remaining unnamed (C262), an absence all the more telling because Hunt had hailed Keats *and* Reynolds as future great poets in his now famous *Examiner* article of 1 December 1816. Reynolds's strategy here may have been to inoculate Keats against future attacks by implicitly admitting to a small degree of the strain of the Cockney school in Keats, but only as a way of throwing into relief how much he has escaped its unnatural influences by virtue of his filial devotion to 'Nature.'

Hunt, Keats's mentor, himself reviewed *Poems* in his influential reformist weekly the *Examiner*. It is on the whole a praising review, although Keats's volume is eclipsed in the first instalment (1 June 1817) by a lengthy discussion of the weaknesses of neoclassical poetry and an admittedly grudging assessment of the merits of the Lake Poets (C428). It is almost as if, in clearing a space for Keats, Hunt pushes his protégé out of the picture, a sign perhaps of the difficulty Hunt faced in writing this piece. Like Reynolds, although to a lesser extent, Hunt feels it necessary to stress the originality of Keats's verse, thus attempting to protect Keats by releasing him from allegiance to any school: '... the work is not one of mere imitation, or a compilation of ingenious and promising things that merely announce better, and that after all might only help to keep up a bad system; but here is a young poet giving himself up to his own impressions, and revelling in real poetry for its' own sake' (C428). Hunt's 'mere' indicates a lingering proprietory impulse on his part towards his protégé, but one that appears in conjunction with a fraternal desire to protect the younger poet.

In the final instalment (13 July 1817) of Hunt's review, however, radical political opinion emerges in the rhetoric used to describe the texts, thus subverting any attempt to present Keats as apolitical: 'The best poem is certainly the last and longest, entitled *Sleep and Poetry* ... Nor do we like it the less for an impatient, and as it may be thought by some, irreverend assault upon the late French school of criticism and monotony, which has held poetry chained long enough to render it somewhat indignant when it has got free' (C430). The decision to reject neoclassical models in favour of a freer verse is here quite deliberately cast as a political act of liberation, reminiscent of Rousseau's revolutionary romanticism: 'Man is born free, yet everywhere he is in chains.' Ironically, 'the late French school' being evoked is the neoclassicism of Corneille and Boileau rather than Rousseau's romanticism, perhaps a deliberately patriotic move on Hunt's part that enables him to *appear* to attack all things French and foreign while clinging to the ideals of the revolution. These sentiments echo Reynolds's claim that Keats's work 'is likely to make a great addition to those who would overthrow that artificial taste which French criticism has long planted among us' (C260). Just as the revolution in France brought an end to oppressive monarchy, so too new literary modes in England are seen as liberating art from neoclassical oppression; art and politics are integrally connected by Hunt, who like Keats hopes that art can act as an agent for change in social conditions.[10] It should come as no surprise, then, that Hunt's radical discourse established Keats as a target for conservative reviewers, even though Hunt seems careful to target *French* neoclassicism as the enemy.

Still, Hunt's comments in this review echo his attack on the monotonous regularity of 'Pope and the French school of versification' in his preface to *The Story of Rimini*. William Keach has pointed out in his illuminating analysis of the political implications of Keats's use of freer verse couplets in 'Sleep and Poetry' and *Endymion* that 'Keats was caught up ... in a squabble between Tory traditionalists [*Blackwood's Magazine* and the *Quarterly Review*], for whom a balanced and closed Augustan couplet had become something of a cultural fetish, and the liberal reformers who set out to establish "a freer spirit of versification," as Hunt says in the Preface to *The Story of Rimini*, along with a freer society' (184). Keach's commentary on Keats's 'liberal' style and on his parody of Pope's couplets in 'Sleep and Poetry' (185–200) leads him to conclude that 'Keats knew what he wanted to do in his 1817 Cockney couplets, and he knew how far beyond the "flowing round of habit and ease" characteristic of Hunt's liberal reform couplets he wanted to go. The *Blackwood's* review is right, given its basic assumption, to assert that "the defects of [Hunt's] system are tenfold more conspicuous in his disciple's work than in his own"' (189).

The liberal *Monthly Magazine*, generally supportive of the second-generation Romantics, whose politics it shared (Hayden, *Romantic Reviewers* 58), printed a very favourable early notice, praising Keats's 'recourse to the age of Elizabeth' in matters of style and claiming that 'the fertile fancy and beautiful diction of our old poets, is not unfrequently rivaled by Mr. Keats' (C659). The reviewer here elides conservative neoclassicism altogether, glancing back instead to an idealized, domestic Elizabethan scene that he hopes can be reproduced in contemporary poetry, thus re-establishing the literary primacy of England while avoiding much of the political discussion of literature so common at the time. Ironically, he praises the very elements of Keats's verse that would come under vicious attack from other quarters for reasons that we will see are profoundly political: 'a rapturous glow and intoxication of the fancy – an air of careless and profuse magnificence in his diction – a revelry of the imagination and tenderness of feeling' (C659).

The *Eclectic Review*, which adopted a tone of enlightened liberalism after it was taken over by Josiah Conder in 1814 – Conder himself wrote the review of Keats's first volume[11] – hailed the promise of this young poet, but qualified the 'promise' itself as 'immature' because of the undeveloped nature of the intellectual and moral ideas in the poetry.[12] Conder judges many of the poems to be poor imitations of Hunt, with 'the affectation which vitiates [Hunt's] style ... aggravated to a ridiculous excess in the copyist' (C331). As Conder admired and usually championed Hunt, such judgment was doubly damning, especially when he pounces upon the very Cockney rhymes that the conservative press attacked and when he describes Keats's imitation of Elizabethan style as 'second hand' and therefore 'simply unpleasing.' What emerges clearly here is Conder's *literary* conservatism: he trounces Keats for the self-consciousness of his art, for producing poetry *'all about* poetry' (C332), the implication being that literature should be representational of the 'real' world rather than auto-representational. Conder thus shows himself to be out of touch with much contemporary literature, although his comment is also a revealing and provocative one when directed at a poet whose stated desire in some of these very poems is to use art to reform material culture. We might speculate on how Keats would react to this criticism that his poetry operates at too much of a remove from material life. Conder predicts that 'a few years hence [Keats] will be glad to escape the remembrance' of these verses, although he closes with praise for the sonnets; ironically, Keats's poetry never ceased, at one level, to be 'all about poetry.'

The strongest censure of Keats's poetry came, again predictably, from the old eighteenth-century monthlies: the *European Magazine* and the *Edinburgh Magazine*. The latter, although liberal in politics, rival to the Tory *Edinburgh Monthly Magazine*, with a number of important liberal contributors, including Hazlitt and Godwin,[13] nevertheless upheld neoclassical literary values. Therefore, while heaping much praise on Keats's sonnets – themselves a conservative and time-honoured form – the reviewer loads his discourse with a particular moralizing weight that becomes highly significant in Keats criticism generally. He begins by describing in apparently neutral tones 'the general character of [Keats's] manner' as that 'which partakes a great deal of that *picturesqueness* of fancy and licentious brilliancy of epithet which distinguish the early Italian novelists and amorous poets' (C807). This sounds initially like it might be praise, except that the adjective 'licentious' marks the start of a tone of moral censure which is expanded on later, after two lengthy quotations, one from 'I stood tip-toe ...' and the other from the epistle 'To My Brother George': 'These specimens will be enough to shew that Mr K. has ventured on ground very dangerous for a young poet; – calculated, we think, to fatigue his ingenuity, and try his resources of fancy, without producing any permanent effect adequate to the expenditure of either' (C808). The discourse here is a striking mixture of science and economics, but the economics of masturbation in which the expenditure of sexual capital cannot produce a return on the investment as procreation is impossible; instead, it fatigues the poet, wasting his resources and casting him in the role of irresponsible, pleasure-seeking adolescent, precisely the role Keats responds to in his *Endymion* preface.

These faults the reviewer traces to Hunt, and he warns Keats against following Hunt's modern example: 'If Mr Keats does not forthwith cast off the uncleannesses of this school [the Cockney], he will never make his way to the truest strain of poetry in which, taking him by himself, it appears he might succeed' (C808).[14] The review concludes with an extremely backhanded compliment: 'We are loth to part with this poet of promise, and are vexed that critical justice requires us to mention some passages of considerable affectation, and marks of offensive haste ... "Leafy luxury," "jaunty streams," "lawny slope," ... these, if not namby-pamby, are, at least, the "holiday and lady terms" of those poor affected creatures who write verses "in spite of nature and their stars"' (C808).

This review signals the start of a sustained attempt to cast the Hunt-influenced Keats style in gendered and class terms, with affectation judged as a form of effeminacy, the preponderance of 'feminine' endings and rhymes, as well as of participles that nominalize verbs and verbalize nouns, being taken to support this interpretation. In ironic and significant opposition to Hunt's rendering of this 'revolutionary' style as a form of 'manly' liberation, the reviewer here marks the same stylistic elements as 'feminine,' thus demonstrating the relative and slippery nature of these terms, which can be arbitrarily assigned differing values for political purposes. Here, what is characterized as the childish ('namby-pamby'), the affected, the unnatural, and the unclean are equated with the feminine and thus dismissed.

The term 'uncleannesses' is also revealing. It evokes notions of low-class squalor and of ritual impurity, thus perpetuating the misconception that art must remove itself from the messiness of the material world. But it also carries suggestions of sexual uncleanness or venereal disease, which is subtly linked to women and the lower classes. In this way the reviewer moves beyond his earlier characterization of Keats's verse as masturbatory, the tone of censure becoming even stronger as the poetry ceases to be simply a waste of creative capital and becomes a potential link in a counter-productive distribution system (the Cockney school) that disseminates disease.

This note of masculinist hysteria against any stylistic innovation – in fact Keats was returning to Elizabethan models – had already been sounded, if in more muted tones, by George Felton Mathew, in his *European Magazine* review in May. Mathew, an early literary friend of Keats who felt rejected when Keats turned his attention to Hunt and his circle, had a personal debt to settle, in addition to upholding the magazine's neoclassical values: he wished to attack Hunt (whose radical politics were opposed to his own), and he actually responds to Reynolds (whose review of *Poems* [1817] had described as inferior the poems composed in 1815 and early 1816, while Mathew was Keats's model). Mathew has some favourable things to say about Keats's verses, but then he rounds on his former friend: 'This fragment ["Calidore"] is as pretty and as innocent as childishness can make it, save that it savours too much, – as indeed do almost all these poems, – of the foppery and affectation of Leigh Hunt ... We might transcribe the whole volume were we to point out every instance of the luxuriance of his imagination, and the puerility of his sentiments' (C422–3). Again, childishness and affectation become equated – in contrast to Wordsworth's equally arbitrary yoking of childhood with naturalness – and are linked to femininity ('foppery') and to sexual extravagance or excess ('luxuriance' with its sense of lasciviousness or lechery). Keats, of course, felt betrayed by his supposed friend. Writing before Lockhart levelled similar charges in his famous 'Cockney School' attack, Mathew here simultaneously proclaims the childish innocence of Keats's poems and suggests that such innocence is only apparent, a mask for a more threatening sexual excess that is quite as dangerous and 'unnatural'/perverse to the conservatives as the political (democratic/republican) excesses of the radicals and the 'loose' style of the Cockneys, to which it becomes linked in a subversive nexus.[15]

The fear of sexual excess as dangerous in its political implications can be traced back, of course, to Malthus's famous *Essay on Population*, in which the political economist despairs of humanity generally, but the uneducated lower classes in particular, ever overcoming their addiction 'to an immoderate indulgence in the pleasures of sensual love' (217), an appetite that he presents as a threat to the prosperity of the realm – that is, to those who hold property – because it leads to an increase in population, among whose members wealth must be spread ever more thinly.[16] It is not far-fetched, I think, to detect Malthusian thought behind these assaults on Keats, who is seen as pandering to the desires of sensual pleasure and supporting the aspirations of political reformers who wish to widen the democratic franchise. This depiction of Keats-as-threat is 'bolstered' by his association with Hunt's *Examiner*, a newspaper the conservative press figured as appealing to and inciting the lower classes.[17]

The linking of loose language, loose morals, the uneducated reader (from the lower classes), and women reveals the matrix of fear and disdain under which many of these reviews operate, and which reaches its apotheosis in the famous reviews of *Endymion*. Unstated but clearly implied here is the recognition that maintaining rigid control of the language – if such a thing were possible – is essential to continued control of political power. Permitting the infiltration of Cockney slang into poetic discourse is tantamount to political revolution, a situation to be avoided at all cost.

IV

> Keats appears to have been of opinion that I ought to have taken more notice of what the critics said against him. And perhaps I ought ... But in truth, as I have before intimated, I did not see a twentieth part of what was said against us; nor had I the slightest notion, at that period, that he took criticism so much to heart.
>
> Leigh Hunt, *Autobiography* 275

Although most of the reviews were generally favourable, they did little or nothing to help the sale of *Poems* (1817), a problem compounded by the fact that the two major reviewing periodicals – the *Edinburgh Review* and the *Quarterly Review*, with a combined circulation of about 25,000 during 1817–18 (Altick 319, 392) – completely ignored the volume. The neglect of the staunchly Tory, establishment *Quarterly* is understandable given Keats's political affiliations; but Keats felt bitterly betrayed by the neglect of the Whig, liberal *Edinburgh*, as is evident from a later letter to

George and Georgiana (*Letters* 2:200). Being ignored not only implied that his contribution to liberal causes was insignificant but also resulted in very poor sales for Keats's initial publication; as Cowden Clarke later observed, 'Alas! the book might have emerged in Timbuctoo with far stronger chance of fame and approbation' (quoted in Matthews 7). As with all of Keats's books published in his lifetime, no more than the small first edition was printed, and even that did not sell out.[18] Keats himself remarks, not without bitterness and sarcasm, in his proposed – and finally rejected – preface to his next work, *Endymion*: 'About a twelvemonth since, I published a little book of verses; it was read by some dozen of my friends who lik'd it; and some dozen whom I was unacquainted with, who did not' (quoted in Stillinger edition 739). Apart from this cutting remark and the later expression of betrayal by the *Edinburgh Review*, no specific comments of his on the reviews are extant.

The poor reception accorded this early volume was a portent of Keats's future sales, which were uniformly bad. As late as 9 January 1835, John Taylor, Keats's publisher, wrote to John Clare:

[Woodhouse] has left me all his MS. papers containing unpublished Poems of Keats, but I don't know when it will be possible for me to do anything with them. I should like to print a complete Edition of Keats's Poems, with several of his Letters, but the world cares nothing for him – I fear that even 250 copies would not sell. (Quoted in Blunden, *Shelley and Keats* 82)[19]

The effect of this praise for an unknown poet in the liberal periodical press (five of the reviews appeared in liberal or, in the case of the *Examiner*, radical publication) was to confirm Keats's position in the reformist/Huntian camp – a position he had already been placed in by virtue of his inclusion in Hunt's December 1816 notice of 'Young Poets' (Shelley, Reynolds, and Keats) in the *Examiner*. Keats, an avid reader of the *Examiner* for years and a supporter of liberal political causes, can hardly have failed to recognize that, by throwing in his lot with Hunt he was setting himself up as a reformer in politics and in poetry, and thus exposing himself to the attack of the conservative periodicals. Such an attack was not long in coming: in October 1817 *Blackwood's Edinburgh Magazine* launched its famous assault, to which I have already alluded, the first in its series 'On the Cockney School of Poetry,' in which Keats was linked to Hunt from the start, in the epigraph.

Lockhart and Wilson's Cockney School invective – it hardly qualifies as a review, even by the partisan standards of the early nineteenth century – is highly inflected with a rhetoric of class, gender, and race superiority. Hunt is attacked personally as a man 'of exquisitely bad taste, and extremely vulgar modes of thinking and manners, in all respects. He is a man of little education' (C49). Hunt, in other words, was not a member of the public school–Oxbridge elite, whose values *Blackwood's* claimed to be defending. The denigration of the author as a member of the lower orders (literally 'vulgar') continues: 'All the great poets of our country have been men of some rank in society, and there is no vulgarity in any of their writings; but Mr Hunt cannot utter a dedication, or even a note, without betraying the *Shibboleth* of low birth and low habits. He is the ideal of the Cockney poet. He raves perpetually about "green fields," "jaunty streams," and "o'er-arching leafiness," exactly as a Cheapside shop-keeper does about the beauties of his box on the Camberwell road.' Both Levinson and Wolfson, quoting from the *OED*, have recently reminded us that Cockney here means '"A child that sucketh long," ... a mother's darling; pet, minion; "a child tenderly brought up"; hence a squeamish or effeminate fellow'; it is also used as 'a derisive appellation for a townsman, as the type of effeminacy in contrast to the hardier inhabitants of the country' (Levinson i; Wolfson, 'Feminizing Keats' 319). Once again, 'childishness,' 'effeminacy,' and 'unnaturalness' (urban rather than rural) are subtly linked and dismissed.

Not surprising, then, is the reviewer's claim that reading Hunt's *Story of Rimini* evokes the same disgust as entering 'the gilded drawing-room of a little mincing boarding-school mistress, who would fain have an *At Home* in her house. Every thing is pretence, affectation, finery, and gaudiness. The beaux are attorneys' apprentices, with chapeau bras and Limerick gloves – fiddlers, harp teachers, and clerks of genius: the belles are faded fan-twinkling spinsters, prurient vulgar misses from school, and enormous citizens' wives' (C50). It is the aspiration to upward mobility from those on the fringes of the middle class, their pretention to upper-class behaviour, that is seen as particularly odious, precisely because their vulgarity is threatening to the values of 'the man of fashion' who deigns to enter/read Hunt's text. In this figuration based on gender and class hierarchy, the aristocratic reader (to whom *Blackwood's* desires to appeal) is a wealthy and penetrating *male*, while Hunt's text is 'a little mincing boarding-school mistress' looking to please. Finally, this linking of class and gender – with its obvious misogyny – becomes a triadic union of lower class, effeminacy, and immorality:

His poetry resembles that of a man who has kept company with kept-mistresses. His muse talks indelicately like a tea-sipping milliner girl. Some excuse for her there might have been, had she been hurried away by imagination or passion; but with her indecency seems a disease, she appears to speak unclean things from perfect inanition. Surely they who are connected with Mr Hunt by the tender relations of society, have good reason to complain that his muse should have been so prostituted. (C51)

The figures here are complex. On the one hand, Hunt's muse is measured and found wanting at the level of language; but her language is then presented as intimately entangled with, perhaps even the result of, the uncleanness of her body: the diseased female body is blamed for infecting and corrupting the language. In a move typical of the time's patriarchal values, the reviewer also suggests that the behaviour of this low-class girl could be excused had her seducer been an upper-class gallant ('imagination or passion'),[20] but her lover is the Cockney Hunt, who is figured as a pimp, the disseminator of the intellectual equivalent of venereal disease through selling the services of his vacuous and unclean muse-prostitute. He is said to lack 'the dignified purity of thought, and the patriarchal simplicity of feeling with which [Wordsworth's poems] are throughout penetrated and imbued.' The masculinist discourse is again revealing – the patriarch Wordsworth has penetrated and thus taken possession of and legitimized, made pure, the female muse principle – with the author assuming that his readership will share his equation of effeminacy with intellectual, physical, and moral weakness.

The comparison with Wordsworth is significant for the shift it reveals in gender classifications. In the 1790s, as Clifford Siskin and Alan Richardson have demonstrated, Wordsworth, Coleridge, and other male poets were actively colonizing for their own poetic purposes the traditional domain of 'feminine' writing – the emotions, tenderness, softness, the imagination, the irrational – in the same way that they appropriated the lower classes as poetic subjects, writing about the lower orders from above, as outsiders looking in, or, more aptly, superiors looking down. At the same time as he andronogized the poet by claiming for him certain 'feminine' attributes, however, Wordsworth was careful to categorize him as 'a *man* speaking to *men*,' thus trying to ensure – in the face of evidence to the contrary – that the circuit of exchange between poet and reader remained an exclusively masculine domain. By the

1810s this colonization was so complete – 'the *center* of that which is written [had been] feminized' (Siskin 172) – that Wordsworth is reinscribed by the critics as the centre of masculinity, the patriarch of contemporary poetry, which claims 'imagination' and 'passion' as its prime attributes. Such a reinscription could occur only by displacing and redefining, thus remarginalizing, the 'feminine,' which now became equated with 'weak' poetic diction (Hunt's stylistic 'faults'), with 'minor' subjects (urban and domesticated as opposed to rural and wild), and with the urban lower classes (those economically and politically disenfranchised). Keats, by virtue of his lower-class origins (recently become middle-class) and his Cockney style, fell squarely into this category.

At this point of comparison with Wordsworth, racism slips into the barrage against Hunt – and by implication Keats: 'For the person who writes *Rimini*, to admire the Excursion, is just as impossible as it would be for a Chinese polisher of cherry-stones, or gilder of tea-cups, to burst into tears at the sight of the Theseus or the Torso' (C51). The apparent cultural relativity expressed here is not predicated on a belief in equality through difference, but on a violent hierarchy that assumes European superiority. In all these comparisons, the Cockneys are cast as 'other' to true poets and intellectuals: low-class, effeminate, immoral, and now 'Oriental'/foreign, thus incapable of sensitively appreciating, far less generating, cultural greatness. The charge of being foreign-by-analogy is especially damaging in the atmosphere of patriotism engendered by the Napoleonic wars. Hunt's poetry is said to lack 'the two great elements of all dignified poetry, religious feeling, and patriotic feeling' (C50). The inferiority of the lower classes, the feminine, and the foreign (in this case the non-European) is held to be self-evident, in need of no justification since it is assumed that these groups are incapable of defending themselves. As a final reprimand, the reviewers chastise Hunt for 'the insult which he offered to Lord Byron in the dedication of Rimini, – in which he, a paltry cockney newspaper scribbler, had the assurance to address one of the most nobly-born of English Patricians ... as "My dear Byron" ... [thus] excit[ing] a feeling of utter loathing and disgust in the public mind' (C51–2). This attack on Hunt as a subaltern is loaded with unconscious irony, for in expressing their horror at Hunt's deeming himself *Lord* Byron's equal, the reviewers reveal their own sense of inferiority, the self-hatred produced in an economy of rigid class consciousness where democracy is an evil.

Although reticent about the reviews of *Poems*, Keats is fairly profuse in his comments on the *Blackwood's* article:

There has been a flaming attack upon Hunt in the Edinburgh Magazine – I never read any thing so virulent – accusing him of the greatest Crimes – dep[r]eciating his Wife his Poetry – his Habits – his company, his Conversation – These Philipics are to come out in Numbers – calld 'the Cockney School of Poetry' There has been but one Number published – that on Hunt ... In the Motto they have put Hunt and Keats in large Letters – I have no doubt that the second Number was intended for me: but have hopes of its non appearance ... I dont mind the thing much – but if he [Z] should go to such lengths with me as he has done with Hunt I mu[s]t infalibly call him to account – if he be a human being and appears in Squares and Theatres where we might possibly meet – I dont relish his abuse. (*Letters* 1: 179–80)

Keats's brave face – 'I dont mind the thing much' – is a mask designed to hide the profound effect on him of the attack. The courtly and masculine bravado exhibited at the close of this passage, where Keats asserts he will challenge Z to a duel, demonstrates how deeply he has been affected by the aspersions cast on his class and gender by the reviewers. Even for Bailey he must overcompensate in this verbal display.

As if this barrage from a hostile review were not enough, October 1817 also brought a review from the newly named, liberal *Edinburgh Magazine*, which, as outlined above, fell into the same sexist and narrowly moralizing rhetoric as *Blackwood's* had used. All of this partisan reviewing came too late, however, to influence Keats's relationship with his original publishers, Charles and James Ollier. For some reason Keats had decided to break with them by April 1817,[21] less than a month after publication and when only the favourable review by Reynolds and the brief notice in the *Monthly Magazine* had appeared. The Olliers, who also published Shelley at this time, can hardly have been put off by Keats's political views or affiliations since Shelley was also friendly with Hunt – as were the Olliers themselves – and was much more overtly radical than Keats; yet they seem to have encouraged Keats's decision to leave, judging from their acerbic response of 29 April to George Keats's letter severing the tie:

Sir, – We regret that your brother ever requested us to publish his book, or that our opinion of its talent should have led us to acquiese in undertaking it. We are, however, much obliged to you for relieving us from the unpleasant necessity of declining any further connexion with it, which we must have done, as we think the curiosity is satisfied, and the sale has dropped. By far the greater number of persons who have purchased it from us have found fault with it in such plain terms, that we have in many cases offered to take the book back rather than be annoyed with the ridicule which has, time after time, been showered upon it. In fact, it was only on Saturday last that we were under the mortification of having our own opinion of its merits flatly contradicted by a gentleman, who told us he considered it 'no better than a take in.' (Quoted in Matthews 7)

The Olliers' motivation seems to have been primarily economic: they were glad to be rid of an unmarketable author; although they may also have been somewhat disgruntled at Keats's defection to Taylor and Hessey. Still, the Olliers remained on cordial terms with Keats, as a curious, self-mocking letter of 14[?] February 1818 from Keats to his brothers makes clear: 'Richards tell[s] me that my Poems are known in the west country & that he saw a very clever copy of verses, headed with a Motto from my Sonnet to George – Honours rush so thickly upon me that I shall not be able to bear up against them. What think you, am I to be crowned in the Capitol, am I to be made a Mandarin – No! I am to be invited, Mrs Hunt tells me, to a party at Ollier's to keep Shakespeares birthday' (1:227).

V

> Keats wrote a strange and rash preface – and I prevailed on him to cancel it – & place the inscription the book now bears.
>
> Reynolds to Milnes, 30 December 1846

His faith in his own abilities unshaken, Keats pressed ahead with his next project, the long romance *Endymion*. More than ever he was determined to work independently, such resolve probably resulting in part from the reviewers' linking him unfavourably to Hunt. Keats therefore kept *Endymion* away from Hunt, a decision that led to a breach in their relationship when he did finally seek Hunt's opinion: 'Leigh Hunt I showed my Ist Book [of *Endymion*] to, he allows it not much merit as a whole; says it is unnatural & made ten objections to it in the mere skimmimg over ... the fact is he & Shelley are hurt & perhaps justly, at my not having showed them the affair officiously & from several hints I have had they appear much disposed to dissect & anatomize, any trip or slip I may have made. – But whose afraid Ay! Tom! demme if I am'

(*Letters* 1:213–14). This account may explain why Hunt did not review *Endymion*. Keats must also have felt some resentment at being lumped with Hunt in *Blackwood's* Cockney School articles (mentioned later in this letter to his brothers) at the very time that Hunt was criticizing his work.

Keats's relationship with the reading public *had* been shaken, however, by the reception of *Poems*, so that he felt the need to justify this new publication with an apologetic preface. He begins tentatively: 'A preface however should be down in so many words; and such a one that by an eye glance over the type, the Reader may catch an idea of an Author's modesty, and non opinion of himself – which I sincerely hope may be seen in the few lines I have to write' (Stillinger edition 738–9). Of *Endymion* he says: '... this Poem must rather be consider'd as an endeavour than a thing accomplish'd; a poor prologue to what, if I live, I humbly hope to do. In duty to the Public I should have kept it back for a year or two, knowing it to be so faulty: but I really cannot do so: – by repetition my favorite Passages sound vapid in my ears, and I would rather redeem myself with a new Poem – should this one be found of any interest' (739). The advance critique of his own work employed as a strategy to forestall the criticism of others, the self-pitying hint of his own ill health, the humility worn too much on the sleeve, and the final appeal for the poem despite his own harsh judgment – all indicate how uncertain Keats was as he faced the reading public once more, although the possiblity exists that the tone here is mocking and ironic from the start, as indicated by the excessive humility so uncharacteristic of Keats.[22] The ambiguities of this preface reveal a conflicted mixture of fairly harsh self-criticism and mocking disdain towards the public. Keats seems to have wanted to escape the kind of criticism he knew his poem deserved, while at the same time carefully crafting his reception by a public he projects as gullible.

Keats does, however, seem genuinely concerned in his preface with what the reviewers will say about this new work: 'I would fain escape the bickerings that all Works, not exactly in chime, bring upon their begetters: – but this is not fair to expect, there must be conversation of some sort and to object shows a Man's consequence.' Keats admits reluctantly what he had earlier championed: the need for conversational give-and-take between writer and reader (see *Letters* 1:231–2); still, he hopes to mount a defence, however temporary, against the attacks of the London and Edinburgh reviews: 'In case of a London drizzle or a scotch Mist, the following quotation from Marston may perhaps stead me as an umbrella for an hour or so: "let it be the Curtesy of my peruser rather to pity my self hindering labours than to malice me"' (739). The appeal for pity is again overt – Keats knew this poem was highly smokeable – but the source of the Marston quotation, from the prefatory 'To My Equal Reader' in *The Fawn* (1606), ironically hints at a good deal of respect for his readership. Perhaps the ambiguity of tone here stems from Keats's belief that dialogue between text and audience is productive and from the knowledge that he cannot – should not be able to – pull the wool over the public's eyes: his cynical desire is in conflict with his better judgment.

Not surprisingly, Taylor and Hessey did not like this preface when Keats sent it to them on 21 March 1818 (*Letters* 1:253); apparently using Reynolds as an intermediary, they asked Keats to revise it, as Keats's letter to Reynolds of 9 April 1818 indicates: 'Since you all agree that the thing [the preface] is bad, it must be so – though I am not aware there is any thing like Hunt in it, (and if there is, it is my natural way, and I have something in common with Hunt)' (*Letters* 1:266). Taylor and Hessey thought it politically and financially wise to erase any connection with Hunt, whom they – along with some of Keats's friends – viewed as having been a liability in the publication of Keats's first volume of poetry, an opinion unconscious of the irony that without Hunt's influence Keats's first volume might not have been published. In late April 1817, just after becoming Keats's publisher, Taylor had written to his father about Keats's *Poems* (1817): 'I agree with you in finding much fault with the Dedication [to Hunt], etc. These are not likely to appear in any other of his publications' (quoted in Bate 156). If they did not exactly want to pander to public taste, Taylor and Hessey at least sought with *Endymion* to avoid overt political gestures like the dedication of the earlier volume. Keats himself may have come around to Taylor's point-of-view fairly early on; on 27 February 1818, he writes to Taylor: 'I am extremely indebted to you for this attention [to the punctuation in book 1 of *Endymion*] and also for your after [father's?] admonitions – It is a sorry thing for me that any one should have to overcome Prejudices in reading my Verses – that affects me more than any hypercriticism on any particular Passage' (*Letters* 1:238). Is he here agreeing that Hunt's political position establishes too prejudicial a situation for his readers to overcome? If so, the reviews were having an insidious effect on Keats.

Keats eventually conceded to his publishers' objections, writing a new preface on 10 April and submitting it to Reynolds on the 17th for further revisions by Taylor, but not before he expressed to Reynolds his dissatisfaction with preface writing in particular and with the public in general:

I have not the slightest feel of humility towards the Public – ... When I am writing for myself for the mere sake of the Moment's enjoyment, perhaps nature has its course with me – but a Preface is written to the Public; a thing I cannot help looking upon as an Enemy, and which I cannot address without feelings of Hostility – If I write a Preface in a supple or subdued style, it will not be in character with me as a public speaker – I wo^d be subdued before my friends, and thank them for subduing me – but among Multitudes of Men – I have no feel of stooping, I hate the idea of humility to them –
I never wrote one single Line of Poetry with the least Shadow of public thought.
Forgive me for vexing you and making a Trojan Horse of such a Trifle, both with respect to the matter in Question, and myself – ... I hate a Mawkish Popularity. – I cannot be subdued before them – My glory would be to daunt and dazzle the thousand jabberers about Pictures and Books – I see swarms of Porcupines with their Quills erect 'like lime-twigs set to catch my Winged Book' and I would fright 'em away with a torch – You will say my preface is not much of a Torch. It would have been too insulting 'to begin from Jove' [to have taken a superior attitude] and I could not [set] a golden head [a strong/proud preface] upon a thing of clay [*Endymion*] – if there is any fault in the preface it is not affectation: but an undersong of disrespect to the Public. – if I write another preface. it must be done without a thought of those people – I will think about it. (1:266–7)

The cynicism and bitterness expressed here may be a reaction to criticism of his preface, but they also reveal how strongly he felt towards the public by this time. The depiction of the issue as a Trojan horse is especially telling: on the surface the phrase appears to be nothing more than a substitute for 'making a mountain out of a molehill,' but it also reveals Keats's deep-seated desire to get behind the defences of the public and the jabbering critics in order to disarm them before they can attack him. He hopes the preface will achieve such a victory, although by labelling it 'a Trifle' he mockingly undermines his faith in his own abilities to do so.

The images of conflict and power struggle between the writer and his reading public that follow reinforce this idea, demonstrating how vulnerable Keats felt as an aspiring bourgeois poet: he fears his preface-torch will be ineffective in subduing the quills-pens of the porcupine-public and critics, who have the power – through the media and market demand – to make or break his career. He also recognizes, however, that this state of conflict is in contradiction to his ideal of reading as co-creativity and dialogue between writer and audience, so much so that he feels it necessary to reject adopting a Jove-like position of superiority which would reveal 'an undersong of disrespect to the Public.' The very need for such a rejection, however, uncovers the compelling appeal of a hierarchical poet-audience relationship to a bourgeois poet like Keats. It would be so much easier to be an aristocratic poet (Jove), like Shelley or Byron, who can lecture from on high; but he cannot bring himself to insult his audience in public by adopting such a superior attitude, not least because he is dependent on them if he hopes to make a living from his art. Economic circumstances not only rob him of the necessary leisure and ease for composition taken for granted by poets like Byron and Shelley; they make him cruelly dependent on the very public he scorns in practice while he claims to respect the individual reader in principle. In the end, he can only write a preface by deflecting this conflict through a refusal to think about the public – 'I had an idea of giving no Preface,' he tells Reynolds – and a conscious effort to 'not be too timid – of committing fault' (*Letters* 1:269).

The new preface to *Endymion* is cast in the discourse of 'developmental desire,' a term I borrow from Siskin (172):

... the manner in which this Poem has been produced ... will be quite clear to the reader, who must soon perceive great inexperience, immaturity, and every error denoting a feverish attempt, rather than a deed accomplished ... The imagination of a boy is healthy, and the mature imagination of a man is healthy; but there is a space of life between, in which the soul is in a ferment, the character undecided, the way of life uncertain, the ambition thick-sighted: thence proceeds mawkishness ... (Stillinger edition 102–3)

By way of examining this preface, I return to Siskin, who quotes Philippe Aries on adolescence:

Aries points out that before the advent of development and age consciousness, human life was understood to be divided into two stages: youth and adult. 'People had no idea,' he observes, 'of what we call adolescence' (29). Once the self was rewritten ... with consciousness and time newly interrelated within the work of endless self-revision, the making of identity proceeded ... through the identification of stages: parts multiplied as wholes became 'something evermore about to be.' As adolescence thus became the crucial passage between childhood and adulthood, the hormonal metamorphosis of the body was psychologized as the act of maturing, and sexuality became an essential condition of the maturity of individual identity. (172)

Siskin goes on to point out that the feminine condition was treated as analogous to adolescence: an incomplete stage on the trajectory to a higher, 'masculine' condition of maturity.[23] This may explain why Keats was, with the 1817 volume and, as we see later, with *Endymion*, attacked for his profuse but immature sexuality and for his 'femininity,' a criticism he anticipates, almost invites, in his preface, where he casts himself as the dis-eased adolescent. He thus sets himself up for the attacks on his youthful hormonal excess and his 'femininity.' By pre-emptively discussing his own stages of development, however, he hopes to present himself as now beyond that stage of adolescence.

After submitting the new preface, Keats seems to have trusted the rest of the book's production to Taylor, who suggested certain omissions to the new preface (*Letters* 1:272). He apologizes for leaving Taylor 'all the trouble of Endymion' (1:270), citing youthful aversion to such work as an excuse. Still, the fact that Keats carefully proofread his advance copy, providing Taylor with a list of errors and suggesting changes in the use of quotation marks to avoid confusion for the reader, indicates that his deferring to his publisher in production matters may have stemmed from a desire for a better reception from the public this time around. He went to considerable effort to secure a favourable reception for his romance, even to the point of entering enthusiastically into Taylor's plan to 'publish it in Quarto if Haydon would make a drawing of some event therein, for a Frontispiece' (*Letters* 1:213); they would thus afford this volume an expensive gloss absent from *Poems* (1817). The intended shift from a dedication of the earlier volume to radical Hunt to a frontispiece by conservative Haydon summarizes the insidious effect of the reviews on Keats. However, after agreeing to provide a signed engraving of an original sketch for the frontispiece, Haydon failed to fulfil his promise and Taylor did not publish a high-quality quarto. In the end, all Keats's efforts were to no avail, as we know only too well from the famous reception of *Endymion*. What we as late-twentieth-century readers looking back at 'Keats' recognize is the constriction he felt at being placed in the subject positions carved out for him by the reviewers, even though some of those positions – for example, reformer in politics – were ones he had enthusiastically adopted. As we examine his attempts to negotiate from/out of those positions in order to balance his own values with his desire for literary success, we see to what extent Keats was/is written by his readers, the very readers he hoped to change with his poetry.

NOTES

Research for this paper was undertaken with the generous support of the Social Sciences and Humanities Research Council of Canada. I wish to thank David L. Clark, whose close reading and rigorous criticism helped improve the paper.

1 Levinson's Keats emerges as a weird reincarnation of Yeats's famous schoolboy with his nose pressed to the glass of a sweetshop. To be sure, Levinson herself attempts to correct 'Yeats's patronizing caricature' by claiming that 'instead of looking *out* with Yeats from his cosy inside station ... at that embarrassingly squashed nose, we should look through Keats's alienated eyes at that conspicuously structured array, the Tradition' (89); but this revision maintains intact Yeats's narrative of envy and also produces its own form of condescension: pity. Levinson cannot conceive of a Keats who wishes to throw a stone through the window.

2 By critiquing Levinson's position, I do not mean to imply that I support *in toto* the Harvard Keats – itself something of a phantom construct given the large and significant variations within the criticism of the Harvard scholars. What I would stress is the impossibility of escaping their profound influence on all Keats criticism, as Levinson's own preoccupation with them indicates.

3 The tendency of the Harvard Keatsians to downplay Keats's social status so as to ease his passage into the Great Tradition echoes the position of the liberal reviewers of Keats's day, while the Ricks-Bayley emphasis on the vulgar infelicities of Keats's style comes dangerously close to reinscribing the opinions of the early-nineteenth-century Tory reviewers. Levinson herself falls into such a reinscription of the rhetoric of the early Tory reviewers when she casts Keats as representing the entire class of the 'petty bourgeoisie' that constitutes a threat to the 'legitimate bourgeoisie' to which the reviewers belong: '"Keats" was the allegory of a man belonging to a certain class and aspiring, as that entire class was felt to do, to another' (4–5).

4 See my 'Keats on Reading: "Delicious Diligent Indolence."' William Keach's illuminating analysis of the ideological implications of Keats's early style and Susan Wolfson's brilliant explication of the gendering of Keats by reviewers and critics have the most direct influence on my present study, although neither focuses extensively on reviews of the first volume of poetry. I am interested in tracing how quickly in his career Keats was thrust into certain subject positions, from which he needed to negotiate in order to achieve what today we conceive as literary greatness.
5 Quotations of Keats's poetry are from *The Poems of John Keats*, ed. Jack Stillinger (1978); line numbers appear in parentheses.
6 For a concise and illuminating discussion of the political implications and material conditions of publishing in Hunt's *Examiner*, see Hoagwood 687–9. He concludes: 'Whether by personal choice or under the press of circumstances that surrounded him and his poems, Keats's works were delivered to the world in a context charged with political urgency, and it is important to perceive that political dimension internalized in the poems themselves.'
7 Quotations from Keats's letters are from *The Letters of John Keats, 1814–1821*, ed. Hyder Edward Rollins, 2 vols (1958).
8 All quotations from the reviews of Keats's *Poems* (1817) are from *The Romantics Reviewed*, ed. Donald Reiman, Part C (1972).
9 See Reiman C256; Redpath 134; and Hayden, *Romantic Reviewers* 68–70.
10 The all-too-painful irony here is that, caught in the web of representations of him by conservative reviewers as a Cockney reformer, Keats's desires for political reform became further entangled with his desires to escape the figures created for him. This conflict emerges in much of his later poetry, where the Cockney style and the political statements are curbed, and demonstrates how much Keats – a poet who sought at one level to use art to change life – was himself changed by the material conditions of the literary industry in which his own life was embedded.
11 See Reiman C319; Redpath 77–8; Hayden, *Romantic Reviewers* 48–9.
12 This criticism that the sentiments 'sometimes border on childishness' (C331) seems the focus of Keats's discussion of the process of maturing in his Preface to his next published poem, *Endymion*, to which I will turn presently.
13 See Reiman C806; Redpath 134; and Hayden, *Romantic Reviewers* 56.
14 It becomes abundantly clear why Reynolds and Hunt had made such an issue of asserting Keats's independence from any school.

15 David Bromwich points out that G.M. Hopkins would later be critical of 'an unmanly and enervating luxury' in Keats's verse, although Hopkins interpreted this as a sign of the apolitical nature of the poetry (199).
16 Malthus's full statement, connected with his central proposition in the essay, runs as follows:

> It is a truth, which history I am afraid makes too clear, that some men of the highest mental powers, have been addicted not only to a moderate, but even to an immoderate indulgence in the pleasures of sensual love. But allowing, as I should be inclined to do, notwithstanding numerous instances to the contrary, that great intellectual exertions tend to diminish the empire of this passion over man; it is evident that the mass of mankind must be improved more highly than the brightest ornaments of the species at present, before any difference can take place sufficient sensibly to affect population. I would by no means suppose that the mass of mankind has reached its term of improvement; but the principal argument of essay tends to place in a strong point of view, the improbability, that the lower classes of people in any country, should ever be sufficiently free from want and labour, to attain any high degree of intellectual improvement. (217–18)

17 Jon Klancher points out that, in fact, the *Examiner* appealed to a readership of 'middle-class intellectuals ... a small audience of liberal reformers whom Hazlitt and Shelley adressed, a readership parallel to [but not the same as] the radical artisan public' who read Cobbett's *Political Register* (101). Its readership came, then, from the same class as did most of its conservative opponents, although the conservative periodicals preferred to create a false polarity by presenting themselves as the defenders of aristocratic values and tastes while figuring magazines like the *Examiner* as the repositories of demagogy.
18 An anecdote concerning Keats recounted in W. Carew Hazlitt's history of his family may be relevant here: 'Edward Stibbs, the bookseller, mentioned that, when he was in business in Holywell Street, he bought the remainder of Ollier's original edition of *Endymion* at three-halfpence a copy in quires, paid twopence-halfpenny for boarding, and sold the lot very slowly at eighteenpence' (Hazlitt 1:276). (This at a time when the average cost of a 12mo novel had risen to 5–6s. [Altick 260–2].) As the Olliers published *Poems* (1817), not *Endymion* (published by Taylor and Hessey), Stibbs may have been referring to Keats's first volume.
19 Blunden observes that 'perhaps this gloomy view of Taylor's was not

quite the true one' and cites the publication of the Galignani edition in 1829 as evidence of Keats's growing reputation (*Shelley and Keats* 82); but the Galignani edition was published in Paris, not in England, and Keats remained more popular in the United States than in his native country.
20 Roy Porter points out that in the eighteenth century 'certain forms of sexual permissiveness were taken as the order of things. It was taken for granted that maid-servants were fair game for philanderers; the gentlemen were thought gallants so long as they made arrangements for resulting bastards' (262).
21 Gittings speculates that the Olliers, who were novices in the publishing world – Keats's *Poems* being one of their first ventures – 'clearly dropped some expressions of alarm or even resentment' at the low sales (179–80).
22 Compare this public stance with what he was saying privately in letters at this time; for example, to Reynolds on 9 April 1818 (*Letters* 1:266–7).
23 Aries traces this association of male adolescence with femininity to physical conditions: 'since social life began at a very early age, the full, round features of early adolescence, about the age of puberty, gave boys a feminine appearance' (29).

WORKS CITED

Altick, Richard D. *The English Common Reader: A Social History of the Mass Reading Public 1800–1900*. Chicago: U of Chicago P, 1957.
Anonymous. *The Periodical Press of Great Britain and Ireland*. London, 1824.
Aries, Philippe. *Centuries of Childhood: A Social History of Family Life*. Trans. Robert Baldick. New York: Vintage, 1962.
Bate, Walter Jackson. *John Keats*. Cambridge: Harvard UP, 1963.
Bayley, John. *The Uses of Division: Unity and Disharmony in Literature*. London: Chatto and Windus, 1976.
Bewell, Alan J. 'The Political Implication of Keats's Classicist Aesthetics.' *Studies in Romanticism* 25 (Summer 1986): 220–9.
Blunden, Edmund. *Leigh Hunt's 'Examiner' Examined*. London: Cobden-Sanderson, 1928.
– ed. *Shelley and Keats As They Struck Their Contemporaries*. 1925. New York: Haskell House, 1971.
Briggs, Harold E. 'Keats's Conscious and Unconscious Reactions to Criticisms of *Endymion*.' *PMLA* 60 (1945): 1106–29.
Bromwich, David. 'Keats's Radicalism.' *Studies in Romanticism* 25 (Summer 1986): 197–210.
Bush, Douglas. *John Keats*. New York: Macmillan, 1966.

Dickstein, Morris. 'Keats and Politics.' *Studies in Romanticism* 25 (Summer 1986): 175–81.

Fry, Paul H. 'History, Existence, and "To Autumn."' *Studies in Romanticism* 25 (Summer 1986): 211–19.

Gittings, Robert. *John Keats*. 1968. Harmondsworth: Penguin, 1971.

Goellnicht, Donald C. 'Keats on Reading: "Delicious Diligent Indolence."' *JEGP* 88 (April 1989): 190–210.

Hayden, John O. *Romantic Bards and British Reviewers*. London: Routledge and Kegan Paul, 1971.

– *The Romantic Reviewers 1802–1824*. Chicago: U of Chicago P, 1968.

Hazlitt, W. Carew. *Four Generations of a Literary Family: The Hazlitts in England, Ireland, and America*. 2 vols. London: G. Redway, 1897.

Heinzelman, Kurt. *The Economics of the Imagination*. Amherst: U of Massachusetts P, 1980.

– 'Self-Interest and the Politics of Composition in Keats's *Isabella*.' *ELH* 55 (Spring 1988): 159–93.

Hoagwood, Terence Allan. 'Keats and Social Context: *Lamia*.' *Studies in English Literature* 29 (Autumn 1989): 675–97.

Huang, Tsokan. *The Magazine Reviews of Keats's 'Lamia' Volume (1820)*. Salzburg: Universitat Salzburg, 1973.

Hunt, Leigh. *The Autobiography of Leigh Hunt*. Ed. J.E. Morpurgo. London: Cresset P, 1948.

Jauss, Hans Robert. 'Literary History as a Challenge to Literary Theory.' *Toward an Aesthetic of Reception*. Trans. Timothy Bahti. Minneapolis: U of Minnesota P, 1982. 3–45.

Keach, William. 'Cockney Couplets: Keats and the Politics of Style.' *Studies in Romanticism* 25 (Summer 1986): 182–96.

Keats, John. *The Letters of John Keats, 1814–1821*. Ed. Hyder E. Rollins. 2 vols. Cambridge: Harvard UP, 1958.

– *Letters of John Keats*. Ed. Robert Gittings. Oxford and New York: Oxford UP, 1970.

– *The Poems of John Keats*. Ed. Jack Stillinger. Cambridge: Belknap-Harvard UP, 1978.

– *The Poems of John Keats*. Ed. Miriam Allott. London: Longman, 1970.

Kelley, Theresa M. 'Poetics and the Politics of Reception: Keats's "La Belle Dame Sans Merci."' *ELH* 54 (Summer 1987): 333–62.

Klancher, Jon. *The Making of English Reading Audiences, 1790–1832*. Madison: U of Wisconsin P, 1987.

Levinson, Marjorie. *Keats's Life of Allegory: The Origins of a Style*. Oxford: Basil Blackwell, 1988.

Malthus, Thomas. *First Essay on Population, 1798*. Notes by James Bonar. London: Macmillan, 1926.

Marsh, G.L., and N.I. White. 'Keats and the Periodicals of His Time.' *Modern Philology* 32 (August 1934): 37–53.

Matthews, G.M., ed. *Keats: The Critical Heritage*. New York: Barnes and Noble, 1971.

McGann, Jerome. 'Keats and the Historical Method in Literary Criticism.' *MLN* 94 (1979): 988–1032.

Perkins, David. *The Quest for Permanence*. Cambridge: Harvard UP, 1959.

Porter, Roy. *English Society in the Eighteenth Century*. Rev. ed. Harmondsworth: Penguin, 1990.

Redpath, Theodore. *The Young Romantics and Critical Opinion 1807–24*. New York: St Martin's P, 1973.

Reed, Thomas A. 'Keats and the Gregarious Advance of Intellect in *Hyperion*' *ELH* 55 (Spring 1988): 195–232.

Reiman, Donald H., ed. *The Romantics Reviewed: Contemporary Reviews of British Romantic Writers. Part C: Shelley, Keats, and London Radical Writers*. 2 vols. New York and London: Garland, 1972.

Richardson, Alan. 'Romanticism and the Colonization of the Feminine.' *Romanticism and Feminism*. Ed. Anne K. Mellor. Bloomington and Indianapolis: Indiana UP, 1988. 13-25.

Ricks, Christopher. *Keats and Embarrassment*. Oxford: Clarendon P, 1974.

Schwartz, Lewis M. *Keats Reviewed by His Contemporaries: A Collection of Notices for the Years 1816–1821*. Metuchen, N.J.: Scarecrow, 1973.

Siskin, Clifford. *The Historicity of Romantic Discourse*. London: Oxford UP, 1988.

Vendler, Helen. *The Odes of John Keats*. Cambridge: Belknap-Harvard UP, 1983.

Ward, William Smith. 'Some Aspects of the Conservative Attitude toward Poetry in English Criticism, 1798–1820.' *PMLA* 60 (1945): 586–98.

Wasserman, Earl. *The Finer Tone: Keats' Major Poems*. Baltimore: Johns Hopkins UP, 1953.

Watkins, Daniel P. *Keats's Poetry and the Politics of the Imagination*. Rutherford: Fairleigh Dickinson UP, 1989.

Wolfson, Susan J. 'Feminizing Keats.' *Critical Essays on John Keats*. Ed. Hermione de Almeida. Boston: G.K. Hall, 1990. 317–56.

– 'Introduction' to 'Keats and Politics: A Forum.' *Studies in Romanticism* 25 (Summer 1986): 171–4.

PART THREE

The Scene of Displacement

J. DOUGLAS KNEALE

Symptom and Scene in Freud and Wordsworth

One can study only what one has first dreamed about.

Bachelard, *The Psychoanalysis of Fire*

In his 1896 paper 'The Aetiology of Hysteria,' Freud presented for the first time a fully developed analytic model based on a binary trope of what he calls 'symptom' and 'scene' (*SE* 3:187–221). This archaeological figure, which contains layers upon layers of memories, defences, and repressions, offers both a historical view of the development of the unconscious and a structural design of how the various layers fit together in a model that is at once diachronic and synchronic. At each level of Freud's palimpsestic figure is a 'scene of reading,' to borrow Paul de Man's phrase (*Allegories* 162) – a physical or psychological text that demands interpretation. Only by tracing a figural path descending from the surface 'symptom' (*semeion*, or sign) to the psychical ground or 'scene,' Freud suggests, can a successful reading occur: the effacement of the surface by the depth.

Freud's early paper is significant not only for what it achieves and adumbrates for psychoanalysis, but also for the interpretive model it offers literary critics. Freud provides us with a hermeneutic that can be applied to other (non-hysterical) texts. His paired terms 'symptom' and 'scene' generate analogous couplets that still carry considerable theoretical force in criticism today: manifest/latent, signifier/signified, readable/unreadable. In what follows, I describe the rhetorical operation of these paired terms in Freud and Wordsworth in order to show how their texts use and put in question the binary oppositions on which their analytic model (therapeutic or autobiographical) depends. That rhetorical operation, I suggest, necessarily involves a function of repetition, whereby surface symptoms repeat or reproduce an underlying scene, itself a repetition, and thus challenge the opposition between experience and imagination, or between history and textuality. On my way to Wordsworth, I pause to examine how these ideas of history and textuality operate in a recent study by Alan Liu, which, though not explicitly psychoanalytic, nevertheless is relevant to the questions I pursue. The obvious example in Wordsworth is *The Prelude*, his autobiographical poem on the 'growth of a poet's mind.' Crossing the Alps in book 6, Wordsworth encounters what I call The Symptom Pass, in which surface text and deep structure collide in a scene of self-reading crucial to the poet's composition and the reader's understanding of the text. More elaborately in book 4, and even more problematically in a manuscript draft for book 14, Wordsworth's narrative pauses to consider how its own textual self-analysis moves from the readable to the unreadable, or from symptom to scene. How Freud can help us read Wordsworth reading himself, and how Wordsworth, who was there before Freud, can put in question the tropes of symptom and scene, or of history and textuality, are the issues I wish to address.

I. FREUD: THE SENSE OF HYSTERIA

> And almost make remotest infancy
> A visible scene
>
> *The Prelude*

Freud's 'Aetiology of Hysteria' begins with an elaborate analogy that poses a hermeneutical problem:

Imagine that an explorer arrives in a little-known region where his interest is aroused by an expanse of ruins, with remains of walls, fragments of columns, and tablets with half-effaced and unreadable inscriptions. He may content himself with inspecting what lies exposed to view, with questioning the inhabitants – perhaps semi-barbaric people – who live in the vicinity, about what tradition tells them of the history and meaning of these archeological remains, and with noting down what they tell him – and he may then proceed on his journey. But he may act differently. He may have brought picks, shovels and spades with him, and he may set the inhabitants to work with these implements. Together with them he may start upon the ruins, clear away the rubbish, and, beginning from the visible remains, uncover what is buried. If his work is crowned with success, the discoveries are self-explanatory: the ruined walls are part of the ramparts of a palace or a treasure-house; the fragments of columns can be filled out into a temple; the numerous inscriptions, which, by good luck, may be bilingual, reveal an alphabet and a language, and, when they have been deciphered and translated, yield undreamed-of information about the events of the remote past, to commemorate which the monuments were built. *Saxa loquuntur!* (*SE* 3:192)

This astonishing paragraph, if itself quarried, would yield considerable material to help us understand the psychoanalytic methodology. Freud's rhetorical strategy repeats with a difference his theme, in its deliberate movement from the 'superficial' method in the first half of the paragraph to the 'deep' method in the second half, in its interest in both 'history and meaning,' and in its emphasis on language and interpretation. The text even includes an example of the bilingualism Freud describes in his hypothetical scene: the final epigrammatic sentence itself poses an interpretive problem which the *Standard Edition* feels sufficiently difficult to warrant translation in a footnote. '*Saxa loquuntur!*': '"Stones talk!"' (*SE* 3:192n1).

While this reading of Freud the rhetorician may be promising – and here I refer to a variety of similar work by Peter Brooks, Stanley Fish, Patrick Mahony, and Michel de Certeau – I am for the present more interested in the implications of Freud's rhetoric for reading Romantic poetry. If, as Lionel Trilling said in 1940, 'psychoanalysis is one of the culminations of the Romanticist literature of the nineteenth century' (35), then one may legitimately hope to hit interpretive pay dirt at the bottom of Freud's archaeological analogy. Let me consider it briefly.

As a self-declared archaeologist of the mind, Freud in the paragraph just quoted is committed to a rhetoric that favours depth over surface, scene over symptom. Yet it is not just Freud who is locked into such a theoretical scheme, but the reader of Freud too: when seeking figurative expressions of value judgments, we necessarily privilege what is 'deep' over what is 'superficial'; we appreciate profundity over shallowness; we try to get to the 'bottom' of things. Yet while this logocentric valorization, in an inescapable tropological structure, implies setting one thing *over* another, paradoxically what is always placed over is the thing that is under. Thus, traditionally, the received scheme of things looks like the following:

surface	manifest	external	behaviour	symptom
depth	latent	internal	motivation	scene

– in which the lower or second term of each pair is privileged. We might illustrate this with examples from many different fields, but let us choose an instance from the clinical world, to remain close to the terms of Freud's text.

A patient comes to a doctor with a complaint, a presenting symptom: headaches, tiredness, nervousness or, as in the case of Lisa Erdman in D.M. Thomas's *The White Hotel*, a mysterious pain in the left breast and ovary. We all know that the doctor diagnoses the symptom, that is, reads the *semeion*, to determine its cause, and then prescribes something to treat the cause so as to remove its effect. Kathryn Montgomery Hunter, in her book *Doctors' Stories: The Narrative Structure of Medical Knowledge*, has explored this aspect of medical semiotics, showing how a 'diagnostic circle' operates in medicine analogously to the hermeneutic circle in the interpretation of texts (9). Tracing parallels between medical and textual hermeneutics, Hunter shows how understanding, whether of patients or of literary texts, 'is narratively constructed and transmitted' (xvii). To put it in our terms, the scene of reading in medical diagnostics begins with a symptom that is already *in medias res*: it is a sign with a past and future history, or an aetiology and a prognosis. Obviously, the doctor does not treat the symptom merely, though there are plenty of products on the market nowadays advertising 'symptomatic' relief for certain ailments. Rather, the doctor attempts to treat the illness that is causing the symptom, thereby eliminating both of them at the same time. Now Freud, applying this standard diagnostic technique to the treatment of hysteria, translates it this way: 'What we have to do,' he writes, is

to lead the patient's attention back from his symptom to the scene in which and through which that symptom arose; and, having thus located the scene, we remove the symptom by bringing about, during the reproduction of the traumatic scene, a subsequent correction of the psychical course of events which took place at the time. (*SE* 3:193)

From symptom to scene: it sounds simple. Yet we've only scratched the surface.

Examining the metaphor of psychoanalysis as *depth* in his book *The*

Writing of History, de Certeau says:

> Such is the way Freudian therapeutics proceeds: analysis discerns organizations in the words of patients that 'betray' a genesis; it refers them to events that they hide and which become – as *both* absent and present – a past ... Through a study of the text, the analysis will transform the surface of verbal elements into a network of interrelations that organize this surface, that articulate words as a function of lost or effaced things, and that turn the text into a deceptive sign of past events. (292)[1]

What complicates or makes 'deceptive' the apparent directness of Freud's approach is the fact that the path from point A to point B is never a straight line. The backward tracing from symptom to scene always contains detours and retracings, which involve what Freud calls 'overdetermination' (*SE* 3:216, 216n1) and 'nodal points' (*SE* 3:198, 198n1). He writes: 'The path from the symptoms of hysteria to its aetiology is more laborious and leads through other connections than one would have imagined' (*SE* 3:193). The reason for the analytic journey's tortuousness lies in the two criteria that Freud stipulates in order for the scene to qualify as the 'right' scene: (1) *'suitability to serve as a determinant'*; and (2) sufficient *'traumatic force'* (*SE* 3:193). Specifying these two requirements, Freud argues that what may *appear* as a ground or scene often turns out to be a false bottom, insufficient to explain or explain away the surface symptom. Hysterical vomiting, to use Freud's example, might be traced back to a scene in which the patient ate a rotten apple. Such a scene qualifies as a suitable determinant – that is, it could explain the vomiting – but it hardly has sufficient traumatic power to induce hysterical symptoms. By contrast, a serious train wreck involving the patient might be sufficiently traumatic, but its precise connection to vomiting is not immediately determined or motivated. In each case, something remains unexplained, and analysis must push on. As Freud elaborates his method in the essay, he constructs a vertical palimpsest in which symptom and scene are not present in a simple pairing, but rather are part of a long and tangled web of signification. Freud's disentangling of the chain of associations is linear, that is, ultimately from point A to point B, but he reminds the reader of the crossovers and intersections that are always present. Yet there is no mistaking Freud's direction. 'Whatever symptom we take as our point of departure,' he writes, the destination is always the same: 'the field of sexual experience' (*SE* 3:199). Or to make explicit the vertical and spatial rhetoric governing Freud's discourse: 'At the bottom of every case of hysteria there are *one or more occurrences of premature sexual experience*, occurrences which belong to the earliest years of childhood' (*SE* 3:203).

From the symptom, then, we are led back, structurally, to a memory, which hides a deeper memory. Historically, we move from a present symptom to a previous scene, usually in puberty, which masks an even earlier scene, always in infancy. My concern here is not to debate the accuracy or usefulness of Freud's argument regarding infantile seduction – in any event, he would radically revise the sexual theory in a year, by the fall of 1897 – but rather to explicate his method as such.[2] In Freud's summary of the retrograde analytic trail there are at least six distinct stages. 'We have come to know,' Freud writes, that

in order to form a hysterical symptom [1] a defensive effort [2] against a distressing idea [3] must be present, that this idea must exhibit a logical or associative connection with an unconscious memory [4] through a few or many intermediate links, which themselves, too, remain unconscious at the moment, that this unconscious memory must have a sexual content [5], that its content must be an experience which occurred during a certain infantile period of life [6]. (*SE* 3:213)

The careful and patient way that Freud rhetorically unfolds this palimpsestic tissue of memories, defences, and repressions – repeatedly reaching conclusions in his paper that intentionally turn out to be disappointments or dead ends – enacts the difficulty of the interpretive process itself. In the essay as a whole, as much as in the opening analogy, Freud's style repeats the manoeuvres of the psychoanalytic method.

For Freud in 1896, the scene is historical, the symptom is textual. However, in his own dismantling of this hierarchical opposition a year later, the crucial discovery Freud made – and the discovery that allowed psychoanalysis proper to develop, distinct from a sociology of incest – was that *the scene or ground of historical event also turned out to be textual*, that is, fantasy, wish, or myth. Freud never at any point in his career denied the actuality of infantile seduction in certain cases, but the difference between actual and fantasized seduction makes no difference for the inauguration of psychoanalysis, since it is precisely how these real or imagined events *work themselves into the unconscious* that psychoanalysis addresses.[3] This point has been misunderstood to mean that Freud (or psychoanalysis) didn't care about child abuse, that by eliding the psychoanalytic significance of the difference between the actual and the fantasized, or between the historical and the textual, he trivialized the awful seriousness of sexual crimes against children. Such a view shows a genuine concern for the victims of sexual assault but little understanding of the origins of psychoanalysis.

Of central significance in Freud's model is the way that interpretation always keeps reaching what looks like a limit. You never actually reach a limit, however; the ground or bottom repeatedly falls away, so that even the final or primal scene is rendered textually. Stanley Fish, in an essay on Freud's case of the Wolf-Man, claims that this primal scene is always a 'scene of persuasion' (*Doing What Comes Naturally* 547). 'Now if at bottom,' Fish writes, 'the primal scene is the scene of persuasion, then the one thing you cannot do is get to the bottom of it; for as the bottom or bottom line, it underwrites everything, including whatever efforts one might make either to elude it or achieve distance from it.'[4] As persuasion, therefore, the scene is thoroughly rhetorical or textual. Again we have the rhetoric of 'bottoms,' especially appropriate for an essay that argues for Freud's rhetorical retentiveness as a repetition of the Wolf-Man's inhibitions. In fact, one of Fish's epigraphs for the essay is taken from 'a report by the Wolf-Man of what he thought to himself shortly after he met Freud for the first time: "this man is a Jewish swindler, he wants to use me from behind and shit on my head." This paper is dedicated to the proposition that the Wolf-Man got it right' (*Doing What Comes Naturally* 526). As we shall see, for Wordsworth as for Freud, the repetition can be traced all the way down: like its symptom, the scene is always a scene of reading.

II. LIU: THE AETIOLOGY OF DENIAL

> to detect
> Some inner meanings which might harbour there
>
> *The Prelude*

To show how this (Freudian) hermeneutic of symptom and scene both has been and could be adapted, I turn now to a recent study of Wordsworth, a book which is in my opinion one of the strongest readings of Wordsworth in the last decade. I refer to Alan Liu's *Wordsworth: The Sense of History*, published in 1989. No brief summary could do justice to either the scope or the detail of Liu's book of more than seven hundred pages, but let me try, as I did with Freud, to explicate very briefly some aspects of his rhetoric and show their implications for a psychoanalytic reading of Wordsworth. By doing so, I shall be applying a 'symptomatic analysis' to Liu, not in the Marxist sense of the term, but in a manner that seeks to question the fundamental assertions of Liu's model.[5]

In *Wordsworth: The Sense of History* Liu constructs, in opposition to the conventional Romantic dialectic of Imagination versus Nature, a triangulation of what he calls 'history, nature, self' (4). 'In *The Prelude*,' Liu writes,

> history is the base upon which the issue of nature's sourcehood is worked out. *The Prelude* organizes the 1790 tour [through the Simplon Pass] so that 'nature' is precipitated in Book 6 only as a denial of the history behind any tour, and the goal of the denial – not fully effective until the purge of Books 9 and 10 – is to carve the 'self' out of history. The theory of denial is Imagination. (*Sense* 4–5)

What is interesting in this excerpt is not only Liu's triangulated thesis of 'history, nature, self,' and the deconstructive potential of such a system, but the implicit hierarchical structure of the three terms. The rhetorical strategy of selectively putting certain terms in quotation marks, as Liu does, has the effect of giving them a kind of figural distance, as if at this point they are not to be taken literally; yet the same figurality given to 'nature' and 'self' is not accorded to the terms 'history,' 'base,' 'behind,' or even 'out,' terms which are, as we have just seen, the index to the same conceptual scheme as Freud's.[6] In other words, Liu's terms are offered as

History – Nature – Self

on one level, yet are really constructed hierarchically as

Self
Nature
History.

History, for Liu, is the 'base' or ground upon which both nature and self are built, and here, as in Freud's model, depth is privileged over surface, history valorized over nature and self. The two upper levels become 'denials' or repressions or 'symptoms' for the real 'scene' of history.[7] Liu elaborates: 'Wordsworthian nature,' he says, is

> an imaginary antagonist against which the self battles in feint, in a ploy to divert attention from the real battle to be joined between *history* and self. Whatever the outcome of the skirmish (called dialectic) between nature and self, history, the real antagonist, is thus momentarily denied ... (*Sense* 31)

A revealing example that Liu uses to argue his case for the primal scene of history is derived from Virgil's first book of the *Georgics*, in which 'a plowman working in the field ... suddenly turns up rusting armor and heroic bones' (*Sense* 18).[8] Read in a palimpsestic way, the pastoral georgic from Virgil to Wordsworth, Liu argues, becomes 'the supreme mediational form by which to bury history in nature, epic in pastoral' (*Sense* 18). Thus, he concludes, beneath landscape poetry, beneath the eighteenth-century topographical or tour genres, lies a buried or denied or repressed history; and, as with any repressed content, it must return. History will out. Liu is explicit on this point: 'If we penetrate deeply enough,' he writes, what we discover in Wordsworth's poetry is 'the moving agon of the sense of history in its original power.' And again, on the same page: 'Penetrate deeply enough under the rhetorical ambition and hardened ideology ... and we can recognize the original sense of history, inchoate, terrifying, and brutal, underlying Wordsworth's poetry' (*Sense* 499).

This is a strong reading, nor terrifying nor brutal, though of ample power to chasten the post-structuralist critic. Yet I must question the ultimate validity of it. Is it true that in Wordsworth the 'real' battle is not, as Paul de Man put it, between the priority of self and the priority of natural objects (*Blindness* 196–7), but rather between the self and history? Is it true that, at bottom in Wordsworth's poetry, both self and nature are merely veils or screens that mask the scene of history? Yet if history isn't rock bottom, then what is? What's deeper than history?

A psychoanalytic reply might be that we face such questions when we mistake an imagistic or thematic ground for an interpretive ground. As an alternative, we might try to read the 'history, nature, self' economy, not in vertical and hierarchical terms – Self over Nature over History – but rather in terms of an economy of difference. By doing so, we would see the dynamic of Wordsworth's poetry, not as a journey of discovery that seeks the goal or ground of interpretation, but rather as a tour, all surface and no depth, where one term or event or sign displaces the next only for it to be displaced in turn. If the hermeneutic in Wordsworth's poetry *is* a voyage of discovery, it is a discovery that discovers it is really a tour, and Wordsworth forever the tourist, the *spectator ab extra*.⁹ In other words, when you uncover the bones or the helmets while ploughing in the rain, when you exhume the body, you have not discovered or recovered history as a ground; at most you have found an index or trace of history, a sign or symptom or, as Cynthia Chase might say, a 'decomposing figure.' History is not discovered as a presence, but only as an absence.¹⁰ Liu does not exactly say that, well, once you've found the body, there's an end of it. Such an attitude would be the *habeas corpus* theory of history. But it is interesting that Paul de Man says just the opposite, that when you do find the corpse, that is precisely when the interpretive problems begin: How, he asks, do you read the textuality of such an event? How do you dispose of the body?

Interestingly, de Man poses these questions in the course of an essay on Shelley that takes as its epigraph a passage from Thomas Hardy dealing with archaeology and reading ('Shelley Disfigured' 39).¹¹ Describing the 'archeological labor' of critics on Shelley's poem *The Triumph of Life*, de Man writes that 'such an attitude coincides with the use of history as a way to new beginnings, as "digging in the grounds for the new foundation." Much is invested in these metaphors of architecture and of statuary on which seems to hinge our ability to inhabit the world' ('Shelley Disfigured' 39, 40). Not *interpret* the world, de Man says, but 'inhabit' the world: the difference is not just semiotic. Disposing of the body, of one's own body not least, has both rhetorical and existential dimensions, though to separate their interdependence, to try to disengage the inhabitation of the world from its interpretation, would be a misguided and futile effort. In de Man, a corpse is no more reduced to the status of a decomposing rhetorical figure than it is elevated to the position of embodying 'the original sense of history'; but at the same time it is impossible to determine whether the literal historical event cannot be prevented from being read rhetorically, or the rhetorical figure from being experienced literally, 'felt in the blood.' 'Reading as disfiguration,' de Man concludes, 'to the very extent that it resists historicism, turns out to be historically more reliable than the products of historical archeology' ('Shelley Disfigured' 69).

Such a statement clearly challenges the method of *Wordsworth: The Sense of History*, in which Liu is explicitly and elaborately self-conscious in his theorizing of historicism. Who else has made the annotated footnote such an egotistically sublime art? Yet there is a tension or contradiction, which Liu is aware of, stemming from his mix of deconstructive and new historicist methodologies. Twice he cites approvingly Marjorie Levinson's formulation of a 'deconstructive materialism' (*Sense* 39, 312) in an attempt to find an interpretive cooperation between considerably different post-structuralisms.[12] Yet even as history becomes the ground of interpretation for Liu, new historicism 'grounds' deconstruction, or grounds it out. Thus Liu's quarrel with the anti-historical turn of some post-structuralist readings, those that share an aversion to what Stephen Greenblatt has facetiously called the 'slime of history' (101), contains its own form of denial. Liu writes:

We flinch before the topical – the apparition of Napoleon in Imagination, for example – as before a devil; we seek ways to textualize it, to exorcise the mundane demon through phenomenal, psychic, or metaphoric displacement. (*Sense* 35)

This statement – which is only *half*-ironic, I think – betrays the assumption that 'the topical,' or history itself, is somehow pre-textual and therefore unproblematic; Liu says that 'we seek ways to textualize' history, as if it were not always already textual through and through. Elsewhere Liu accepts the post-structuralist notion that, as Roland Barthes in 'The Discourse of History' writes, 'fact never has any but a linguistic existence' (138) – but here, at least, Liu denies the textuality of history in order to assert the history of textuality.[13] Such a denial on Liu's part carries with it, as Jacques Derrida has said of historical logocentrism generally, 'the theme of a final repression of difference' (*Speech and Phenomena* 141). In Liu's version of the battle between history and textuality, or between presence and difference, textuality is wrestled to the ground of history. Difference meets its WaterLiu. For all the impressive historical details that Liu amasses – family statistics, topographical aesthetics, and French revolutionary politics – there is still a sense of history as something transcendent, pure, absolute: in Liu's theory, history has less to do with race, class, and gender than with a consummate sense of the strength of usurpation in contemporary experience for Wordsworth. There are, however, other senses of history, and other histories, yet to be understood in Wordsworth, senses excluded by Liu's grammar of definite articles and singular number ('Wordsworth: *The Sense* of History'; 'Wordsworth: *The History* in "Imagination"'). For example, we still need to assess how Wordsworth's later turn to Roman and classical history might be read as a swerve from contemporary history--that is, as an attempt to contain, to contextualize, or just *to comprehend* (make 'sense' of) history as such. The paradox is that while for Liu 'History' is abstractly immaculate in its own way, it is seen, as with Greenblatt, as being a dirty word in other critical minds. Thus rhetorical figuration by anti-historical critics is viewed as an attempt to purify or even cleanse altogether the stain of history that spoils the white radiance of textuality. As for this figurative – that is, 'phenomenal, psychic, or metaphoric' – displacement, Liu concludes: 'That such figuration denies history is indisputable. But surely such denial is also the strongest kind of engagement with history' (*Sense* 35). For the new historicist as for the psychoanalyst, where denial was, there engagement shall be – or rather, where denial was, there engagement always already was too.

III. WORDSWORTH: HISTORY AND REPETITION

> stumbling on, at length
> Came to a bottom
>
> *The Prelude*

I have juxtaposed Freud and Liu in this way because they share a common rhetoric. Freud is absent for the most part from Liu's book, but the fact that its argument depends, at the very least, on a symptomatology of denial opens it up to psychoanalytic readings.[14] At the same time, Freud's archaeological rhetoric of discovery, unearthing, and reconstruction of a particular 'scene' has everything to do with a 'sense of history,' though not necessarily, as I have suggested, with an end *in* history.[15] In turning now to Wordsworth, let me try to focus this topos of symptom and scene by means of a couple of brief readings.

We might begin with the conclusion to book 1 of *The Prelude*, where, like Freud *avant la lettre*, Wordsworth says that 'remotest infancy' becomes 'A visible scene, on which the sun is shining' (1.635, 636). We might equally turn to the description of the 'virgin scene' in the poem 'Nutting' (*Poems* 1: 368), or to the 'wild scene' and the 'visible scene' in the early version of 'There Was a Boy' (*Norton Prelude* 492), about which Coleridge had so much to say in chapter 20 of the *Biographia Literaria*.[16] Let me start instead on different ground, with a passage in Wordsworth's *Prelude*, book 4, in which the poet thematizes these levels of surface and depth. I quote from the 1850 version of the poem:

> As one who hangs down-bending from the side
> Of a slow-moving boat, upon the breast
> Of a still water, solacing himself
> With such discoveries as his eye can make
> Beneath him in the bottom of the deep,
> Sees many beauteous sights – weeds, fishes, flowers,
> Grots, pebbles, roots of trees, and fancies more,
> Yet often is perplexed and cannot part
> The shadow from the substance, rocks and sky,
> Mountains and clouds, reflected in the depth
> Of the clear flood, from things which there abide
> In their true dwelling; now is crossed by gleam
> Of his own image, by a sun-beam now,
> And wavering motions sent he knows not whence,
> Impediments that make his task more sweet;
> Such pleasant office have we long pursued
> Incumbent o'er the surface of past time
>
> (4.256–72)

As I have noted elsewhere, this passage is one of only three epic similes in the whole of the 1850 *Prelude*.[17] As such, it invites consideration first in formal rhetorical terms such as I.A. Richards's tenor and vehicle (96). The figure is structured conventionally, with the comparison making a simple claim: 'As one who hangs down-bending from the side / Of a slow-moving boat ... Such pleasant office have we long pursued / Incumbent o'er the surface of past time ...' 'The *surface* of past *time*': in its union of spatial and temporal dimensions, overdetermined by the earlier association of 'down-bending' and 'slow-moving,' the image nostalgically implies the inaccessibility or pastness of the past, the inevitability that the poet cannot get beneath the surface in his retrospective tour. He remains, like Freud's original traveller, in the position of *spectator ab extra*. Yet this position is an 'office,' as he calls it, in which, as 'incumbent' – Wordsworth's pun is surely motivated by the Shakespearean 'Impediments' two lines earlier[18] – he has been both 'perplexed' and 'solac[ed].' As epic simile, the entire passage conforms to the convention that the vehicle should for the moment usurp the tenor, that the means of conveying the comparison should temporarily overshadow the larger function of the comparison – except that here, the figural means of conveyance is literally a means of conveyance: the vehicle is a vehicle, a 'slow-moving boat.' The passage begins to thematize its own rhetoric; distinctions between literal and figurative levels of meaning become uncertain, even as optical differentiations between surface and depth, between 'the shadow and the substance,' or the actual and the virtual image, are blurred. This interpretive impediment, however, is itself read by the poet, not as something to be lamented, but rather as something that makes 'his task more sweet' – his 'task' being reading itself. We have a moment here which has the force of a paradigm: whenever interpretation reaches what appears to be a limit, whenever Wordsworth experiences perplexity or bafflement – as he does in the 'spots of time' (*Prelude* 12.208), for example – that is precisely when interpretation itself becomes interpreted.[19] Reaching a limit – an impasse, an aporia, even a reflective mirror – disturbs otherwise transparent assumptions about the literal and the figural. What is paradigmatic about the 'spots of time' is that they are, in a sense, *about* impediments – that is, textual reflexiveness, thwarting, or unreadability.

In this passage these *impedimenta* are thematized through certain rhetorical figures, chief of which is chiasmus. The thematic crossover or interpenetration of surface and depth, like the union of space and time at the end of the passage, is imaged in the form of a *rhetorical* crossing, a visual and verbal marriage that is not without its own impediments. Hanging over the side of his own wandering bark, the poet gazes:

> ... now is crossed by gleam
> Of his own image, by a sun-beam now,
> And wavering motions sent he knows not whence

To be 'crossed' can suggest a thwarting, as in the Ravine of Gondo passage in book 6, where the crosswinds in the Alps are felt 'at every turn' as 'Winds thwarting winds, bewildered and forlorn' (6.627, 628). But the crossing here specifically takes the form of a rhetorical cross, or chiasmus: 'now ... gleam ... image ... beam ... now.' The palindromic structure of the figure, in which the word 'image' functions as a nodal point, attempts to distinguish the surface symptoms from those things 'in the bottom of the deep,' 'things which there abide / In their true dwelling.' Strangely, the reflection of the self – the 'gleam / Of his own image' – does not, at first glance, seem valorized here (we would expect that it would be, that a narcissistic moment would be the text's aim);

Symptom and Scene in Freud and Wordsworth   149

rather, the image of the self operates on the same level as the other reflections of natural phenomena – mountains, clouds, sun-beams. The thrust of the passage instead seems to be to discriminate two different levels of interpretation.

What introduces a 'wavering motion' into this binary opposition, however, is a curious phrase that Wordsworth added in revision. The viewer, he says,

> ... often is perplexed and cannot part
> The shadow from the substance, rocks and sky,
> Mountains and clouds, *reflected in the depth*
> Of the clear flood ...   (emphasis added)

'Reflected in the depth,' not reflected on the surface? The perplexity of this *mise en abyme*, in its deeper entanglement, works to confuse the two separate levels of reading on which the whole argument depends. Surface and depth not only have usurped each other's place, but the very distinction between 'shadow' and 'substance' is put in question. What such a crossing, as both rhetorical figure and interpretive impasse, might mean for the notion of reflection or the larger issue of representation, especially self-representation, in *The Prelude* is a question that is continually posed by Wordsworth's text.

This much, however, seems clear: in any structure of surface and depth – Freud's as well as Wordsworth's – repetition plays a crucial role. In the Freudian model, the critical insight is the concept of the symptom *as a repetition* of the scene. Instead of 'working through' the trauma, the patient repeats or reproduces it, symptomatically at first, and then transferentially with the analyst. As Freud said of the 'compulsion to repeat' in *Beyond the Pleasure Principle*, repetition substitutes for memory (*SE* 18:19). The patient, he writes, 'is obliged to *repeat* the repressed material as a contemporary experience instead of, as the physician would prefer to see, *remembering* it as something belonging to the past' (*SE* 18:18).[20] But this repetition is thoroughly rhetorical and semiotic; it has always already textualized the 'experience' or scene that it purports to repeat. Symptoms never have any but a linguistic existence. Rhetorically, the Wordsworthian symptom emerges as that scheme of repetition called chiasmus.[21]

If now we attempt to map this boating scene onto the earlier relation between history and textuality, or onto the three levels of 'history, nature, self' in this palimpsest, we discover that Wordsworth's text does not seem to cooperate. The self appears to want to gaze *through* nature to the rock bottom of history –not 'the surface of past time,' but its very depths – yet is prevented, double-crossed, by both language and nature. For what does the poet hope to see? What is he looking for? The image of hanging over the side of a boat is not limited to this episode of *The Prelude* but is repeated in the next book in a significant context:

> ... some looked
> In passive expectation from the shore,
> While from a boat others hung o'er the deep,
> Sounding with grappling irons and long poles.
> At last, the dead man, 'mid that beauteous scene
> Of trees and hills and water, bolt upright
> Rose, with his ghastly face, a spectre shape
> Of terror ... (5.444–51)

Like Virgil's 'heroic bones,' this moment can be read as an eruption of history into nature, yet the 'textuality of this event,' to recall de Man's phrase ('Shelley Disfigured' 67), the characteristically Wordsworthian aspect of this epitaph, remains to be interpreted. How does Wordsworth dispose of the body? The 'beauteous scene' here, echoing the 'beauteous sights' in the earlier 'surface of past time' episode (4.261), turns out to be hardly a ground, even less a limit, but rather a repetition of something deeper:

> ... my inner eye had seen
> Such sights before, among the shining streams
> Of faery land, the forests of romance. (5.453–5)

Like the Boy of Winander, whose name also was writ in water, the drowned man is a reflection of the spectator. We have at least three moments in the text that are superimposed: the trope of the 'still water' and the 'incumbent' poet; the experience of 'the deep' yielding up its contents; and the memory of earlier 'shining streams' in imagination. The text is awash with its own analysis. Even if we could touch bottom, we would discover that for Wordsworth, experience evokes a repetition of something already written, a historical replay of an imaginative text.

IV. WORDSWORTH: IMAGINATION AND HISTORY

> even then I felt
> Gleams like the flashing of a shield
>
> *The Prelude*

Here might we pause, while still on familiar ground. But I wish to pursue this line a bit further to consider another, somewhat more speculative example of the symptom/scene model. By moving in this direction, we emulate the manoeuvres of the psychoanalytic method, proceeding from certainty to deliberate uncertainty, facing interpretive risks but confident of a return at the end. I conclude, therefore, with an out-of-the-way piece by Wordsworth in which the quarrying method of Freud again turns up some interesting but problematic artefacts. It is a curious text, part of a fragment of MS. W, written in early 1804, and originally intended to follow the Snowdon episode in the final book of *The Prelude*, but never included (see *Norton Prelude* 496–9). A rhetorical set-piece that easily could have been inserted at any of a number of places in *The Prelude*, it advertises its own status as a distinct imaginative exemplum in the growth of a poet's mind and thus bears analysis in isolation as well as in its surrounding context. Perhaps what attracts the critic initially is the way the episode both resists and challenges the opposition between experience and imagination, or between history and textuality:

> One evening, walking in the public way,
> A peasant of the valley where I dwelt
> Being my chance companion, he stopped short
> And pointed to an object full in view
> At a small distance. 'Twas a horse, that stood
> Alone upon a little breast of ground
> With a clear silver moonlight sky behind.
> With one leg from the ground the creature stood,
> Insensible and still; breath, motion gone,
> Hairs, colour, all but shape and substance gone,
> Mane, ears, and tail, as lifeless as the trunk
> That had no stir of breath. We paused awhile
> In pleasure of the sight, and left him there,

> With all his functions silently sealed up,
> Like an amphibious work of Nature's hand,
> A borderer dwelling betwixt life and death,
> A living statue or a statued life. (MS. W 57–73)

To perform a 'textual peel' of this fragment, hermeneutically stripping away different layers of meaning in the manner of Freud, we might begin with the characteristically Wordsworthian poetics of encounter, as definitively treated by Geoffrey Hartman (1–30). My immediate interest, however, is not in the theme of self-consciousness so much as in the way that the self here, as in the 'surface of past time' passage, does not appear foregrounded to the extent it is in such scenes as the blind Beggar in London (*Prelude* 7.619–49). Wordsworth's claim that the encounter with the horse is meant 'to embody / [The] pleasing argument' of an 'analogy betwixt / The mind of man and Nature' (MS. W 33, 27–8) does not make interpretation any easier, though it perhaps justifies a psychoanalytic rhetoric. The episode begins in its 'chancy' way, not with 'a leading from above,' as in 'Resolution and Independence' (*Poems* 1:553), but with a more human contingency, with the speaker's attention being directed to the scene in front of him by 'a peasant of the valley.' Like the 'surface of past time' episode, the text emphasizes its own margins, its boundary layers between 'life and death,' as the poet says, or between nature and art, the object and the image. The peculiar adjective 'amphibious,' by no means common in Wordsworth, recalls a passage from *The Prelude* in which the poet's life at Cambridge is 'compared / To a floating island, an amphibious spot / Unsound, of spongy texture' (3.335–7). A fair surface belies a foul depth, no grounding at all, either personal or interpretive. Whether the poet sails 'upon the breast / Of a still water' or sees a horse standing 'upon a little breast of ground,' something symptomatically floats or remains precariously suspended, like a horse's leg in air. Though Wordsworth uses no interjective signposts here such as 'Lo!' or 'Behold!' the shock of mild surprise is familiarly Wordsworthian. Yet the speaker's response is not just surprise, but pleasure: 'We paused awhile / In pleasure of the sight.' But what exactly in this 'pleasing argument' is pleasurable about this horse? Is it merely, as one critic suggests, its ordinariness? 'What the Grasmere peasant points out to the poet,' Jonathan Wordsworth writes, 'is a horse in the moonlight, sleeping as horses often do sleep, on three feet' (2).

Yet there is nothing so ordinary about Wordsworth's rhetoric in this passage, with its carefully wrought examples of anaphora, epistrophe, and chiasmus. Repetition of certain phrasings – 'stood ... stood'; 'breath ... breath'; and 'gone ... gone' – not only rhetorically overdetermines the text but also creates a sense of hermeneutic closure, as if interpretation kept circling around the object without getting any closer, its own powers of explication being 'silently sealed up.' The stylization of description reflects the aestheticization of the horse itself, as a 'living statue or a statued life.' Like Freud's archaeological artefacts, this statue might provide an index to history, to 'the events of the remote past ... *Saxa loquuntur!*' If stones can talk, maybe horses can, and not just in the way that the 'Horse of knowledge' in book 7 of *The Prelude* communicates 'by stamping out ... answers' on the ground (*Norton Prelude* 262n6). Here is a horse, Wordsworth's fragment implies, and thereby hangs a tale. 'My present aim,' he writes, 'Is to contemplate for a needful while / (Passage which will conduct in season due / Back to the tale which I have left behind) ...' (MS. W 6–9). While among other tales *The Winter's Tale* stands as an obvious hintertext here in relation to living statues, the final epigrammatic verse, in its deliberately sculpted chiasmus ('living statue ... statued life'), verges on that central Wordsworthian genre of the epitaph. One almost expects a rhetorical figure linking 'horse' and 'corse,' in the spirit of a Lucy poem: A slumber did my palfrey seal ... No motion has it now, no force.

The emphasis on sight calls attention to the episode as something of an optical puzzle. Demarcations of foreground and background, lighting, attitude, and perspective cast the horse as 'an object full in view,' and thus place this text within the purview of the picturesque. Like the Wanderer in the first book of *The Excursion*, the horse is locodescriptively 'stationed' (*Poems* 2:41); it is posed as just a silhouette, illuminated by 'a clear silver moonlight sky behind.' The reader sees only its contours, its 'shape and substance' alone:

> breath, motion gone,
> Hairs, colour, all but shape and substance gone,
> Mane, ears, and tail, as lifeless as the trunk
> That had no stir of breath.

In this anti-blazon, all horses are grey in the dark. Given the silhouetting of this horse, as well as its explicitly statuesque aspect, we are encouraged to approach it from the perspective of the visual arts, as either sculpture or a type of 'still life.' The passage is a powerful *ekphra-*

sis, a rhetorical flourish that delights in its own descriptiveness as it pauses awhile 'in pleasure of the sight.' The poet tropes the horse as a strange 'work of Nature's hand.' It is art, or an artefact, though one made by Nature. What is it about this horse that catches the viewer's eye?

We know that elsewhere in this fragment of MS. W (75–130) Wordsworth got both matter and manner from specific travel and history books. He 'drew, at times verbatim, on Ferdinand Columbus, *Life and Actions of Christopher Columbus* ... Richard Hakluyt's *Principall Navigations* ... Mungo Park, *Travels in the Interior of Africa* ... and William Dampier, *A New Voyage round the World*' (*Norton Prelude* 496; see also de Selincourt 623–8). With so much historical texture, and so many explicit references to historical explorers, it can hardly be said that Wordsworth here in MS. W denies history. Yet his engagement with history, through its textual mediations, could still be read as repression and denial. An adaptation of a Lacanian joke is apropos here: Wordsworth, why do you tell me you are engaging history so I'll believe you are denying it, when you really are engaging it?[22] 'Surely such denial is also the strongest kind of engagement with history,' we recall Liu saying (*Sense* 35). Wordsworth's use of history might be neither advocacy nor suppression, yet it still runs the risk of being read as a swerve from the very thing it appears to invoke and encounter.

In the context of MS. W, lines 1–33, and their later transformation into *The Prelude* 14.78–95, the only 'history' in the horse appears to be the one related to 'the history of a Poet's mind' (14.414), since the purpose of this scene, like the following ones dealing with Columbus, Gilbert, Dampier, and other explorers, is to provide the 'analogy betwixt / The mind of man and Nature' (MS. W 27–8). In this episode we clearly have two components, self and nature, with that third element, history, apparently elided or at least subsumed under the aspect of personal imaginative history. Yet if this alleged incorporation of history into self can be read as 'the strongest kind of engagement with history,' it is not an engagement untroubled by its own textuality. What history is not inhabited by difference? The question is at once symptomatic and fundamental, and disturbs the assumption of an original or final scene of history as the unassailable limit of reading. But what about this dark horse? Where is the history in it?

Let us imagine that it resides in the deliberate military pose of the creature. It stands like a stylized horse in a military painting or war memorial, one leg raised, not quite rampant, on 'a little breast of ground.' In his description of the 'Armoury' (1805 *Prelude* 7.135) in the Tower of London, Wordsworth views

> ... Statues – man,
> And the horse under him – in gilded pomp
> Adorning flowery gardens, 'mid vast squares;
> The Monument, and that Chamber of the Tower
> Where England's sovereigns sit in long array,
> Their steeds bestriding ... (*Prelude* 7.133–8)

Yet precisely what is missing from this statued horse is its rider, as though the animal had wandered 'out of Romance,' as Hartman might say (xx) – or perhaps out of battle, or myth. No Bellerophon here; no 'apparition of Napoleon' either (Liu, *Sense* 35). The horse is closer to the riderless ass in *Peter Bell*, likewise standing motionless in the clear moonlight. 'Insensible and still,' the horse is staged as one more of the 'living pictures' (MS. W 32) that illustrate the mind in creation.[23]

Still, that one raised hoof raises speculations. What if the horse were to stamp? Would a fountain of poetic inspiration spring up? Or is the hoof an index to some imagined military exploit, itself a memory or self-echo of a childhood scene in which the poet on horseback 'beat with thundering hoofs the level sand' (*Prelude* 2.137; 10.603)? What have we here – a naturalized Pegasus, a Marengo, or some other beast from out the 'Augean stable' (*Prelude* 10.585)?[24] The bare simplicity of the scene belies a complex archaeology of reading. The horse is poised at an interpretive crossroads, an interface between history and textuality, or the intersection of 'history, nature, self.' Each step recovers the ground of something already written: dream, fantasy, wish, myth. At bottom, for Wordsworth, 'history' is a repetition of 'imagination.'

NOTES

1 De Certeau considers at length the question of history in Freud's writings in chapters 8 and 9. To compare the Lacanian perspective on the concept of the symptom in Freud, see the discussion of '*le symptôme*' (or '*le sinthome*') in Ragland-Sullivan.
2 See Freud's important letter of 21 September 1897 to Wilhelm Fliess (*Origins* 215–18), in which he says he is 'ready to abandon two things – the complete solution of a neurosis and sure reliance on its aetiology in infancy' (216).

3 See, for example, the second of Freud's *Three Essays on the Theory of Sexuality*, in which he states, in reference to 'The Aetiology of Hysteria,' that he did not there exaggerate 'the frequency or importance' (*SE* 7:190) of sexual influence of adults on children. See also chapter 6 of *The Interpretation of Dreams*, where Freud states that 'real and imaginary events appear in dreams at first sight as of equal validity; and that is so not only in dreams but in the production of more important psychical structures' (*SE* 4:288). The footnote in the *Standard Edition* (4:288n1) suggests, I think correctly, that Freud is likely referring to his earlier work on the aetiology of hysteria.
4 This sentence does not appear in the revised version of Fish's essay in *Doing What Comes Naturally*; it occurs in the earlier version published in *TLS* (938).
5 My procedure, to the extent that it adapts a symptomatology of reading, evokes certain Marxist methodologies, especially the kind practised by Fredric Jameson in *The Political Unconscious*, where Freud, subjected to what Jameson, after Marx, calls a 'symptomal' analysis (57), is shown to repress History (see also Dowling's helpful discussion of 'symptomatic analysis' [78–80, 90–3]). However, while certain aspects of the two approaches are similar in the particular textual features they choose to highlight, my aim, obviously, is to put in question some of the grounding certitudes inherent in Jameson's and Liu's approaches.
6 It is interesting to note how Liu's use of quotation marks changes from the first appearance of this portion of the book as an article in *ELH* to its later book form. Whether the changes can be ascribed to a difference in house style between the Johns Hopkins University and Stanford University presses (the publishers of the original article and the later book, respectively), the impression remains that 'history,' 'nature,' and 'Imagination' have shifting status between the figural and the literal.
7 For example, see Liu's claim that 'Book 6's description of the 1790 tour, read in its own context, is a sustained effort to deny history by asserting nature as the separating mark constitutive of the "egotistical" self' (*Sense* 518). Liu speaks of the repression of history in connection with the Simplon Pass (*Sense* 539).
8 I add further that this moment of surmise by Virgil has, in Dryden's translation, several similarities with Freud's archaeological analogy:

> Then, after length of Time, the lab'ring Swains,
> Who turn the Turfs of those unhappy Plains,
> Shall rusty Piles from the plough'd Furrows take,

And over empty Helmets pass the Rake.
Amaz'd at Antick Titles on the Stones,
And mighty Relics of Gygantick Bones.   (662–7)

9 I am revising a distinction that Liu makes in his discussion of the Simplon Pass episode: the autotelic 'tour' versus the telic 'voyage of exploration' (*Sense* 4). The phrase *spectator ab extra* is Coleridge's description of Wordsworth's quintessential imaginative stance (*Table Talk* 189, 210–11).

10 See Liu, *Sense* 620n5, for his distinction between 'enactive history' and 'epitaphic history': 'If enactive history brings the past into the present, epitaphic history effects precisely the reverse: it displaces even the living present into the undisturbed past.' As I have discussed elsewhere, binary oppositions of this sort, between past and present, or between life and death, voice and silence, and speech and writing, are the very structures that Wordsworth's texts continually dismantle. As far as Liu's example of Virgil's *Georgics* is concerned, I do not think that an uncovered corpse 'brings the past into the present' in the way that Liu suggests.

11 Of the business of finding corpses in interpretation, de Man later says: 'The final test of reading, in *The Triumph of Life*, depends on how one reads the textuality of this event, how one disposes of Shelley's body ... The apparent ease with which readers of *The Triumph of Life* have been able to dispose of this challenge demonstrates the inadequacy of our understanding of Shelley and, beyond him, of romanticism in general' ('Shelley Disfigured' 67).

12 See Levinson 8–10. Levinson's phrase 'deconstructive materialism' is meant to have oxymoronic or dialectical power, but as her list of critics alleged to be 'at once materialist and deconstructive' (9) demonstrates, Levinson has a curious idea of what constitutes a deconstructive criticism. To take one example, she includes Kenneth Johnston (along with Liu) in her roster of deconstructive materialists! Now, Johnston, one of our finest historical scholars working on Wordsworth, is anything but deconstructive, as he himself admits in his book *Wordsworth and 'The Recluse.'* By the same token, not surprisingly, there is nothing deconstructive about Levinson's readings.

13 In her essay 'History as Gesture; or, The Scandal of History,' Lynn Hunt recounts how critics have justifiably 'accuse[d] the new historicists of gesturing toward history as if it were an unproblematic ground of truth without paying adequate attention to the ways in which history itself was constructed and reconstructed both by those who framed the original

documents and those who later interpreted them' (100). Her argument that 'many historians believe in the existence of history standing outside of interpretation' (100) can be taken to include the assumption of a history outside of textuality too.

14 There are other good methodological reasons for juxtaposing Freud and Liu. As Slavoj Zizek, among others, has noted, 'there is a fundamental homology between the interpretative procedure of Marx and Freud – more precisely, between their analysis of commodity and of dreams' (11). Strictly speaking, in the case of Liu we could substitute 'historicism' for 'Marx,' and still keep the parallelism intact. See Zizek 11–84 for a discussion of the symptom in Marxist and Lacanian terms. In his review of Liu's book, Kurt Heinzelman makes an observation on Liu vis-à-vis psychoanalysis and materialism: 'Although Liu's critical quest is psychological, his method is not psychoanalytical, both because he wants to historicize causality materialistically and because he is not arguing for inadvertent or repressed denial but for a psychodynamic more deliberate, intentional, and authored' (134–5).

15 To recall Liu's opposition between the journey and the tour (*Sense* 4), we see where Freud stands in 1896 when he writes, with deliberate emphasis: 'Whatever symptom we take as our point of departure, *in the end we infallibly come to the field of sexual experience*' (*SE* 3:199). Freud obviously casts his analytical project in the form of the voyage of discovery – as in his opening archaeological analogy – and characterizes himself as the discoverer. He does not, like Wordsworth in France during the early stages of the Revolution, play the tourist.

16 I pause first over the literal word 'scene' because of its resonances in both Wordsworth and recent criticism – for example, de Man's 'scene of reading' again (*Allegories of Reading*, passim); Bloom's 'scene of instruction' (52–82), or even Derrida's 'fabulous scene' (*Margins of Philosophy* 213). In the *Biographia Literaria*, chapter 20, Coleridge argues, not entirely persuasively, for the use of the word 'scene' in a strict theatrical sense, as he claims both Shakespeare and Milton had used it. Wordsworth's 'austerely accurate' diction in 'There Was a Boy,' Coleridge suggests (2:103), judiciously respects this usage, so that the dramatic context is always present or implied in any scene. One could say, after Robert Greene, that 'the onely Shake-scene in a countrey,' for Coleridge, is the one that is genetically theatrical (Shakespeare 13).

17 See my *Monumental Writing* 49, 191n17. It is relevant to note the provenance of this topos of the poet as sailor; see, for example, Curtius's claim that 'the epic poet voyages over the open sea in a great ship, the

lyric poet on a river in a small boat ... the poet becomes the sailor, his mind or work the boat' (128, 129). The rhetorical structuring of this image as an epic simile clearly aligns Wordsworth with this tradition. Liu mentions this boating scene in the context of a 'locodescriptive moment' (*Sense* 553n113).

18 The word 'Impediments' recalls Shakespeare's Sonnet 116 ('Let me not to the marriage of true minds admit / Impediments'), with its intersection of marriage, a 'wandering bark,' and both legal and nautical impediments; and the impediment/marriage topos in *Much Ado about Nothing* 2.2.1–7, where we find a rhetorical cluster of impediments – that is, crossing, coming athwart, and barring:

> DON JOHN: It is so; the Count Claudio shall marry the daughter of Leonato.
> BORACHIO: Yea, my lord; but I can cross it.
> DON JOHN: Any bar, any cross, any impediment will be medicinable to me: I am sick in displeasure to him, and whatsoever comes athwart his affection ranges evenly with mine. How canst thou cross this marriage?

See also *Measure for Measure* 3.1.242 for the image of 'an impediment in the current' evoked in the context of marriage. Shakespeare plays with the legal and nautical connotations of the trope in all cases (see also *Much Ado* 3.2.93, 4.1.12, and 5.2.85). 'Incumbent' is by contrast a Miltonic word – see *Paradise Lost* 1.226, where Satan is 'incumbent on the dusky Air'; Wordsworth invokes it in book 3.119 of *The Prelude* ('Incumbencies more awful') in a Miltonic context. I suggest that 'impediments' and 'incumbent' are linked because of the intertextual play of Shakespeare and Milton as contraries in Wordsworth's own imagination.

19 See Hertz, especially his chapter 'The Notion of Blockage in the Literature of the Sublime' (40–60), for a discussion of blockage as a literary topos that 'reestablishes boundaries between representor and represented' (60).

20 Freud's footnote (*SE* 18:18n1) usefully directs the reader to his paper 'Recollecting, Repeating, and Working Through' (*SE* 12:145–56). For one succinct description of the transference and its textual nature, see Brooks ('Idea'), who explores the implications of the encounter between literature and psychoanalysis for a theory of reading.

21 Chiasmus in Wordsworth, in its reflexive A-B-B-A form, is conventionally a figural marriage, a trope for how, as the Prospectus to *The Recluse* puts it, 'the discerning intellect of Man ... [is] wedded to this goodly universe' (*Poems* 2:38–9). Wordsworth celebrates this 'great consummation' (*Poems*

2:39) in terms that, while making Blake protest, nevertheless enact the union:

> How exquisitely the individual Mind
> (And the progressive powers perhaps no less
> Of the whole species) to the external World
> Is fitted: – and how exquisitely, too –
> Theme this but little heard of among men –
> The external World is fitted to the Mind (*Poems* 2:39)

What is significant in this passage is the rhetorical structuring of the marriage as chiasmus: 'Mind ... World ... World ... Mind.'

22 See Lacan's version of 'the sad plaint of the Jew to his crony: "Why do you tell me you are going to Cracow so I'll believe you are going to Lvov, when you really are going to Cracow?"' (173). Lacan uses the joke as an illustration of the signifying conventions of 'game-strategy, where it is a rule that I deceive my adversary' (173).

23 Within MS. W there is recurrent mention of horses and their riders. The pattern begins with the description of the traveller in the storm: 'The horse and rider staggered in the blast' (45); it continues fifteen lines later with the stationary riderless horse that I discuss; and it concludes with the account of 'that traveller' who 'did find when he awaked / His horse in quiet standing at his side, / His arm within the bridle ... (95, 100–2; *Norton Prelude* 498–9). Whether there is a narrative here within the obvious one is a question that deserves separate discussion.

24 On Mount Helicon, Pegasus's stamping hoof creates the Hippocrene, 'a new fountain that gushed out of the earth at a blow from the hard hoof of the winged horse Pegasus, Medusa's offspring' (Ovid 123). For a later variation on the myth of Pegasus, compare the closing lines of e.e. cummings's poem 'what a proud dreamhorse': 'o what a proud dreamhorse moving (whose feet / almost walk air). now who stops. Smiles.he / stamps' (*Poems* 313). Wordsworth's horse is crossed with both mythical and historical intertexts: as a Pegasean figure, child of Medusa (with its rider, as in *Paradise Lost*, being 'unrein'd' and 'dismounted' [7.17, 19]), it is overdetermined by Medusa's power to turn humans to stone, to 'a living statue or a statued life': 'Everywhere, all through the fields and along the roadways [Perseus] saw statues of men and beasts, whom the sight of the Gorgon had changed from their true selves into stone ... The fleet-winged steed Pegasus and his brother were born then, children of the Gorgon's blood' (Ovid 115). At the same time, the contemporary

context is present, evoking military scenes similar to displays in the Tower of London, and anticipating the actual exhibition of Napoleon's white charger Marengo in London after the Battle of Waterloo. See Altick 239, 300, for an account of the various shows of Napoleonana in nineteenth-century London. Wordsworth, writing in 1804, might have known about Napoleon's famous horse, although he could not have seen it on exhibition. I leave aside the intertext of Swift's Houyhnhnms, but recall Freud again, thinking of Schiller: 'Pegasus yoked to the plow!' (*Origins* 170).

WORKS CITED

Altick, Richard D. *The Shows of London*. Cambridge: Belknap, 1978.

Bachelard, Gaston. *The Psychoanalysis of Fire*. 1938. Trans. Alan C.M. Ross. Pref. Northrop Frye. Boston: Beacon P, 1964.

Barthes, Roland. 'The Discourse of History.' *The Rustle of Language*. Trans. Richard Howard. New York: Hill and Wang, 1986. 127–40.

Bloom, Harold. *Poetry and Repression: Revisionism from Blake to Stevens*. New Haven: Yale UP, 1976.

Brooks, Peter. 'The Idea of a Psychoanalytic Literary Criticism.' *Critical Inquiry* 13 (1987): 334–48.

– *Reading for the Plot: Design and Intention in Narrative*. New York: Alfred A. Knopf, 1984.

Chase, Cynthia. *Decomposing Figures: Rhetorical Readings in the Romantic Tradition*. Baltimore: Johns Hopkins UP, 1986.

Coleridge, Samuel Taylor. *Biographia Literaria*. Ed. James Engell and W. Jackson Bate. 2 vols. Princeton: Princeton UP, 1983.

– *The Table Talk and Omniana of Samuel Taylor Coleridge*. London: Oxford UP, 1917.

cummings, e.e. *Poems 1923–1954*. New York: Harcourt, 1968.

Curtius, Ernst Robert. *European Literature and the Latin Middle Ages*. Trans. Willard R. Trask. New York: Pantheon, 1953.

de Certeau, Michel. *The Writing of History*. Trans. Tom Conley. New York: Columbia UP, 1988.

de Man, Paul. *Allegories of Reading: Figural Language in Rousseau, Nietzsche, Rilke, and Proust*. New Haven: Yale UP, 1979.

– *Blindness and Insight: Essays in the Rhetoric of Contemporary Criticism*. 2d ed. Introd. Wlad Godzich. Minneapolis: U of Minnesota P, 1983.

– 'Shelley Disfigured.' *Deconstruction and Criticism*. By Harold Bloom et al. New York: Seabury P, 1979. 39–73.

Derrida, Jacques. *Margins of Philosophy*. Trans. Alan Bass. Chicago: U of Chicago P, 1982.
- *Speech and Phenomena, and Other Essays on Husserl's Theory of Signs*. Trans. David B. Allison. Pref. Newton Garver. Evanston: Northwestern UP, 1973.
de Selincourt, Ernest, ed. *The Prelude, or Growth of a Poet's Mind*. By William Wordsworth. 2d ed. rev. Helen Darbishire. Oxford: Clarendon, 1959.
Dowling, William C. *Jameson, Althusser, Marx: An Introduction to 'The Political Unconscious.'* Ithaca: Cornell UP, 1984.
Fish, Stanley. 'Withholding the Missing Portion: Psychoanalysis and Rhetoric.' *Doing What Comes Naturally: Change, Rhetoric, and the Practice of Theory in Literary and Legal Studies*. Durham: Duke UP, 1989. 525–54.
- 'Withholding the Missing Portion: Power, Meaning, and Persuasion in Freud's "The Wolf-Man."' *TLS* 29 August 1986: 935–8.
Freud, Sigmund. *The Origins of Psychoanalysis: Letters to Wilhelm Fliess, Drafts and Notes: 1887–1902*. Ed. Marie Bonaparte et al. New York: Basic Books, 1954.
- *The Standard Edition of the Complete Psychological Works of Sigmund Freud*. (*SE*). Trans. and ed. James Strachey. 24 vols. London: Hogarth, 1953–76.
Greenblatt, Stephen. 'Shakespeare and the Exorcists.' *After Strange Texts: The Role of Theory in the Study of Literature*. Ed. Gregory S. Jay and David L. Miller. University, Alabama: U of Alabama P, 1985. 101–25.
Hartman, Geoffrey H. *Wordsworth's Poetry 1787–1814*. 1964. Cambridge: Harvard UP, 1987.
Heinzelman, Kurt. Review of *Wordsworth: The Sense of History*. By Alan Liu. *Wordsworth Circle* 21 (1990): 134–7.
Hertz, Neil. *The End of the Line: Essays on Psychoanalysis and the Sublime*. New York: Columbia UP, 1985.
Hunt, Lynn. 'History as Gesture; or, The Scandal of History.' *Consequences of Theory*. Ed. Jonathan Arac and Barbara Johnson. Baltimore: Johns Hopkins UP, 1991. 91–107.
Hunter, Kathryn Montgomery. *Doctors' Stories: The Narrative Structure of Medical Knowledge*. Princeton: Princeton UP, 1991.
Jameson, Fredric. *The Political Unconscious: Narrative as a Socially Symbolic Act*. Ithaca: Cornell UP, 1981.
Johnston, Kenneth R. *Wordsworth and 'The Recluse.'* New Haven: Yale UP, 1984.
Kneale, J. Douglas. *Monumental Writing: Aspects of Rhetoric in Wordsworth's Poetry*. Lincoln: U of Nebraska P, 1988.
Lacan, Jacques. *Ecrits: A Selection*. Trans. Alan Sheridan. New York: Norton, 1977.

Levinson, Marjorie. *Wordsworth's Great Period Poems: Four Essays*. Cambridge: Cambridge UP, 1986.

Liu, Alan. 'Wordsworth: The History in "Imagination."' *ELH* 51 (1984): 505–48.

– *Wordsworth: The Sense of History*. Stanford: Stanford UP, 1989.

Mahony, Patrick J. *Freud as a Writer*. Expanded ed. New Haven: Yale UP, 1987.

Milton, John. *Complete Poems and Major Prose*. Ed. Merritt Y. Hughes. New York: Odyssey, 1957.

Ovid. *The Metamorphoses of Ovid*. Trans. Mary M. Innes. Harmondsworth: Penguin, 1955.

Ragland-Sullivan, Ellie. 'Lacan's Seminars on James Joyce: Writing as Symptom and "Singular Solution."' *Psychoanalysis and ...* Ed. Richard Feldstein and Henry Sussman. New York: Routledge, 1990. 67–86.

Richards, I.A. *The Philosophy of Rhetoric*. 1936. New York: Oxford UP, 1965.

Shakespeare, William. *The Complete Works*. Ed. Alfred Harbage. Baltimore: Penguin, 1969.

Thomas, D.M. *The White Hotel*. Harmondsworth: Penguin, 1981.

Trilling, Lionel. 'Freud and Literature.' *The Liberal Imagination: Essays on Literature and Society*. New York: Scribner's, 1940. 34–57.

Virgil. *The Georgics, with Dryden's Translation*. Introd. Alistair Elliot. Ashington, Northumberland: MidNorthumberland Arts Group, 1981.

Wordsworth, Jonathan. *William Wordsworth: The Borders of Vision*. Oxford: Clarendon, 1982.

Wordsworth, William. *The Prelude: 1799, 1805, 1850*. Ed. Jonathan Wordsworth, M.H. Abrams, and Stephen Gill. New York: Norton, 1979.

– *The Poems*. Ed. John O. Hayden. 2 vols. Harmondsworth: Penguin, 1977.

Zizek, Slavoj. *The Sublime Object of Ideology*. London: Verso, 1991.

DAVID L. CLARK

Against Theological Technology: Blake's 'Equivocal Worlds'

> The conditions which compose a moral practice are not theorems or precepts about human conduct, nor do they constitute anything so specific as a 'shared system of values': they compose a vernacular language of colloquial intercourse ... Each such vernacular of moral converse is a historic achievement of human beings ... It emerges as a ritual of utterance and response, a continuously extemporized dance whose participants are alive to one another's movements and to the ground upon which they tread. This language ... is never fixed or finished, but (like other languages) it has a settled character in terms of which it responds to the linguistic inventions, the enterprises, the fortunes, the waywardness, the censoriousness, and sometimes the ridicule of those who speak it. It *is* its vicissitudes, and its virtue is to be a living, vulgar language articulating relationships, responsibilities, duties, etc., recognizable by its speakers as reflections of what, on earth, they have come to understand themselves to be ... Moral conduct is not solving problems; it is agents continuously and colloquially related to one another in the idiom of a familiar language of moral converse.
>
> Michael Oakeshott, *On Human Conduct*

Blake no doubt felt strangled by the Great Chain of Being, and by the myriad onto-theological systems whose underlying purpose it was to promote the dead certainties of essence at the expense of the liveliness of existence. He resists the coercive force of these systems, not because he thinks that eternity is an illusion or that the world in its present condition is all that is the case, but because he believes that 'metaphysics' (*MHH* 19, E 42)[1] – in Hegel's definition, the 'range of universal thought-determinations ... the diamond-net into which we bring everything in order to make it intelligible' (Petry 202) – has grievously misunderstood the true nature of perfection. *Meta*-physics: the very word marks and enforces the hierarchical division between the fractious complexities of the world's body and their rightful sublation into the serene realm of thought and spirit. Like Nietzsche, Blake sees that the strict discrimination between being and becoming leads inevitably to two 'Great errors':[2] first, the denunciation of difference, contrariety, and relation as marks of falsehood; and second, the identification of 'purity in holiness' (J 86.7, E 244) with the masterful ascension to a world of 'joy without pain' (BU 4.10, E 71).

In an epigram entitled 'The Root of All Evil,' Hölderlin asks: 'Whence comes among humankind the cursed wish that there should only be the one and that everything should come from the one?' (36; translation modified). What I want to argue is that in answering his German contemporary's searing question, Blake retains the classical metaphysical opposition of essence and existence, but crucially displaces its moral valuations; for him, the relation-less, undifferentiated world of the 'One' is the weary projection of the mind blinded to the differentiated possibilities of the Many, not the simple form and truth of which the Many are a feeble shadow. Although I shall refer to passages drawn from across Blake's *oeuvre*, three texts are crucial to this discussion: *The Four Zoas*, providing as it does a critical rhetoric with which to discuss Blake's notion of apocalypse; *Jerusalem*, whose written accounts of 'the Four-fold Humanity' (J 78.20, E 234) augur a revisionary Christianity founded upon the dialogical principle of 'mutual interchange' (J 88.5, E 246) rather than the monological principle of 'undivided Essence' (FZ 84.5, E 359); and the illustrations to the Book of Job, one plate of which strikingly visualizes both Blake's ideal world and the totalitarian cosmos that it interrogates. The fact that 'the dreadful state / Of Separation' (FZ 87.32–3, E 369) between the One and the Many constitutes the inaugural condition of philosophical and theological thinking points to the depth and originality of Blake's critique. But Blake is not, or not merely, a metaphysician; he also objects more pertinently to the fatal complicity between the assertive, classificatory idiom of Western ways of knowing and being, with its emphasis on the containment of the Other and the absolute sublation of contrariety, *and* the calculated distribution of power and knowledge within any given social formation or institution. For Blake, meta-physical thinking is in this sense always also a form of social practice. He wanders through the 'charter'd street[s]' (SI, E 26) of

London, and everywhere he looks he sees the agonistic clash of wills, the endlessly repeated structures of domination and techniques of correction. Whenever he hears talk of Christian forbearance and charity, whenever he encounters angels with bright keys who teach the virtue of obedience, sacrifice, and discipline, he hears only the punitive language of *ressentiment*. To paraphrase Foucault, in the absence of other voices, the voices of the Other, all that is audible is the monologue of identity about difference (*Madness* x–xi).

In *Jerusalem* Los proclaims that he 'must Create a System, or be enslav'd by another Mans' (J 10.20, E 153). The curiously self-qualifying nature of this declaration of independence deserves pause: the imperative to be free compels Los, but that law is expressed in the form of a compulsion to reinvent his slavery. In other words, *what* Los says does not quite match *how* he says it, and this disparity between script and performance helps clarify what I perceive to be two competing understandings of subjection and revolutionary change in Blake, one of which will be more to my purposes than the other. We should see right away that the liberty about which Los speaks cannot be the same as that pictured in paintings like *Glad Day* (fig. 1), whose titular subject stretches muscularly outwards in a thrilling gesture that appears to vanquish all forms of containment: as the artist's inscription simply declares, 'Albion rose from where he labourd at the Mill with Slaves / Giving himself for the Nations he danc'd the dance of Eternal Death' (E 671). Freedom is more complexly figured in Los's claim: here Blake's incredulity is not directed towards metaphysics as such, which he frankly concedes is inescapable, but to the carceral implications of 'another Mans' systematic thinking for the life-world human beings inhabit now and in the future. But how can Los so enthusiastically endorse a position which amounts to celebrating the liberty to create one's *own* form of incarceration? What can it mean for the purposes of revolutionary thought and action merely to substitute one kind of 'System' for another, as if – to cite Hegel's description of the 'unhappy consciousness' – 'freedom [were] still enmeshed in servitude' (119)?[3] Los's double gesture makes sense, it seems to me, if it is treated as a critique of the 'repressive hypothesis':[4] in Foucault's analysis, this is the single vision and Marx's sleep which dreams of discrete coercive agencies – the State apparatus, the super-ego – blocking the spontaneous overflow of unfettered human energy. It is a hypothesis to which Blake sometimes seems naïvely attracted, drawn towards a Hegelianism that imagines the destiny of consciousness to be

Against Theological Technology 167

Fig. 1. *Glad Day, Albion Rose,* or *The Dance of Albion*

fulfilled only when human beings wholly realize themselves as free, self-determining agents. In his equivocal (de)valuation of 'System,' however, Blake's 'Prophet of Eternity' (*M* 7.36, E 101) hints instead that slavery is more than freedom's determinate negation, the two notions having another and finer connection than that of contrast. Free creation is unavoidably the reinscription of coercive systematization, Los suggests, even if that compromise is his alone to make. Read against the grain of its own idealism, Los's position comes perilously close to Foucault: 'to imagine another system is to extend our participation in the present system.'[5] We might even say that 'there is nothing outside "System" [no outside-"System"],' if it were not for the fact that this Derridean phrasing, already a quarter-century old, continues to be more scandalous than understood. But if all systems are equal, perhaps it is the case that some are more (or less) equal than others; a crucial task of this essay will be to demonstrate how Blake, in full knowledge of the fundamental pervasiveness of 'System,' pursues the difficult task of imagining *otherwise*, which is to say, of envisioning other configurations and economies of power, and thus other kinds of subjects, where the carceral *frame*-work of system might give way to the *borders* of vision.

In the language that this essay will develop, struggling 'against' techniques of subjection cannot therefore simply mean overthrowing them, as if the release of an un-subjected subject were the proper or even coherent end of revolution. Foucault's critique of the 'repressive hypothesis' brings out the phantasmic nature of that absolute 'freedom,' reminding us that Blake had already determined as much in *The Marriage of Heaven and Hell*, where he determines that no quantum of 'Energy' can exist independently of its 'outward circumference' (*MHH* 4, E 34).[6] And if Foucault proves useful by way of a supplementary reading of Blake, then the reverse may also be true. Insofar as Foucault's writings tend not to involve emancipatory narratives, containing nothing of the fabulous kind that we see at the conclusion of *The Four Zoas* or *Jerusalem*, they are fundamentally unlike Blake's. Yet reading *Discipline and Punish after* Blake, I have found, helps retrieve from that text the residua of a certain revolutionary, liberationist desire. As Charles Taylor has rightly observed, the imposition of power, even of the highly generalized kind that Foucault evokes, is unintelligible without a concomitant notion of 'freedom' (174–7). Let us say, then, that Foucault's spectacles of subjection are at the very least haunted by a picture of freedom – if only in the form of a resistant after-image, an after-image

Against Theological Technology 169

of resistance. It is the fitful emergence of this difficult liberty, beyond the 'repressive hypothesis,' that I want to discuss in the context of Blake's work. Blake does not simply oppose the totalizing pretensions of metaphysics to postmodernist free-play; he instead pursues what amounts to a nascent philosophy of finitude (in the manner of Schelling, for example, and anticipating Heidegger and Derrida) – a philosophy which, very simply put, recognizes that knowledge and the knowing subject are always in arrears vis-à-vis the structuring principle of their articulation. As Manfred Frank cogently argues, 'It is ... a commonplace of late idealist philosophy and romantic philosophy ... that consciousness (including self-consciousness) is not the author of itself, but rather that it experiences itself as inescapably thrown into the determination of being a self. To that extent it is not master of itself' (283). In eschewing the seductions of Urizenic self-mastery for the contingently ecstatic life of what Heidegger calls 'thrownness [*Geworfenheit*]' (*Being and Time* 329), Blake paradoxically finds the grounds for a new kind of freedom. The path to this discovery, I wish to argue, is through an analysis of the 'range of universal thought-determinations' that underwrites Judeo-Christianity, 'the diamond-net' that simultaneously captures, disciplines, and fashions the *theological* subject, bewitching it under the immediate eye of heaven. In his writings and in his pictures, Blake asks how *on earth* the carceral experiences of this regimen have come to reflect what the subject understands *itself* to be. What is the relationship between the 'german forged links' (E 796) – the poet's figure, abandoned in manuscript, for the despotism of the Hanoverian kings – and the less tangible but equally coercive 'manacles' that are 'forg'd' in the 'mind' (*SI*, E 27)? How is onto-theological oppression the alibi or origin of social oppression?[7] What is the connection between 'violence and metaphysics' (to cite the title of a relevant essay by Derrida)? What changes in the structure of thought itself will best ensure the triumph of Christian liberty – even a revisionary understanding of 'liberty' – and the realization of what Kant describes as 'the highest end' intended for humankind, 'namely, sociability [*Geselligkeit*]' (54)?

I. 'UP' AND 'DOWN' IN THE NON-MORAL SENSE

> 'Whither is God gone?' he called out ... 'Who gave us the sponge to wipe away the entire horizon? What were we doing when we loosened this earth from its sun? Whither is it now moving? Whither are we moving? Away from all suns? Are we not lunging unceasingly? Back-

wards, sideways, forwards, in all directions? Is there still an up and down?'

Friedrich Nietzsche, *The Gay Science*

'Sociability,' or what I will call, after Foucault, the notion of human communities organized according to the principle of 'horizontal conjunctions' rather than 'verticality' (*Discipline* 219–20), is an ideal that surfaces early on in Blake's work, but perhaps most polemically in *The Marriage of Heaven and Hell*. There he asserts that the 'history' of the spectacularly unhappy process by which human beings came to renounce the progressive life of the 'Contraries,' in favour of conforming to the hegemonic demands of the 'One,' is 'written in Paradise Lost' (*MHH* 5, 3; E 34). In Milton's poem Raphael learnedly instructs a suitably docile Adam on how creation is structured 'by degrees,' each element fitted to the next in a serviceable order that easily becomes the promise of a seamless whole: 'One Kingdom, Joy and Union without end' (7.161).[8] If there is change or movement among the created, it is meticulously controlled, a careful proceeding up the scale of nature within predetermined bounds. Under these conditions, creative acts of the individual, in a repetition of Christ's triumph over Satan's armies, affirm the deep structures shaping the cosmos and organizing it into hierarchies of being. Acts of rebellion, by contrast, constitute a fundamental refusal to conform to these hierarchies: *Paradise Lost* tells the story of how the original whole exorcized those elements which threatened the body of truth with the contagion of dissent. As the Devil's remarks in *The Marriage of Heaven and Hell* imply, Milton is never more a member of the angels' party – and thus more aberrant in his thinking – than when he demands that the proper pattern of human experience is to internalize that originary police action, and to do so by handing the disorderliness of devilish energy over to the rule of angelic rationality.

Milton's creation provides the righteous with the option of 'open[ing] ... at length the way / Up' (7.158–9) to God, whereas it is important to remember that in Blake's myth the notion of an Absolute condescending to the graduated ascent of humankind is at best the 'pernicious' (*VLJ* 91, E 563) sign of fallen thinking, and at worst a humiliating illusion that closes the imagination off from the shape of the true reality. For Blake, as for the Gnostics by whom he was complexly influenced, creation is the violently illegitimate imposition of hierarchical structures on a universe that was originally and energetically non-hierarchical in nature.[9]

In Blake's apocalyptic politics, the goal of imagination – in Raphael's terms, the 'way / Up' – is more properly the revolutionary break *out* of the vertical, totalitarian structures which so powerfully obtain in *Paradise Lost*, or in any other text which promotes the fearful symmetry of Milton's 'architecture of ... space and being' (B. Rajan, *Lofty* 62). As Blake says, flatly rejecting what he sees as Dante's similarly maniacal adherence to the perpendicular design of the cosmos: 'In Equivocal Worlds Up & Down are Equivocal' (E 690). Blake is not known for his positive reception of European science, but in this instance he does not hesitate to draw a figure from it in order to unsettle what he could only have felt was the 'moralizing sadism'[10] of Dante's world-view. Just as Copernicus had introduced early modern astronomy to the vertiginous notion of a universe in which there is no above and below, Blake asks us to imagine the dizzying prospect of counter-worlds lacking a firmly fixed orientation point with which to get one's moral bearings. Where do human beings fall *from* or ascend *to* if 'Up & Down are Equivocal'? He consequently conceives of 'equivocality,' not negatively as a condition of ambiguity or ambivalence, but positively as a state of creative instability, a rootlessness founded upon a deep wariness about the coercively centring powers of the *un*equivocal.

Blake is a close enough reader of Dante and Milton to see that the moral intelligibility of their 'univocal' worlds is indistinguishable from their disciplinary organization. Although neither precursor is entirely without visionary strengths, both suffer from what Nietzsche calls an 'arbitrary incarceration in the pre-Copernican prison and field of vision' (*Will* 417). (We shall have reason to return to this penal metaphor, and to the identification of confinement with a regime of visibility.) In *Paradise Lost* and *The Divine Comedy*, knowledge and power, the promise of comprehension and the expression of divine authority, jointly rest with the stringent discrimination between 'Up' and 'Down,' a place for everything and everything in its place: *where* one is, is a measure of *what* one is. The exclusionary structure of this cosmos calls out for 'reorganiz[ation],' as Albion argues in a crucial passage from *The Four Zoas*:

> If Gods combine against Man Setting their Dominion above
> The Human form Divine. Thrown down from their high Station
> In the Eternal heavens of Human Imagination: buried beneath
> In dark oblivion with incessant pangs ages on ages
> In Enmity & war first weakend then in stern repentance

> They must renew their brightness & their disorganizd functions
> Again reorganize till they resume the image of the human[.]
>
> (126.9–15, E 395)

Albion's account remembers the story of the fallen angels in *Paradise Lost*, but reverses and disrupts its spatial and moral dynamics: here, it is the 'Gods' who are disobedient and who deface the 'Human' in whose 'image' they have been made. By 'Setting their Dominion *above* / The Human form Divine,' Albion suggests, the 'Gods' behave in a way that is paradoxically *beneath* their 'high Station'; they consequently find themselves cast into a place analogous to Milton's hell. Blake's syntax conveniently lacks a subject to name who it is that has actually 'thrown' the 'Gods' out of 'the Eternal heavens of human Imagination,' making it seem that they have somehow managed to expel themselves. Brian Wilkie and Mary Lynn Johnson point out that this 'lecture sums up the theme' of *The Four Zoas* (223), but it might just as easily be argued that it embodies a distrust of vertically organized structures that reverberates throughout Blake's work, from *The Marriage of Heaven and Hell* to *Jerusalem*, and from the frontispiece to *Europe* (*The Ancient of Days* [fig. 2]) to the illustrations for the Book of Job. What is curious about the passage from *The Four Zoas* is that in reversing the moral polarities of Milton's universe, Albion clearly reinscribes the very 'Up & Down' (E 690) organization he would unsettle: that the hero of the poem should himself be drawn back into the disciplinary possibilities of this design suggests both its inherent seductiveness and the difficulty of imagining worlds founded upon wholly different principles.

In 'Equivocal Worlds,' however, the regulative force of pyramidal structures no longer obtains because the hierarchical valuations upon which these structures depend, beginning with the distinction between 'the higher' and 'the lower' as the proper and the improper, are no longer given, but construed, not univocally enforced but equivocally interpreted. To put it in Nietzschean terms, in an equivocally re-organized universe, terms like 'Up & Down' can only be understood in their 'extra-' or 'non-moral sense.'[11] Without a higher place from which to feel the burden of a sustained moral surveillance, or a lower place in which to suffer the 'pangs' of 'Enmity' and 'repentance,' life is liberated from the traditional metaphysical compass points with which it orients itself. Not surprisingly, the immanent loss of these points triggers the onto-theological equivalent of vertigo, as Urizen feels in the Ninth Night of *The Four Zoas*:

Against Theological Technology 173

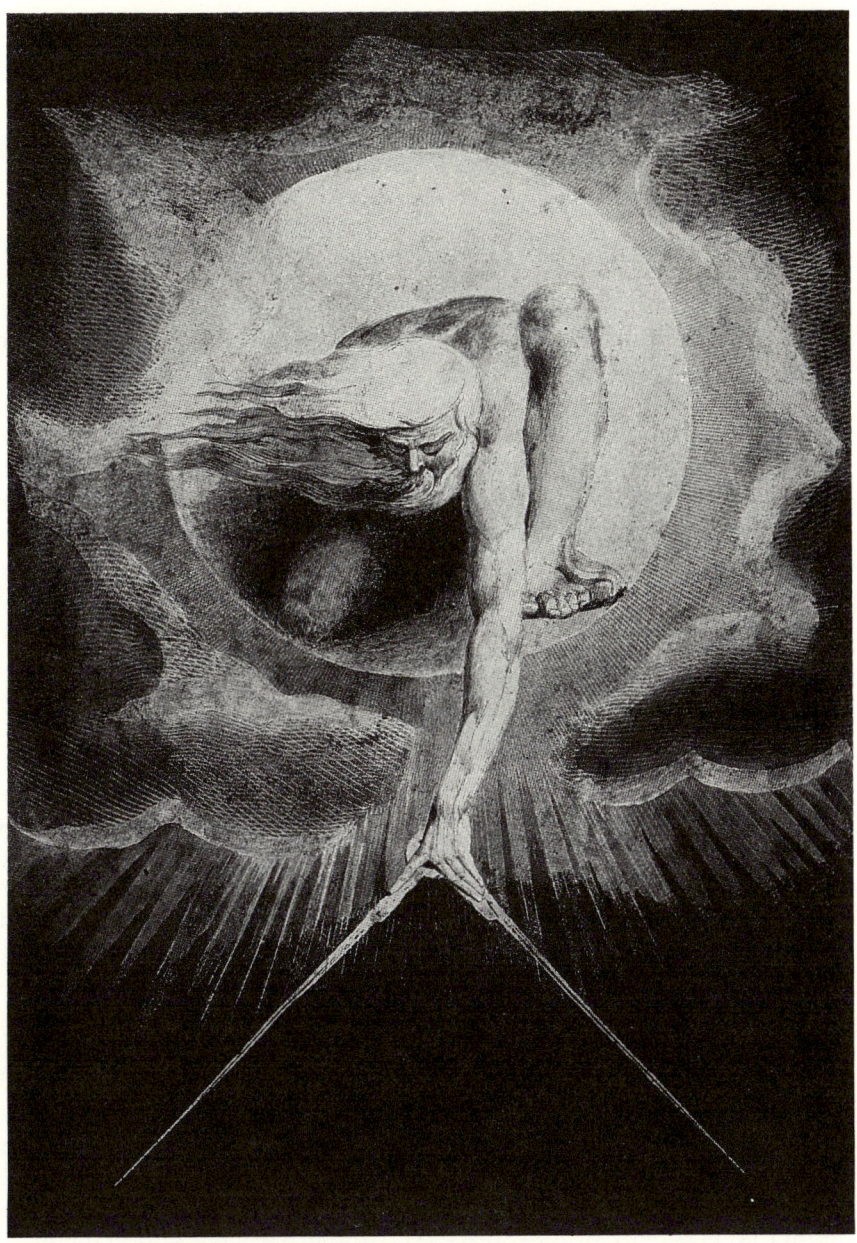

Fig. 2. 'Europe,' Plate i; Frontispiece: *The Ancient of Days*

> ... I have Erred & my Error remains with me
> What Chain encompasses in what Lock is the river of light confind
> That issues forth in the morning by measure & the evening by carefulness
> Where shall we take our stand to view the infinite & unbounded
> Or where are human feet for Lo our eyes are in the heavens[.]
>
> (122.21–5, E 391)

Urizen's nervous questions anticipate those of Nietzsche's madman in the third book of *The Gay Science*, for whom the immanent collapse of metaphysics leads to a moment of profound disorientation. Remembering Copernicus, he asks: 'What were we doing when we loosened this earth from its sun? ... Is there still an up and down?' (181). So afraid that the demise of the old metaphysical order can only mean the end of the world, and unable to imagine the absence of the centre except as the advent of utter darkness, the madman lights a lantern even though it is a bright morning. As Urizen comes to the threshold of his regeneration in *The Four Zoas*, his sense of moral direction becomes similarly confused. On the one hand, he knows that while 'our eyes are in the heavens,' we inevitably reinscribe the vertical design of the cosmos, setting the 'Dominion' of the 'Gods ... *above* / The Human form Divine' (*FZ* 122.22–4, E 391). Looking skyward rather than at the other Zoas with which he is irrevocably bound, and unable to see where the true, 'human' ground lies, he can only stumble blindly into an in-human future – which is to say, into a future determined in 'heaven.' On the other hand, in asking anxiously after the fate of the 'Chain' that 'encompasses' the order of things, Urizen betrays a residual faith in the disciplinary structure of a univocal world: there, at least, the line dividing 'morning' from 'evening' is carefully maintained, there the 'river of light' is properly 'confind.' More important, the prospect of apprehending absolute knowledge, of commandeering the absolutely unconditioned and dominating stance from which to 'view the infinite & unbounded' (*FZ* 122.22–4, E 391), continues to tantalize and distract his imagination. Urizen here evokes the oldest, and, one might say, the founding dream of metaphysics: namely, to know and to see the world from an Archimedean point. As the position from which all other positions can be seen, this 'stand' is, precisely, a non-place, an *ou tópos* or utopia. It is the stance that Blake portrays in *The Ancient of Days* (fig. 2), a painting whose ironic intent does not quite succeed in undercutting the heroic grandeur of its subject, as if the artist were simultaneously repulsed and captivated by the possibility of absolute knowledge. Blake also represents Urizen's aggressively panoptic fantasy of bringing the entire universe into view in an illustration to the Book of Job (fig. 3), to which I want to return; for now it is sufficient to note how the myth's most recalcitrant Zoa teeters aporetically between two worlds, at once cognizant of the 'Error' of imagining the Absolute as absolute relationlessness,[12] but as yet unable to think *otherwise*: as he concedes, his 'Error remains with' him (*FZ* 122.21, E 391).

The irony is that Urizen's dizziness only augurs a more profound displacement. In a moment, the Great Chain of Being begins to disintegrate, 'rivn link from link' (*FZ* 122.26, E 392). Although Blake's account of the unravelling of the architecture of space and being is dense with allusions to Revelation, it begins with a detail that is conspicuously alien to that text: 'the bursting Universe explodes,' he writes, 'All things reversd flew from their centers' (*FZ* 122.26–7, E 392). Apocalypse *begins*, in other words, with a liberating flight outwards from the centre rather than an inward gravitational collapse towards that placeless place where 'things' are said simply to *be*, unequivocally present to themselves in the sanctity of their own essence. Since Plato, mental travellers have conventionally conceived of the apprehension of knowledge as the penetration to just such a *punctum saliens*. But Blake is suspicious of what he calls 'concentering vision' (*FZ* 87.30, E 369), and of the totalizing notion that to know something is to master what it *is* at the point of its elemental and undifferentiated ground, unconditioned by or related to any other 'thing.' As Urizen more than any other figure in the myth demonstrates, the 'conglobing' (*J* 38.16, E 184) desire to suppress otherness and to trace a path back to an underlying epoch is in fact a concealed craving after 'a world of the constant.'[13] Whatever 'Heaven' is, it cannot possibly lie in the 'holiness' and 'purity' of an inner sanctum against which the contingent, various life of human beings is measured and invariably found wanting: so conceived, the origin is a terrible delusion, an 'Inner Sanctuary: a False Holiness hid within the Center' (*J* 69.40, E 223). As Urizen's experience of the reversed centres in 'Night the Ninth' suggests, Blake's revisionary response is to displace the hallucinatory hold which that 'Center' has always had over imagination by turning the false heaven *inside out*, exactly as the annotations to *The Divine Comedy* urge his readers to turn Dante's univocally organized world upside down: in 'Equivocal Worlds' 'within & without' (*J* 12.15, E 155) are also equivocal. (In a declaration whose invaginated topography is not without relevance here, Blake writes: 'From every-one of the Four Regions of Human Majesty, / There is an Outside spread Without, &

an Outside spread Within' [J 18.1–2, E 162].) Explosively wrenched away from the self-centred centre, in the boundary region of the circumference, 'All things' are necessarily exposed to the contextualizing presence of 'all [*other*] things' (FZ 122.27, E 392). In *Jerusalem*, the displacing force of this 'de-concentering vision' is even more clearly articulated; as Blake argues, it is the function of Jesus to remind us that the search for an epochal truth is inherently misleading: 'the Sanctuary of Eden' lies not in some mysterious centre, but in the equivocal region of the *parerga*: 'in the Camp: in the Outline, / In the Circumference' (J 69.41–2, E 223).

II. 'A BECOMING GOD'[14]

> Apart from a fallen confinement in an isolated selfhood there could be no awareness of God as Wholly Other.
>
> Thomas Altizer, *The New Apocalypse*

For all of his idealism, however, Blake harbours few illusions about the difficulty of achieving or sustaining 'de-concentering' vision, a fact put to us by the degree to which *Jerusalem* is taken up with representing not the equivocal life of Eden, but the viciously embroiled world of fallen consciousness. The desire to escape the nightmare of history is human, all-too-human; what Blake objects to is the theological transformation of this desire into the denunciation of difference, or what he calls 'Striving to Create a Heaven in which all shall be pure & holy' (J 49.27, E 198). When 'The Twenty-eight' cathedral cities despair to see each of the Four Zoas 'dreadfully plotting against each other' (J 37.23, E 183; J 38.4, E 184), their prayer for intervention from an outside realm makes a certain, undeniable psychological sense. But Los's 'furious' and 'raging' reply is revealing:

> ... Why stand we here trembling around
> Calling on God for help; and not ourselves in whom God dwells
> Stretching a hand to save the falling Man: are we not Four
> Beholding Albion upon the Precipice ready to fall into Non-Entity[?]
> (J 38.12–15, E 184)

Significantly, Los's rhetorical questions do not condemn a providential rescue so much as a rescue of a conventional 'metaphysical' kind. Whatever 'help' is available will not come from some dimensionless, non-perspectival point beyond the Zoas, before which they can only 'tremble' in meek acknowledgment of their creaturely dependence. '[A]re we not Four[?]' Los asks, reminding his counterparts not only of their fundamentally horizontal and pluralistic make-up, but of the more difficult fact that *being* a Zoa irreducibly means being-in-the-midst-of the other Zoas: which is to say, absorbed into a structure of sociable (*gesellig*) relation and difference. Los's question reaches back to Blake's earliest suspicions about the identification of self-sameness with truth and multiplicity with falsehood; in *The Marriage of Heaven and Hell*, for example, it is the Angel who appeals to the unity of God as a way of underlining the derivative condition of the Many. Adopting the self-abasing posture of what Nietzsche called Christian *ressentiment*, it is the Angel who asks, '[I]s not God One?' (*MHH* 23, E 43), naïvely oblivious to the Devil's counter-affirmation of the duplicity at the heart of things, of the fact that everything that *is* – reason, energy, spirit, body, heaven, hell – is ineluctably bound up with its contrary in a field of forces that is irreducible to any original simplicity. As Blake's contemporary Friedrich Schelling convincingly demonstrates, God himself was originally not one but at least two.[15] Or perhaps more – as Los insists, redemption is constituted not by the re-collection of our absolute dependence on an Absolute which is wholly other than 'ourselves,' but in reaffirming the original coexistence of the 'Four' that is our truest self. Indeed, the syntax of Los's plea suggests that the self-effacing gesture of 'Calling on God for help' is itself symptomatic of (or perhaps even responsible for) the 'conglobing' of the universe into the brutalist architecture of 'Heaven & Hells.' To be sure, the imagination continues to strive for perfection; but Blake feels compelled to distinguish this ideal from a root univocality which would silence the contention of voices with one voice speaking for all.

The craving after the security of a univocal life, of which Urizen is a kind of limit case, is not living at all, but precisely the systematic denial of life – or 'Eternal Death' (*J* 4.2, E 146 et al.), as Blake calls it – whose names in *Jerusalem* are as various as 'Natural Religion' (*J* 90.66, E 250), 'Demonstrative Science' (*J* 12.14, E 155), and 'Brooding Abstract Philosophy' (*J* 70.19, E 224). Metaphysics is, as Nietzsche declares in *Twilight of the Idols*, so much 'Egyptianism': 'All that philosophers have handled for millennia has been conceptual mummies; nothing *actual* has escaped from their hands alive ... What is, does not *become*; what becomes *is* not' (35). In *Paradise Lost*, Raphael happily anticipates the evolution of the universe into limitless univocality, 'One Kingdom, Joy and Union without end' (7.161). But Urizen exposes that expectation's mortifying subtext, confidently announcing that the beginning and the end of all our exploring should in fact be 'One command, one joy, one desire, / One curse, one weight, one measure / One King, one God, one Law' (*BU* 4. 38–40, E 72). As a blueprint for the order of things, this proclamation frankly identifies the will-to-truth with the will-to-power, and apocalypse with the death of difference. For Blake, the abstraction of particularity and the sublation of the 'Contraries' in the name of 'Negation' orients existence towards a bloodless essence and compels the mind's eye to turn, with a self-destructive mixture of nostalgia and abnegation, to 'that sweet golden clime / Where the travellers journey is done' (*SI*, E 25). Under the auspices of this 'Egyptianism,' this worship of the dead, fourfold vision degenerates into mere memory, imagination into the mindless heliotropism of Blake's sunflower.

Rather than ceaselessly recalling ourselves back to some 'undivided Essence' (*FZ* 84.5, E 359), Blake's notion of 'Equivocal Worlds' calls for an energetic leap into an undetermined future. In this way, his position most closely resembles the radical elements of Søren Kierkegaard's Christian existentialism. In the opening paragraph of *Repetition*, published only fifteen years after Blake's death, Kierkegaard mocks those thinkers who pretend to celebrate the noisy flux of human becoming while covertly returning philosophy and theology to the quiet consolations of being: as the ironically named 'Constantin Constantius' says, the metaphysician always 'find[s] an excuse to sneak out of life again, for example, that he has *forgotten* something' (*Repetition* 131; emphasis mine). Against this subtle treachery, whose roots lie in Plato, Kierkegaard asserts a theology of *kinesis* or Christian repetition. As John D. Caputo cogently argues, 'In repetition, eternity is not something lost but something to be attained, not a lost actuality but a possibility yet to be seized, not something passed (past) but something to come, not something to recover but something toward which we must press forward' (14–15). Like Kierkegaard, Blake opposes the 'Greek' fascination with 'Memory,' with the recollection of what eternally *is*, to the dynamism of Christian becoming, the arduous and continually recreated faith in what could be: the object of vision is not what was forgotten but what can be imagined. Nowhere is this advancing dynamism more evident than in the concluding plates of *Jerusalem*, where Blake's accounts of life in eternity give a form and a face to Kierkegaard's somewhat abstract notion of *kinesis*. Here redemption is not the 'Safe' return to an 'eternal Paradise of rest' (12.314), as Michael promises Adam in Milton's poem, but an electrifying deliverance into an unsaturable condition of being ever more about to be, an 'irresistible' motion *'from* Eternity *to* Eternity' (emphasis mine), neither up nor down, neither inside nor outside, but a region of connectedness and circulation, a 'going forward' which is always also a 'living going forth & returning' (J 98.27, E 257; J 99.2, E 258). In 'Equivocal Worlds' life is fundamentally one of unending *doings*, as the predominance of verbal constructions attests even at the level of Blake's syntax. Where 'metaphysics puts becoming under the protective rule of essence so that nothing genuinely new can emerge' (Caputo 33), Blake represents perfection as a process of producing and reproducing ever new configurations of reality: 'creating exemplars of Memory and of Intellect / Creating Space, Creating Time' (J 98.30–1, E 258).

The dis-oriented and pluralistic shape of Blake's 'Equivocal Worlds' suggests what this recreated 'Space' might look like. The nature of an analogously recreated 'Time' is somewhat more difficult to imagine. But temporality remains crucially important to Blake, as it does to Kierkegaard, because it is the condition of meaningful transformation. Without the contingent possibility of change, human freedom is an illusion, a hallucinated space carved out from the realm of Necessity. Constantin: 'Therefore, when Aristotle long ago said that the transition from possibility to actuality is a *kinesis* [motion, change], he was not speaking of logical possibility and actuality but of freedom's, and therefore he properly posits movement' (*Repetition* 310). The violence of metaphysics is that it leaves human beings 'killing' time rather than 'making' or 'creating' it, waiting for the end of change rather than affirming it as the mark of true Christian liberty. Blake is so concerned to restore a certain innocence to the non-closural liveliness or kinetic movement of becoming, and thus to rescue motion and change from its ancient defamation at the hands of being, that his accounts often make redeemed existence seem uncannily similar to the 'fluctuation' of the temporal world: as the concluding plates of *Jerusalem* make clear, life in the 'Sanctuary of Eden' is a furious *mélange* of sex, sacrifice, singing, weaving, hunting, walking, fighting, and, above all, talking (see Clark, 'Innocence' 103). Characterized by 'the hardiness of Christian, existential advance,'[16] Blake's ideal is fundamentally an on-going project rather than a withdrawal into an immutable realm like Urizen's 'solid without fluctuation' (*BU* 4.11, E 71). Manfred Frank points out that metaphysics conventionally 'orients the decentering power of time around the concept of a unity that history always and unforgettably imagines as its final aim' (77). If historical life is considered metaphysically significant at all, it is as the means or medium by which the spirit is finally made present to itself – at the end of history. To those who are 'weary of time' (*SI*, E 25), however, Blake offers no respite, no escape from 'life' in the manner of Constantin's 'sneaky' philosophers or Nietzsche's 'Egyptians'; to the extent that he insists upon preserving the ardour of becoming and the mutability of temporality, he resists the classical metaphysical subordination of existence to essence and the temporal to the timeless, and asks us instead to think of redemption in terms of an agonistic immersion *in* a form of idealized temporality. The radical contingency which is temporality's fundamental nature, the moment-by-moment 'transition from possibility to actuality' (*Repetition* 310), guarantees human freedom from the 'rule of essence' (Caputo 33). For this reason, recreated 'Time' cannot be mere duration, the period of spirit's servitude or rectification, from which it is eventually freed as a prisoner is from incarceration; ideal temporality is instead the condition of the possibility of the 'genuinely new' (Caputo 33), not a time in the service of Platonic recollection but of human invention, a *'creating'* – as opposed to a *re-membering* – 'time.'

Just how it is that 'Eternity is in love with the productions of time,'[17] even as the Devil had once elliptically announced (*MHH* 7, E 36), is largely put to us in the charged life of the Four Zoas. Using the complex figure of the Zoas in an economic circulation of 'mutual interchange' (*J* 88.5, E 246), Blake decisively shifts thinking about the origin from metaphors of substance and identity to that of force and thus of difference and displacement. The 'Human form Divine' (*FZ* 126.10, E 395) is not simple, a locus of indivisible singularity; in fact, by refiguring the metaphysical ground as non-hierarchically plural in nature, the Four Zoas precisely rule out singularity as such. As Leopold Damrosch argues, the 'Zoas are not faculties, and certainly not discrete beings; they are an ever-shifting *system* of relationships within the self' (128; emphasis mine). In *The Marriage of Heaven and Hell*, Blake had first posited the notion of a complex rather than integral subjectivity in the form of a duplicitous knot of 'Reason' and 'Energy.' Moreover, inasmuch as 'Reason' is there described as the 'bound or outward circumference of Energy' (*MHH* 4, E 34), it is compelled to recognize the containment of the Other by which it has constituted itself. By quadrupling the origin into fourfold *logoi*, Blake develops the most radical features of his earlier position. In 'mutual interchange' the Other is not what dispossesses the self from itself, as if to block its path towards inward and absolute self-relation; because no Zoa is absolutely relation-less but acquires its significance in relation to the remaining three, Otherness is patently ineradicable in nature. Continually generating new 'exemplars of Memory and of Intellect' (J 98.30, E 258), the Four Zoas are never fully present; irreducibly in excess of themselves, they are therefore the site and source of a perpetual unfolding towards the future. To put it another way, because the Zoas are unable to close up into a unity, but instead project anticipatorily ahead of each other, they themselves ecstatically perform a temporalizing structure of *espacement* and delay: precisely, in Blake's words, 'Creating Space, Creating Time' (J 98.31, E 258).[18] Any attempt by one Zoa 'to Create a Heaven in which all shall be pure & holy' (J 49.27, E 198) is therefore automatically illegitimate, the imposition of a hierarchical containment upon a horizontally organized field which precludes the origin from ever coinciding unequivocally with itself. In the unending and essentially differential activity of the Zoas, Blake signals his most complex refusal to 'sneak out of life' (Kierkegaard, *Repetition* 131), preferring instead to affirm multiplicity over self-sameness, the equivocality of dissent over the commanding power of the 'Omnific Word' (7.217), and the 'mutual interchange' of the Many over the mute inertia of the One. By making a virtue of equivocality, Blake in effect dis-orients the polarities governing the order of things: just as the fall of consciousness is not from univocality to a benighted state of difference, as is the case in *Paradise Lost*, but from the original, creative difference represented by the Four Zoas to the absolutist order of the Great Chain of Being, so too the goal of imagination is not to renounce life by securing a frame of reference beyond difference, but much rather to immerse oneself utterly in its fundamentally productive equivocality. Under these conditions, true knowledge is indistinguishable from its differential circulation, visionary *gnosis* from all manner of dialogical *praxis*.

III. CONVERSING WITH ETERNAL REALITIES

> The prison must be the microcosm of a perfect society in which individuals are isolated in their moral existence, but in which they come together in a strict hierarchical framework, with no lateral relation, communication being possible only in a vertical direction.
>
> Michel Foucault, *Discipline and Punish*

In *Jerusalem* Blake puts the differential aspect of 'mutual interchange' to us in many different ways: I have elsewhere discussed how he characterizes the dialogical instability of 'Eden' as a special form of contrariety called the 'wars of life, & wounds of love,' a reciprocally sustaining condition of attraction and repulsion in which life is lived 'Mutual in one anothers love and wrath all renewing' (J 34.14, 16; E 180); perfection is also figured forth as an agonistic process of 'Perpetual Mutual Sacrifice' (J 61.23, E 212), which is Joseph's name in *Jerusalem* for a profitless economy of atonement that frees human beings from the absolute cost incurred by the original and unrepeatable sacrifice of the Son to the Father (see Clark, 'Innocence' 104–11). Blake's metaphors of dialogue are similarly revealing because they place individuals in intertextures which disperse or 'disseminate' their significance into fields of active relation, rather than allow any single entity to arrogate to itself a metaphysical priority or centrality. It is worth emphasizing that the Blakean paradigm for error in the fallen world lies in exactly that arrogation. But each time the life of the unfallen Four Zoas is described, the same revisionary strategy is in place: the possibility of arresting all motion, of saying the last word, of securing an everlasting peace, is aggressively deferred in favour of bringing elements into a 'Perpetual' relation in which there is no certainty of a simple ground, no chance of finding a resting place in the absolutely unequivocal.

In its local context, Los's evocative phrase 'mutual interchange' refers specifically to the eternal conversation at work in a redeemed world of *Geselligkeit*. Eternity is not a question of being absorbed into what Coleridge once described as an 'energy divinely languageless' (*Notebooks* no. 3401). Blake's view of language and truth could not be more different from that of Augustine, for whom (as Joseph Mazzeo argues) 'all dialectic, true rhetoric, and thought itself were but attempts to reascend to that silence from which the world fell into the perpetual clamour of life as fallen men know it' (23). Blake certainly finds the noisy fractiousness of the fallen Zoas reprehensible; yet he also condemns the notion that the object of imagination is properly the return to a univocal presence beyond language. The first descriptions that we get of Urizen in Blake's *oeuvre* underline the nightmarish character of this silence:

Dark revolving in silent activity:
Unseen in tormenting passions;

> An activity unknown and horrible;
> A self-contemplating shadow,
> In enormous labours occupied[.]   (BU 3.18–22, E 71)

Present only to himself in his self-contemplation, and thus without need of conversation, Urizen embodies the tortured autism of pure intellection, the involuted energy of a divinity trapped in its own muteness.

For Blake, however, the movement of imagination is not from the clamour of life to the calm silence of life everlasting; it is instead a translation of uncreative into creative difference and debate, both a defibrillation (to follow the implications of Blake's own mixed metaphors) of the 'heart ... shut up in integuments of frozen silence' (J 38.33, E 185) and an opening out into the give and take of a dialogue with and of God. In *A Vision of the Last Judgment*, Blake imagines 'Paradise' as a pastoral landscape of 'tents & pavilions Gardens & Groves'; yet rather than picturing its 'Inhabitants' in quiet repose, as we might expect, Blake has them 'walking up & down' in

> Conversations concerning Mental Delights.
> Here they are no longer talking of what is Good & Evil or of what is Right or Wrong & puzzling themselves in Satans [*Maze*] Labyrinth But are Conversing with Eternal Realities as they Exist in the Human Imagination[.]   (85, 90; E 562)

The reference to 'Satans [*Maze*] Labyrinth' recalls the activities of Milton's fallen angels, some of whom debate amongst themselves 'And found no end, in wand'ring mazes lost':

> Of good and evil much they argu'd then,
> Of happiness and final misery,
> Passion and Apathy, and glory and shame,
> Vain wisdom all, and false Philosophie[.]   (2.561–5)

But Blake's allusion to *Paradise Lost* amounts to more than a verbal echo; it brings out what Milton had already invited us to hear in 'the great consult' (1.798): namely, that the appearance of dialogue does not guarantee its substance. In the passage from *A Vision of the Last Judgment*, the poet distinguishes between a genuine dialogue with God and those conversations which remain caught up in the belief that truth-seeking is strictly a matter of un-puzzling what is assumed to be the *un*equivocal answer. But for Blake the belief that coherence and truth are grounded in binary structures of 'Good & Evil or ... Right or Wrong,' like that of 'Up & Down' (E 690), risks reinscribing the hierarchical organization of the fallen universe. That the misguided devils wandering around 'Satans ... Labyrinth' concern themselves exclusively with moral discriminations thus plays out an irony with which Milton had also undercut the pretensions of his fallen angels: even though they rebel against the Father's exclusionary metaphysic, their conversation remains conspicuously theological, centred on the nature of the very deity they would decentre.

In 'Paradise,' however, the question of 'what is Right or Wrong' is replaced by perpetual dialogue: 'Conversing with Eternal Realities as they Exist in the Human Imagination' (*VLJ* 90, E 562). To evoke a contemporary *theological* equivalent to Blake's dialogical understanding of eternity, we could turn to the 'Rabbinic' hermeneutic of Emmanuel Levinas, in whose writings Derrida discovers deep resonances: 'the route followed by Levinas's thought,' Derrida points out, 'is such that all our questions already belong to his own interior dialogue, are displaced into his discourse and only listen to it, from many vantage points and in many ways' ('Violence' 109). The metaphors of audition and conversation, notwithstanding their phonocentric bias, do not appear in Derrida's text unreflectively. As Susan Handelman argues, Levinas's critique of ontology, to which Derrida acknowledges his indebtedness (*Grammatology* 70), is 'structured not around a hierarchical great chain of being, but ... conceives of metaphysics as a discourse with God, an endless dialogue and disputation, interpretation and reinterpretation' (116).[19] The trope of '"inter-subjective space"'[20] would seem to appeal to Levinas, Derrida, and Blake for quite similar reasons: it is the means by which to reconceive the fundamental relationship between humankind and the absolute Other signified by 'God,' and thus to think the 'liberat[ion]' of human beings from 'the Greek domination of the Same and the One (other names for the light of Being and of the phenomenon) as if from oppression itself – an ... ontological or transcendental oppression, but also the origin or alibi of all oppression in the world' (Derrida, 'Violence' 83). The irreducible mediation of dialogue, in other words, threatens and displaces the concept of plenitude as unified, autonomous, free-standing presence and stages it instead as an intersubjective space, as site and condition of mutual interchange in which the issuance of a single subsuming voice is creatively deferred rather than obsessively sought: the latter mode of thinking constitutes the real hellishness of 'Satans ... Labyrinth.'

Dia-logos – a speaking between – displaces *Logos*:[21] 'When in Eternity Man converses with Man,' Los says to Enitharmon, 'they enter'

> Into each others Bosom (which are Universes of delight)
> In mutual interchange ...   (J 88.3–5, E 246)

The mutual entry of beings 'Into each others Bosom' recalls Los's explicitly dialogical assertion that 'Contraries mutually Exist' (J 17.33, E 162). But it also echoes the promise that Jesus gives Blake at the start of *Jerusalem*: 'Within your bosoms I reside, and you reside in me' (J 4.19, E 146); and, as is the case in that passage, Blake's rhetoric of chiasmic reversal and economic transaction resists allowing the terms of this interchange to coalesce into a univocal presence. In eternity, both 'Man' and his 'Four-fold Forms' (J 88.7, E 246) are first characterized by their desire for combination: 'they embrace & comingle ... in thunders of Intellect' (J 88.3, 7, 6–7; E 246), Los says. But Blake also delicately underlines the simultaneous pressure of their differences, for 'Man ... unite[s] with Man' not by collapsing into an undifferentiated whole but by engaging one another through 'their Emanations' (J 88.10, E 246): as he asserts earlier in the poem, 'Man is *adjoind* to Man by his Emanative portion' (J 39.38, E 187; emphasis mine). Of course, Blake's androcentric rhetoric reminds us that his resistance to the dominant ideology is hardly complete, or unproblematical. Alan Richardson claims that 'Blake's conception of "emanation" as feminine belies his utopian vision, for here again we see woman's sympathetic, maternal capacities subordinated to a male agenda' (20); but this assessment of the poet's position within the dominant ideology is undoubtedly too unequivocal, for it ignores the critical power that the concepts of 'sympathy' and 'maternality' assume *within* the larger context of *Jerusalem*'s opposition to the coercive effects of the logic of identity. To be sure, the feminine is subordinated to 'Man' as 'his Emanative portion.' If Blake's strategy is to trivialize women by feminizing the emanations, however, that may remain troublesome only for those who think that 'sympathy' and 'maternality' are trivial. Moreover, as Nancy Chodorow has observed, the masculinist derogation of relationality as a 'feminine' quality serves and enhances the interests of industrial capitalism (180–90), whose atomistic and utilitarian ethic had swept England during Blake's formative years as an engraver's apprentice (King 27). In the poem, it should be remembered, Blake is massively critical of a world that has been subordinated to the 'male agenda' of loveless, Promethean self-sufficiency. His suspicion of this position helps explain why he refrains from developing the notion of male emanations in any detailed way. To the degree that 'sympathy' and relationality are 'feminine' qualities, they function as part of Blake's criticism of the Urizenic obsession with the sovereign self, 'free' from the contextualizing presence of other selves. The poet's emphases lie less in the efficient subordination of the female emanations to their male sources and more with their affirmative role in bringing selves into sociable relation, adjoining them like links in a chain or stitches in a weave, while also insisting on the differences between each self, the fact that only a 'portion' has been adjoined. Damrosch suggests that 'Blake can come to terms with the Emanation only by seeing it as a mode of activity rather than as a part of the self' (346), but I would go further and suggest that in this case, the emanation is a trope for the possibility of relationship itself, for the principle of adjoining which inscribes entities in the web of difference. In the midst of Edenic dialogue, human beings are necessarily disseminated into a self-complicating intertexture of words, 'Forms,' and 'Emanations' (J 88.7, 10; E 246), or what Jesus calls 'Fibres of love from man to man thro Albions pleasant land' (J 4.8, E 146). Searching for a language with which to describe eternity as a site of *dialogos*, Los (who is not without his own Promethean qualities) understandably moves with ease from a metaphor of conversation to one of weaving. 'When Souls mingle & join thro all the *Fibres* of Brotherhood,' he concludes, 'Can there be any secret joy on Earth greater than this' (J 88.14–15, E 246; emphasis mine)?

But why only a 'secret joy'? And why only a 'Brotherhood'? Perhaps echoing the ideals of the French Revolution (*liberté, egalité,* and, especially, *fraternité*), Los imagines the true community as one that is possible between men, but not necessarily between men and women or women and women. His language remains both conspicuously patriarchal and faintly homoerotic in nature, and it is impossible not to ask whether there would be less need for 'secrecy' had he instead imagined a horizontally structured and truly *gesellig* society composed of both 'Sisterhood' *and* 'Brotherhood.' The privative nature of Los's mingling of 'Souls' in 'Brotherhood' inevitably recalls the unequivocally exclusionary and hegemonic shape of a 'joy[less]' community described earlier in *Jerusalem*:

Then all the Males combined into One Male & every one
Became a ravening eating Cancer growing in the Female[.]   (J 69.1–2, E 223)

It would be hard to imagine a more gruesome warning against the dangers of the consolidation of power in the hands of men. Left to fulfil their Urizenic desires, men would reduce the world to a homogeneous mass, the featureless shape of the (male) Same. As Blake clearly understands, this anti-community, founded as it is on the suppression of sexual difference, only 'Devour[s] Jerusalem' (J 69.5, E 223), the true embodiment of sociability. Blake's rhetoric of parasitism characterizes 'Brotherhood,' not positively as the gathering of a visionary company, but negatively as a hegemony carelessly secured and maintained at a horrifyingly destructive cost for women. And when women deflect that violence, it is easily translated into more overt forms of hostility. In the previous plate, for example, the 'Warriors' culminate their 'Songs' by openly admitting to the masculinist identification of sexual gratification with fighting: because they are 'drunk with unsatiated love,' the brothers in arms cry, they 'must rush again to War' (J 68.10, 62, 63; E 221–2). These passages bring out the limitations of Los's vision of 'secret joy,' as does Blake's description of redeemed sexuality. In the 'Sanctuary of Eden,' we are told,

> Embraces are Cominglings: from the Head even to the Feet;
> And not a pompous High Priest entering by a Secret Place.
> (J 69.41, 43–4; E 223)

Here Blake figures forth patriarchal conceptions of sexuality as a duplicitous form of subjection: the feminine is simultaneously *constructed* as 'Mystery' (J 93.25, E 255) – hallucinated as the Holy of Holies – and *regulated* by a class of men whose arrogant privilege it is to command the power to penetrate this occult site, surveying and apprehending it, and thus to possess it absolutely. Against the techniques of this sort of *assujettissement*, Blake insists upon a revision of sexual relations in which one sex neither 'combine[s]' against the other nor clandestinely invades the other, but in which each mingles with the other according to horizontal rather than hierarchical principles of human relations. Against the masculinist ethic of utility and exploitation, where men are 'higher,' spiritualized entities who reduce women to 'lowly,' fleshly orifices, Blake's redeemed community briefly evokes what Carol Gilligan would call a feminist 'ethic of care,' whose motivating premise is 'nonviolence – that no one should be hurt' (174).

Jerusalem implies more interesting insights into the disfiguring effects of a masculinist culture than it pursues, no doubt because Blake is too often caught up in that same culture, teetering between denouncing the female as either passive or aggressive, Beulah or the Female Will. The fact that he considers the relationship between violence and metaphysics in gendered terms at one point in *Jerusalem* and not at another forces us to read each plate as part of a weave of differences, and to consider it in terms of its paradigmatic relationship with other plates in the poem. In other words, it is possible that the principle of dialogue inadvertently applies to the structure of *Jerusalem* as a poem in conversation with itself over the question of gender and the 'Sanctuary of Eden.' Notwithstanding the ideological limitations of Blake's vision, the interchange and the intercourse of Edenic life remain ennobling to the degree that they prevent the 'One Male' from having the final say and thus from 'Devouring Jerusalem' (J 69.1, 5; E 223). For Blake, the last word too closely resembles the omnipotent 'Word' of the 'great Work master' Urizen (FZ 24.6, 5; E 314). As the original utterance marking the end of difference, it is the death sentence – *l'arrêt de mort* – or closural gesture that 'shut[s] up' the 'open heart ... in integuments of frozen silence' (J 38.33, E 185). In a perpetual, mutually sustaining conversation, no speaker can claim for himself or herself an independence from every other speaker, no more than a stitch in a weave can be considered outside of the warp and woof by which it is made. Dialogue, like mutuality, forces us to reconsider truth as a site of relation and displacement rather than identity, as a presence or self-sameness always crossed by otherness, always somehow related to other elements, anticipating them or coming after them, resembling them or differing from them, as a text suspended in and intersected by a context. That the highest imaginative experience possible sees humanity inserted into a charged space of dialogue is vividly confirmed by the text's concluding images, where Blake's masculinist rhetoric mostly falls away. In Eden, 'The Four Living Creatures Chariots of Humanity Divine Incomprehensible / ... expand'

> ... going forward forward irresistible from Eternity to Eternity
> And they conversed together in Visionary forms dramatic which bright
> Redounded from their Tongues in thunderous majesty ...
> (J 98.24, 25, 28–30; E 257)

Repeating the word 'forward,' the visionary's tongue redounds upon itself, perhaps tripped by the precipitous momentum of the energetic world it articulates. Here, as elsewhere in *Jerusalem*, we are asked to consider the paradox of being 'in Eternity' (*J* 71.6, E 225) while also advancing upon it, as if by permanently deferring the closure of arriving, imagination kept itself from ever grasping a single, totalized meaning. Carrying themselves ever ahead of themselves, the 'Living Creatures' (*zoa*) constitute Jerusalem as a place ever more about to be: theirs is always 'the coming community.'[22]

Eternity is a perpetual conversation between the Four Zoas, a 'thunderous' intertexture woven by the shuttling '[t]o & Fro' (*J* 98.39, E 258) motion of their walking and talking. Blake describes the texts that they create as 'Visionary forms dramatic' – dramatic, I would argue, because drama is a genre which calls explicit attention to itself as a tissue of differences, each voice played off against the next and thus entirely dialogized by its context.[23] As Keats more than any of the other Romantics affirmed, successful drama effaces the 'concentering' (*FZ* 87.30, E 369) or 'egotistical' (Rollins 387) presence of the author.[24] Blake himself scoffed at readers who nevertheless continued to ground out the positions of dramatic characters in the author who created them (E 601). In Eden, the Four Zoas compose the drama of their own fourfold composition, performing what they produce and producing what they perform, folding author into text and being into language, all in a self-recharging nexus of living forces. 'Visionary forms dramatic': like 'Human Form Divine' (*SI*, E 32), the phrase is itself the site of significant cross-talk, one adjective, 'dramatic,' gently contesting the monological associations of the other, pulling the 'Visionary' claim to substance, origin, and the self-presence of a thing to sight into the mutual interchange and displacement of conversation.[25]

Perhaps not surprisingly, the implicit dialogue with Milton that I have identified as functioning all along as the framework for Blake's revisionary stance against the architecture of space and being is carried over into this concluding account of the Four Zoas. Their description as 'The Four Living Creatures Chariots of Humanity Divine' (*J* 98.24, E 257) declares its affiliation with the 'four Cherubic shapes' that convey Milton's similarly unstoppable 'Chariot of Paternal Deity' in *Paradise Lost* (6.753, 750) – but with a significant modification. Missing from this apocalyptic scene is an emphasis on the inviolate Godhead, making it appear that the fatherly divinity has been diffused, without loss of power, into the multiple visage of its conveyance, and the focus of the vision thereby shifted from the First Mover to the movement itself. 'The Four Living Creatures' appear for a moment to bear something other than and superior to themselves, the 'Humanity Divine,' until we realize that what they carry is – precisely – themselves, the 'Humanity Divine' being indistinguishable from 'the *Four*-fold Humanity' (*J* 78.20, E 234; emphasis mine) in Blake's myth. Neither the multiple image of God, nor God himself, the Four Zoas are both ground and figure at once in a shimmering, horizontally organized motion of 'living going forth & returning' (*J* 99.2, E 258).

IV. VIOLENCE AND METAPHYSICS: THE REGIME OF SIGHT[26]

> The entire parapenal institution, which is created in order not to be a prison, culminates in the cell, on the walls of which are written in black letters: 'God sees you.'
>
> Michel Foucault, *Discipline and Punish*

The assimilative design of the metaphysic of the One, its preoccupation with the scrupulous determination of identity as that which simply (rather than complexly) *is*, the inside inside and the outside outside, is everywhere apparent in Blake's representation of the fallen world: in Milton's violent expulsion of the devils, in Urizen's desire for a world 'without fluctuation' (*BU* 4.11, E 71), in the narrowing effects of 'concentering vision' (*FZ* 87.30, E 369), and in the Four Zoas' longing for what William James once described as 'that sense of a perfected Being with all its otherness soaked up into itself.'[27] The significance that Blake attaches to the non-hierarchic equivocality of the Zoas over the hegemonic authority of the 'Paternal Deity' (6.750) is perhaps no more powerfully evident than in the late illustrations to the Book of Job,[28] and it is to one of these designs (fig. 3) that I want to turn in order to provide a visual focus for my remarks. *When the Morning Stars Sang Together* depicts a crucial moment in the narrative of the Old Testament story. Tortured in mind and in body, his family destroyed and his wealth decimated, Job understandably calls divine justice into question. In response to the senselessness of his suffering, he bluntly accuses God of apathy and carelessness with respect to his human subjects. Feeling himself unjustly wronged, he insists upon knowing the crimes with which he has been charged. Although he risks outright blasphemy, Job goes so far as to demand an audience before which he might argue his innocence and reassert his righteousness. In Blakean terms, Job resists his invisible accuser and implies that 'Conversing with Eternal Realities' (*VLJ* 90, E 562) must include debate about the nature of providence itself.

Fig. 3. *When the Morning Stars Sang Together*, illustration to the Book of Job

With an indifference to Job's terrifying predicament that Blake no doubt found cruelly paradigmatic of a certain Judeo-Christian conception of the deity, God refuses either to entertain his righteous subject's questions or to respond in kind to the debate that had hitherto been conducted between him and his friends. Jehovah chooses instead to make a series of severely – even absurdly – ironical pronouncements from the whirlwind. Of course, the whirlwind is the conventional medium of theophanies, but it is also a metaphor throughout Blake's work for the deity's most vicious qualities, the qualities that identify him as Urizen: his self-obscuring aloofness and abstraction, his defensiveness, and his faceless malevolence towards humankind. God refrains from physically destroying Job, though the threat of that annihilation unavoidably forms the disciplinary background in which this scene of instruction is set. Yet his pronouncement from the sanctuary of the whirlwind is not without its own remarkable violence; it could be argued that it is the nature of this less spectacular brutality which is the real target of Blake's curious illustration. As if to mock Job's profound and profoundly felt questions, God answers with a ferocious counter-interrogation whose sole purpose it is to intimidate Job into dutiful silence. Who is Job to 'darken' God's design with a cloud of thoughtless words? Who is this man who speaks from ignorance? What could he possibly know of the creation of the world, the taming of the oceans, and the ordering of the constellations? Can he grasp the expanse of the earth, the source of the rivers, the depth of the seas, the beauty of the snow, the nature of death, the fate of the wicked? Where were you during the laying of the foundations of the world, he charges his paralysed listener, 'when the morning stars sang together, and all the Sons of God shouted for joy' (38.7)?

Job had demanded answers from his Lord, but at this point receives only questions about the spectacle of creation and the origin of its coherence, questions for which he cannot possibly provide replies. As God well knows, when the world was created only the angels were in a position to stand together amongst the dawn's constellations and sing songs of holy adoration. Job, like all human beings, was absent from this primal scene, and something of that lack remains with him still as the mark of his relative insubstantiality and ignorance. By virtue of his simple creatureliness, all the riddles of creation exceed his puny grasp. To be human is fundamentally to be lowly and in the dark, as Blake's depiction of Job and his circle in a dim grotto at the bottom of the design literally suggests. To the extent that Job's pleas are addressed at all, it is by way of suggesting that the burden of the mystery of suffering is to be born by human beings but never explained. The heartless rhetorical question forming the caption to Blake's design decisively fixes Job's position within the Great Chain of Being by registering both his belatedness and inconsequentiality in the order of things. Not surprisingly, the effect of Jehovah's counter-interrogation is immediate and complete: Job humbly acknowledges God's omnipotence and his own unworthiness, vowing never to question the deity's wisdom again.

Needless to say, it is a strange and violently hierarchical vision of the shape of the true reality, and Blake could not help but be repulsed by every aspect of it. What does not escape his critical eye is that Job's accusation of God's indifference to human suffering is in fact proven by the deity's intimidatory tactics. In this univocal world, God's assertion of his own omniscience immediately translates into an act of power, absolute knowledge being precisely the means by which the deity enforces total control over even the most insignificant signs of dissent. The assertion of such knowledge primarily serves the purpose of *exposing* Job's near total ignorance about the world whose design he has dared to question. And indeed, as Blake's illustration grimly suggests, while Jehovah pronounces upon the extent and the mystery of creation, arms outstretched in order to contain all things in a single, totalizing gesture, Job and his circle find themselves silhouetted by and imprisoned within a band of clouds. We see this space in the form of a 'cut-away,' as if Job were an animal or a prisoner, and the world a cell or a cage in which – as with all cells and cages – confinement is indissociable from the humiliating experience of being rendered absolutely visible to the outside observer. Human beings thus share the carceral exposure that Behemoth and Leviathan must suffer in the design (fig. 4) immediately following *When the Morning Stars Sang Together*. In this illustration, God points muscularly downward into the creation of which Job is surely a part, compelling him to observe the earth's greatest creatures stuffed into similarly constricting circumstances. Because Jehovah watches Job looking at the strangely compressed vista below, the disciplinary intent of this scene of instruction appears to be to make human beings see and feel an exaggerated re-presentation of their own condition. To be sure, Jehovah contrasts the immenseness of the beasts to the smallness of Job. Yet Blake's side-by-side designs also bring out their common condition, at once captured and inescapably visible. What René Girard says of Behemoth and Leviathan holds equally true for Job and his followers: they are 'les grandes vedettes de cette

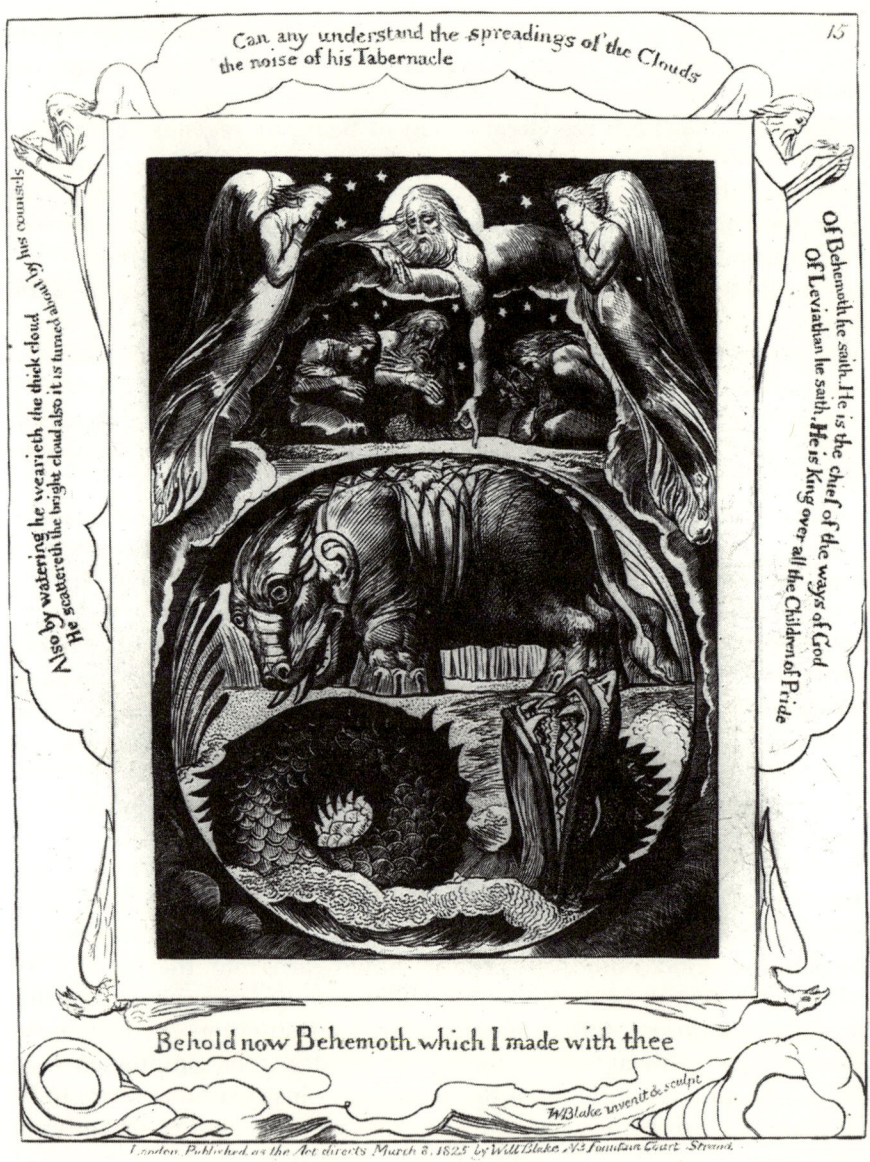

Fig. 4. *Behemoth and Leviathan*, illustration to the Book of Job

ménagerie,' that is, 'the stars of this zoo' (208). By implication, Jehovah is the 'zoo-keeper' and the world merely a place in which to show off his most interesting creatures.[29] The speech from the whirlwind therefore provides a spectacular instance of what Foucault calls 'the superimposition of the power relations and knowledge relations' (*Discipline* 185).[30] In a cosmos properly governed by the principle of unconditional love rather than discipline, life under the immediate eye of heaven would mean the reassurance of God's sustained and sustaining providence; in Blake's picture, however, providence is supplanted by penetrating surveillance. Limitlessly available to the sight of the Creator, but, like all lesser beings, himself unable to see the source of that surveillance, Job and his circle are immobilized within a space of domination carved out from the basement of the world.

From his vantage point of his perch atop Job's cell (fig. 3), Jehovah claims that the mysteries of the universe are illuminated only by himself. Blake's response is to show how that bright design is characterized by its own pervasive darkness. God demands that Job imagine creation as a building, constructed with foundation stones and a measuring line; what Blake's illustration brings out is how that edifice, imbued as it is with the imposition and effects of power, and clearly structured for the purpose of subjecting its occupants to unequivocal mastery, is nothing less than penal in nature. For this reason, Jeremy Bentham's specifications for an imaginary prison – published in a series of letters in the same year (1791) that *The Marriage of Heaven and Hell* was probably completed – seems uncannily apposite to Blake's illustration; as Foucault points out, the design for the new penitentiary or 'Panopticon' is not so much a cultural artefact in the history of penal architecture as a 'diagram of a mechanism of power reduced to its ideal form' (*Discipline* 205). Its central principle is control through segregation and observation; its purpose is to make it possible, through the orderly arrangement of spaces, to keep its inmates under sustained, centralized, intimidating surveillance: *pan-opticism*. The 'Panopticon' therefore differs from the prisons it was to replace in one crucial respect: rather than hiding prisoners away within a dark fortress, the masters place them in a structure of limitless visibility. Under these conditions, the inmate experiences incarceration not actively, at the hands of the master's crushing violence, but passively, by being placed, seen, and known to all who would observe. As Foucault argues, a panoptic disciplinary structure is designed 'to permit an internal, articulated and detailed control – to render visible those who are inside it; in more general terms, an architecture that would operate to transform individuals; to act on those it shelters, to provide a hold on their conduct, to carry the effects of power right to them, to make it possible to know them, to alter them' (*Discipline* 172). In Blake's illustration to the Book of Job, Jehovah occupies the masterful position equivalent to the prison warden of Bentham's 'Panopticon.' The cosmos is represented as a gigantic 'instrument of subjection' (*Discipline* 224) in which nothing, no matter how small or how large, can escape Jehovah's keen gaze. The design's details are appropriately sweeping in their reach, from the great sea monsters in the churning oceans below to the limitless reaches of the stars above, and from the first fiat announcing the advent of 'Light' to the sixth fiat decreeing the creation of the living creatures, the *zoa*. Blake's severely foreshortened perspectives flatten out the design and give it a certain frozen and cartographic quality: what we see here is a schematic diagram, so to speak, of the mechanism of theological power reduced to its ideal form. Literalizing the penal and disciplinary nature of the architecture of space and being, Blake's illustration is unusually busy with frames and with the cellular distribution of spaces, all of them radiating outwards from the Urizenic figure whose backlit face forms the dead centre of the design. The outside border is itself inscribed with individually framed depictions of the originating bounds of the cosmos, each fiat 'fram[ing]' the universe with a 'fearful symmetry,' even as Blake had suggested twenty years earlier in a poem whose hysterical series of rhetorical questions also remembers the Book of Job (*SI*, E 24-5). Blake gives these fiats an undeniably sinister context by locating them in the same parergonal space as the coiled, headless serpent at the bottom of the illustration and the constellations at the top: in the artist's visual language, these are unhappy figures for the fission of the universe into brute matter and a volatilized heaven. Within this complex frame lies another frame, conspicuously blank. And inside that border, the design's lower region is made up of three cramped tableaux. Immediately beneath one of Jehovah's ruling hands, Helios and his dutiful horses struggle to part the circling clouds; beneath the other, a winged goddess drives the dragons of passion before the cusps of a waning moon (Butlin, *Text* 415). The disposition of Blake's visual figures puts to us that under the auspices of Jehovah, even our psychological lives are scrupulously compartmentalized, like this picture, into Platonic dualisms of spirit and flesh, the hard daylight of bridled intellect and the dark place where worms fly in the night. Jehovah's unnaturally long and muscular arms seem indistinguishable from the thick cord of clouds which shut humanity up in a subterranean cavern. From the grotto of the world, Job, his wife, and his comforters are compelled to worship a creation whose very vastness isolates and objectifies them in their creatureliness.

For Blake, the unhappiest fact is that Jehovah's techniques confine Job and his followers at the same time as they instil within them the feelings of self-loathing (or what Nietzsche denounced as Christian *ressentiment*) which internalize this discipline and make it indistinguishable from being human. Here Job is controlled by the manipulation of his own feelings of responsibility and guilt; here, humankind is enlisted as its own jailer, a horrifying effect of coercion that Blake had earlier explored in 'The Chimney-Sweeper' of *Songs of Innocence*. The scene is paradigmatic not only of a certain Judeo-Christian view of the relationship between the One and the Many, but also of a transitional moment between two forms of discipline by which that relationship is established and executed. Earlier in the narrative Job and his family experience the rule of their sovereign in the form of brute, concentrated force. With a kind of lurid intensity, power is exercised directly over Job through a series of ritualistic disasters: the slaughter of his servants, the abduction of his cattle and camels, the sudden electrocution of his sheep, the death of his children by the whirlwind, and finally the affliction of the boils and 'loathsome sores.' (Blake reserves one of his most grisly Job illustrations for the last form of subjection.) The cruel irony is that Job's objection to this torture leads, not to the end of his suffering, but to a subtle shift in the means by which his subjugation is carried out. For Job, the corporal ritual of torture is superseded by the non-corporal ritual of inspection. Jehovah's intimidatory questions perform the disciplinary function of the examination: as Foucault remarks, the examination combines 'the ceremony of power and the form of the experiment, the deployment of force and the establishment of truth' (*Discipline* 184). Under interrogation, Job is confined to a single place in the Great Chain of Being, where every aspect of his smallness and creatureliness is brought into the light, silhouetted against the glare of creation in all its regulated mystery. As Blake's illustration suggests, insofar as the architecture of space and being is itself entirely penal in nature, and every feature of it, whether distant in time or large in size, instantly available to the panoptic gaze of its creator, power need not be expressed through spectacular acts of localized violence; the very arrangement of the cosmos, a place for everything and everything in its place, automatically registers and carries out this discipline. For this reason, Jehovah looks away from the very human subjects whom he has fixed and objectified for the purposes of examination. His indifferent stare reminds the viewer that power is no longer concentrated in single acts of punishment meted out by a guardian, but rather lies in the disciplinary structure which governs the cosmos down to its smallest details. Jehovah imagines a univocal cosmos that is subjugated by hierarchies, bounding lines, and regulating fiats. Here, disciplinary force need not be brought to bear all at once, as it were, in exceptional acts of subjection, for the very *form* of the cosmos as it is experienced by human beings, the crowded, anxious, and entirely carceral experience that is represented in Blake's design, passively *performs* this discipline as a matter of fact. This is an *over-looked* universe, where the architecture of surveillance has come to replace the surveillance itself. Like the prison master in Bentham's 'Panopticon,' Jehovah could, paradoxically, withdraw from this penitential structure, and the imposition of power, the play of its coercive effects upon the personal and the social body, would remain entirely intact. To be sure, Jehovah initially permits Satan to exercise sudden and arbitrary power over Job; but the narrative of the Old Testament story turns at the point when Job is compelled to see that power also functions continuously in the structure of the universe, subtly present in the very orderliness of the order of things.

For Blake, as for the Gnostics, creation is the originary Great Confinement, after which all other illegitimate forms of exclusion and imprisonment are patterned. We see why Blake frames the scene of Job's incarceration and instruction with depictions of scenes from the opening chapters of Genesis. As Blake had seen in engravings after Michelangelo's frescoes on the Sistine Ceiling, the opening book of the Old Testament presents 'primal acts of binary differentiation as the essential feature of divine creativity' (La Belle 76). The marginal 'quotations' form a backdrop reminding the viewer that the disciplining of Job is not merely negative and repressive; the moment of his subjugation is also, 'positively,' the momentous occasion of his production or creation as a specifically *theological* subject. (For this reason, perhaps, Blake's marginal illustrations from Genesis do not include a depiction of God's final fiat announcing the creation of humankind; the unhappy scene of Job and his followers in their subterranean cavern takes its place and functions as a severely ironic refiguring of the command 'Let us make man in our image, after our likeness; and let them have dominion over ... every creeping thing that creepeth upon the earth' [Gen. 1.26]. The artist's bitterly critical point here would seem to be that under Jehovah's discipline, it is humanity which has been turned into a 'creeping thing.') As we see in Job's upturned eyes, his confinement not only excludes and isolates, it is also responsible for generating a particular experience of faith: the moralizing sadism of the carceral universe produces human subjects who excel through obedience and who are emptied of any positive content that is not directed towards fulfilling that 'ennobling' end. Job is therefore not unlike Winston Smith at the conclusion of *1984*; at the instant that he comes to 'love' his overlord, he is re-created into an unmediated effect of the State. The Job who cowers reverentially in the cave at the bottom of Blake's illustration is similarly re-produced, but under the auspices of a theological rather than political technology where divine knowledge, power, and human being intersect. Jehovah's normalizing orthopaedics, which effectively shame Job into 'discovering' his true self, *open up* the docile region of the human subject as a space of subjection. What Job *is*, here, now, at this relatively late point in his examination, is irreducible to his being-surveyed and being-arraigned, fixed in the 'penal mapping' (Foucault, *Discipline* 78) of an infinitely juridical cosmos. Jehovah would have us believe that Job's discipline is no more contingent than the discipline of chaos is in Genesis; in both cases, the acts of subjugation are *constitutive* in nature, a making that is somehow always also a breaking. Job's individual subjection/invention is in this way located within a universal context, and his particular discipline connected to the generally disciplinary nature of a cosmos which of course *began* with extraordinary acts of containment: not only the unequivocal separation of the light from the dark, the firmament from the waters, and the sun from the moon, which is to say, the subject of the scenes that fill the outer frame of Blake's design, but also the taming of the oceans, the ordering of the constellations, and the laying of the foundation of the world, the latter being the scenes of power that Jehovah specifically conjures up in the Book of Job. From Jehovah's commandeering perspective, all of these first fiats are recalled so as to remind Job of his finite humanity; from the point of view of the Blakean spectator, however, the visual and verbal allusions to Genesis in the illustration's margins recall quite another truth, one that Job cannot afford to imagine: while he crouches in the cramped prison for which he is deemed responsible, he is kept from seeing that it is creation in its entirety which is carceral.[31]

200   David L. Clark

V. LIVING ON/BORDER LINES: BLAKE'S 'EQUIVOCAL WORLDS'

> Am I in Jerusalem? This is a question to which one will never respond in the present tense ...
>
> Jacques Derrida, 'How to Avoid Speaking: Denials'

Across the centre of *When the Morning Stars Sang Together* (fig. 3), Jehovah's outstretched arms divide the illustration into two distinct areas. As I have argued, the partitioning of the illustration into upper and lower sections rehearses Job's lesson in the hierarchical organization of the order of things: in the world below, humanity is circumscribed in place and in time; but in the world above, beyond the limited vision of Job and his circle, the angels and stars joyfully witness the foundation of the cosmos. Given Blake's suspicion of this sort of vertical organization, however, we have reason to ask whether the illustration also works in more complex ways. With Blake's admonition about 'Equivocal Worlds' in mind, let us look at the design again, this time paying closer attention to the way in which it is transected by axes that run left and right as well as top to bottom. In the grotto below, Job and his companions gaze prayerfully upwards towards God, their sight-lines marking the up*right* construction of the universe in which they live; by contrast, in the constellations and morning stars above, the world is conspicuous for its lateral rather than perpendicular shape. Because of the imposing form of their jailor, however, they are unable to discern these starry expanses. What is the significance of that unseen sky? What is the meaning of its textured infinity? Four winged angels, their mouths open in song, gaze outwards into the space shared by the viewer. Their limbs are raised in celebration, each crossing the other in a woven chain of mutual interchange whose lateral direction visualizes a non-hierarchical world founded upon horizontal rather than vertical principles of human relations. In other words, Blake subtly contrasts two representations of the shape of the true reality within one picture, playing the desire for containment and control in the lower realm against the infinitely expansive possibilities that are depicted in the upper portion of the illustration. Rather than all of a whole, the design is therefore itself equivocal: to use the language of *Jerusalem*, the lower portion reflects Los's fear of assimilation into the undifferentiated unity of the Godhead, while the upper part embodies his hopes for a world in which the 'One' is creatively exposed to the ongoing dissent of the

'Four.' In the water-colour version of this plate (fig. 5), Blake paints only four figures, but in the engraving he has the presence of mind to add the arms of two more angels in the left and right margins – thereby auguring a potentially endless sequence, limited only by the boundaries of the illustration's inner blank borderline. The change between the water-colour and engraved versions is small, but its implications for Blake's critique of the metaphysics of the One are large and complex.[32] Because the unengraved version depicts four and only four angels, it is more easily interpreted as representing Blake's ubiquitous Zoas or perhaps the four evangelists. But by adding the liminal limbs in the engraved version, the artist shifts the focus from what the angels might *mean* as a group of four to the importance of their *position* in the structure of mutual interchange which clearly exceeds them.

What the artist finds repulsive about the Urizenic figure who intimidates Job is that he lords his mastery over his subjects by reminding them that he alone is in a position to comprehend creation, and thus to make visible what will forever remain hidden to humanity. Yet the upper portion of the design interrogates Jehovah's pretensions to the unequivocality of absolute knowledge by pointing to the inescapable *excess* which the articulation of that knowledge mobilizes. In this illustration we are not offered an intimidating glimpse of creation in its entirety, but a 'window' or perhaps 'clearing' [*Lichtung*] whose limiting border forms an 'event horizon' – a term I borrow from theoretical physics (J. Taylor 53–6) – which reminds the spectator that everything cannot be seen all at once, as it were, and in one go. The four angels which are wholly visible do not simply appear, innocent of any context, but come into appearance as a framing *effect* precisely because this context is blanked out. Heidegger is helpful in this regard when he argues that '[a] boundary is not that at which something stops but ... is that from which something *begins its presencing*' (*Poetry* 154). That is to say, the visibility of the angels depends on the invisibility of the chain or unarticulated background within which their articulation is possible. What lies inside the frame is constituted by the trace of its difference from what lies without, in this case a trace quite literally marked by the angelic bodies which the illustration's blank border transects and leaves as mere residua. This can be expressed differently: because the border is crucial in making the four 'stand out' (*ex-sistere*), but is not itself *of* the four, it points to the fact that an 'ex-sisting' being can never be in full possession of itself – in much the same way that the eye's field of vision can never so widen as to include the sight of itself seeing. (Blake's

Fig. 5. *When the Morning Stars Sang Together*, illustration to the Book of Job

contemporary, Fichte, had come to consider the impossible notion of a gaze capable of bringing itself into view as *the* central philosophical question.)[33] It is not the first time that Blake has evoked this epistemological knot of blindness and insight, of a certain blindness *enabling* insight. Towards the conclusion of *Jerusalem*, for example, Blake's 'Prophet of Eternity' and his dark double peer into the night sky, at once seeing and not seeing: 'Los reads the Stars of Albion!' whereas 'the Spectre reads the Voids / Between the Stars' (J 91.36–7, E 251). As in the Job illustration, Blake turns to the stellar field as a way of evoking an interdiction that is hidden from the eye of reason. As Derrida describes it: *'blindness to the supplement* is the law' (*Grammatology* 149). Despite, or rather, because Blake's figures insist that they are reading antithetically opposed scripts, they are prevented from seeing that the two texts by which they are separately captivated combine into one complex inscription. But this blindness or aphasia is inescapable, indeed, to the exact extent that the combination of the scripts is unavoidable: the 'Stars' and 'Voids' appear as distinct objects of apprehension only because of the 'prior' blanking out of the semiotic economy – illegible as such – that brings them into visibility and legibility in the first place. The fact that the diacritical spacing of the two texts remains illegible to both figures *even while they continue to read* suggests how their identically reversed blindnesses produce a deeper insight: namely, insofar as knowledge is inscribed in and articulated by systems of signification it can never be absolutely in possession of itself. The play of signs and the inscriptive organization of blank spaces, *as* play and *as* inscription, are always illegible to readers who after all read 'only' signs and to knowers who know 'only' knowledge, just as the structure of difference that mutually implicates Los and the Spectre remains inaccessible to them precisely because they are situated *within* it. Neither 'Voids' nor 'Stars,' but the enabling 'principle' of their intertexture, the 'structural unconsciousness' (Derrida, 'Signature' 192) of Blake's night sky, marks the condition of the possibility of articulated knowledge; as such, however, it will always be elsewhere and out of reach, an irreducible remainder and supplementary in-between that remains radically un-known and un-read. In an analogous way, Jehovah cannot realize the panoptic position of absolute knowledge that he claims is his privilege in the Book of Job because his very positioning – the 'stand' he must 'take' (FZ 122.24, E 391), somewhere – prohibits him from broadening his visionary powers to the point that he can grasp what, in himself and in all others, necessarily exceeds and precedes these powers. No vantage point is so univocally secure, or, more precisely, so removed from structures of difference that it contains all other vantage points. As Blake never tires of saying, to pretend to occupy such a (non-)place leads only to the death of the imagination. It is for this reason, perhaps, that Jehovah appears massively rooted into his perch atop the cave that imprisons Job and his followers, in effect reminding the viewer that his putatively absolute vision is irreducibly relative.

Blake's illustration represents the character of knowledge that the mind achieves in fundamentally different ways. In the design's lower region, Jehovah's words and actions evoke the intimidating possibility that creation could be exhaustively grasped and known. But the upper portion of the illustration suggests otherwise: because it is here faced with a potentially limitless chain of angels, knowledge is necessarily incomplete. Significantly, this in-completeness is structural in nature, and not to be confused with a sublimity of infinitude, the very exorbitancy with which Jehovah threatens Job. The distinction between these two forms of 'non-totalization' is crucial to Derrida, who radicalizes Claude Lévi-Strauss's notion of *'bricolage'* as a way of distinguishing his project from that of the 'engineer[s]' ('Structure' 285–6). As Gayatri Spivak remarks, Lévi-Strauss makes a strong advance against the totalizing pretensions of the engineer by conceding that 'it is in fact impossible for him to master the whole field':

Derrida, by important contrast, suggests that the field is *theoretically*, not merely empirically, unknowable. Not even in an ideal universe of an empirically reduced number of possibilities would the projected 'end' of knowledge ever coincide with its 'means.' Such a coincidence – 'engineering' – is an impossible dream of plenitude. (xix)

As the cellular mapping of the cosmos in Blake's Job illustration suggests, Jehovah has a special stake in a meticulously 'engineered' creation. Above his weary or anxious gaze, however, the interlocked angels effortlessly transgress the design's tabular spaces, forever just out of range of his vision. And beyond the left and right border lines, the same angels extend outwards past *our* view as well. To the extent that the four angels are brought into sight, they are already marked by the trace of excess by which they are shaped and upon which they are dependent. By relying on the articulating force of the border, the four are fundamentally in excess of what they appear to be, never absolutely or unequivocally present to themselves. Exceeded by the principle of their articulation, they stretch forever ahead of themselves into an unfinishable future: 'Eternity ... in love with the productions of time' (*MHH* 7, E 36). The presence of residual limbs in the left and right margins marks this excess, reminding the viewer that the border could always transect the angels *elsewhere*, at some other point. The point seems to be that a border will always transect them *somewhere*; there will always be some form of articulation where knowledge is concerned, since articulation is what makes knowledge possible, but is also what makes it *absolutely* impossible. The root epistemological question is, then: at what point does one draw the line? Where to begin, or end? For Derrida's *'bricoleur,'* the answer is fundamentally equivocal: here, or there, more to the left or to the right, with whatever comes to hand. 'We must begin *wherever we are* and the thought of the trace ... has already taught us that it was impossible to justify a point of departure absolutely. *Wherever we are*: in a text where we already believe ourselves to be' (*Grammatology* 162). Only engineers like Urizen and Jehovah dream of absolute visibility, which is to say, of grasping knowledge that has turned back upon itself to incorporate the principle of its own articulation, knowledge so expansive as to apprehend *without remainder* or *excess* or *over-run* its own determining ground. Only Urizen dreams of appropriating the absolutely unconditioned and masterful stance from which to 'view the infinite & *unbounded'* (FZ 122.24, E 391; emphasis mine).

The un-viewable remainder at the point of the border's blankness brings Blake to the threshold of illustrating what amounts to the 'structural unconsciousness' (Derrida, 'Signature' 192) of all that is seen and known. In doing so, he risks a scandal that is not so much irrational as *other* than rational in kind. As Derrida writes in an essay whose title – 'Living On / BORDER LINES' – is not without significance here: 'Visibility should – not be visible. According to an old, omnipotent logic that has reigned since Plato, that which enables us to see should remain invisible: black, blinding ... To see vision, to see on beyond sight: this abyss-like madness of an utterly primal scene, the scene of scenes, stages, representation' (90–1). Blake might say: 'According to an old, omnipotent logic that has reigned since Jehovah's inaugural fiat, "Let there be light," that which enables us to see should remain invisible.' From the beginning, *Fiat lux* has meant *Fiat lux et veritas*: God's inaugural command flushes the universe with that brightness in which all beings are presented to knowledge. Truth must be its own irradiated appearance, the transparency of the seen to seeing, the luminous clearing where what *is* is what stands out before God's great, pure, sunny contemplation. Blake puts this paradox to us in the illustration of *fiat lux* in the design's upper left margin. 'Let there be light': what lets light be? How to illustrate – better, illuminate – this letting-be of light, this originary moment of utter illumination? Light *there is*: what is the un-lit (darkness [visible]) that underwrites that visibility, gives the givenness of light the force of law by setting it irretrievably upon its way? In this marginal 'quotation' from Genesis, Blake looks into the sun ... and envisions nothing, a shape, all light whose blankness he can visualize only supplementarily, that is, by surrounding it with a sort of radiant outline. That, and by writing the word 'Light' across this blankness, thereby making the sheer featurelessness of the inaugural scene of illumination *invisible*. What strange economy of blindness and sight is here at work? We 'see,' as it were, that when light is made visible (by becoming legible in the word 'Light'), its luminosity is extinguished, its blankness blanked out, filled in; the word literally performs the erasure of what it signifies, as though the bringing into light necessarily brought with it a deprivation, a sightlessness, and a hidden invisibility.[34] What can it mean to cast one's eye back to that first fiat and first dawn? Metaphorically speaking, does Blake not risk a certain blindness and lunacy, precisely in order to disclose something that is neither light nor dark, visibility nor invisibility? 'During one of the first American expeditions to the moon,' Geoffrey Bennington writes,

a careless astronaut pointed his camera at the sun, which immediately burned out its cells. The camera cannot tolerate the source or purity of what is its only *raison d'être* to capture and relay. This lunar drama of reflected light, of a burning that leaves only ash, of the sun and death that cannot be looked at directly, haunts all Derrida's thought. We should follow all the suns that figure this blinding source of what allows us to see. (137–8)

How, then, to make appearing appear, to bring into visibility that which goes without seeing – *must* go without seeing – for the integrity and distinctness of the *logos* to remain lucid and intact? As the condition of the possibility of that which appears, *appearing* as such is radically invisible, a blind spot escaping even Jehovah's absolutely discerning eyes. Appearing cannot be seen, except, perhaps, in the incalculably 'thin' line, visible only in its transecting effects, joining the four which are framed to those which are not. Both this line and the blank frame, which is its shadow, augur in their very emptiness a conception of the bounding gesture which does not admit a strictly exclusionary distinction between inside and outside, *ergon* and *parergon*. Jehovah apprehends the shape of the true reality through violently exclusionary acts; but Blake asks us to consider the frame as a border, neither entirely inside nor outside, 'where' that shape is at once articulated and cleft. Inasmuch as the true reality is a totality, it is a structured totality, which is to say, irreducible to its differential articulation and consequently at no single point unequivocally visible – that is, *present* – to itself.

In an artist who always insisted on the imaginative efficacy and clarifying power of the 'distinct, sharp, and wirey ... bounding line' (*DC* 63–4, E 550), the revisioning of the frame as border and frontier is not a matter of dissolving boundaries, but much more a question of investigating their nature and of reassessing their use. To return to a point made at the start of this essay: Blake resists the allure of the 'repressive hypothesis,' and thus the temptation to think of freedom as the condition of unboundedness. However, the principle of articulation that Blake figures forth in the border cannot, as the condition of visibility and specificity, form a part of the visual system and be 'situated as an object in its field.' This does not mean, as Derrida warns, that it has a 'real field *elsewhere, another* assignable *site*' (*Grammatology* 60). Because the articulating force of the border, or rather, of bordering in general, operates as the 'infrastructural possibilit[y]' (Gasché 160)[35] of all particular boundaries, distinctions, and differentiations, and because this 'already' at once opens the space of the human *and* renders the human irretrievably derivative, belated, with respect to that opening, one could be forgiven for calling it *God*.[36] Bordering renders things visible, makes them 'ex-sist,' but does not strictly speaking belong anywhere to the order of visibility; to the extent that it lights up all the world but itself, which is to say, remains necessarily in-visible to itself, a black sun, the tain of the mirror, bordering in general is at the very least God-like. To imagine the inscription of the border (beyond the imposition of the frame) is to envision the unseen ground of seeing. It is to understand what it means for the human to be 'sighted,' if by this term we mean not the anxious condition of being-surveyed but, as Fichte says of absolute self-consciousness, the apprehension and letting-be of the 'power *into which* an eye is implanted':[37] beyond panoptic domination, then, the eye that finds its *ethos*, its true dwelling-place, *in-the-midst-of* the production of the visible. Jerusalem: a clearing, *wherever we are.*

What Blake calls 'fourfold vision' (E 722) cannot simply be an increase in acuity or resolution, a quadrupling of the capacity to see – as if two eyes were not enough with which to be blind. It is rather the capacity to glimpse 'around' glimpsing, to 'see' the logos at the fundamentally equivocal point of its coming into sight, the 'blind spot' or 'not-seen that opens *and* limits visibility' (Derrida, *Grammatology* 163; emphasis mine). This vision – folded into itself, into its own indiscernible folds – peers without seeing into a certain 'bottomless fund [*fonds sans fond*],' a 'store of deep background,' which Derrida will call 'the *pharmacy*' (*Dissemination* 127, 128). Indeed, *Plato*'s pharmacy. Its viewless 'reserve' resists the 'omnipotent logic that has reigned since Plato' (Derrida, 'Living' 90), embarrassing the metaphysic of the One with the trace of an excess that transgressed that logic from the beginning. The *total* shape of the true reality is therefore 'incomprehensible' (J 98.11, 24; E 257), even as Blake says twice at the conclusion of *Jerusalem*. But here incomprehensibility is not the measure of an in-human magnitude; non-closure is brought about not by the size of the field, but rather by its character, whose irreducible excess makes all frames, systematizations, and unifications provisional and open to being differently redrawn.

Blake's transected angelic chain greets our gaze and draws us into a reciprocal form of visibility: as spectators of the illustration, we are asked to imagine the networks of differences in which we are also situated, and to discern the borders – or what Blake calls the 'lineaments divine of human beauty' (FZ 25.2, E 314) – that make them come into appearance. In a pictorial equivalent to dramatic irony, then, *we* see so much more than Job, who must look fearfully from the bottom 'Up' (even as Milton's Raphael had said to Adam) and whose only source of light comes significantly from the halo behind Jehovah's imposing head. This scene of subservience captures the power-knowledge nexus that Job duly rehearses in his final words:

I know that thou canst do everything, and that no thought can be withholden from thee.
 Who is he that hideth counsel without knowledge? therefore have I uttered that I understood not; things too wonderful for me, which I knoweth not.
  I have heard of thee by the hearing of the ear: but now mine eye seeth thee.
  Wherefore I abhor myself, and repent in dust and ashes.   (42.2–3, 5–6)

Job begins by frankly acknowledging his utter visibility before God. But the carceral physics of Jehovah's universe are so efficiently manipulative that he experiences this surveillance as its opposite – as the sight of God. But Job's momentary reversal of perspectives serves to identify the apprehension of God's face with the confirmation of human worthlessness: according to the implacable logic of his imprisonment, glimpsing God automatically translates into despising oneself. The end of Job's moral examination – insofar as it could ever come to an end – is realized in the form of a gesture that seamlessly combines adoration with self-abasement. What keeps Job from attaining *four*fold vision, that is, from escaping his 'arbitrary incarceration in the pre-Copernican prison and field of vision' (Nietzsche, *Will* 417) and from apprehending the fundamentally non-hierarchical shape of the true reality, would seem to be concentrated in the alien figure of Jehovah. As the illustration attests, however, Job's face is indistinguishable from that of his jailor. From Blake's point of view, the God that Job thinks he sees is his own invention, a hallucinatory product of his inability to imagine the *Geselligkeit* of 'equivocal worlds' founded upon 'horizontal' rather than 'vertical' principles of human relations.

Blake's illustration contrasts two ways of living in and knowing about the world: on the one hand, life under the auspices of a certain 'Egyptianism,' as Nietzsche puts it, in which knowledge involves the grim entombment and silent exchange of so many 'conceptual mummies,' the chastening re-collection of what is and what has always been (*Twilight* 35). By compelling Job to recall the origin and orderliness of creation, and to feel the cold heart of sameness to which all difference is compelled to return, Jehovah instils in his human subjects a form of metaphysical necromancy and nostalgia. His is the fiat underwriting all fiats, the imperative driving all catechisms: *'Don't forget'* or *'You must remember this.'* In the design's upper portion, on the other hand, Blake represents the subject living a life of what Kierkegaard calls repetition, as opposed to re-memoration. As Kierkegaard's work of the same name promises in its opening pages, repetition frees the Christian from turning resolutely from the sensible to the intelligible, which is to say from the domination of the metaphysical and the theological as these terms have governed thinking since Plato. Not the narcotic gaze upwards to the word and the face of God, but the shared look outwards to us. Not the *frame* that cleanly separates the forms of heaven from the dwellers of the cave, but the *border* that always and already exposes the light to the dark, the stars to the voids between the stars, eternity to the productions of time. Not the intimidating recollection of a frozen *eidos*, but the repetition of a work of weaving whose warp and woof run off the margins of knowledge in a 'textual ... in-finity' (Caputo 150). Here the adjoined, singing angels are inscribed like musical signs, their 'dynamics ... always oriented towards the future of their repetition, never toward the consonance of their simultaneity' (de Man 129). Here the border-line embodies the forward motion of *kinesis* or Christian becoming, human being pulled ceaselessly towards the frontier of an absolute future. Do these angels trace the lineaments of Jerusalem? This is a question to which one could never respond in the present tense.

NOTES

Versions and portions of this paper were given at conferences at Stanford University, Queen's University, and the University of Toronto. Robert Alexander, Peter Babiak, Stephen Barber, Donald Goellnicht, Barbara Havercroft, James King, and Ross Woodman all read drafts of this paper, and I am very grateful for their invaluable criticisms and suggestions. The paper was prepared for publication with the able assistance of Susan Murley, and with the generous support of the Social Sciences and Humanities Research Council of Canada.

1 Blake is quoted from David V. Erdman (1982). In citations in the text, the following abbreviations will be used: *Jerusalem* (J); *The [First] Book of Urizen* (BU); *The Marriage of Heaven and Hell* (MHH); *Milton* (M); *Europe* (E); *The Four Zoas* (FZ); *Songs of Innocence and of Experience* (SI); *Vision of the Last Judgment* (VLJ); *Descriptive Catalogue* (DC). The abbreviations are followed by numbers indicating plate and/or line; then by 'E' and numbers indicating page references to the Erdman edition.
2 My phrase recalls Nietzsche's numerous references to the fundamental or 'Great Errors' which underwrite what is said to be 'truth.' See, for example, 'The Four Great Errors,' in *The Twilight of the Idols* 47.
3 I am grateful to Judith Butler, whose essay 'Stubborn Attachment, Bodily Subjection: Rereading Hegel on the Unhappy Consciousness' pointed me to Hegel's curious phrase.
4 Perhaps the clearest articulations of Foucault's position vis-à-vis the 'repressive hypothesis' are in part 2 of his *History of Sexuality, Vol. 1: An Introduction* 17–49, and in 'Truth and Power,' the interview conducted by Alessandro Fontana and Pasquale Pasquino, collected in *Power/Knowledge* 109–33.
5 Cited in Michael Walzer, 'The Politics of Michel Foucault,' in Hoy 60.
6 See Clark, 'The Innocence of Becoming Restored.'
7 In a discussion of Emmanuel Levinas to which I want briefly to return,

Derrida notes that the Jewish thinker seeks to liberate onto-theology 'from the Greek domination of the Same and the One ... as if from oppression itself – an ... ontological or transcendental oppression, but also the origin or alibi of all oppression in the world.' See 'Violence and Metaphysics: An Essay on the Thought of Emmanuel Levinas' 83.

8 All references to Milton's *Paradise Lost* are from the Hughes edition, and will be cited in the body of the essay by book and line number.

9 Harold Bloom remarks: 'From a normative Jewish or Christian point of view, catastrophe is allied to the abyss, and creation is associated with an order imposed upon the abyss. But from a Gnostic perspective, catastrophe is true creation because it restores the abyss, while any order that steals its materials from the abyss is a sickening to a false creation' (20). Bloom's comments of course recall *The Marriage of Heaven and Hell*, in which Milton's 'Messiah' is condemned as 'Satan' for 'form[ing] a heaven of what he stole from the Abyss' (*MHH* 5, 6, E 34, 35).

10 I borrow Foucault's description of the will-to-power disguised as altruism, in this case the 'philanthropy' of the 'liberation' of the mad in the nineteenth century (*Mental* 73).

11 My argument alludes here to the title and substance of Nietzsche's essay 'On Truth and Lies in a Nonmoral Sense.' As Nietzsche argues, the stable distinction between truth and falsehood – upon which the intelligibility of metaphysics rests – begins to disintegrate once truth is freed from its moral valuation as a positivity, and instead revalued as a special category of lying. See Nietzsche 79–81.

12 My characterization of Urizen recalls Heidegger's description of what he calls 'totality': 'In accordance with its nature, this totality can no longer be determined by *relations, in terms of* relations *to something else* – otherwise it wouldn't be a totality. This totality of Being lacks a relation to other things, is not relative, and is in this sense absolutely *absolved* from everything else, released from all relations because it doesn't admit of any such thing at all. This absolute *relationlessness* to anything else, this absolutely absolved is called the *Ab-solute*' (*Treatise* 43).

13 Nietzsche argues that 'the will to truth is ... merely the desire for a world of the constant.' See *The Will to Power* 317.

14 'Thus a *becoming* God! [*Also ein* werdender *Gott!*]': so Heidegger (*Treatise* 190) exclaims over Friedrich Schelling's highly unconventional representation of God as a site of conflicting forces rather than a stable substance. The German is cited from Heidegger (*der Menschlichen* 109).

15 'Duality must therefore be just as original as unity' (Brown 157n12), Schelling says in a lecture given to supplement *Of Human Freedom*. In that

text, Schelling argues that God's self-revelation is always a process of inward displacement and self-repetition, the production of an intertexture of darkness and light rather than the unveiling of a pre-existent identity. Like Blake, the later Schelling demonstrates the profound influence of Boehme, perhaps no more tellingly than in the German philosopher's sense of the Godhead as a 'nexus of forces.' See *Philosophical Inquiries into the Nature of Human Freedom* 41. For an English translation of a portion of Schelling's Stuttgart lecture, see Robert Brown 157n12. See also n22.

16 So Caputo (14) characterizes Kierkegaard's process of repetition.
17 Kierkegaard similarly writes: 'The moment is that ambiguity in which time and eternity touch each other, and with this the concept of *temporality* is posited, whereby time constantly intersects eternity and eternity constantly pervades time.' See *The Concept of Anxiety* 89. For Kierkegaard's 'ambiguity' we might substitute Blake's 'equivocality.'
18 Derrida's account of the relationship between time and space is useful: 'I often talk about spacing, but this is not simply space as opposed to time, but a mode of producing space by temporalizing it. Temporization, to temporize, means waiting or expecting, postponing or delaying. Temporizing is spacing, a way of making an interval, and here again with the idea of differance the ideas of spacing and temporization are inextricably linked' (Mortley 100).
19 Derrida summarizes Levinas's position as one arguing for 'Discourse with God, and not in God as *participation*. Discourse with God, and not discourse on God and his attributes as *theology*' ('Violence' 108).
20 Derrida cites Levinas's phrase from *Totality and Infinity*.
21 I borrow these terms from Tilottama Rajan, who argues that Nietzsche's 'On Truth and Lies in a Nonmoral Sense' 'replaces truth as identity with truth as difference, *logos* with *dia-logos*.' Rajan suggests that for Nietzsche 'figured language is seen as true precisely because it unsettles without dissolving the identity of the signifier and signified, and makes the idea a network of differences, a summa of human relationships' ('Displacing' 467).
22 I borrow this phrase from the evocative title of Giorgio Agamben's *The Coming Community*, a book whose vision of radically new forms of *Geselligkeit* has no doubt influenced my thinking here.
23 My argument adapts to a dialogical or semiological context Joseph Anthony Wittreich's conclusion that Blake emphasizes the specifically dramatic structure of prophetic vision. As Wittreich notes, the conception of revelation as a '"high and stately Tragedy"' would have come to Blake in part through Milton's discussion of the biblical commentator

David Pareus in *Reason of Church Government*. 'With greater precision than Milton,' Wittreich writes, 'Blake defines multiple perspectives contending with one another as characters in a drama ...' (34, 43). It is important to emphasize, however, that for Wittreich these contentions are 'complementary' (42), related in a complex harmony whose unity is confirmed rather than dislocated by the differences in perspective. Balachandra Rajan responds to this point by asking about the 'extent to which even a mode as self-confident as the prophetic may be beset with uncertainty and the extent to which that uncertainty may be implicit in the "contending perspectives" the prophetic voice struggles to establish as "complementary"' (*Form* 140n). My point is that whatever the nature of the prophetic text in terms of its multiple layers of voices and narrative strands, Edenic dialogue is 'complementary' insofar as it is creatively confrontational, but 'uncertain' because it must resist the mute certainty of totalization.

24 See, for example, Keats's letter to Richard Woodhouse (27 October 1818) on 'the poetical Character' (Rollins 386–8).

25 Robert N. Essick has noted that 'Blake's famous phrase, "Visionary forms dramatic," offers one relatively simple example of his management of language so as to involve the reader in structural transformations. The syntactic order of the three signifiers is only one of three arrangements that yield meaning (although perhaps only versions of the same meaning) because of the grammatical indeterminacy, and hence fluidity, of each. This opening up of determinate structures, penetrating beyond tropological inventiveness and into the most basic elements of language, should offer opportunities for investigation by those schools of modern criticism founded on linguistics and semiotics' (398).

26 This is not the place to discuss in any extended way the philosophical-historical context for Blake's revisionary metaphysics. But it should be said that he is hardly alone in his exploration of structures of difference as a way of delegitimizing the metaphysics of the 'One,' whether those structures are overtly thematized, as in the case of the notion of the Four Zoas in a relationship of 'mutual interchange' (J 88.20, E 234), or whether they are articulated in more subtle ways, as in the scene of reading involving Los and his Spectre (see the discussion in part 5 of this essay). In characterizing the shape of the true reality in terms of difference and relationality rather than self-sameness and exclusion, Blake closely resembles a number of late eighteenth- and early nineteenth-century thinkers who, in different ways, and with varying degrees of insight into the radical implications of their own work, similarly jettison pretensions to absolute knowledge.

In lectures delivered at the University of Edinburgh during the latter half of the eighteenth century, for example, Hugh Blair speaks of relationality as an irreducible feature of mental life. 'Every object which makes any impression on the human mind,' he argues,

> is constantly accompanied with certain circumstances and relations that strike us at the same time. It never presents itself to our view, *isolé*, as the French express it; that is, independent on, and separated from, every other thing; but always occurs as somehow related to other objects; going before them, or following them; their effect or their cause; resembling them, or opposed to them; distinguished by certain qualities, or surrounded with certain circumstances. By this means every idea or object carries in its train other ideas ... (354)

What is intriguing is that Blair makes this remark in the midst of a discussion of the origin and nature of figural language *but does not take the next logical step and theorize consciousness in linguistic terms.* Compare Derrida's well-known description of 'the play of differences,' a play that

> supposes, in effect, syntheses and referrals which forbid at any moment, or in any sense, that a simple element be *present* in and of itself, referring only to itself. Whether in the order of spoken or written discourse, no element can function as a sign without referring to another element which itself is not simply present. This interweaving results in each 'element' – phoneme or grapheme – being constituted on the basis of the trace within it of the other elements of the chain or system ... Nothing, neither among the elements nor within the system, is anywhere ever simply present or absent. There are only, everywhere, differences and traces of traces. (*Positions* 26)

As both Tilottama Rajan (*Supplement* 281) and Jerrold E. Hogle have recently argued, Shelley also acknowledges the non-closural play of difference and similarity in which and by which consciousness is articulated but goes much further than Blair inasmuch as he identifies 'dissemination as a source of imaginative power.' '[T]he logic of transposition,' as Hogle puts it, 'is primal and constantly active in Shelley's portraits of sensation, perception, association, recollection, anticipation, inspiration, conception, declaration, allusion, and communication' (13).

Analogous claims for the creatively disruptive power of relationality are also made by contemporaneous German philosophers, notably by

Schleiermacher and Schelling. Schelling's case is particularly instructive. During the last years of the eighteenth century, the German philosopher developed a theory of natural phenomena that emphasized the interchange of dynamically opposed forces. As Robert Stern argues, in *Ideas for a Philosophy of Nature* (1797) Schelling 'stands opposed to the Newtonian picture of matter as made up of hard, impenetrable, inert particles ... and argues instead that matter is an equilibrium of active forces that stand in polar opposition to one another' (x). In the years that followed, culminating with the publication of his treatise on human freedom in 1809, Schelling came to similar conclusions regarding the nature of primordial being. In an attempt to break with what Rodolphe Gasché calls 'German Idealism's pretensions to have deduced the oneness of origin' (181), Schelling turns to Jacob Boehme's theosophical speculations, not to abandon Enlightenment rationality for mysticism, but to displace the classical metaphysical presupposition that difference derives from an original simplicity in God. For Schelling, as for Boehme before him, God's appearance as the 'One' is indistinguishable from his irreducibly differential interplay with an equally original 'Other,' thereby making 'Duality ... as original as unity' (Brown 157n12). In *Of Human Freedom*, Schelling neutralizes the moral opposition of identity as good and difference as negation and reinscribes it as the difference between the 'light' centre and the 'dark' (38). Beyond good and evil, these centres form the bivalent sub-version of the origin, now conceived not as a simple substance but as a circulating relationship or 'cycle.' As Schelling writes, at the origin neither one centre nor the other possesses

> precedence in time [or] ... priority of essence. In the cycle whence all things come, it is no contradiction to say that that which gives birth to the one is, in its turn, produced by it. There is here no first and no last, since everything mutually implies everything else, nothing being the 'other' and yet no being being without the other. (33)

Schelling's case is apposite to Blake's for several reasons, not the least of which is their shared interest in Boehme, especially his representation of primordial being as a 'nexus of living forces' (*Of Human Freedom* 41). As in the case of Blake's Four Zoas, the shift from figures of substance to figures of force is important because it enables the German philosopher to map reality not only positively in terms of discrete entities but differentially in terms of the relationship between entities. Under these conditions, there is no 'precedence in time' because the 'cycle whence all things come' is *itself* the origin of non-self-coincidence, spacing, and temporality. Moreover, Schelling's critical reception shares certain features with that of his English contemporary. In both cases, the most far-reaching implications of their revisioning of classical metaphysics have up until relatively recently been ignored. Like Blake, the German philosopher has more often been celebrated as one of the last great systematizers. With the exception of a recent reassessment by readers under the influence of de Man and Derrida, Schelling continues to be read as the 'Prince of the Romantics,' and as one of German idealism's foremost champions of the mind's unequivocal power to apprehend presence. M.H. Abrams is representative of an analogously idealistic strain of Blake criticism when he argues that it is 'very dubious indeed that Blake ... can be read by a deconstructor as paradigmatic; beyond most poets, he is an essentialist who claims that his fundamental assertions disclose presence' (169). The limitations of this position have only recently been the subject of critical discussion. Arguably the most significant of these reassessments is Peter Otto's powerfully illuminating and scrupulously argued *Constructive Vision and Visionary Deconstruction*. Other readers of both the deconstructive and non-deconstructive persuasion have emphasized the artist's disseminative play with the graphic and phonic substance of his visual and verbal languages, as well as the pervasively anti-systematic character of his narrative, hermeneutical, and illustrative strategies. [See, respectively, Nelson Hilton, Donald Ault, Tilottama Rajan (*Supplement*), and David Clark ('How to Do Things').] But the resistance to interpretations by what Abrams rather cavalierly calls 'deconstructor[s]' is not difficult to understand: for Blake may affirm the equivocality of differential structures, but he does so with a prophet's univocal confidence that his words and pictures are of one's 'eternal Salvation' (*M* 4.20, E 98). If there is a developing methodological division in Blake studies, it is because the texts *themselves* embody a theoretical tension between the claims of *logos* and *dialogos*, essentialism and an incredulity towards essence conceived as univocal in nature. Revolutionary in his time for pluralizing the origin and for affirming the constitutive significance of difference and relationality, he remains conservative for confidently reifying 'the logocentrism of the Bard' (T. Rajan, *Dark* 264). For this reason, as I have argued elsewhere, 'Blake cannot be translated into Nietzsche and one post-structuralist law applied to both' ('Innocence' 111).

27 James is discussing – no doubt mistakenly – the 'mystical' element in Hegel's treatment of the self (298–9n).

Against Theological Technology 217

28 For an interpretation diametrically opposed to the one that I offer here, see S. Foster Damon.
29 I am grateful to Professor Janine Langan for pointing out this passage from Girard.
30 My remarks here and throughout this section of the essay owe a great deal to Foucault's *Discipline and Punish*, especially part 3,' entitled 'Discipline.'
31 The human world thus resembles what Jean Baudrillard would call the 'order of the hyperreal and of simulation' in which 'prisons are there to conceal the fact that it is the social in its entirety, in its banal omnipresence, which is carceral' (25).
32 There are many other significant changes between the two versions of Blake's illustration, including alterations to Jehovah's and Job's hand-signs, and to Job's sight-lines. Discussion of these changes must await another essay.
33 Dieter Henrich (33) argues that this optical trope, and the philosophical problem it expresses, dominated Fichte's thought during the last thirteen years of his life – the years that Blake was creating *Jerusalem*.
34 The (re)visionary optics of this scene recall the situation of the actor playing Jack the Giant-killer in Wordsworth's *Prelude* (1805, 7.310), whose invisibility is at once represented and disguised – in a redoubled motion that de Man would call 'disfigurement' – by the word 'INVISIBLE' written 'upon his chest.'
35 Gasché writes: 'Deconstruction reinscribes the origin into the context or text of its infrastructural possibilities. To speak the language of philosophy, one could say that this context of infrastructures – the space of inscription of the function of origin – is an *absolute passivity*, if it did not also anticipate the metaphysical difference between active and passive ... The system of infrastructural possibilities inscribes both the origin and its function of command, and even though this system of possibility does not control or command the origin, the origin presupposes it as its (limiting) possibility. An origin presupposes this play as a text presupposes its context, *a book its margins, a painting its frame, or any unity its border*' (160; emphasis mine).
36 Mark C. Taylor notes that there is 'a striking similarity between Derridean *différance* and what theologians have traditionally called "God"' (99). In a relatively recent discussion which sketches out the complex relationship between, on the one hand, the '"already there" (*déja-là*)' of *différance* as that which 'will have rendered speech possible' and, on the other hand,

the '*Christian* apophatics of Dionysus,' Derrida writes: 'Language has started without us, in us and before us. This is what theology calls God, and it is necessary, it will have been necessary, to speak' ('How to Avoid' 28, 29).

37 Emphasis mine. Manfred Frank quotes and discusses Fichte's curious phrase from *Darstellung der Wissenschaftslehre* (1801) in *What Is Neostructuralism?* (89).

WORKS CITED

Abrams, M.H. 'Construing and Deconstructing.' *Romanticism and Contemporary Criticism*. Ed. Morris Eaves and Michael Fischer. Ithaca: Cornell UP, 1986. 127– 82.

Agamben, Giorgio. *The Coming Community*. Trans. Michael Hardt. Theory Out of Bounds 1. Minneapolis: U of Minnesota P, 1993.

Altizer, Thomas J.J. *The New Apocalypse: The Radical Christian Vision of William Blake*. East Lansing: Michigan State UP, 1967.

Ault, Donald. 'Re-Visioning *The Four Zoas*.' *Unnam'd Forms: Blake and Textuality*. Ed. Nelson Hilton and Thomas A. Vogler. Berkeley: U of California P, 1986. 105–39.

Baudrillard, Jean. *Simulations*. Trans. Paul Foss, Paul Patton, and Philip Beitchman. New York: Semiotext(e), 1983.

Bennington, Geoffrey. *Jacques Derrida*. Chicago: U of Chicago P, 1993.

Blair, Hugh. *Lectures on Rhetoric and Belles Lettres*. 1785. Facs. rpt. Vol 1. New York: Garland, 1970.

Bloom, Harold. 'Freud's Concepts of Defense and the Poetic Will.' *The Literary Freud: Mechanisms of Defense and the Poetic Will*. Psychiatry and the Humanities 4. Ed. Joseph H. Smith. New Haven: Yale UP, 1980. 1–28.

Brown, Robert F. *The Later Philosophy of Schelling: The Influence of Boehme on the Works of 1809–1815*. Lewisburg: Bucknell UP, 1977.

Butler, Judith. 'Stubborn Attachment, Bodily Subjection: Rereading Hegel on the Unhappy Consciousness.' *Intersections: Nineteenth-Century Philosophy and Contemporary Theory*. Ed. David L. Clark and Tilottama Rajan. Albany: SUNY P, forthcoming.

Butlin, Martin. *The Paintings and Drawings of William Blake*. *Plates* and *Text*. New Haven: Yale UP, 1981.

Caputo, John D. *Radical Hermeneutics: Repetition, Deconstruction, and the Hermeneutic Project*. Bloomington: Indiana UP, 1987.

Chodorow, Nancy. *The Reproduction of Mothering: Psychoanalysis and the Sociology of Gender*. Berkeley: U of California P, 1978.

Clark, David L. 'How to Do Things with Shakespeare: Illustrative Theory and Practice in Blake's *Pity*.' *The Mind in Creation: Essays on English Romantic Literature in Honour of Ross G. Woodman.* Ed. J. Douglas Kneale. Kingston and Montreal: McGill-Queen's UP, 1992. 106–33, 167–73.

– '"The Innocence of Becoming Restored": Blake, Nietzsche, and the Disclosure of Difference.' *Studies in Romanticism* 29 (1990): 91–113.

Coleridge, Samuel Taylor. *The Notebooks of Samuel Taylor Coleridge.* Vol. 3. Ed. Kathleen Coburn. Princeton: Princeton UP, 1973.

Damon, S. Foster. *William Blake's Illustrations of the Book of Job.* Providence: Brown UP, 1966.

Damrosch, Leopold, Jr. *Symbol and Truth in Blake's Myth.* Princeton: Princeton UP, 1980.

de Man, Paul. *Blindness and Insight: Essays on the Rhetoric of Contemporary Criticism.* Rev. 2d ed. Theory and History of Literature 7. Minneapolis: U of Minnesota P, 1983.

Derrida, Jacques. *Dissemination.* Trans. Barbara Johnson. Chicago: U of Chicago P, 1981.

– 'How to Avoid Speaking: Denials.' *Languages of the Unsayable: The Play of Negativity in Literature and Literary Theory.* Ed. Sanford Budick and Wolfgang Iser. New York: Columbia UP, 1989. 3–70.

– 'Living On / BORDER LINES.' Trans. James Hulbert. *Deconstruction and Criticism.* New York: Seabury P, 1979. 75–176.

– *Of Grammatology.* Trans. Gayatri Chakravorty Spivak. Baltimore: Johns Hopkins UP, 1976.

– *Positions.* Trans. Alan Bass. Chicago: U of Chicago P, 1981.

– 'Signature Event Context.' Trans. Samuel Weber and Jeffrey Mehlman. *Glyph* 1 (1977): 172–97.

– 'Structure, Sign and Play in the Discourse of the Human Sciences.' *Writing and Difference.* Trans. Alan Bass. Chicago: U of Chicago P, 1978. 278–93.

– 'Violence and Metaphysics: An Essay on the Thought of Emmanuel Levinas.' *Writing and Difference.* Trans. Alan Bass. Chicago: U of Chicago P, 1978. 79–153.

Erdman, David V., ed. *The Complete Poetry and Prose of William Blake.* By William Blake. Rev. ed. Berkeley: U of California P, 1982.

Essick, Robert N. 'Blake Today and Tomorrow.' *Studies in Romanticism* 21 (1982): 395–9.

Foucault, Michel. *Discipline and Punish: The Birth of the Prison.* Trans. Alan Sheridan. New York: Vintage, 1979.

– *History of Sexuality, Vol. 1: An Introduction.* Trans. Robery Hurley. New York: Pantheon, 1978.

- *Madness and Civilization: A History of Insanity in the Age of Reason.* Trans. Richard Howard. New York: Vintage, 1988.
- *Mental Illness and Psychology.* Trans. Alan Sheridan. New York: Harper & Row, 1976.
- 'Truth and Power.' *Power/Knowledge: Selected Interviews and Other Writings 1972–1977.* Ed. Colin Gordon. Trans. Colin Gordon, Leo Marshall, John Mepham, and Kate Soper. New York: Pantheon, 1980. 109–33.

Frank, Manfred. *What Is Neostructuralism?* Trans. Sabine Wilke and Richard Gray. Theory and History of Literature 45. Minneapolis: U of Minnesota P, 1989.

Gasché, Rodolphe. *The Tain of the Mirror: Derrida and the Philosophy of Reflection.* Cambridge: Harvard UP, 1986.

Gilligan, Carol. *In a Different Voice: Psychological Theory and Women's Development.* Cambridge: Harvard UP, 1982.

Girard, René. *La Route antique des hommes pervers.* Paris: B. Grasset, 1985.

Handelman, Susan. 'Jacques Derrida and the Heretic Hermeneutic.' *Displacement: Derrida and After.* Ed. Mark Krupnick. Indianapolis: Indiana UP, 1983. 98–129.

Hegel, G.W.F. *Phenomenology of Spirit.* Trans. A.V. Miller. Oxford: Clarendon P, 1979.

Heidegger, Martin. *Being and Time.* Trans. John Macquarie and Edward Robinson. New York: Harper & Row, 1962.
- *Poetry, Language, Thought.* Trans. Albert Hofstadter. New York: Harper & Row, 1971.
- *Schelling: vom Wesen der menschlichen Freiheit (1809). Gesamtausgabe.* Vol. 42. Frankfurt: Klostermann, 1988.
- *Schelling's Treatise on the Essence of Human Freedom.* Trans. Joan Stambaugh. Athens: Ohio UP, 1985.

Henrich, Dieter. 'Fichte's Original Insight.' Trans. D.R. Lachterman. *Contemporary German Philosophy.* Ed. D.E. Christenson et al. Vol. 1. University Park: Pennsylvania State UP, 1982. 15–53.

Hilton, Nelson. *Literal Imagination: Blake's Vision of Words.* Berkeley: U of California P, 1983.

Hogle, Jerrold E. *Shelley's Process: Radical Transference and the Development of His Major Works.* New York: Oxford UP, 1988.

Hölderlin, Friedrich. *Selected Verse.* Ed. and trans. Michael Hamburger. London: Anvil P, 1986.

Hoy, D.C., ed. *Foucault: A Critical Reader.* Oxford: Basil Blackwell, 1986.

Hughes, Merritt Y., ed. *John Milton: Complete Poems and Major Prose.* By John Milton. Indianapolis: Odyssey, 1957.

James, William. *The Varieties of Religious Experience: A Study of Human Nature.* New York: Mentor, 1958.

Kant, Immanuel. *On History.* Ed. Lewis White Beck. Trans. L.W. Beck, R.E. Anchor, and E.L. Fackenheim. Indianapolis: Bobbs-Merrill, 1963.

Kierkegaard, Søren. *Fear and Trembling / Repetition.* Trans. Howard V. Hong and Edna H. Hong. Princeton: Princeton UP, 1983.

– *The Concept of Anxiety: A Simple Psychologically Orienting Deliberation on the Dogmatic Issue of Hereditary Sin.* Ed. and trans. Reidar Thomte and Albert Anderson. Princeton: Princeton UP, 1980.

King, James. *William Blake: His Life.* New York: St. Martin's, 1991.

La Belle, Jenijoy. 'Michelangelo's Sistine Frescoes and Blake's 1795 Color-Printed Drawings: A Study in Structural Relationships.' *Blake: An Illustrated Quarterly* 14 (1980): 66–84.

Levinas, Emmanuel. *Totality and Infinity.* Trans. A. Lingis. Pittsburgh: Duquesne UP, 1969.

Mazzeo, Joseph Anthony. *Renaissance and Seventeenth-Century Studies.* New York: Columbia UP, 1964.

Mortley, Raoul, ed. *French Philosophers in Conversation: Levinas, Schneider, Serres, Irigaray, Le Doeuff, Derrida.* London: Routledge, 1991.

Nietzsche, Friedrich. 'On Truth and Lies in a Nonmoral Sense.' *Philosophy and Truth: Selections from Nietzsche's Notebooks of the early 1870's.* Trans. Daniel Breazeale. Atlantic Highlands, N.J.: Humanities P, 1979. 79–97.

– *The Gay Science.* Trans. Walter Kaufmann. New York: Vintage, 1974.

– *The Twilight of the Idols / The Anti-Christ.* Trans. R.J. Hollingdale. Harmondsworth: Penguin, 1968.

– *The Will to Power.* Trans. W. Kaufmann and R.J. Hollingdale. New York: Vintage, 1968.

Oakeshott, Michael. *On Human Conduct.* Oxford: Oxford UP, 1975.

Otto, Peter. *Constructive Vision and Visionary Deconstruction: Los, Eternity, and the Productions of Time in the Later Poetry of William Blake.* Oxford: Oxford UP, 1991.

Petry, M.J., ed. and trans. *Hegel's Philosophy of Nature.* By G.W.F. Hegel. Vol. 1. London: George Allen, 1970.

Rajan, Balachandra. *The Form of the Unfinished: English Poetics from Spenser to Pound.* Princeton: Princeton UP, 1985.

– *The Lofty Rhyme: A Study of Milton's Major Poetry.* Coral Gables, Fla.: U of Miami P, 1970.

Rajan, Tilottama. *Dark Interpreter: The Discourse of Romanticism.* Ithaca: Cornell UP, 1980.

- 'Displacing Post-Structuralism: Romantic Studies after Paul de Man.' *Studies in Romanticism* 24 (1985): 451–74.
- *The Supplement of Reading: Figures of Understanding in Romantic Theory and Practice*. Ithaca: Cornell UP, 1990.

Richardson, Alan. 'Romanticism and the Colonization of the Feminine.' *Romanticism and Feminism*. Ed. Anne K. Mellor. Bloomington: Indiana UP, 1988. 13–25.

Rollins, H.E., ed. *The Letters of John Keats: 1814-1821*. By John Keats. Vol. 1. Cambridge: Harvard UP, 1958.

Schelling, F.W.J. *Philosophical Inquiries into the Nature of Human Freedom*. Trans. James Gutmann. Chicago: Open Court, 1936.

Spivak, Gayatri Chakravorty. Translator's Preface. *Of Grammatology*. By Jacques Derrida. Trans. Gayatri Chakravorty Spivak. Baltimore: Johns Hopkins UP, 1976. ix–lxxxvii.

Stern, Robert. Introduction. *Ideas for a Philosophy of Nature*. By F.W.J. Schelling. Trans. Errol E. Harris and Peter Heath. Cambridge: Cambridge UP, 1988. ix–xxiii.

Taylor, Charles. *Philosophy and the Human Sciences: Philosophical Papers* 2. Cambridge: Cambridge UP, 1985.

Taylor, John. *Black Holes: The End of the Universe?* London: Souvenir P, 1973.

Taylor, Mark C. *Deconstructing Theology*. Chico, Calif.: Scholars P, 1982.

Wilkie, Brian, and Mary Lynn Johnson. *Blake's 'Four Zoas': The Design of A Dream*. Cambridge: Harvard UP, 1978.

Wittreich, Joseph Anthony, Jr. 'Opening the Seals: Blake's Epics and the Milton Tradition.' *Blake's Sublime Allegory: Essays on 'The Four Zoas,' 'Milton,' 'Jerusalem.'* Ed. Stuart Curran and Joseph Anthony Wittreich, Jr. Madison: U of Wisconsin P, 1973. 23–58.

Wordsworth, William. *The Prelude: 1799, 1805, 1850*. Ed. Jonathan Wordsworth, M.H. Abrams, and Stephen Gill. New York: Norton, 1979.

PART FOUR

Gender, Language, Power

IAN BALFOUR

Promises, Promises: Social and Other Contracts in the English Jacobins (Godwin/Inchbald)

I

'Society indeed is a contract.' These blunt words come not from Rousseau or Locke but from Edmund Burke in his epoch-making *Reflections on the Revolution in France*.[1] They display none of the laboured eloquence one comes to expect from the premiere political rhetorician of his day. The pronouncement is not even as nuanced as something like 'society is founded on a contract' or 'society is structured like a contract': simply 'society *is* a contract.'

In an essay entitled 'Of the Original Contract,' Hume noted how Tory and Whig political philosophy could be distinguished according to doctrines of passive obedience and primeval contract respectively.[2] One might suppose that the conservative, indeed reactionary, Burke of the *Reflections* would go against the grain of this tendency here, until we recall that Burke was indeed a Whig, at least technically.[3] Even so, Burke's promotion of a social contract might still seem the reverse of what one would expect. Was not the thinking of the social contract so thoroughly inscribed in the tradition of Locke and Rousseau that a progressive political thinker should be aligned with it and a reactionary one opposed? Despite Hume's suggestive analysis, philosophies of the social contract did and do not always divide neatly along party lines. The metaphor of the contract – though it is not simply a metaphor – spans a good deal of the spectrum of political discourse in Britain in the 1790s. But the instance that will first occupy this paper – the most famous political treatise of the decade – is one in which the social contract appears primarily in a negative mode. In his *Enquiry Concerning Political Justice* Godwin notes how 'friends of equality of justice' tend to promote the idea of the social contract, and this at a time when the word 'equality' was virtually of itself a revolutionary slogan.[4] Certainly the contract model seems to imply a real or possible equality of relations that could be used to counter the not yet passé doctrines of the *anciens régimes*. Nonetheless, there is ultimately no identifiable politics of the social contract as such. The political, and more than political, stakes lie rather in the terms of the contract to be negotiated, or, as in Godwin's case, in the rejection of the social contract, period.

It is perhaps primarily in opposition to Burke that Godwin argues so stridently against the very notion of the social contract, because the most notorious version of the day was Burke's codification of the contractual relation as the handing down of power and property from literal and figurative fathers to their literal and figurative sons. Burke goes so far as to claim the following for his genealogical conception of the contract:

As the ends of such a partnership cannot be obtained in many generations, it becomes a partnership not only between those who are living, but between those who are living, those who are dead, and those who are to be born. Each contract of each particular state is but a clause in the great primaeval contract of eternal society, linking the lower with the higher natures, connecting the visible and the invisible world, according to a fixed compact sanctioned by the inviolable oath which holds all physical and all moral natures, each in their appointed place. This law is not subject to the will of those, who by an obligation above them, and infinitely superior, are bound to submit their will to that law.[5]

The contract envisioned by Burke is thoroughly spectral, with two of the three signatory groups no longer or not yet among the living. The *Ur*-contract binds together the visible world and the ghostly, unrepresentable world of the invisible. Moreover, one signs this primeval contract before one is capable of signing, one promises obedience before one is able to promise.[6] Such a contract can never be an empirical one, particularly in its positing of a divine law beyond law, a law spoken into being by an 'inviolable oath' before any human language. But it is nonetheless, for Burke, the paradigm under which all the empirical contracts – and not only contracts – of history are to be understood.

In his *Enquiry Concerning Political Justice*, Godwin reviews the three principal models proposed for the origin and regulation of political institutions, namely, the rule of the strongest, divine right, and the social contract, and finds only the last worthy even of refutation. The questions he asks of the social contract are as pertinent to its Lockean as to its Burkean formulation. Who signs this contract? For whom does one sign? How long is the contract binding? How and how often is it to be renegotiated? These last questions are among many which address the problematic temporality of the social contract and of politics more generally. The Burkean contract is remarkable for the way it determines the lines of history as the binding of one generation to the next, of father to son. Succession is the ruling principle of Burke's discourse, the principle that determines the genealogy and development of societies, indeed nothing less than the narrative of history as such. (One might note parenthetically that it is no exaggeration to say that a crucial problem the French Revolution posed for Burke was that of its narratability: how to account – in a story – for the 'most astonishing' revolution 'that has hitherto happened in the world.')[7] For Godwin, the contracts of the fathers are not to be visited upon their sons. He opposes any philosophy positing an originary institution that would choose a system of regulations for posterity and 'barter away the understandings and independence of all that came after them, to the latest posterity' (1:188).[8] And even a more pragmatic vision of contractual relations renegotiated in every generation is rejected by Godwin as still fraught with inequities. The Tory doctrine of tacit obedience is dismissed on class grounds, because those without sufficient property or means are not truly free to choose whether or not to remain in any given body politic. But a similar institution of inequality plagues the social contract as well. Here Godwin is not far from the Marquis de Sade, who, in his 'Français, encore un effort,' argues against the oath taken by all Frenchmen to respect the property of the nation, an oath which Sade takes as the paradigm of the social contract:

God forbid that I should here wish to assail the pledge to respect property the Nation has just given: but will I be permitted some remarks upon the injustice of this pledge [*serment*]? What is the spirit of the vow [*serment*] taken by all a nation's individuals? Is it not to maintain a perfect equality amongst citizens, to subject them all equally to the law protecting the possessions of all? Well, I ask you now whether that law is truly just which orders the man who has nothing to respect another who has everything? What are the elements of the social contract [*pacte social*]? ... Certainly, nothing is more unjust: an oath [*serment*] must have an equal effect upon all individuals who pronounce it; that it bind him who has no interest in its maintenance is impossible, because it would no longer be a pact among free men; it would be the weapon of the strong against the weak, against whom the latter would have to be in incessant revolt.[9]

This version of the social contract is not a codification of revolutionary principles but is taken by Sade as an incitement to revolution against the 'contract.' In its levelling of all differences among 'men' before the law, this social contract reinscribes pre-existing inequities even as it appeals to a universal equality: the universality of the law remains largely a formal matter.[10] The protection of property – which, strangely enough, to Godwin the atheist was 'sacred' – served in Sade's France to sustain especially the most propertied people and thus, for him, constituted only a semblance of social justice. The same was surely true in Godwin's England, where the notorious Black Act – invoked explicitly in *Caleb Williams* – stipulated absurd penalties for crimes against property, precisely because those secure in their property would hardly be in a position to commit them.[11] The Black Act was a codification of class warfare under the guise of a legal equality and a formal universality. Thus for several reasons Godwin wished to abandon the social contract: its vexed temporality and its codification of asymmetries of power in the name of universal equality.

Not content to dismantle only the social contract as such, the privileged model under which to think the structure and history of politics in his day, Godwin finds it necessary to supplement that argument with a similar one on the character of promises. Jeremy Bentham, for one, would define a contract as 'a pair of promises,' underscoring the status of the promise as the linguistic mode of that contract.[12] More fundamental still than the social contract, the institution that some would contend constitutes society as such, lies, for Godwin, the promise. What then is to be said of the promise and its consequences for politics and political theory?

A promise, Jacques Derrida maintains, cannot be kept. Or, in a slightly different formulation in *Mémoires*, he writes that one could 'almost say': 'even if a promise could be kept, it would matter little.'[13] In this formula, already termed excessive by Derrida himself, there is not the slightest advocacy of an abandonment of responsibility, even as traditionally understood. Nor does Derrida deny the possibility that the content of a given promise might actually be fulfilled. The emphasis is rather on the movement, the act of the promise. 'Keep' translates the word 'tenir': a promise cannot be 'held,' 'main-tained,' so to speak, for the promise, insofar as it is an act, is untenable. Uttered in a moment, enacting itself in a moment, whether or not it corresponds to the integrity of an intention or a will, the promise is oriented towards an unknown future that has already been changed by its very utterance. The promise is an event and not merely a linguistic marker. It has consequences – nothing but consequences – but ones that are unpredictable, even if the promise itself promises to predict.

In the chapter devoted to 'Promises' in the *Enquiry Concerning Political Justice*, the promise and its repercussions unfold in what Godwin calls the 'theatre of time.'[14] Nothing is more sacred, he contends, than the right 'disposal' of our time, time in which, in order to act on behalf of the general good, we are 'bound to acquire all the information which our opportunities enable us to acquire' (1:198). This imperative for knowledge has serious implications for the performance of promises, since according to Godwin 'we abridge, and that in the most essential point, the time of gaining information, if we bind ourselves to-day to the conduct we will observe two months hence' (1:199). Thus the temporality of knowledge need not converge with the arc of futurity cast by the promise, and in Godwin's economy, knowledge must take priority over the speech-act, even if the promise comes first in time.[15]

What disturbs Godwin about the promise is not so much its potential 'infelicity,' in J.L. Austin's term – whether or not it can go wrong – as its very existence in the first place.[16] Godwin reasons along these lines: 'What I have promised is what I ought to have performed, if no promise had intervened, or it is not. It is conducive, or not conducive, to the generating of human happiness. If it be the former, then promise comes in merely as an additional inducement, in favour of that which, in the eye of morality, was already of indispensable obligation' (1:197). Thus the promise can be a *mere* supplement, wholly unnecessary to the cause of morality. Any yet it can also be something much more than sheerly external: the promise is, in Godwin's words, 'absolutely considered, an evil' and it stands 'in opposition to the genuine and wholsome exercise of an intellectual nature' (1:196). As a supplement that nonetheless intervenes, codifying and projecting a prior unspoken obligation, the promise teaches one 'to do something from a precarious and temporary motive, which ought to be done for its intrinsic recommendations. If therefore right motives and a pure intention are constituent parts of virtue, promises are clearly at variance with virtue' (1:197). Godwin in no way seeks to eschew responsibility; indeed, he displays a kind of hyper-responsibility that calls for constant vigilance, the following of an imperative requiring the incessant reinvention of politics and a negotiation of what is just. But that justice is threatened by the very institution of the promise, the evil promise, that would have seemed to be one of the mechanisms for its fulfilment.

In *Political Justice*, Godwin explicates the notion of 'evil' in quasi-physiological terms as pain, much in the mannner of Burke in his treatise on the sublime and the beautiful. But the word 'evil' – highly charged for someone educated as a Calvinist – does not lose all of its ethical pathos, for Godwin uses it in numerous contexts remote from anything physiological. Indeed, it is a word he had already applied to government in general. 'Promises, in the same sense as has already been observed of government, are an evil, though it may be, in some cases a necessary evil' (1:200). Godwin's link between the promise and government under the same rubric makes clear what one could demonstrate from other sources as well, that the promise is the exemplary speech-act of government. (This is not just because what politicians famously do is make promises, more often than not ones that will not be kept; rather, it is because the promise is the linguistic structure of the law.)[17] Thus Godwin's anxiety about institutions extends from the actual practices of government to individual promises, speech-acts that posit and institute (rather than represent or refer), especially in that they perform in excess of what needs to be performed.

That the same problem of the institutional and institutionalizing character of the promise plagues government in general as well as the individual subject is one reason for the relatively unproblematic transitions between the discourses of government and subject in Godwin's texts. This state of affairs also goes some way towards explaining how Godwin could translate so successfully from the theoretical program of *Political Justice* to the narrative of *Caleb Williams*. 'The spirit and character of government,' we are told in the preface to *Caleb Williams*, 'intrudes itself into every rank of society.'[18] Similarly, in *Political Justice* we learn how government 'insinuates' itself into the private transactions of individual subjects (1:4). Both texts pursue these concerns in different ways, to some extent corresponding to the time-honoured but tenuous opposition between 'abstract' philosophy and 'concrete' narrative. Another related and almost equally clichéd opposition, that between the public and the private, is much less pertinent, especially in Godwin's work: a rigorous distinction between the two is untenable, not least because of his thinking on and through language, for the very operation of language always threatens that distinction.[19] Indeed the passage between the public philosophy of concepts and private narrative of individual characters in Godwin is such that the distinction between the two wavers and all but collapses.

The passage from *Political Justice* to *Caleb Williams* would not be a simple one from philosophy to fiction, or from theory to narrative. *Political Justice* is already a narrative of sorts, recounting the story of concepts and the history of institutions rather than the lives of characters.[20] Within the grand story of the 'progress of truth' that Godwin tells in *Political Justice*, two narratives stand out: its history of political institutions and the one I will focus on, its history of language.[21]

The first moment in Godwin's account of the origin and development of language is the involuntary cry, soon transformed into linguistic gestures supposed to excite pity or procure assistance, moments not yet associated with the cognitive or representational clarity that will become Godwin's Enlightenment *telos* for language. Much like the original utterances in Rousseau's divided origins of language (in the North the primal proposition is *aidez-moi* ['help me'] and in the South *aimez-moi* ['love me']), Godwin's originary forms of language would seem to be, in Austin's terms, more performative than constative: linguistic or proto-linguistic gestures like a plea for help, a command, a threat, a warning.[22] These original gestures of language are already 'communicative,' but in Godwin's abridged history, it is not long before language becomes essentially the means of conveying information, 'communication' in a more restricted sense. Eighteenth-century theorists of the origins of language were divided in their speculations on the primal unit of language: Herder arguing for the verb, a good many arguing for the noun, Diderot perversely and ingeniously contending for the adjective. Godwin is circumspect on the original moment of language, avoiding the often lurid narratives that distinguish so many treatises before his (one thinks especially of Herder's repeated encounters with soft, woolly sheep): one can nonetheless infer in Godwin a certain primacy of the noun, or the name, in Aristotle's terms, the *onoma*. In the key passage in question Godwin moves rather quickly from the 'involuntary cry' to the conveying of information, even as he acknowledges the immense distance between them. He says of the first language:

Its beginning was probably from those involuntary cries, which infants, for example, are found to utter in the earliest stages of their existence, and which, previously to the idea of exciting pity or procuring assistance, spontaneously arise from the operation of pain upon our animal frame. These cries, when actually uttered, become a subject of perception to him by whom they are uttered; and, being observed to be constantly associated with certain antecedent impressions and to excite the idea of those impressions in the hearer, may afterwards be repeated from reflection and the desire of relief. Eager desire to communicate information to another, will also prompt us to utter some simple sound for the purpose of exciting attention: this sound will probably frequently recur to organs unpracticed to variety, and will at length stand as it were by convention for the information intended to be conveyed. But the difference is extreme from these simple modes of communication, which we possess in common with some of the inferior animals, to all the analysis and abstraction which languages require. (1:112)

Thinking within the tradition of Locke, Godwin posits language as essentially cognitive and communicative, and as such a privileged vehicle for the progress of understanding that motors his Enlightenment myth of perfectibility. (Indeed, this discussion of language and writing is the *sole* topic of the section on 'Human Inventions Susceptible of Perpetual Improvement,' whereas the history of politics recounted elsewhere is essentially a history of crime.) Virtually all the key moments that Godwin goes on to single out in his history of language – abstraction, or the invention of hieroglyphics as picture-writing – are of the order of the name and the constative, inscribed in a fundamentally representational economy. That is to say, Godwin's history of language narrates, among other things, the supercession of the performative by the constative. It is no wonder, then, that there is little room left for the social contract, much less for the performative promise, in Godwin's scheme of politics, which is supposed by him to be more a matter of truth than of power. (One might note here that Godwin's account of language at the end of book 1 immediately precedes the opening of book 2 on the 'Principles of Society.' That is, the analysis of language directly prepares the way for the theory of politics.) Godwin inherits from Aristotle the topos of 'the true politician' but posits this same figure as the politician of the true. He repeatedly has recourse to the notion of what he calls, in a striking phrase, 'political truth' (1:119). Politics for Godwin is not opposed to science: it *is* science, which is to say, a coherent body of knowledge. Strange as it may sound to contemporary ears, there is no sustained distinction in Godwin between politics and political science: the former is the latter. That politics is of the order of knowledge and its acquisition – and not just of the order of timeless reason – is one factor that allows him not only to argue in terms of principles and concepts but to narrate the movement of knowledge. This itinerary Godwin frequently terms 'the progress of truth.' It is a complicated progress because it is based on the acquisition of knowledge, especially given that language is the prime medium for that acquisition. In dismissing the social contract, Godwin complained that a principal obstacle to its realization was the inability of different people to agree on the terms of the 'agreement.' So Godwin, at least for strategic purposes, admits that language is an uncertain ground for this construct, though it is not clear how he can confine the vicissitudes of language to the domain of contracts, whereas elsewhere it serves as the adequate medium for the protocols of reason. Rather like Locke, who accounts for various abuses of language and then proposes remedies for them, Godwin acknowledges what is problematic about language, epistemologically and socially, and then proceeds with a calculus for the steady progress of truth based on a number of immutable principles, such as man's perfectibility and his infinite susceptibility to the advance of reason.

But from within this history of progress, the promise intervenes. As an evil, necessarily. Though Godwin does his level(ling) best to delimit the sphere of the promise, it continues to surface in his treatise, most notably in the chapter on 'Legislation,' which follows that on 'Political Authority.' (The sequence of chapters is thus: 'Social Contract,' 'Promises,' 'Political Authority,' and 'Legislation.') The core of Godwin's enigmatic pronouncements on the character of the law, or rather of legislation, is given as follows: 'Legislation, as it has been usually understood, is not a matter of human competence. Immutable reason is the true legislator, and her decrees it behooves us to investigate. The functions of society extend, not to the making, but the interpreting of law; it cannot decree, it can only declare that, which the nature of things has already decreed, and the propriety of which irresistibly flows from the circumstances of the case' (1:221). The law thus precedes legislation and precedes all government.

That the originary law necessarily comes in the form of language is underscored through Godwin's citation of a passage from a sermon by Laurence Sterne on 'Good Conscience,' where he speaks of the office of conscience which must determine matters 'not like an Asiatic cadi, according to the ebbs and flows of his own passions, but like a British judge, who makes no new law, but faithfully declares that which he finds already written' (1:222). This empirical instance of the 'already written' serves as the model for the more purely speculative notion of the law that precedes government, indeed that antedates all society. Immutable reason, which can be neither identified with nor abstracted from any individual or group of individuals, *decrees* the law in advance of any actual government. Thus one has to acknowledge a law before the law, and a realm of the performative prior to the cognitive interpretation or reinscription of it. In this regard, Godwin is close to a fragment of Rousseau on law where he claims that of necessity laws were prior to government and, more than that, that laws were prior even to leaders (*chefs*).[23] Rousseau insists on the independence of law from government, not in the modern sense of a separation of powers, but as an absolute theoretical independence. This priority of the law can itself be understood as a law of language, law as language subject to the law of language. For Godwin as for Rousseau, language performs law prior to government.

If the discourse of politics, for Godwin, is essentially a language of meaning and of truth, one nonetheless has to recognize that before language means, language promises meaning. The primacy of positing – rather than referring or representing – is one thing the chapter on legislation makes clear. It is to Godwin's credit, and it is a sign of the complexity and strange rigour of his work, that he allows so much about language, politics, and their mutual imbrication to see the light of day. Yet Godwin seeks ultimately to determine language as essentially cognitive and communicative of information, by circumscribing, by delimiting the performative and by subordinating power to truth, only to find that the promise, the law of the promise, intervenes and does not cease to intervene.

II

The transition from the theoretical program of the *Enquiry Concerning Political Justice* to the fictional narrative of *Caleb Williams* is not as problematic as one might expect, partly because *Political Justice* was a story to begin with, a grand story of the tortuous but inexorable progress of truth. Thus when Godwin speaks in the preface to *Caleb Williams* of its review of 'domestic and unrecorded despotism ... as far as the progressive nature of a single story would allow,' he acknowledges one aspect of the novel's identity with his political treatise.[24] We noted above how, in Godwin's view, the forces of government insinuated themselves into the most private transaction of individuals. It is to Godwin and Wollstonecraft that we owe a version of the insight that the personal is the political, since any subject, for them, is a political subject from the start.

But if the transition from *Political Justice* to *Caleb Williams* is unproblematic in some respects, we by no means find in the latter simply the fictional mirror-image of the former. Instead of a steady progress of truth and its triumph over error, we seem to encounter in Godwin's novel an endless series of catastrophes after an initial period of innocence and grace when the young Caleb is employed as secretary and librarian, a transcriber and keeper of the books for his master Falkland. The latter – an apparently noble aristocrat who revels in his Ode to the Genius of Chivalry resonant with the rhetoric and values of Edmund Burke – soon emerges as one villain of the piece.[25] Caleb finds information suggesting that Falkland, in a moment of passion, murdered his nemesis, Tyrrel, and, further, that he caused the death of others as a result. Falkland discovers Caleb's discovery and seeks to ensure his silence about these facts known to no one else. To guarantee Caleb's future obedience, Falkland first forces Caleb to swear – in unconditional fashion – that he will never reveal what Falkland is about to disclose to him, and upon obtaining this promise, proceeds to confess his crime (*CW* 135). Caleb has no intention of ever disclosing what he knows, but the aftermath of the confrontation is enough for him to wish to leave the employ of Falkland, which becomes the occasion for the master's relentless and obsessive persecution of his servant.

Caleb Williams is quite literally a story of trial and error: virtually all the decisive scenes take place in the numerous courtroom trials or in public hearings, and both Falkland's and Caleb's actions that precipitate those confrontations are characterized in terms of 'error.' We shall take up the question of the trial momentarily and look first at the way 'error' unfolds in novelistic terms. Here, for example, is one of Caleb's reflections after he recognizes how far things have degenerated:

I have now every thing to fear. And yet what was my fault? It proceeded from none of those errors which are justly held up to the aversion of mankind; my object had been neither wealth, nor the means of indulgence, nor the usurpation of power. No spark of malignity had harbored in my soul. I had always reverenced the sublime mind of Mr. Falkland. I reverenced it still. My offence had merely been a mistaken thirst for knowledge. (*CW* 133)

It is striking how the gap between 'error' and 'mistake' in this passage collapses, for the more purely epistemological or even pragmatic function of the mistake cannot quite be separated from 'error' understood in an ethical register with which the passage began in a negative mode.

The vocabulary of error is entirely consistent with Godwin's attempt to think political justice in terms of truth: error, for Godwin, is as much an epistemological category as it is an ethical one. It is 'error' – rather than, say, evil, self-interest, or power – that lies at the root of the whole organization of society in terms of masters and slaves.[26] As Caleb reflects in a heady moment after he has just been liberated:

I looked back with abhorrence to the subjection in which I had been held. I did not hate the author of my misfortunes; truth and justice acquit me of that; I rather pitied the hard destiny to which he seemed condemned. But I thought with unspeakable loathing of those errors, in consequence of which every man is fated to be more or less the tyrant or the slave. (*CW* 156)

The very incongruity of the invocation of error here as a means of understanding no less than the tyrant/slave relation is one sign of that category's ubiquity. Godwin's novel is a philosophical 'romance' of error, a programmatic variant of the genre on which Caleb was weaned.[27] But error is also on trial in *Caleb Williams*, for side-by-side with passages like the one just quoted stands one character's conviction that the 'true state of things will always come to light' (*CW* 118). Godwin's text, if not Godwin himself, is not naïve enough to assume that truth will always triumph, even though the Godwin of *Political Justice* could proclaim apodictically that 'truth is omnipotent' (1:91). What is important about this configuration is less the alteration between truth and error than its omnipresence as *the* framework for political analysis, whether in a fictional or a philosophical mode. But what are the limits of such a grid for understanding politics and the political?

The promise, as Austin demonstrates, is not itself subject to criteria of truth and falsity: a promise is a promise regardless of whether or not it is fulfilled, and regardless of whether the promise is 'true' to a speaker's intention. Indeed, the impossibility of a promise being true or false may well be one reason why Godwin is so suspicious of this speech-act. Moreover, the promise, once uttered, takes on something of a life of its own, and to an extraordinary degree Caleb is a victim not just of Falkland, but of his oath to him. Long after it seems reasonable for Caleb to be bound by an oath to a person unjustly terrorizing him, Caleb still feels obligated, perhaps perversely so, by the promise not to reveal Falkland's secret. Much is made of Caleb's readiness to tell only a 'mangled' or adulterated tale, as opposed to a coherent but trumped-up story like the one that Falkland concocts in blaming a robbery on Caleb.

And to undercut in advance any possibly cogent defence by Caleb in the crucial trial scene, Falkland draws attention to his secretary's ability to spin a plausible tale, one of many ways that Caleb is constructed as a maker of texts, a composer of fictions. Yet Caleb's 'inability' to tell the truth is still in no small measure the result of his promise: the performative disrupts the smooth functioning of the constative.

Caleb's resistance to breaking his promise and to telling what is repeatedly called 'the whole story' forces his escape from imprisonment and the adoption of an extended series of disguises. These disguises – the very existence of which is anathema to Godwin's politics of truth – do double duty in the novel. They not only provide necessary complications for the prosecution of the plot, but the roles of beggar, Irishman, and Jew also emphasize Caleb's alignment with other outcast victims of a Christian society that persists in honouring the likes of Falkland. In this sequence of disguises, the nadir may well arrive when Caleb is forced to earn a living as a writer, first as a poet, and then, lowest of the low, as a writer of prose. So successful is Caleb in this last role that we begin to wonder whether we are not reading one more of Caleb's fictions, and not merely one of Godwin's.

The original ending of *Caleb Williams* – the more powerful and consequential one – closes with Caleb as yet another kind of writer, coming full circle to the mechanical transcriber of texts that he was at the outset. His old friend Collins tells him in a penultimate scene that he is 'as a machine'(*CW* 310), and what Caleb mechanically produces in his last, mad days is an epitaph, identical to the cipher to which he has been reduced. The last lines of the text read: 'true happiness lies in being like a stone – Nobody can complain of me – all day long I do nothing – am a stone – a GRAVE-STONE! – an obelisk to tell you, HERE LIES WHAT WAS ONCE A MAN!' (*CW* 326). This hardly seems the fictional equivalent of Godwin's story of the grand progress of truth recounted in *Political Justice*. Rather it stands as its negative version: Things As They Are (the original title of the novel) as a provocation to Things As They Ought To Be.

The revised, published ending of the text is much closer to Godwin's programmatic narrative of politics in *Political Justice* in that the truth does eventually see the light of day. In an unexpected reversal of fortune, Caleb is vindicated, Falkland publically confesses his crime and embraces the man he had spent a good part of his life persecuting. The final courtroom scene is the last in a long series of public hearings and trials, none of which had contributed much to the production of truth or justice. Though on the face of it at odds with the progress of truth announced by Godwin, this comes as no surprise to the reader of the chapter on oaths from the *Enquiry Concerning Political Justice*. If promises are, absolutely considered, evil, oaths are somehow an even more radical evil. 'Can there be a practice more pregnant with false morality,' Godwin asks, 'than that of administering oaths' (2:265)? 'It treats veracity,' he goes on to say, 'in the scenes of ordinary life, as a thing not to be looked for.' To be forced to speak the truth primarily because the government demands it is, for Godwin, the ultimate perversion of an institution already intrinsically evil. He has nothing but contempt for whoever 'contaminates his lips with an oath' (2:266): the very act is an affront to society and to the God whose name is taken in vain. And thus the courtroom, paradoxically, is the last place one would go in search of truth. The trial is not only the scene of error, it *is* error.

What the spectacle of the trials makes painfully clear, in their confrontation of word against word, is the dependence of justice not so much on truth as on rhetoric. If Caleb's disarming address to the court in the revised finale is persuasive – with its unexpected praise of Falkland as a great man together with the latter's self-deprecation for having forced such an encounter – it is so partly by accident. Falkland effects an about-face only when he senses Caleb is succeeding in persuading the courtroom audience of the truth of his tale, and thus is undone by what he terms Caleb's 'artless and manly story' (*CW* 324). It is, however, no accident – in this narrative much preoccupied with the categories of accident and necessity – that what triumphs in the end is a rhetoric of non-rhetoric, an artless story, about which one can say, in more than one sense, that justice is done. Godwin uses the phrase 'to do justice' repeatedly, and it is telling that it occurs almost only in reference to language, that is, apropos the description of a certain state of affairs represented accurately and to be judged accordingly. The truth of justice is linked, in the end, to the truth of representation, but virtually the entire preceding narrative has shown the reception of a story as true has little or nothing to do with its truth. (There is, however, throughout the novel a moral hierarchy established whereby those who believe Caleb's tale, like the head of the gang of thieves, rank higher than those who do not.) Doing justice in language is no guarantee that justice will be done. The outcome of rhetoric remains radically unpredictable, as unpredictable as the ending of *Caleb Williams*, which could always go, as they say, either way. And in fact did.

In a world of enforced oaths, whether Falkland's or those of courtroom witnesses, there is no telling what will happen. What does happen will necessarily be arbitrary, but 'arbitrary' in the twin and not entirely compatible senses of that term in the eighteenth century: the random and the wilful. As much as Godwin's novel insists on a rigorous causal nexus organizing the succession of events, a good deal of the action is impervious to that logic, though it is often here that the 'arbitrary' exercise of power enters the scene to fill up the void of explanation. It is partly because Godwin imagines a social action based on truth that he has such deep reservations about the linguistic action of the performative promise and the oath. These speech-acts, not subject to the criteria of truth and falsity, exceed the representational frame of Godwin's ideal politics. Godwin may well want to rid society of these disfiguring acts at odds with the exercise of virtue, yet they keep reasserting themselves in the practice of things as they are.

III

The fateful consequences of the promise mark too Elizabeth Inchbald's *A Simple Story*, a novel composed in the early 1780s but not published until 1791, when its author was established as a member of the circle of English 'Jacobins' that included Godwin and Wollstonecraft. Thus this novel, produced by the first English woman to earn a living as a drama critic (as well as being an actor and dramatist), predates both *Political Justice* and *Caleb Williams*, and it is not fanciful to think that Inchbald's work had a considerable influence on Godwin's, not least regarding his reflections on the promise.[28] It is no exaggeration to say that the whole of the not-so-simple plot of *A Simple Story* revolves around a series of promises, vows, and oaths, made and broken. The story is set in motion when Dorriforth, a Roman Catholic priest, is asked by a certain Mr Milner, expiring on his deathbed, to be the guardian of his surviving daughter. The Milner children had been raised in the different religions of their parents, the girls as Protestants like their deceased mother, the boys as Catholics like their expiring father. The opposition between Roman Catholic and Protestant frames a good deal of the action of the novel and builds a real tension into the relationship of Dorriforth and his ward Miss Milner, a tension that informs also the hermeneutics internal to the novel, pitting a Protestant spirit of individualism against a Catholic reverence for authority and tradition.[29]

The plethora of promises throughout *A Simple Story* have consequences for the reader's sense of narrative progress, not unlike with the oracles of classical epic, or the witches' predictions in *Macbeth*: they all cast a line of futurity over the plot to come. A good part of the suspense of reading lies in finding out if the promise will converge with its forecast outcome further down the line. The movement in Inchbald is rarely one of simple fulfilment: the promises function more often than not as obstacles to the resolution of the plot. Their very existence forces characters into untenable situations that were precisely not inevitable. As in *Caleb Williams*, the promises seem to take on lives of their own, and characters operate as much as victims as they do as makers of their own speech-acts.

Early on in *A Simple Story*, the rakish Lord Frederick remarks that 'monastic vows, like those of marriage, were made to be broken,'[30] and this dictum opens up the possibility, perhaps even desirability, of the broken promise that will facilitate the marriage at the novel's centre. At the opposite end of the spectrum of conventional ethical wisdom stands Miss Woodley's claims for the heinousness of broken vows. As the narrator summarizes on her behalf: 'Education, is called second nature; in the strict (but not enlarged) education of Miss Woodley, it was more powerful than the first – and the violation of oaths, persons, or things consecrated to Heaven, was, in her opinion, if not the most enormous, the most horrid among the catalogue of crimes' (*SS* 73). The intrigue of the novel is by no means confined to duelling conceptions of the promise: the most exacting complications of the novel turn on the precise promises made by each of the leading characters. We are told in the very first sentence of *A Simple Story* of the solemn vows that Dorriforth has taken as a member of his order. And in the initial meeting between Dorriforth and Miss Milner, no sooner has she been informed of his acceptance of her as a ward, then she promises to obey him in no uncertain terms:

The instant Dorriforth was introduced to her by Miss Woodley as her 'Guardian, and her deceased father's most beloved friend,' she burst into a flood of tears, knelt down to him for a moment, and promised ever to obey him as her father. (*SS* 13)

Neither of the two promises would be so problematic were not a romantic relationship to develop between the guardian and her ward, who are from the outset, in figurative terms, father and daughter. At the end of the tortuous process by which the protagonists discover their own and each other's feelings – and their promises are major obstacles in the way of that discovery – all of a sudden Dorriforth's perpetual vow of celibacy and Miss Milner's promise to obey him *as a father* take on new and wholly unexpected meanings. These two promises stand temporarily in the way of the one promise at the centre of the novel: the marriage vow.[31]

It is not a matter of indifference that in the inaugural text of speech-act theory, Austin's *How to Do Things with Words*, the privileged example of the performative is the marriage promise: the 'I do' of the marriage ceremony that Austin misquotes in an attempt to emphasize its character as an act.[32] Austin is concerned not just with grammatical and rhetorical formulae as such, but with what he calls the 'total speech-act,' the analysis of which requires attention to the social frame in which any speech-act occurs, even if it can and does exceed the frame of its utterance. The marriage promise is arguably the speech-act that guarantees the very coherence of certain kinds of society: certainly it holds for the worlds of Inchbald and Austen.[33] In *A Simple Story*, what seems an unthinkable eventuality – the marriage of Dorriforth and Miss Milner – is made possible by his inheritance of the Elmwood estate. This admits him to the peerage and simultaneously forces him to come up with an heir, necessitating a shotgun wedding of sorts, though there is as yet no offspring, only the need to come up with one. And in this case the bride is to be named later, so to speak, because no one, not even the groom, has a clue about her identity.

A special papal dispensation is ultimately procured to release Dorriforth from his vows, thus doing away with the major hurdle in the way of marriage and permitting the exchange of the lovers' vows. Yet long before the occurrence of the deferred marriage ceremony proper, the reader is privy to a remarkable scene in which Dorriforth delivers a promise even more 'unconditional' – because less determinate – than Caleb's fateful oath to Falkland. Here is the account of a conversation between Miss Woodley, a companion of Miss Milner's, and Dorriforth now free of his religious vows:

'Heaven is my witness, if I knew – if I could conceive the means how to make her [Miss Milner] happy, I would sacrifice my own happiness to her's.'

'My lord,' cried Miss Woodley with a smile, 'perhaps I might call upon you hereafter, to fulfill your word.'

He was totally ignorant what she meant, nor had he leisure from the confusion of his thoughts to reflect upon her meaning; he nevertheless replied, with warmth, 'Do – you will find I'll perform it. – Do – I will faithfully perform it.' (*SS* 112)

At the moment of his promise, Dorriforth has no conception of Miss Milner's feelings for him, but he has, in effect, just promised to marry her.

But the plot thickens a good deal between this promise and the official exchange of wedding vows. Much of the novel's first half involves the display of the vanity and impetuousness of Miss Milner, who seems to delight in trying the patience of the saintly Dorriforth. The principal act of transgression is her attendance at a masquerade ball against her guardian's wishes. The masquerade, the history of which has been well charted by Terry Castle, provides a setting which thematizes the problem of deception already much at work in Inchbald's fictional world. Miss Milner's transgression – which is coloured by more than a suggestion of gender-crossing, as some descriptions of her costume fix it as male rather than female – would be the act that 'totally reversed the prospect of all future accomodation,' as the narrator informs us (*SS* 151). The drama of the masquerade does indeed rupture relations between Dorriforth and Miss Milner, but not so permanently that they cannot discover their deep feelings for each other, such that on the verge of their parting for ever they can be almost miraculously reconciled.

We have noted that the marriage scene proper does not appear as such, but the moment of reconciliation is staged in such a way that it constitutes a second 'marriage' before the fact. As Lord Elmwood's carriage is waiting at the door of the manor for his departure that would spell the end of his relation to Miss Milner, his confessor and mentor, Sanford, forces a resolution of the crisis by saying to the two of them: 'Separate this moment ... Or resolve never to be separated but by death' (*SS* 190). Then, seizing 'a book,' this man of the cloth asks:

'Lord Elmwood, do you love this woman?'
 'More than my life,' replied the lordship, with the most heartfelt accents.
 'He then turned to Miss Milner – 'Can you say the same by him?'
 She spread her hands over her eyes, and cried, 'Oh, heavens!'
 I believe you *can* say so,' returned Sanford, 'and in the name of God, and your own happiness, since this is the case, let me put it out of your power to part.' (*SS* 190–1)

Though not technically a marriage, this odd 'exchange' of vows orchestrated by a priest in the name of God is the closest thing to it. The very proliferation of pre-nuptial agreements in effect does away with the need to represent the marriage ceremony itself. (One interesting consequence is that Miss Milner does not – so far as we know – promise to obey her husband, a promise that indeed would have been hard to keep.)[34] No one is quite prepared for the wedding and so Lord Elmwood in the confusion places a ring at hand on Miss Milner's finger, only to discover too late that it was really a mourning ring. This ominous sign turns out to be prophetic, as the marriage cannot survive his long trip to the West Indies, during which the former Miss Milner becomes 'involved,' as we might now say, with another man. One could rehearse along the same lines the promises that organize the intrigues of the second half of the novel, in which the daughter of their union, Matilda, becomes the female lead and Dorriforth's nephew Rushbrook her frustrated suitor. Both the principles and mechanisms of the promise are precisely the same, as characters move through a labryrinth of vows, threats, and commands, all still haunted by those original promises that generated the plot in the first place.

Is the problematic of the promise in *A Simple Story* largely a matter of plot mechanics or is there some political valence to the promise, such that it makes particular sense for it to figure so prominently in what will come to be known as a Jacobin novel? Might it even, in its insistence of the complexities of the promise, be considered a precursor to Godwin's project in both fiction and philosophy? In an early confrontation between Dorriforth and the studiously impulsive Miss Milner, the guardian asks his ward if she has given her suitor Lord Frederick her 'promises' (SS 56), to which she can respond with an unequivocal 'No.' When Dorriforth persists in asking her if it is her intention 'never to become his wife,' she counters by saying, 'At present it is.' Her guardian is taken aback by this response of a Godwinian *avant la lettre*. Miss Milner does not want to 'abridge' the time, as Godwin would say, that would enable her to make such a promise. It is precisely ignorance of the future that requires her not to promise in the present. This situation, together with a simultaneous imperative for knowledge, is perhaps best understood as the ethical precondition for a Godwinian politics of truth and justice.[35]

Inchbald seems to anticipate the Godwinian insight into the promise as mere supplement – a dangerous supplement, to borrow Rousseau's phrase from a different context – that leads characters into all kinds of predicaments, including deception and even self-deception.[36] Like Godwin, she queries the putative equality of contractual relations and finds them wanting as vehicles for truth and social justice. What the novels of Godwin and Inchbald elaborate is a 'domestic' version of the more purely political discourse of the social contract, even if they engage it primarily in a negative mode. In reading the novels of Inchbald and Godwin together with the *Enquiry Concerning Political Justice*, one can perhaps glimpse something of the continuum of the language of government as thematized and performed in English Jacobin writing, a spectrum extending from individual promises to governmental legislation to the model of the social contract itself. One can understand why the English Jacobins, reacting against the massive injustices of regimes at home and abroad, would not want simply to argue word against word, power against power, but rather to ground their cause in nothing less than truth. Though Godwin and Inchbald share with their fellow Jacobins a suspicion of legal despotism common to the left, they go further than most of their radical contemporaries in their questioning of the very structures of contractual relation.

A science of politics is what Godwin desparately wants, but the performance of his treatise as well as its fictional counterpart shows how the vicissitudes of the political complicate the science of politics that would encompass it. The dream of a politics of truth and a conceptual language of representation wakes up to find the promise, the performative, a language of government that always exceeds representation. Indeed 'theory' itself, understood as a language of representation, is disarticulated by its object of inquiry. As Paul de Man has commented apropos Rousseau: '... the theory of politics inevitably turns into the history, the allegory of its inability to achieve the status of the science.'[37] The same would hold true for the theory of literature. The dream of theory always risks being dissipated by the singularity and unpredictability of any truly political event or act of reading, and thus the discourse of theory – however rigorous or necessary – produces, in the end, histories, allegories of knowledge and of something other than knowledge.

NOTES

1 Edmund Burke, *Reflections on the Revolution in France*, ed. Conor Cruise O'Brien (Harmondsworth: Penguin, 1969), 194
2 David Hume, 'Of the Original Contract,' in *Essays: Moral, Political, and Literary*, ed. Eugene F. Miller (Indianapolis: Liberty Classics, 1987), 465–87.

See also the other relevant essays in the same collection: 'Of Passive Obedience,' 'Of the First Principles of Government,' 'Of the Origin of Government,' and 'That Politics May Be Reduced to a Science.'

3 The portrayal of Burke here cannot be generalized to the whole of his politico-literary career. Indeed the letter from France that provoked Burke's *Reflections* assumed from the outset that Burke, as a former champion of the American revolutionary cause, would be in sympathy with the French revolutionaries. Nor did the 'revolutionary' character of his thinking and work simply come to a halt in 1790. On the later Burke, see David Bromwich, 'Edmund Burke, Revolutionist (1795),' *Yale Journal of Criticism* 4.1 (Fall 1990): 85–108.

4 William Godwin, *Enquiry Concerning Political Justice*, ed. F.E.L. Priestley (Toronto: U of Toronto P, 1946), 1:186. Priestley's text is based on the third edition of the *Enquiry* and includes notes on the variants from previous editions, as well as omitted chapters. Further citations to the *Enquiry* will be given in the text by volume and page number.

5 Reflections on the Revolution in France, 194–5.

6 The problematic of the signature complicates each formulation of the social contract and needs to be read each time in its specificity. For an exacting analysis of this issue in Rousseau, see Peggy Kamuf, *Signature Pieces: On the Institution of Authorship* (Ithaca: Cornell UP, 1988), especially chapter 2 'Contracting the Signature,' 42–78.

7 On the narrativity of the revolution, see, for example, Marlyn Butler, 'Telling It like a Story: The French Revolution as Narrative,' *Studies in Romanticism*, 28.3 (Fall 1989): 345–64. Butler is right to point out how often this passage from Burke is misquoted, with the word 'revolution' elided, as if to say that the revolution was the most astonishing *thing* that had ever happened.

8 Though Godwin in principle rejects the language of contracts altogether, he reserves a particular animus against the doctrine of the *original* contract.

9 Marquis de Sade, *The Complete Justine, Philosophy in the Bedroom and Other Writings*, trans. Richard Seaver and Austryn Wainhouse (New York: Grove, 1966), 312–13. For the French version, see *Oeuvres complètes de Marquis de Sade*, vol. 3, ed. Annie Le Brun and Jean-Jacques Pauvert (Paris: Pauvert, 1966), 508.

10 Slavoj Zizek appeals to this Sade text in his 'Formal Democracy and Its Discontents,' *American Imago* 48.2 (1991):181–98. But Zizek does so primarily in a wild psychoanalytic framework, virtually confining himself to the function of fantasy. For a suggestive reading of questions of law and

literature in Sade, see Thomas Keenan, 'Freedom, the Law of Another Fable,' *Yale French Studies* 79 (1991) [*Literature and the Ethical Question*]: 231–51.

11 On the emblematic history of the Black Act, see the excellent account by E.P. Thompson, *Whigs and Hunters: The Origins of the Black Act* (New York: Pantheon, 1975).

12 See the section by Bentham in 'The Fiction of an Original Contract,' in C.K. Ogden, *Bentham's Theory of Fictions* (London: Kegan, Paul et al., 1932), 123.

13 Jacques Derrida, *Memoires for Paul de Man*, trans. Cecile Lindsay, Jonathan Culler, and Eduardo Cadava (New York: Columbia, UP, 1986), 98. The French version of the passage can be found in *Mémoires pour Paul de Man* (Paris: Galilée, 1989), 102. The first formulation, that a promise cannot be kept, is one I recall from a seminar at Yale University on this same material. To the best of my knowledge, it does not occur in that form in Derrida's writings.

14 This essay will not be much preoccupied with questions of theatricality, though their analysis in Godwin would repay attention. From its opening sentence ('My life has for several years been a theatre of calamity') *Caleb Williams* is marked by a concern with representation and public staging. By way of summary, one could say that a principal goal of Godwin's politico-epistemological project is to overcome theatricality and all it represents to the extent that it is antithetical to the discourse of sincerity and truth he advocates.

15 For a complementary reading of the consequential temporality of a promise in novelistic narrative, see Deborah Esch, 'Promissory Notes: The Prescription of the Future in *The Princess Cassamassima*,' *American Literary History* 1.2 (Summer 1989): 317–38. There is more than just a structural similarity between the promises in James and Godwin. James's novel turns on his hero's promise to do whatever he is called upon to do by an anarchist organization, one which could well claim Godwin as a philosophical precursor.

16 On the promise and its status as a performative speech-act, see the classic analysis by J.L. Austin, *How to Do Things with Words*, 2d ed., (Cambridge: Harvard UP, 1975).

17 On the structure of the law as promise, see Paul de Man, 'Promises,' in *Allegories of Reading* (New Haven: Yale UP, 1979), 246–77. My approach to the Godwin and Inchbald material is informed by de Man's elaboration of a similar problematic in Rousseau's *Social Contract*.

18 William Godwin, *Caleb Williams*, ed. David McCracken (Oxford: Oxford UP, 1970), 1. Further citations will be given in the text, with the title abbreviated as *CW*.
19 Jacques Derrida makes this point in 'La démocratie ajournée,' in *L'Autre Cap* (Paris: Editions de Minuit, 1991), 110–11.
20 A number of essays on *Caleb Williams* have illuminating things to say, if sometimes only in passing, on the relation between Godwin's narrative and philosophical projects. See, for example, the opening pages of the chapter on Godwin and Wollstonecraft and the question of political fiction in Tilottama Rajan's *The Supplement of Reading* (Ithaca: Cornell UP, 1990), 167–94. Rajan is particularly illuminating on the hermeneutics internal to the novel, in their own terms and in the light of Godwin's explicit remarks in his essay 'A Choice in Reading.' See also Kevin Everest and Gavin Edwards, 'William Godwin's *Caleb Williams*: Truth and "Things As They Are,"' in *1789: Reading Writing Revolution*, ed. Francis Barker et al. (Essex: U of Essex, 1982), 129–46. This article attends to the complications of the problem of truth in Godwin, especially with regard to the rhetoric of persuasion, but does not take up the question of performative or non-constative language. On the dialectic of romance and history (or fiction and politics), see the thorough chapter on *Caleb Williams* in Eric Rothstein, *Systems of Order and Inquiry in Later Eighteenth-Century Fiction* (Berkeley: U of California P, 1975).
21 The history of political institutions that is the first section of Godwin's treatise is an unrelieved catalogue of crime. Thus Godwin, the philosopher of perfectibility, does not see political improvement issuing from the history of institutions. As we shall see, language becomes the privileged locus and the medium of amelioration.
22 Though almost a taboo subject some decades ago, there is now a rich literature on theories of the origins of language, especially in the eighteenth century. For Derrida's meticulous reading of Rousseau, see *Of Grammatology*, trans. Gayatri Spivak (Baltimore and London: Johns Hopkins UP, 1977). For superbly informed histories of ideas on the topic in general, see Hans Aarsleff, *The Study of Language in England, 1780–1860* (Minneapolis: U of Minnesota P, 1983) and the same author's *From Locke to Saussure* (Minneapolis: U of Minnesota P, 1982).
23 The fragment reads as follows: 'In returning to the origin of political right one finds that before there were leaders [*chefs*] there necessarily were laws. There had to have been at least one law in order to establish the public confederation; there had to have been a second to establish the

form of government; and the two suppose numerous intermediaries of which the most solemn and sacred was that by which one pledged [*s'engagea*] obedience to all the others. If laws exist before government and they are thus independent of it, government itself depends on laws because it is from them alone that it derives its authority, and far from being the author or the master, it is only the guarantor, the administrator or at most the interpreter' (*Oeuvres complètes de Jean-Jacques Rousseau* [Paris: Pléiade, 1964], 3:491; my translation).

24 It is for good reason that Nancy Armstrong begins her study of 'domestic' fiction in the English eighteenth- and nineteenth-century novel with a review of notions of the social contract. See the first chapter of her *Desire and Domestic Fiction: A Political History of the Novel* (New York: Oxford UP, 1987).

25 On the place of Burke in Godwin's thinking, see Marilyn Butler, 'Godwin, Burke, and *Caleb Williams,*' *Essays in Criticism* 3.3 (July 1982): 237–56.

26 The plot of *Caleb Williams* virtually calls out for a reading along the lines of Hegel's dialectic of master and slave in the most famous chapter of the *Phenomenology*. Not only does the Caleb-Falkland relationship exhibit the paradoxical reversal of master and slave in a fight to the death, very much as in Hegel, it does so quite explicitly at the level of consciousness. That consciousness could also be well examined in terms of the framework established by John Bender, who in his *Imagining the Penitentiary: Fiction and the Architecture of Mind in Eighteenth-Century England* (Chicago: U of Chicago P, 1987) demonstrates how closely the thematics and the actual social practice of imprisonment were tied to the empirico-utilitarian philosophy of mind articulated from Locke to Bentham. For reasons of economy, Bender omitted a chapter on Godwin from his text, but see his related essay 'Impersonal Violence: The Penetrating Gaze and the Field of Narration in *Caleb Wiliams,*' forthcoming in *Critical Reconstructions: The Relationship of Fiction and Life*, ed. Roger B. Menkle and Robert M. Polhemus (Stanford: Stanford UP, 1993).

27 See, however, Falkland's comments in an exchange with Caleb, when the latter is obliquely alluding to his possible crimes: 'Error, once committed, has a fascinating power, like that ascribed to the eyes of the rattle snake, to draw us into a second error' (*CW* 112–13). The irony that haunts Godwin's project in *Caleb Williams* is that if truth appears, it does so primarily in the mode of error, which is often to say, of fiction. One cannot overlook that all our knowledge is filtered through Caleb, who is literally the first to admit that he has been raised on romance and is an accomplished maker of fictions. For a comprehensive study of the 'error'

of romance in general, see Patrica Parker, *Inescapable Romance* (Princeton: Princeton UP, 1976).

28 Ronald Paulson goes so far as to say that 'without *A Simple Story* Holcroft's *Anna St. Ives* and Godwin's *Caleb Williams* would have been inconceivable' (*Representations of Revolution [1789–1820]* [New Haven: Yale UP, 1983], 230). Paulson is entirely correct to include a discussion of *A Simple Story* in a book on the representation of revolution, even though the text has nothing explicitly to do with the French Revolution. There is no doubt that Godwin knew Inchbald's text well, and some reason to believe that he aided Inchbald in the preparation of the second edition. Paulson follows the lead of Gary Kelly, who conducted the first thoroughgoing discussion of *A Simple Story* in his *The English Jacobin Novel, 1780–1805* (Oxford: Clarendon P, 1976). Kelly calls the novel 'pre-Jacobin' but also terms it 'the beginning and the basis for the English Jacobin novel' (92–3). He argues for its profound influence on Godwin, Holcroft et al.

29 Siobhan Kilfeather has explored the importance of Catholicism as an ideological frame and its bearing on Inchbald's narrative in an unpublished paper 'Roman Catholicism as the Symbolic Structure of *A Simple Story*.'

30 Elizabeth Inchbald, *A Simple Story*, ed. J.M.S. Tompkins (Oxford: Oxford UP, 1988), 21. Further citations will be given in the text with the title abbreviated as *SS*.

31 Terry Castle, in the fullest and most generous reading of the novel, remarks on the absence of the scene of betrothal in her *Masquerade and Civilization: The Carnavalesque in Eighteenth-Century English Culture and Fiction* (Stanford: Stanford UP, 1986), 304. The proof of this is the lapidary rendering of the scene as follows: 'He [Dorriforth/Lord Elmwood] turned to Sanford – then placing her by his own side, as the form of matrimony requires, gave this as a sign for Sanford to begin the ceremony. – On which, he opened the book, and – married them' (*SS* 192). And yet, as I will try to show, the traditional scene of betrothal may be omitted because it has already taken place, more than once, in different modes.

32 On this matter see the editor's note to *How to Do Things with Words*, 5. Though Urmson categorically describes it as a misquotation, he is perhaps forgetting the fact that *How to Do Things with Words* was based on lectures given in North America (at Harvard), where some marriage ceremonies do employ the 'I do' formula.

33 For our historical moment, the primacy of the marriage vow may seem a bit outdated, since now what often matters is not so much the marriage ceremony itself as the pre-nuptial agreement.

34 Terry Castle points to the importance of this absence in making the case for *A Simple Story* as a feminist text.

35 Perhaps the political character of *A Simple Story* surfaces most prominently in its thematics of education. Much like the novels of the other English Jacobins, Inchbald's text explores the parameters of individual liberty, and if Miss Milner, with all of her impulsiveness and impertinence, exceeds the bounds of ethical decorum, she will be exonerated after the fact by a virtual blanket excuse delivered in the final sentence of the novel:

> And Mr. Milner, Matilda's grandfather, had better have given his fortune to a distant branch of his family – as Matilda's father once meant to do – so he had bestowed upon his daughter

A PROPER EDUCATION

The coda of *A Simple Story* reads like a concrete instance of the general program of *A Vindication of the Rights of Woman*, which sees in education the principal medium for social acculturation and the locus of ethical *habitus*. Insofar as it is conspicuously only the women who have been deprived of the benefits of a proper education in Inchbald's novel, the plot emerges as 'incorrigibly' feminist, in Terry Castle's phrase. Though Inchbald and her fellow Jacobins inherit much from the Lockean tradition of bourgeois liberalism (largely still for them the 'heroic' phase of the bourgeoisie), they refuse to decide questions simply in terms of 'structure' or 'agency,' to invoke categories anachronistic to the period, and try to confront rather the specific entanglements of their mutual determination without assigning priority to either term. In this way, too, Inchbald's story is not so simple.

36 The complicated thematics and semiotics of inside and outside in the novel, enlisting the rhetoric of physiognomy to catalogue and correlate outer features and inner character, are partly enabled but also disabled by the language of promises whose external form need not coincide with the interiority of an intention. This is one aspect of a larger preoccupation in the novel with correlating the visual and the verbal or the visual (in the sense of what appears to be the case) and the realm of action, with attention to discrepancies between one's words and one's looks.

37 *Allegories of Reading*, 271

JEAN WILSON

Romanticism's Real Women

In the first part of *Don Quixote*, that brilliantly parodic work of romance so admired by the Romantic writers (Close 29–67), we are told the story of the student Grisóstomo, who dies of love for the 'cruel and ungrateful' Marcela, a proud, disdainful creature of 'matchless beauty.'[1] One of the best moments in this highly ironic account of unrequited love involves the unexpected appearance of the object of desire: 'Marcela herself,' so the text reads, 'more beautiful even than she was reputed to be' (103). The 'real' woman, then, whose beauty ironically, impossibly, exceeds all idealized portraiture, goes on to offer a defence, not of poetry, but of herself: 'I come to defend myself and to demonstrate how unreasonable all those persons are who blame me for their sufferings and for Grisóstomo's death' (104). Like Francesca in the fifth canto of Dante's *Inferno*, albeit for rather different reasons, Marcela shifts the blame for what has gone wrong away from herself, and like Francesca, though less explicitly, she blames literature, in this case, the absurd conventions of the amorous pastoral. The disastrous plot, Marcela insists, was one of Grisóstomo's own making; although she 'disillusioned him, he persisted,' and 'if he with all this plain-speaking was still stubbornly bent upon hoping against hope and sailing against the wind, is it to be wondered at if he drowned in the gulf of his own folly?' (105). The implications of this for Don Quixote's analogous relationship to Dulcinea are clear, especially given the self-proclaimed knight-errant's description of his own 'sweet enemy':

... her name is Dulcinea, her place of residence El Toboso, a village of La Mancha. As to her rank, she should be at the very least a princess, seeing that she is my lady and my queen. Her beauty is superhuman, for in it are realized all the impossible and chimerical attributes that poets are accustomed to give their fair ones. Her locks are golden, her brow the Elysian Fields, her eyebrows rainbows, her eyes suns, her cheeks roses, her lips coral, her teeth pearls, her neck alabaster, her bosom marble, her hands ivory, her complexion snow-white. (96)

While the speeches of both Francesca and Marcela reveal the potentially fatal consequences of life uncritically imitating art, readers of Dante's text are meant to recognize Francesca's blind complicity and beware the dangers of similar textual seductions, whereas in Cervantes, the woman herself sees through the process of idealization, meeting rhetoric with 'plain-speaking,' in the hope of 'disillusion[ing] with [her] words' (105). A resisting reader (Fetterley), as it were, she feels compelled to 'speak the truth' (104), to identify, expose, deflate, correct false notions about who she, in fact, is. Marcela's stance can be seen as protofeminist, in its opposition to the ultimately enslaving tendencies of Grisóstomo's idealizing discourse: 'My life is a free one, and I do not wish to be subject to another in any way' (106). Hers, in short, is the 'reasonable' voice of demystification, a voice that can be heard – and this brings me, more specifically, to my topic – in much prose fiction of the Romantic period.[2]

In 'the Romantic reading of gender,' as Margaret Homans, among others, has argued, woman is 'the other and the object,' 'associat[ed] with nature and exclu[ded] from speaking subjectivity' (*Women Writers* 12, 215). Goethe's *Die Leiden des jungen Werther* (*The Sorrows of Young Werther*) provides an example of this in Lotte, that lovely, ideal image of unaffected simplicity, the creation of the male hero's imagination. Werther writes:

Einen Engel! – Pfui! das sagt jeder von der Seinigen, nicht wahr? Und doch bin ich nicht imstande, dir zu sagen, wie sie vollkommen ist, warum sie vollkommen ist; genug, sie hat allen meinen Sinn gefangengenommen.

So viel Einfalt bei so viel Verstand, so viel Güte bei so viel Festigkeit, und die Ruhe der Seele bei dem wahren Leben und der Tätigkeit. –

Das ist alles garstiges Gewäsch, was ich da von ihr sage, leidige Abstraktionen, die nicht einen Zug ihres Selbst ausdrücken. (6:19)

An angel! – Nonsense! Everyone calls his loved one thus, does he not? And yet I cannot describe to you how perfect she is, or why she is so perfect; enough to say that she has captured me completely.

So much innocence combined with so much intelligence; such kindness with such firmness; such inner serenity in such an active life.

But all this is foolish talk – pure abstract words which fail to describe one single feature of her real person. (20)[3]

Werther's rhetorical strategy here – his insistence on the ineffability of Lotte's true nature – works precisely to establish the credibility of his own fanciful description of her 'real' person. There are, however, repeated indications that Werther's perception of Lotte is nothing more than a pretty picture of his own making. For instance, at the end of the letter immediately preceding the one just cited, Werther writes that he will avoid meeting the woman with whom an acquaintance of his is in love, for 'Es ist besser, ich sehe sie durch die Augen ihres Liebhabers; vielleicht erscheint sie mir vor meinen eigenen Augen nicht so, wie sie jetzt vor mir steht, und warum soll ich mir das schöne Bild verderben?' (19) ['It is better that I see her through the eyes of her lover; she might not appear to my own eyes, in reality, as I now see her; and why should I destroy the lovely image I already possess?' (20)]. Although the text achieves an ironic perspective on the subjectivity of the hero in a number of ways, evidence of what one might call the strategy of plain-speaking is found in Lotte's straightforward pronouncement to the tormented soul: '"Werther," sagte sie mit einem Lächeln, das mir durch die Seele ging, "Werther, Sie sind sehr krank"' (92) ['"Werther," she said with a smile that went deep to my heart, "Werther, you are very sick"' (124)].

If we turn to Goethe's *Faust*, we find a similar dynamic. In the scene 'Hexenküche' ('Witch's Kitchen'), Faust contemplates in the magic mirror the image of ideal feminine beauty,[4] and is thus primed to remake the first woman he meets in that image. Accordingly, he accosts Gretchen: 'Mein schönes Fräulein, darf ich wagen, / Meinen Arm und Geleit Ihr anzutragen?' (2605-6) ['My fair young lady, may I make free / To offer you my arm and company?']. To which Gretchen replies, 'Bin weder Fräulein, weder schön, / Kann ungeleitet nach Hause gehn' (2607-8) ['I'm neither fair nor lady, pray, / Can unescorted find my way']. This clear example of plain-speaking relates to the strong critique of romantic egotism and narcissistic desire offered throughout the play as a whole. Faust has already been told in no uncertain terms of the folly of his imaginative projections: 'Du gleichst dem Geist, den du begreifst, / Nicht mir!' (512-13) ['Close to the wraith you comprehend, / Not me!'], declares the Earth Spirit, who then abruptly vanishes, as if to emphasize his point, just as Gretchen quickly exits immediately after she has rebuffed Faust. However, beyond the irony of the fact that Faust is too busy inventing Gretchen to see her as she 'really is' – beyond, in other words, the sharp critique of romantic idealism – lie fundamental problems concerning the status of the 'real' in this text. For even as boundless male aspiring is put in critical perspective here – Faust's eternal striving after 'jenem schönen Bild' (3248) ['that fair image' of the feminine] – so the category of the 'real' in opposition to the ideal becomes problematic, particularly through its association with Mephistophelean cynicism: 'Du bist am Ende – was du bist' (1806) ['You are, all told – just what you are']. Thus, the disillusioning voice which exposes the trap of idealization risks entrapment of a different, but equally confining, sort.

Both works by Goethe contain striking examples of idealizing discourse. In Werther's first glimpse of his beloved, the woman is, quite properly speaking, framed. What Bakhtin has identified as the love idyll and the family idyll converge in the picture of Lotte amicably distributing bread to the children, an image[5] which indeed emphasizes, in Bakhtin's words, an 'utterly conventional simplicity of life in the bosom of nature' (226). Even more remarkable, perhaps, is the episode of Faust alone in Gretchen's 'clean little room' ['ein kleines reinliches Zimmer'], where we witness his imaginative transformation of her bedroom into a 'shrine':[6]

> Wie oft, ach! hat an diesem Väterthron
> Schon eine Schar von Kindern rings gehangen!
> Vielleicht hat, dankbar für den heil'gen Christ,
> Mein Liebchen hier, mit vollen Kinderwangen,
> Dem Ahnherrn fromm die welke Hand geküßt
> Ich fühl', o Mädchen, deinen Geist
> Der Füll' und Ordnung um mich säuseln,
> Der mütterlich dich täglich unterweist,
> Den Teppich auf den Tisch dich reinlich breiten heißt,
> Sogar den Sand zu deinen Füßen kräuseln.   (2697–2706)

> To think, about this patriarchal throne[7]
> Time and again has swarmed a throng of children!
> I seem to see my little darling stand
> As she, round-cheeked, with joys of Christmas thrilling,
> Devoutly kissed her grandsire's withered hand.

> I sense, dear girl, your very spirit
> Of plenitude and order all about,
> Benignly counseling domestic merit,
> Seeing the tablecloth all tidily spread out,
> Even the sanded floor in patterns fine.

In constructing this image of his beloved, it helps, of course, that Faust has exchanged with Gretchen only the few lines cited above. He is obviously carried away by his own pleasure in aesthetic creation, seduced by his own imaginative construct. This leads to the strong sense of a discrepancy between Faust's vision of Gretchen (i.e., Gretchen constructed as the embodiment of 'artless innocence')[8] and the 'real' woman (Gretchen as she 'actually is'). Ironically, however, our idea of who Gretchen 'really is' doubtless resembles the picture of innocence and simplicity that Faust paints for us – except that there is less likelihood of our recognizing the equally constructed nature of this idea of the 'real' Gretchen.

Both Romanticism's idealization of women and its self-critique in this regard figure centrally in another key work in the German tradition: E.T.A. Hoffmann's 'Der Sandmann' ('The Sandman'). From the beginning, the text sets up an opposition between word and picture,[9] between, for instance, the images the imaginative Nathanael creates and the rational explications of these images offered by the clear-sighted Clara, true to her name. Nathanael's preoccupation with the hideous image of the sandman begins in his childhood. Most evenings, Nathanael's father cheerfully entertained the children by telling them stories, but on certain occasions, when 'the sandman' came, he would simply put picture books in the children's hands and sit silently in his armchair. Significantly, the nights of storytelling were punctuated by the repeated extinguishing and relighting of the father's pipe, whereas the evenings spent looking at picture books typically involved the father's continuous smoking: he would sit 'stumm und starr' ['silently'] in his chair, 'und [er] blies starke Dampfwolken von sich, daß wir alle wie im Nebel schwammen' (332) ['blowing out billows of smoke till we all seemed to be swimming in clouds' (94)]. Obsessed with the image of the sandman, Nathanael finally finds himself 'festgezaubert' (335), 'spellbound,' captivated, transfixed (97) by the medusifying power[10] of a picture he himself has drawn; like Victor Frankenstein in Mary Shelley's tale – written the same year as 'The Sandman' (1816) – Nathanael becomes enslaved, the victim of his own creation.

At least this is Clara's interpretation. Clara, the bright-eyed, plain-speaking spokesperson for the 'real' world ['die wahre wirkliche Außenwelt'], banishes Nathanael's nightmarish images with a narrative of rational explanation:

Geradeheraus will ich es Dir nur gestehen, daß, wie ich meine, alles Entsetzliche und Schreckliche, wovon Du sprichst, nur in Deinem Innern vorging, die wahre wirkliche Außenwelt aber daran wohl wenig teilhatte ...
Natürlich verknüpfte sich nun in Deinem kindischen Gemüt der schreckliche Sandmann aus dem Ammenmärchen mit dem alten Coppelius, der Dir, glaubtest Du auch nicht an den Sandmann, ein gespenstischer, Kindern vorzüglich gefährlicher, Unhold blieb. Das unheimliche Treiben mit Deinem Vater zur Nachtzeit war wohl nichts anders, als daß beide insgeheim alchimistische Versuche machten, womit die Mutter nicht zufrieden sein konnte, da gewiß viel Geld unnütz verschleudert und obendrein, wie es immer mit solchen Laboranten der Fall sein soll, des Vaters Gemüt ganz von dem trügerischen Drange nach hoher Weisheit erfüllt, der Familie abwendig gemacht wurde. Der Vater hat wohl gewiß durch eigne Unvorsichtigkeit seinen Tod herbeigeführt ... (339–40)

I will frankly confess that in my opinion all the fears and terrors of which you speak took place only in your mind and had very little to do with the true, external world ...
Naturally, your childish mind associated the dreadful Sandman of the nurse's tale with old Coppelius – who would have been a monster particularly threatening to children even if you had not believed in the Sandman. The sinister business conducted at night with your father was probably nothing other than secret alchemical experiments, which would have displeased your mother because not only was a great deal of money being squandered, but, as is always the case with such experimenters, your father's mind was so imbued with an illusory desire for higher knowledge that he may have become alienated from his family. Your father, no doubt, was responsible for his own death through some carelessness or other ... (101)

The import of Clara's account closely resembles what Gary Kelly identifies as the moral of the series of confessional narratives in *Frankenstein*: 'passion, that inward imperative and sign of authentic selfhood in Romantic fiction, isolates the individual from society, destroys the domestic affections, and brings the individual to the edge of self-obliteration' (188).

Clara is the sensible, perceptive, even proto-Freudian figure,[11] whose penetrating gaze 'sees through' the gloomy dreamer Nathanael and all his wild imaginings. Indeed, she analyses things so masterfully that Nathanael accuses her brother of tutoring her in logic – and asks him to stop. The text seems at first sight to privilege Clara's perspective. The narrator, for instance, supports 'die verständige Clara' ['clear-thinking' Clara] in her rejection of Nathanael's disturbing proclivity for 'mystische Schwärmerei' (346) ['mystical nonsense' (107)]. Clara is justified in recoiling from Nathanael's poetic efforts, since they are 'düster, unverständlich, gestaltlos,' 'in der Tat sehr langweilig' (347) ['gloomy, unintelligible, and shapeless,' 'in truth ... really very boring' (108)]. The charge of banality is now properly levelled at the dreamer, rather than at the allegedly 'unimaginative' Clara (106) ['prosaisch' (345)],[12] especially given the fact that 'Die Gestalt des häßlichen Coppelius war ... in [Nathanaels] Fantasie erbleicht und es kostete ihm oft Mühe, ihn in seinen Dichtungen ... recht lebendig zu kolorieren' (347) ['The ugly image of Coppelius had faded in (Nathanael's) imagination, and it often cost him great effort to present Coppelius in adequate vividness in his writing' (108)]. When he does finally become carried away in reading his own poem, when he becomes terrified by something for which he has imaginative responsibility, Clara's no-nonsense reaction causes Nathanael to call her a 'lifeless automaton' (110) ['Du lebloses, verdammtes Automat!' (348)]: cold, unfeeling, limited. The irony, of course, lies in the fact that Nathanael proceeds to fall in love with an actual automaton: Olimpia, the perfectly beautiful, utterly mechanical robot, who neither sees nor speaks, but proves to be 'eine ... herrliche Zuhörerin' (357) ['a splendid listener' (118)], and becomes, in Nathanael's eyes, a *real* woman.

As Mary Jacobus has suggested, Olimpia, 'narcissistically invested with desire' (99), constitutes a 'demonic version' of the Pygmalion myth (95). Despite the text's exposure of the misogynistic underpinnings of this myth, critics have interpreted Nathanael's preference for Olimpia over Clara as 'a satire on the dullness of bourgeois women.'[13] This is possible if one adopts Nathanael's perspective, if, for instance, one reads the tale as a typical *Künstlernovelle*, which presents the dilemma of the artist in an unfeeling, utterly conventional world. In this reading, the temptress is in fact the philistine woman, who poses a 'threat to the artist's creativity,' in opposition to the vision of ideal beauty, which offers 'a source of artistic inspiration.'[14] According to this logic, Clara, upholder of repressive, bourgeois society, actually bears the responsibility for the tragic outcome of the story. She drives Nathanael to fall in love with a wooden puppet, and when he finally perceives what has happened, he loses himself in madness.[15]

However, as Jochen Schmidt has argued, this is a subversive *Künstlernovelle*, whose critique is directed primarily against romantic subjectivity itself, against the imprisoning myth of the autonomous poet, against the madness and destructiveness of solipsism.[16] Clara's voice emerges here as 'the explanatory voice' of reason,[17] which strives to curb romantic imaginings and counter the distortions of narcissistic projection. But this reading is itself not unproblematic. For if we simply reject Nathanael's discourse for that of Clara, we risk ignoring, as Jacobus puts it in a different context, 'the creepiness of [the] story'; we risk missing 'the uncanny altogether' (234). The problems that present themselves here, as in the case of Goethe, have to do with a dualistic structure that thwarts even potentially liberating impulses. However salutary it might initially appear, the opposition to male aspiring provided by the woman's voice in Hoffmann's tale ultimately relates to the restrictive antagonism of the haglike figure of Care in part 2 of *Faust*, 'an alien counter-force to the power of the spirit in its dynamic, creative activity,' indeed, a 'contrast-figure to the Feminine in the drama, a kind of negative ground to the projected goal of Faustian striving ... a destructive power analogous to Mephistopheles himself' (Hamlin 342–3).

It is all the more important to recognize, then, that a closer reading of Hoffmann's text reveals a privileging of neither Nathanael's nor Clara's perspective. Not only is Clara's position presented thoroughly ironically at the end of the tale, but the very picture of 'die verständige Clara' ['clear-thinking' Clara] is shown, in the narrator's quite lengthy address to the reader, to be a constructed image. In this extraordinary passage – which Freud, significantly, as Neil Hertz points out (304), ignores in his reading of 'The Sandman' – the 'image' ['Bild' (344)] of Clara becomes an issue for the narrator, who, like countless painters, poets, and other artists before him, admits to being struck by the woman's matchless, albeit unconventional, beauty. Immediately after suggesting that Clara's true nature is ineffable, the narrator proceeds to describe her – to paint his own portrait of a woman essentially characterized in terms of her 'hellen scharf sichtenden Verstand' (345)] ['clear and discriminating understanding' (106)]. Thus, by way of a complex and exceedingly ironic narrative strategy, the self-conscious literary text exposes the constructed nature of 'reasonable' psychological discourse. As Susanne Asche has argued, the text undermines a psychological reading that would absolutely separate madness from sanity; like the romantic discourse, the analytical narrative is problematized, even as it is staged (164–5). In the end, 'The Sandman' offers polar images of the feminine, only to expose something of the costs involved in all such figuration (Asche 170).

If we turn to women's writing in the Romantic period, we see the centrality of the same polarities of imagination and reason, sense and sensibility, not least, significantly enough, in the relevant literary criticism. For example, the critique of romantic idealism in *Frankenstein* has been explained in terms of Mary Shelley's own alleged inability to 'follow [her husband's mind] to the heights.' Robert Kiely writes that

> ... despite [Shelley's] efforts to form herself after her husband's image, common sense often intruded and made the task difficult ... Her novel, like almost everything else about her life, is an instance of genius observed and admired but not shared ... The arguments on behalf of idealism and unworldly genius are seriously presented, but the controlling perspective is that of an earthbound woman. (161)

Such an emphasis on Mary Shelley's inevitable – and inevitably limiting – 'womanly sense of how things are' (164) brings us back to the problem of Mephistophelean reductionism, a point worth considering, especially given the fact that Kiely's equation of the female voice with 'reasonable statement' (173) accompanies his insight into Victor Frankenstein's bold and patently unreasonable attempt 'to eliminate the need for woman in the creative act,' to produce offspring in isolation (164–5). Indeed, since much has been made of Frankenstein's presumptuous 'circumvention of the maternal,' particularly in feminist criticism of the novel,[18] an awareness of the widely divergent critical contexts within which this idea has been elaborated becomes of no little importance.

An all-too-easy acceptance of the discourse of plain-speaking proves problematic, for if woman as 'the other and the object' is excluded from speaking subjectivity, woman as the 'reasonable' voice of disillusionment risks becoming equally silent – risks never being allowed to say more than is commonsensical, realistic, 'probable' (Kiely 162). Instead of focusing on womanly common sense as the locus of the critique of imaginative projection in *Frankenstein*, we might turn to the new model of creativity suggested in the creature's words to the old man De Lacey, after the latter has received him, in the fullest sense of the word: 'You raise me from the dust by this kindness' (128). This response implicitly points to the fiasco of Frankenstein's display of narcissistic desire, and it acknowledges as an alternative the potentially creative power of reception.[19] Frankenstein's creation of the monster, his single, autonomous, individual 'act of self-assertion' (Poovey 131), constitutes a parody of the biblical myth of creation,[20] itself, as Northrop Frye and others remind us, 'intolerably patriarchal.'[21] Whereas God, however, after each day of carefully ordered labour, looks out at what he has made and '[sees] that it [is] good'[22] – whereas God 'blesses' his creatures and makes a place for them[23] – Frankenstein flees in 'horror and disgust' upon beholding the monster he has created (56–7). In her description of Frankenstein's utter failure as an author, Mary Shelley both articulates a devastating critique of phallic creativity and suggests new possibilities for the exercise of imaginative energies. Most importantly, the latter are shown to be especially required *after* the production of a new life.[24] In a significant gesture, then, when De Lacey invites the creature to share his story, and the wretch replies, 'You raise me from the dust by this kindness,' the focus at least temporarily shifts from an egocentric poetics to a poetics of reception.

Mary Shelley's 'profound ambivalence' about the creative imagination was shared by her mother before her,[25] Mary Wollstonecraft, author of *A Vindication of the Rights of Woman*. In her final work, *The Wrongs of Woman; or, Maria*, Wollstonecraft apparently 'sought to popularize the insights of *The Rights of Woman* by turning to a genre she felt confident women would read: the sentimental novel' (Poovey 95). Although critics generally applaud Wollstonecraft's conversion here to a new voice – to a speaking 'both for and as a woman'[26] – it is also possible to regard the apparent rejection of 'sense' as a dangerous 'fall' back into sensibility (Poovey 98). According to Mary Poovey, Wollstonecraft fails 'to establish a consistent or purposeful attitude toward the subject under consideration,' because of her difficulty in reconciling her intended political purpose[27] with the genre in which she has chosen to write (96). Marilyn Butler, albeit from a quite different perspective, agrees that this conflict between objective political program and subjective fictional style 'damaged Mary Wollstonecraft's coherence as a spokeswoman for her sex' (140). Indeed, Poovey's regret over the lack of a clear development of Wollstonecraft's 'revolutionary insights' (96) is matched by Ralph Wardle's similar desire for coherence, even though he would prefer to have it the other way around: to have a polished sentimental novel rather than an elaboration of what he calls 'the thesis of the book.'[28]

Wollstonecraft's narrative is as much an exploration of romantic idealism as it is a sustained attack on marriage laws and the general oppression of women. The two concerns come together in interesting ways, however, for the dangers of imagination, already considerable, as we know from the example of *Werther*, are rendered more acute in the case of women, 'who have no active duties or pursuits' to 'divert the mind' (Wollstonecraft 87). Maria indulges in reverie, but unlike the solitary walker[29] in Goethe's novel, she has not chosen to flee society; male tyranny has isolated her in the 'infernal solitude' (76) of her cell. The story of Maria's guard further underlines this difference, for Jemima, a poor soul like Rousseau 'sophisticated into misanthropy' (79), indeed achieves her moment of greatest independence as a solitary walker, but one of a very particular kind: a streetwalker or self-employed prostitute (109).

Unlike a dreamer such as Werther, Maria does not succumb to 'self-destructive solipsism,'[30] in part because hers is not the only story to be told. While Maria induces Jemima to 'swerve' from her stony resistance (83) and narratize her experience, Jemima calls Maria both down from 'the clouds' (77) and, in one possible ending of the novel, back to life (203). As Kelly has suggested, the life-stories of both characters possess an important structural complexity (38–42), and it would be a mistake, I believe, to privilege what Poovey calls the 'stark realism' of Jemima's 'radical, indeed feminist, story' (104) over what the same critic terms the 'sentimentalism' of Maria's 'romantic – and escapist – narrative' (107). Ultimately, the two narratives work only in tandem. Like Maria herself, who 'snap[s] the chain of ... theory' to explore what other forms of writing have to offer,[31] Wollstonecraft's novel turns to an exploration of the potentialities of narrative – specifically, to an exploration of the power of women's narrative.

Wollstonecraft encountered a good deal of difficulty in speaking 'with her newfound woman's voice' (she had, for instance, 'composed *The Rights of Men* in less than a month and *The Rights of Woman* in six weeks, but she spent a year working on *Maria*, only to leave the manuscript less than a third finished when she died').[32] However, as critics – such as Poovey – concerned with questions of gender and genre have shown, the resultant text bears witness to the complexities involved in women's writing which resists both the silence imposed by conventional figuration and the merely reasonable voice habitually called forth to challenge that silence. In *The Wrongs of Woman; or, Maria*, Wollstonecraft attempts to escape the established polarities of reason and unreason, sense and sensibility, in a significant effort that ultimately eludes a variety of simplifications and decidedly monological impulses.

This paper will conclude as it began, with a look at a work within the Romantic tradition, but not actually from the Romantic period: Christa Wolf's *Kein Ort. Nirgends* (*No Place on Earth*), written in 1977 in what was then East Germany. Following the Biermann affair in 1976 (that is, the expatriation of Wolf Biermann, criticism of this action on the part of a number of writers, including Christa Wolf, and subsequent reprisals against these critics of the government's decision), Wolf became preoccupied with what she saw as an analogous situation in the Romantic era. The Romantics – the women in particular – also perceived 'that they were outsiders,' 'living on the margins' of a society increasingly dominated by 'instrumental thinking,' 'though from a literary point of view they were at its centre.'[33] In her famous Büchner-Prize acceptance speech, Wolf declares that 'today, literature must be peace-research' (10), and her elaboration of what this might mean is reminiscent of the vision of the literary generation of 1800 in Germany (Kuhn 141), articulated, for example, in Novalis's call to 'romanticize' the world.

The Romantics, of course, did not fare well in an East German cultural context dominated by the Lukácsian realist aesthetic. An important aspect of Wolf's 'rediscovery of Romanticism' (Herminghouse), therefore, involves the rehabilitation of a disparaged writer such as Kleist. The issue of rehabilitation is of particular relevance in the wake of German reunification, a process fraught with ideological significance, which propelled Wolf into the centre of a controversy concerning her own literary, political, and, indeed, moral reputation (Anz). But this is a subject for another paper. Of interest to us here, along with the rehabilitation of Kleist, is the rediscovery of a forgotten woman writer of the Romantic period: Karoline von Günderrode, whose work appeared in a volume edited by Wolf in 1979.[34] Günderrode's writing also finds its way into Wolf's own text, however, for *No Place on Earth*, the fictional account of a meeting between Kleist and Günderrode at a gathering of friends in 1804, includes a good deal of authentic citation (Brandes). This intertextual strategy, combined with considerable innovation in narrative technique,[35] leads to a deconstruction of the dichotomy we have been tracing, in gendered terms, between romantic idealism and the disillusioning voice of reason.

In *No Place on Earth*, Wolf addresses what she elsewhere calls 'a diffuse sense of unease about anything hybrid, about fluid transitions, about things not being simply one thing or the other: friend or foe, male or female ...' ('Romanticism' 102). Her writing generally, as Marilyn Fries has noted, 'displays the searching tentativeness of its own creative process, engages its readers as interlocutory participants in this procedure, vacillates between question and assertion, requires a response' (23). In this case, questions posed explicitly throughout the text – and we are not always certain by whom – problematize traditional notions of authorial voice and procedures of figuration, particularly as they relate to gender relationships: 'Wer spricht?' (6) ['Who is speaking?' (4)]; 'Why is she keeping silent?' (115); 'What were we talking about?' (114); 'What was that you said?' (40); 'Is this woman beautiful?' (8); 'Now, how could that idea be expressed?' (18); 'What's that you say?' (18); 'Who is speaking?' (113) ['Wer spricht?' (113)]. The plot of the novel is minimal,[36] but it involves the brief coming together, at an afternoon gathering, of two characters, a man and a woman, both writers, each deeply troubled and alienated from society. 'Something akin to a lyrical drama is played out, except that it is narrated, and the silent monologues of the isolated main characters flow almost imperceptibly into each other and into spoken dialogue' (Dietrich 212–13).

A utopian moment of what Wolf refers to simply as 'touching,'[37] realized in formal as well as thematic terms, replaces the traditional plot of romantic love. The absence of a proper name in the title of the novel reflects the fact that the controlling subjectivity of the hero gives way here to a process of intersubjectivity – a process, furthermore, which subtly exposes the idealizing and objectifying practices upon which so-called elective affinities usually depend. In her relationships with Brentano and Savigny, Günderrode clearly functions as the idealized object of desire.[38] But even though she does occasionally resist with plain-speaking ('einem Mann hätten Sie das nicht gesagt' [36]) ['you would not have said that to a man' (34)], the trap of mere matter-of-factness is avoided, largely by means of a 'complex, constantly shifting narrative perspective' (Kuhn 146), which undermines dichotomies between subject and object, male and female, and brings Günderrode and Kleist together in mutual acknowledgment of common problems of creativity and reception. A radically interrogative work, *No Place on Earth* constitutes what Adrienne Rich has described as an act of re-vision: 'the act of looking back, of seeing with fresh eyes, of entering an old text from a new critical direction' (35). Writing as revision engages 'the subversive function of the imagination,' the aim being 'to question, to challenge, to conceive of alternatives' (43) –

264   Jean Wilson

indeed, to deconstruct 'false alternatives' (47), to reject dichotomous thinking altogether.

As part of the more general strategy of entering the text of Romanticism from a new critical direction, *No Place on Earth* repeatedly parodies, in Linda Hutcheon's sense of the term,[39] Goethe's *Sorrows of Young Werther*.[40] The triangle Werther/Lotte/Albert becomes Kleist/Günderrode/Savigny, with many important differences deriving from the most crucial change of all: the development of the woman's speaking subjectivity. Günderrode, for instance, asks herself why she has even come to the party in the first place (36/34) – a question conceivable only for Werther in Goethe's novel. Albert and Werther's discussion of suicide is replaced by the incident involving Günderrode's friends' discovery of the dagger she always carries with her, an incident rendered all the more significant given the historical Günderrode's suicide in 1806. Other instances of repetition with critical distance can be found in Günderrode's resistance to Kleist's customary method of picturing women and in Kleist's inability immediately to grasp or comprehend this woman (21/19). By way of contrast, Bettine Brentano is said at one point to understand her friend 'at once' (25) ['Die Bettine verstand sie gleich' (27)]. Perhaps the most striking parodic recall of Goethe concerns that famous scene at the window, in which Lotte, eyes searching the landscape as they fill with tears, lays her hand on Werther's and utters the single word 'Klopstock!' in a moment of apparently perfect communication. In Wolf's novel, this moment is brilliantly evoked, only to be ruptured, 'broken' (there is an extended play on the word 'Gebrechlichkeit'), in Günderrode's sudden and self-conscious shift to absolutely conventional conversation: 'Sie sollen schon hier gewesen sein?' (53) ['I hear that you have been in this area before?' (51)]. Plain-speaking, once again, but here, as throughout the text, Günderrode's words unmistakably form part of a discourse of powerful re-vision.

When the moment of 'touching'[41] finally does occur, it involves two equally reluctant and desiring participants. Günderrode has initiated a solitary walk, which, paradoxically, both is and is not solitary:

Sie bleiben stehn, drehn sich einander zu. Jeder sieht den Himmel hinter dem Kopf des andern. Das blasse spätnachmittagliche Blau, keine Wolkenzüge. Sie mustern sich unverhohlen. Nackte Blicke. Preisgabe, versuchsweise. Das Lächeln, zuerst bei ihr, dann bei ihm, spöttisch. Nehmen wir es als Spiel, auch wenn es Ernst ist. Du weißt es, ich weiß es auch. Komm nicht zu nah. Bleib nicht zu fern. Verbirg dich. Enthülle dich. Vergiß, was du weißt. Behalt es. Maskierungen

fallen ab, Verkrustungen, Schorf, Polituren. Die blanke Haut. Unverstellte Züge. Mein Gesicht, das wäre es. Dies das deine. Bis auf den Grund verschieden. Vom Grund her einander ähnlich. Frau. Mann. Unbrauchbare Wörter. Wir, jeder gefangen in seinem Geschlecht. Die Berührung, nach der es uns so unendlich verlangt, es gibt sie nicht. Sie wurde mit uns entleibt. Wir müßten sie erfinden. In Träumen bietet sie sich uns an, entstellt, schrecklich, fratzenhaft. Die Angst im Morgengrauen, nach dem frühen Erwachen. Unkenntlich bleiben wir uns, unnahbar, nach Verkleidungen süchtig. Fremde Namen, die wir uns zulegen. Die Klage in den Hals zurückgestoßen. Trauer verbietet sich, denn wo sind die Verluste?
Ich bin nicht ich. Du bist nicht du. Wer ist wir?
Wir sind sehr einsam. (108–9)

They stop and turn toward each other. Each of them sees the sky behind the other's head. The pale blue of late afternoon, little processions of clouds. They examine each other candidly, without reserve. Naked gazes. Self-abandonment, a tentative experiment. Smiles, first hers, then his, ironical. Let's pretend it's a game even if it's deadly earnest. You know it, I know it too. Don't come too close. Don't stay too far away. Conceal yourself. Reveal yourself. Forget what you know. Remember it. Masks fall away, superincrustations, scabs, varnish. The bare skin. Undisguised features. So that's my face. This is yours. Different down to the ground, alike from the ground up. Woman. Man. Untenable words. We two, each imprisoned in his sex. That touching we desire so infinitely does not exist. It was killed along with us. We should have to invent it. It offers itself to us in dreams, disfigured, horrible, grotesque. The fear in the pale morning light, after one wakes up so early. We remain unknowable to each other, unapproachable, craving disguises. The names of strangers in which we wrap ourselves. The cry of lament forced back into the throat. Grieving is forbidden, for what losses have we suffered?
I am not I. You are not you. Who is 'we'?
We are very alone. (108–9)

Tentatively, Günderrode and Kleist move towards the overcoming of objectification and alienation,[42] not in a wholly unified vision that would eradicate difference, but rather in the 'invention' of mutual subjectivity, which not only allows, but is predicated on the interrogative and the dialogical. True to its utopian title (Ryan 316), the novel offers a glimpse of a vision Wolf elsewhere describes as the process of 'learning to live with rather than against one another; not in fixed antinomies, but in fluid transitions, in productive alternatives ...' ('Romanticism' 102).

It is noteworthy that Wolf should be, to quote Simone de Beauvoir on Stendhal, 'at once so deeply romantic and so decidedly feministic' (280). To take one last example, Kleist's thoughts (in the form of 'narrated monologue')[43] upon overhearing something Günderrode has said to Bettine: 'Merkwürdig, wie diese Frau, auch wenn sie zu andern spricht, ihn zu meinen scheint, und daß sie ihm als die einzig Wirkliche unter Larven vorkommt' (65) ['Remarkable the way, even when this woman is speaking to other people, what she says appears to be intended for him, and that she seems to him the only person who is truly real in a horde of specters' (64)]. While the egotism of the male Romantic is parodied here, the context also reveals that the two outsiders, Kleist and Günderrode, do in fact communicate in an extraordinary way. Furthermore, Günderrode emerges undeniably as a 'truly real' person against a background of conventional social interaction – the 'real' woman no longer an objectification, however; no longer merely synonymous with the plain-speaking or commonsensical; and certainly no longer in simple opposition to the romantic. Ultimately, the answer to Mephistopheles' categorical statement 'Du bist am Ende – was du bist' ['You are, all told – just what you are'] becomes a series of questions, culminating in the intersubjective 'Wer ist wir?' ['Who is "we"?']. This, indeed, proves to be the point of Wolf's eloquent reading of Romanticism: a sensitive and highly critical probing of our own cultural 'realities.'

NOTES

1 Part 1, chapter 12, 86–90
2 This rational female voice challenges conventional associations of women with unreason. For a discussion of the relation between Romanticism and the traditionally 'gendered opposition of reason and emotion,' see Richardson.
3 Although I find intriguing the translation of 'Selbst' as 'real person' and the appearance of the phrase 'in reality' in the English version of the letter cited below, questions of translation lie beyond the scope of this paper.
4 Note that a certain distance is required to preserve the illusion: 'Ach! wenn ich nicht auf dieser Stelle bleibe, / Wenn ich es wage, nah zu gehn, / Kann ich sie nur als wie im Nebel sehn!' (3:2433–5) ['Alas! but when I fail to keep my distance, / And venture closer up to gaze, / I see her image dimmed as through a haze!']. All references to *Faust* are to line numbers, and translations are from Arndt, in the Hamlin edition.

5 Werther describes 'das reizendste Schauspiel' (21) ['the most charming scene' (22)].
6 See Arndt's translation of line 2708.
7 Faust is referring to an armchair ('Er wirft sich auf den ledernen Sessel am Bette').
8 Faust constructs Gretchen as the desirable opposite of himself. See lines 3007 ('Du gut's, unschuldig's Kind!' ['Dear artless innocence you!']) and 3102–3 ('Ach, daß die Einfalt, daß die Unschuld nie / Sich selbst und ihren heil'gen Wert erkennt!' ['That artlessness, that innocence should never / Respect itself and know its holy worth!']).
9 For a discussion of the complex relation between word and picture in the text, see Lehmann.
10 One of Coppelius's visits causes Nathanael to feel as though he has been 'turned into cold heavy stone' (99) ['Mir war es, als sei ich in schweren kalten Stein eingepreßt' (337)].
11 Prawer points out that Clara's 'rationalizing' anticipates Freud (301).
12 See also Clara's anticipation of Nathanael's reaction to her letter (340 [German], 101 [English]).
13 Sauer, 'Romantic Automata' 305n48. See Sauer, *Marionetten* 236, and the essays by Belgardt and Hayes.
14 I am quoting here the terms of Daemmrich's general discussion of the figure of the artist in Hoffmann's works (25–37).
15 In Wawrzyn's reading of the tale, Clara is identified as 'Agentin der bürgerlichen Gesellschaft,' whose 'Aufforderung zur Verdrängung' is itelf 'krankhaft' (136–40). According to Ellis, Clara ultimately 'deserve[s] th[e] abuse' of being called an automaton (9). She 'directly provokes every violent outburst' on Nathanael's part (10) and 'pushes him into madness' (11); she 'victimizes him ... by behaving like an automaton, and demanding that he be one too' (15).
16 Lilian Furst has discussed these issues with regard to the Romantic hero in general. See *Contours* 40–55, *Perspective* 97 ff., and her article 'The "Imprisoning Self."'
17 Schmidt speaks of 'Claras erklärende Stimme' (370).
18 See, for example, 'Bearing Demons: Frankenstein's Circumvention of the Maternal,' the fifth chapter of Margaret Homans' *Bearing the Word*. Although Homans cites Kiely (302n3), she does not respond to his argument as a whole.
19 The creature's words clearly echo the description of God's creation of man 'of dust from the ground' (Gen. 2.7). All references to the Bible are to the Revised Standard Version.

20 A number of details emphasize the parodic nature of Frankenstein's creative act. For instance, when the minuteness of the parts with which he intends to create a human being forms a hindrance to his speed, Frankenstein simply decides to make a creature of gigantic stature (52). This very haste (his feelings 'bore [him] onwards, like a hurricane') is in marked contrast to the carefully measured and controlled activity of God described in Gen. 1.1–2.3.

21 Frye 37. See also Parker 178 ff. Although there are, as Parker makes clear, 'not one but two creation stories in the Book of Genesis' (178), it is not necessary in this paper to consider the differences between the two accounts.

22 Gen. 1.4, 10, 12, 18, 21, 25, 31

23 Gen. 1.20–2.8, particularly 1.22, 1.28, 2.8

24 Indeed, the focus on Elizabeth as adopted, rather than biological, daughter of Frankenstein's parents helps to shape Shelley's incipient poetics of reception.

25 Poovey 129, 106. I am greatly indebted to Poovey's study, even though at times I take issue with its particulars, as noted below.

26 Jacobus 32. See also Poovey 79–81, 95.

27 That is, to show 'the misery and oppression, peculiar to women, that arise out of the partial laws and customs of society' (Wollstonecraft 73).

28 Wardle 299. It is telling that while Poovey consistently refers to the work as *Maria*, Wardle's short form is *The Wrongs of Woman*. Both critics highlight the part of the text of which they disapprove (in Poovey's case, the 'fall' into sensibility; in Wardle's case, the explicit political agenda).

29 I adopt the term from Rousseau's paradigmatic *Les Rêveries du promeneur solitaire* (*Reveries of the Solitary Walker*), published posthumously in 1782.

30 See Jacobus on the general result of 'the divorce of the Romantic imagination from its revolutionary impulse' (58).

31 Maria begins to read a theoretical analysis of the powers of the human mind, but, the narrator tells us, 'her attention strayed from cold arguments on the nature of what she felt, while she was feeling, and she snapt the chain of the theory' to read more narrative fiction (86). See Kelly on this (39).

32 Poovey 95

33 Wolf, 'Romanticism' 91–3. Wolf uses the term 'instrumental thinking' in her Büchner-Prize acceptance speech, 'Shall I Garnish a Metaphor with an Almond Blossom?' (4). For Wolf's essays in the original German, see *Die Dimension des Autors*. Parenthetical references to *Kein Ort. Nirgends* with

page numbers separated by a solidus are first to the German text and then to the English translation.
34 Karoline von Günderrode, *Der Schatten eines Traumes: Gedichte, Prosa, Briefe, Zeugnisse von Zeitgenossen*, ed. Christa Wolf (Darmstadt: Luchterhand, 1979)
35 For an illuminating discussion of narrative mode in *Kein Ort. Nirgends*, see Dietrich. Kuhn provides an extremely useful general study in English of Wolf's work.
36 Something Wolf says with regard to her novel *Kassandra* applies here as well. 'Questions' – above all questions concerning an androcentric culture – 'constitute the internal "plot" of the book' ('Discussion' 109).
37 Wolf develops this concept in 'Berührung: Maxie Wander,' *Die Dimension des Autors* 196–209. See also Lennox 71 and Kuhn 13–14, 171–2.
38 See Wolf's essay on Günderrode, 'Der Schatten eines Traumes: Karoline von Günderrode – ein Entwurf,' *Die Dimension des Autors* 511–71 (particularly 532–3). See also Kuhn 58–62.
39 Hutcheon redefines parody as 'repetition with critical distance, which marks difference rather than similarity' (6).
40 Although the parody is by no means overt, the specific mention of *Werther* (48/47) is revealing.
41 Note the physical touching which precedes this moment (98, 106 / 97, 105).
42 See Kuhn's discussion of Wolf's relation to Marxist theory (4–6).
43 See Dietrich 214 and Kuhn 146–7.

WORKS CITED

Anz, Thomas, ed. *'Es geht nicht um Christa Wolf.' Der Literaturstreit im vereinten Deutschland*. München: Spangenberg, 1991.
Asche, Susanne. *Die Liebe, der Tod und das Ich im Spiegel der Kunst: Die Funktion des Weiblichen in Schriften der Frühromantik und im erzählerischen Werk E.T.A. Hoffmanns*. Königstein/Ts.: Hain, 1985.
Bakhtin, M.M. *The Dialogic Imagination: Four Essays*. Ed. Michael Holquist. Trans. Caryl Emerson and Michael Holquist. Austin: U of Texas P, 1981.
Beauvoir, Simone de. *The Second Sex*. Trans. H.M. Parshley. 1952. New York: Vintage-Random House, 1974.
Belgardt, Raimund. 'Der Künstler und die Puppe: Zur Interpretation von Hoffmanns *Der Sandmann*.' *German Quarterly* 42 (1969): 686–700.
Brandes, Ute. 'Quotation as Authentication: *No Place on Earth.*' *Responses to*

Christa Wolf: Critical Essays. Ed. Marilyn Sibley Fries. Detroit: Wayne State UP, 1989. 326–48.

Butler, Marilyn. 'The Woman at the Window: Ann Radcliffe in the Novels of Mary Wollstonecraft and Jane Austen.' *Gender and Literary Voice.* Ed. Janet Todd. New York: Holmes & Meier, 1980. 128–48.

Cervantes, Miguel de. *Don Quixote.* Trans. Samuel Putnam. 1949. New York: The Modern Library-Random House, n.d.

Close, Anthony. *The Romantic Approach to 'Don Quixote.'* Cambridge: Cambridge UP, 1977.

Daemmrich, Horst S. *The Shattered Self: E.T.A. Hoffmann's Tragic Vision.* Detroit: Wayne State UP, 1973.

Dietrich, Linda. 'Appropriating Romantic Consciousness: Narrative Mode in Christa Wolf's *Kein Ort. Nirgends.*' *Echoes and Influences of German Romanticism: Essays in Honour of Hans Eichner.* Ed. Michael S. Batts, Anthony W. Riley, and Heinz Wetzel. New York: Lang, 1987. 211–23.

Ellis, John M. 'Clara, Nathanael and the Narrator: Interpreting Hoffmann's *Der Sandmann.*' *German Quarterly* 54 (1981): 1–18.

Fetterley, Judith. *The Resisting Reader: A Feminist Approach to American Fiction.* Bloomington: Indiana UP, 1978.

Fries, Marilyn Sibley. 'Locating Christa Wolf: An Introduction.' *Responses to Christa Wolf: Critical Essays.* Ed. Marilyn Sibley Fries. Detroit: Wayne State UP, 1989. 23–54.

Frye, Northrop. *Creation and Recreation.* Toronto: U of Toronto P, 1980.

Furst, Lilian R. *The Contours of European Romanticism.* London: Macmillan, 1979.

– 'The "Imprisoning Self": Goethe's Werther and Rousseau's Solitary Walker.' *European Romanticism: Literary Cross-Currents, Modes, and Models.* Ed. Gerhart Hoffmeister. Detroit: Wayne State UP, 1990. 145–61.

– *Romanticism in Perspective.* 2d ed. London: Macmillan, 1979.

Goethe, Johann Wolfgang von. *'The Sorrows of Young Werther' and 'Novella.'* Trans. Elizabeth Mayer and Louise Bogan. 1971. New York: Vintage-Random House, 1973.

– *Werke. Hamburger Ausgabe in 14 Bänden.* Ed. Erich Trunz. München: Beck, 1981–6.

Hamlin, Cyrus, ed., and Walter Arndt, trans. *Faust.* By Johann Wolfgang von Goethe. New York: Norton, 1976.

Hayes, Charles. 'Phantasie und Wirklichkeit im Werke E.T.A. Hoffmanns, mit einer Interpretation der Erzählung "Der Sandmann."' *Ideologiekritische Studien zur Literatur.* Ed. Volkmar Sander. Frankfurt am Main: Athenäum, 1972. 169–214.

Herminghouse, Patricia. 'The Rediscovery of Romanticism: Revisions and Reevaluations.' *Studies in GDR Culture and Society 2.* Ed. Margy Gerber et al. Washington, D.C.: UP of America, 1982. 1–17.
Hertz, Neil. 'Freud and the Sandman.' *Textual Strategies: Perspectives in Post-Structuralist Criticism.* Ed. Josué V. Harari. Ithaca: Cornell UP, 1979. 296–321.
Hoffmann, E.T.A. 'Der Sandmann.' *Fantasie- und Nachtstücke.* Ed. Walter Müller-Seidel. München: Winkler, 1960. 331–63.
– *Tales of E.T.A. Hoffmann.* Trans. Leonard J. Kent and Elizabeth Knight. 1969. Abridged ed. Chicago: U of Chicago P, 1972.
Homans, Margaret. *Bearing the Word: Language and Female Experience in Nineteenth-Century Women's Writing.* Chicago: U of Chicago P, 1986.
– *Women Writers and Poetic Identity: Dorothy Wordsworth, Emily Bronte, and Emily Dickinson.* Princeton: Princeton UP, 1980.
Hutcheon, Linda. *A Theory of Parody: The Teachings of Twentieth-Century Art Forms.* New York: Methuen, 1985.
Jacobus, Mary. *Reading Woman: Essays in Feminist Criticism.* New York: Columbia UP, 1986.
Kelly, Gary. *English Fiction of the Romantic Period 1789–1830.* London: Longman, 1989.
Kiely, Robert. *The Romantic Novel in England.* Cambridge: Harvard UP, 1972.
Kuhn, Anna K. *Christa Wolf's Utopian Vison: From Marxism to Feminism.* Cambridge: Cambridge UP, 1988.
Lehmann, Hans-Thies. 'Exkurs über E.T.A. Hoffmanns "Sandmann." Eine texttheoretische Lektüre.' *Romantische Utopie – Utopische Romantik.* Ed. Gisela Dischner and Richard Faber. Hildesheim: Gerstenberg, 1979. 301–23.
Lennox, Sara. 'Trends in Literary Theory: The Female Aesthetic and German Women's Writing.' *German Quarterly* 54 (1981): 63–75.
Parker, Patricia. *Literary Fat Ladies: Rhetoric, Gender, Property.* London: Methuen, 1987.
Poovey, Mary. *The Proper Lady and the Woman Writer: Ideology as Style in the Works of Mary Wollstonecraft, Mary Shelley, and Jane Austen.* Chicago: U of Chicago P, 1984.
Prawer, S.S. 'Hoffmann's Uncanny Guest: A Reading of Der Sandmann.' *German Life and Letters* ns 18 (1964–5): 297–308.
Rich, Adrienne. 'When We Dead Awaken: Writing as Re-Vision.' *On Lies, Secrets, and Silence: Selected Prose 1966–1978.* New York: Norton, 1979. 33–49.
Richardson, Alan. 'Romanticism and the Colonization of the Feminine.' *Romanticism and Feminism.* Ed. Anne K. Mellor. Bloomington: Indiana UP, 1988. 13–25.

Ryan, Judith. 'Twilight Zones: Myth, Fairy Tale, and Utopia in *No Place on Earth* and *Cassandra.*' *Responses to Christa Wolf: Critical Essays.* Ed. Marilyn Sibley Fries. Detroit: Wayne State UP, 1989. 312–25.

Sauer, Lieselotte. *Marionetten, Maschinen, Automaten: Der künstliche Mensch in der deutschen und englischen Romantik.* Bonn: Bouvier, 1983.

– 'Romantic Automata.' *European Romanticism: Literary Cross-Currents, Modes, and Models.* Ed. Gerhart Hoffmeister. Detroit: Wayne State UP, 1990. 287–306.

Schmidt, Jochen. 'Die Krise der romantischen Subjektivität: E.Th.A. Hoffmanns Künstlernovelle "Der Sandmann" in historischer Perspektive.' *Literaturwissenschaft und Geistesgeschichte: Festschrift für Richard Brinkmann.* Ed. Jürgen Brummack et al. Tübingen: Niemeyer, 1981. 348–70.

Shelley, Mary. *Frankenstein; or, The Modern Prometheus.* New York: Signet-NAL, 1983.

Wardle, Ralph M. *Mary Wollstonecraft: A Critical Biography.* 1951. Lincoln: U of Nebraska P, 1966.

Wawrzyn, Lienhard. *Der Automaten-Mensch.* Berlin: Wagenbach, 1976.

Wolf, Christa. *Die Dimension des Autors: Essays und Aufsätze, Reden und Gespräche 1959–1985.* Frankfurt am Main: Luchterhand, 1990.

– 'From a Discussion at Ohio State University: A Conversation with Christa and Gerhard Wolf.' *The Fourth Dimension: Interviews with Christa Wolf.* Trans. Hilary Pilkington. Introd. Karin McPherson. London: Verso, 1988. 103–15.

– *Kein Ort. Nirgends.* 1979. Frankfurt am Main: Luchterhand, 1981.

– *No Place on Earth.* Trans. Jan van Heurck. New York: Farrar, Straus and Giroux, 1982.

– 'Romanticism in Perspective: A Conversation with Frauke Meyer-Gosau.' *The Fourth Dimension: Interviews with Christa Wolf.* Trans. Hilary Pilkington. Introd. Karin McPherson. London: Verso, 1988. 90–102.

– 'Shall I Garnish a Metaphor with an Almond Blossom?' Büchner-Prize acceptance speech. Trans. Henry J. Schmidt. *New German Critique* 23 (Spring/Summer 1981): 3–11.

Wollstonecraft, Mary. *The Wrongs of Woman; or, Maria.* In *'Mary' and 'The Wrongs of Woman.'* Ed. Gary Kelly. Oxford: Oxford UP, 1976. 69–204.

Coda

ASHA VARADHARAJAN

Romanticism Unbound

I find myself in the curious position of offering a concluding cadence to essays which deliberately eschew the temptations of harmony for the risks of productive dissonance. I have made, then, a promise I cannot hope to keep, that I perhaps never intended to keep, or one in the very keeping of which I inadvertently betray. How, then, can I address the promise of these essays or, if I may be pardoned one more metaphoric indulgence, cash in the promissory notes that constitute this text of criticism? I write this piece in a shared spirit of resistance to resounding finales and in response to David Clark's hope that the unbinding of the *book* of criticism might open the volume into the *texts* of Romanticism and of 'theory.'[1]

Contemporary critical discourse is, of course, no stranger to the trajectory of unfulfilled desire, to the gap between intention and execution, or to the inevitability of delay or deferral that I invoke here. I resort to a playful beginning of this sort in order to register the anxiety of Paul de Man's influence or to admit, like the essays in this volume do, to being haunted by his presence. It seems important to indicate this not entirely welcome (at least to my mind) presence because de Man, more than anybody else, perhaps, has been responsible for the production of a 'deconstructive epistemology of perennial disaccommodation' (Radhakrishnan 127). In other words, the disjunction between thinking and willing consequent upon the constituted character of the post-structuralist subject has made it impossible to think a productive relation between the epistemological and the ethico-political. Instead, the task of deconstructive criticism has been to 'highlight ... the profoundly asymmetrical and "interrupted"' (Radhakrishnan 127) character of that relationship.

De Man's readings painstakingly demonstrate the 'necessary exclusion' which forms 'the very originating locus of such insight as they [the readings] achieve or illumination as they can provide' (Godzich 'Introduction' xxi). This exclusion contributes the blindness upon which every insight depends. De Man's reading practice attempts to embody his claim that 'philosophical knowledge can only come into being when it is turned back upon itself' (de Man 16). The self-enclosed quality of his essays reflects their underlying contention: the materiality of the object with which knowledge must come to terms is its own status as representation. Knowledge thus becomes its own object instead of establishing a relation between self and world, while the opacity of the world attests to the '"nothingness of human matters"' (18). De Man writes that the moment of undecidability that thought encounters involves the realization that 'consciousness does not result from the absence of something, but consists of the presence of a nothingness' (18). Consciousness, in de Man, uses objects as mirrors in which to gaze upon its self. Consequently, de Man privileges knowledge which 'knows and names itself as fiction' (18), which is armed with the peculiar courage of a vision that is driven to confront 'the failure [that] lies in the nature of things' (18). I have dwelt on this familiar de Manian posture in order to point out the futility and political quietism of a thought which ceaselessly exposes its own aporias.

The blindness that is inextricable from insight should be cause, not for meditations on the void, but for self-examination which gives 'human matters' their due and holds itself accountable to the world that its blindness fails. I believe that this project reads de Man against the grain. The essays certainly share deconstructive criticism's humble insistence on and scrupulous attention to the blindness which produces insight, but do not, in the process, suggest that the texts of Romanticism are no more than allegories of unreadability. Instead, as Tilottama Rajan's call for a 'phenomenological deconstruction' ('The Future of Deconstruction in Romantic Studies' 131) suggests, criticism which bears testimony to the richness and heterogeneity of history and materiality rather than one which assumes the intractability of reality in advance might actually be possible. If I may draw a different conclusion from Ian Balfour's trenchant awareness that the 'dream of theory always risks being dissipated by the singularity and unpredictability of any truly political event or act of reading,' then, 'theory,' by the same token, might acquire the promise of concretion. It seems appropriate, now, to demonstrate how this volume negotiates the traffic between proximity and distance, between a becoming modesty that refuses totalizations and an imperious refusal *of* position in the name of a 'perilous epistemology' (Radhakrishnan 148).

The invocation of de Man, as I have been suggesting, is unavoidable in the context of a field which he made his particular prerogative, but I, for one, cannot help wondering whether his focus on the destruction of the knowing subject did not serve, paradoxically enough, precisely to restore the numinosity of the Romantic self-made-text, to render it unassailable *because* 'Romanticism theorizes and examines itself from within' ('Introduction'). There is room, therefore, for an examination of the politics of reception which drew a certain kind of post-structuralist critic to the texts of Romanticism. If, in other words, de Man demonstrated that insight and agency were always at odds, did his version of Romantic non-identity divert attention from the political affiliations and 'democratic' aspirations of the Romantics?

De Man's representation of critical consciousness bears a curious affinity to the poetic self constructed in and by Romantic lyric. In Rajan's terms, lyric consciousness exempts itself from the travails of the world. This exemption invites further scrutiny because de Man's insistence on the failure that lies in the nature of things reproduces Romantic disillusionment with the unpredictability of history, with its failure to align itself with the cause of revolution. De Man's rewriting of the crisis of the post-structuralist subject as the absence of the egotistical sublime explicitly severs the practice of poetry from commitment to political revolution. After all, a self that becomes 'the agent of its own instability' (de Man 19) or that recognizes 'that the very basis on which the subject acts is putative, not real' (Radhakrishnan 127) is hardly likely to acquiesce to the exigencies of political subjectivity, to the 'authority of names, identities, and constituencies' (Radhakrishnan 127).

This brief recapitulation of the dimensions of de Man's contribution to critical methodology bears some relation to Frances Ferguson's essay 'Romantic Studies,' which appeared recently in *Redrawing the Boundaries: The Transformation of English and American Literary Studies* (1992). While it is not my intention, as it is Ferguson's, to characterize or even categorize 'the arguments that underlie the disputes [within Romanticism]' (Ferguson 100), I think it might be useful to make discriminations (in the spirit of Lovejoy!) that situate my own invocation of de Man vis-à-vis Ferguson's. These discriminations centre on Ferguson's reconsideration of the problematic of 'the political waged through implicit, aesthetic means' (104).

My retrospective account of the essays in this volume articulates their recasting of the relationship between form and content, of what Ferguson describes as the struggle between Abrams's attempt to discern the implication of politics (in the guise of the French Revolution) in the very structures of Romantic emotion and McGann's refusal to countenance a politics conducted through formal means (105). To my mind, the essays' sensitivity to Romanticism's self-consciousness about its own practice not only demonstrates the inadequacy of what Ferguson, improving upon McGann, describes as 'the formal version of politics [which] continually tends toward the political masquerading as the apolitical' (105), but discerns an equal and opposite danger, that the apolitical might masquerade as the political. In other words, my (unoriginal) charge of political quietism against de Man's critical methodology insists upon the disturbing character of an epistemology whose invulnerability stems from its *radical*, indeed ontological, challenge to all epistemologies. De Man's position, precisely *because* of its Kantian deference to objects which serve as guarantees of nothing other than their own substantial nature (Ferguson 109), applauds a retreat into self-consciousness, as I have been arguing. This point becomes clearer in Ferguson's initial delineation of Geoffrey Hartman's desire to 'epistemologize ontology' as an 'interpenetration between the ways in which one knows and the objects that one can know' (114). 'Interpenetration,' as the progress of Ferguson's argument bears out, is the operative word, because what begins as an attempt to establish a relation between perception and object turns into a fascination, exactly, with the *'appearances* of things' (115. Emphasis mine). In other words, perception becomes its own object. It is this state of affairs that prompts Ferguson's conclusion that Hartman's phenomenology identifies itself with 'the renunciation of claims to knowledge' (117) and my claim that there may not be much to choose between Hartman (the appearances of things as the object of the quest) and de Man (the opacity of objects) after all. I contend that this volume does not need to renounce its claim to knowledge in order to recognize the contingency of such claims.

One more set of discriminations might provide a useful context for the comments I make on grappling with materiality in the interests of political intervention. Ferguson concludes her essay with an illuminating discussion of the deconstructive position as embodied in de Man's contentions regarding the materiality of the letter or the aesthetic as materiality per se (117–18), in the manner in which rhetorical tropes become objects in themselves (117), or in his interest in the ability of consciousness to impersonate thingness (117). The discussion, however, becomes less convincing when Ferguson effects (on Eagleton's own authority) a convergence between Marxist and deconstructive versions of materialism. She locates this convergence in both versions' insistence on concrete particularity. This move, as Ferguson herself acknowledges in her sceptical allusion to a 'thoroughly material world' (122), seems to offer a reductive view of particularity as residing in objects (linguistic or empirical) per se rather than in the particular set of conditions which produce them as objects as such. Moreover, such a move does not account for what Marxist discourse would perceive as the acceptance of reification as the only possible reality. While the absence of thought might have redemptive implications (in the power to imagine the quiddity of things perhaps) for the Romantic poet trapped in self-consciousness, the impersonation of thingness could also imply, as a Marxist critic might argue, the displacement of the reification of the world upon the self or even an abdication from responsibility for that reification.

Ferguson's statement that 'structures of human understanding continually supplement ... objects and make the material count' (109) offers a nice transition to my commentary on the essays that precede mine. The legacy of Romanticism, in Ferguson's view, 'demonstrates how far the nonmaterial extends' (122); these essays, in my view, pay equal attention to how far the material extends. I shall justify this claim in detail in due course; for the moment, however, I want to touch upon Rajan's call for a 'phenomenological deconstruction' whose coordinates, I would suggest, are different from Ferguson's; the persuasive accounts by Wall, Wilson, and Bewell of the masculinity of Romantic self-consciousness that, for all its doubts and self-division, effectively excludes and expropriates the feminine and is far from innocent of the material dimensions of sexual power; Balfour's interest in the performative dimensions of linguistic and social practice as well as Clark's concern with the political and emancipatory possibilities of meta-physical thought and language, who avoid lapsing, as de Man does, into disquisitions on the ontological status of language itself (Ferguson 117); and, finally, Goellnicht's focus on the historical and social factors which produce poetic selves and texts as well as Kneale's desire to negotiate the interface of history and textuality without surrendering to either, which hold out hope for reading Romanticism as an active, if fallible, engagement with the world rather than a retreat from it. In acceding to Ferguson's view that 'trying to have objects without intentions turns out to be having no objects at all (122), the essays intervene in the text of Romanticism not only to supplement its reading of itself, to challenge the unity of its self-perception, but also to make its charting of the relationship between aesthetic experience and the social world *matter*.

The singular achievement of this volume, in my view, is its focus on the *determinate* conditions rather than the inherent limits of the possibility of knowledge and of selfhood. Donald Goellnicht's essay admirably exposes the material conditions and consequences of fashioning poetic selves as discursive effects. Goellnicht attributes the instability of Keats's poetic self to the 'ideological projects' of the latter's critics rather than to any awareness Keats might have had of his own nothingness. By transforming Keats's perceived envy of the Great Tradition into 'an oppositional social perspective from within the historical structure,' Goellnicht reinforces Alan Liu's conception of the '"self" as the register of a dynamic *becoming* of social responsiveness' (173). This strategy enables Goellnicht to tease out the subtle relations between self, text, and context as well as to demonstrate that the dilemma of self or the limits of knowledge are never merely inherent and always overdetermined. What makes this essay more than an exercise in sociological criticism is the attention it pays to the politics of literary production and reception. The careful reading of the rhetoric which animated the periodical reviews of the nineteenth century elicits the age's perceived interconnections among loose morals, loose language, the lower orders, and the en-gendering of the poetic profession as effeminate and sensuous indulgence. Goellnicht, however, does not confine himself to recounting the policing of untrammelled genius; he is equally concerned to show that the fragile and vulnerable Romantic self of de Man's imagining still wielded power unconscionably in its colonization of 'feminine' territory as well as in its representation of rustic simplicity. What is involved here, therefore, is more than the familiar deconstructive practice of laying bare the constitutive contradictions that inhabit constructions of self and world – these contradictions are related to a specific historical context and to the battle in which official culture staved the forces of 'anarchy,' of political revolution.

To return to the self-reflexive nature of the Romantic text, its 'containment' of multitudes in the act of self-division might preclude the consideration of the distinction between difference and dissidence, between a movement which (in Foucauldian terms) generates its own resistance (thereby controlling the terms of that resistance) and one which actively incorporates, rules, or exploits the *conflicting* claims of class, gender, or race. Given my adumbration, thus far, of the essays' sensitivity to the political dimensions of subjectivity and poetic production, I want to register my surprise at the Introduction's benign characterization of the revelation of the Romantic text's 'multiple strands of significance.' While Clark and Goellnicht are right to suggest that these strands 'do not build towards a synthesis,' they seem to mitigate the radical nature of their enterprise when they suggest that these strands 'co-exist.' Since the essays have been instrumental in disclosing the highly conflictual domain that is the Romantic text, it seems important to emphasize the tension between as well as the multiplicity of these strands of significance. In short, I want to suggest that this collection is both radically different and differently radical.

Jean Wilson's interest in Romanticism's 'real women' investigates the possibility of dissidence within the closed circuit of narcissistic desire that informs the male Romantic text. Her essay rightly rejects the false and dichotomous choice between idealizing imagination and disillusioning reason with which the female subject is presented in favour of a more nuanced transaction between masculine and feminine selves. Wilson calls for a poetic (and gendered) subjectivity that is 'predicated on the interrogative and the dialogical' rather than on the static opposition of antinomial subjects; worse, on a system of exchange that continues to produce 'woman' as the object of exchange.

It seems to me, however, that the displacement or unsettling of established polarities is necessary but not sufficient, while the desirability of intersubjectivity does not connote its existence since the process of othering to which the Romantic text subjects the feminine already precludes that possibility. As for the (female) anti-Romantic text, the interrogation of the 'efficacy of the monological' seems incomplete without the concomitant rehearsal of the material conditions under which the reversibility or mutual qualification of oppositions might become a reality. These are early days yet to surrender opposition or resistance to dialogical paradigms of exchange between self and other. Still, Wilson's attempt to write the self as fluid, transgressive, fragmentary, and becoming offers a much-needed utopian or affirmative dimension to reconstituted selves.

Alan Bewell's essay assumes the vexed and crucial (if unfashionable) task of unsettling established polarities in favour of a re-definition of masculinity through a careful examination of Keats's stylistic idiosyncrasies. Bewell's attempt to institute a dynamic and fluid notion of identity and sexuality continues, as it should, to raise perhaps unanswerable questions. Is 'stylistic cross-dressing' more disturbing than it seems because it relinquishes the specificity of sexual difference and is not readily distinguishable from the determinedly masculine masquerading as the radically undecidable? In other words, more work needs to be done, perhaps, on how the process of de-essentializing masculinity and femininity can avoid de-sexualizing either.[2] Indeed, cross-dressing can begin to resemble a kind of androgyny in which the stable opposition between the conventional codes 'masculine' and 'feminine' is merely transcended rather than actively displaced. Keats's continued use of floral imagery can just as easily be construed as the appropriation of the female voice, however conventional women's writing which used such imagery might have been. Despite his awareness of Keats's misogyny, Bewell runs the risk of suggesting that Keats's questionable or self-questioning masculinity was more radical than comparable female poets' efforts to make the floral domain their own. Might it be possible to read the floral imagery of female poets as an active attempt to reclaim the female body and its (conventional) representation?

If the choice between romantic idealization and ironic demystification is, for women, no choice at all, what is the alternative to the 'merely reasonable'? If Romantic imagination functions as a simultaneous provocation to and containment of reason, if it is only one more version of the recurrent crisis of reason, can one contemplate a critique of reason that is not itself a mode of rationality? Jacques Derrida's critique of Michel Foucault's desire to make madness, the other of reason, speak, offers a useful complication of Shelley Wall's insightful interpretation of Percy Shelley's *Julian and Maddalo*. In 'Cogito and the History of Madness' Derrida contends that Foucault cannot escape the paradox that it is the language of reason itself which puts reason on trial. Even though he applauds Foucault's quest for the other of reason, Derrida asks the unanswerable question that Foucault ignores – if discourse delimits the sayable, does it not also structure the possible?[3] In this sense, the Maniac serves not only to baffle Julian's mastery but also to exemplify it. *Julian and Maddalo*, I think, denies the existential reality of 'a country for which no maps exist.' The Maniac represents precisely the impossibility of the escape which madness seems to promise because he cannot sever his present from his past – his past, which includes his lost love and his social and material dispossession, imprisons him in the present. The poem implies that even if the Maniac's reality constitutes the limits of Reason, the representation of that reality does not and cannot disobey the dictates of reason and the conventions of syntax. The Maniac's feminization, his en-gendering, so to speak, as Wall rightly points out, draws attention to the daughter's incarceration; however, this subversive implication does not compensate for the poem's insistence on female responsibility for the Maniac's condition. Interestingly enough, h(i)steria becomes masculine territory, the consequence of betrayal by the feminine. How, then, might an-other story be told?

Even as the text of Romanticism expresses 'a complex incredulity towards the very credal positions that have in the past been identified with [it],' ('Introduction'), does it nevertheless produce violent aporias that become interpretable texts only when read from an-other perspective? In short, do the figures which signal absences that the text of Romanticism cannot contain pre-figure, not something 'other than knowledge,' but an-other knowledge, one that draws attention to what the self does not (as opposed to cannot) know or knows only too well? I want to suggest the possibility that because deconstructive epistemology emphasizes the disseminative potential of language and deprecates the lure of reference, it is often at risk, concomitantly, of leaving unexplored the ideological valency of textual figures that have no apparent objective referent.

Tilottama Rajan's essay demonstrates the manner in which lyric compression 'has the effect of exempting the self from action, from involvement in the complex intertexture of events.' I want to undertake a reading here that explores the implications of the exemption Rajan traces, one that develops the provocations and significant absences in her text as well as Shelley's. For instance, if the (lyric) poetic consciousness is constructed on the trace of its absent other – that is to say, narrative – is there room for a representation of feminine others such as the Arab maiden as figures of *resistance* to containment by lyric consciousness, as others which thwart the desire of the masculine self?

Rajan indicates that one must at all costs avoid sublating 'material circumstance into rhetorical figuration'; however, she prefers to cast the conflict between masculine and orientalist self and feminine/ethnic other as the *generic* struggle between lyric and narrative. Rajan's essay reveals the difficulty of attaching tropes to their referents and, in particular, the masculine lyric self's inability to contend with the other without reproducing that sublation. The female figure is then merely symptomatic of the effacement of being-in-the-world or merely instrumental to the process of repetition and doubling which displaces the self and discloses it as other, to the masculine self's discovery of the difference within. Rajan's privileging of narrative because it is implicated in a future in which the story may be retold or revisioned makes it possible to explore by and for whom that story may be retold. The vacancy which follows the poet's vision of the veiled maid as well as his experience in Ethiopia, I think, could be deployed in the interests of a movement beyond the familiar strategy of containment which produces the other as the ineffable. This movement, or at least the beginnings of one, can be accomplished through developing the connections between the vacancy the poet encounters and imperialist ideology that repeatedly represents its territorial conquests as uninhabited land.

The fragments of another reading of *Alastor* can be discerned within the frame of Rajan's own exemplary version of the poem – one that develops the manner in which the generic struggle between lyric and narrative is itself absorbed into the palimpsest of orientalism and/or imperialism. Within this scheme of things, both lyric and narrative might be equally culpable – one evades while the other effaces the world. I think it is the context of imperialism which demonstrates the particular force and application of Rajan's claim that '... we repeat something ... because what is said is not sufficient: because there is also something else to say.' More to the point, that context attests to the impossibility of the Poet's desire to produce figures upon vacant ground. Rajan's call for a phenomenological deconstruction is an attractive one, precisely because it does more than merely gesture to what it will not explicitly engage as well as refuses to succumb to the desire to transfigure politically charged situations into existential dilemmas; that is, if 'everything is constituted on the trace of its opposite,' critical exposure of the Romantic text's vulnerability to a hermeneutics of difference cannot afford to ignore that a relation of difference inhabits contested terrain, one which entails a struggle for power. The blindness upon which critical and poetic insight depend, it bears repeating, is historically and politically determined and determinable rather than merely logically or epistemologically necessary.

My insistence on the process of overdetermination which produces self, text, and world, of course, bears directly upon Douglas Kneale's desire to discover an alternative to history as absent cause and to challenge the trite opposition between history and textuality. If the self can no longer serve as the legitimating basis of knowledge and action, Kneale seems to be suggesting, an appeal to history will not help matters either. It is not so much that access to history is always mediated but that event and trope are, in the end, indistinguishable. The history which 'hurts' (in Fredric Jameson's formulation) will always turn out to be a false bottom, another symptom rather than the longed-for primal scene. If history is no more than a decomposing figure which chastens and eludes the most intrepid explorer, the event, Kneale argues, cannot but be read rhetorically and the rhetorical figure, in its turn, cannot but be experienced literally. This provocative overlapping and displacement of figure and ground, however, still does not explain why 'experience,' which Kneale describes as 'a historical replay of an imaginative text,' cannot also be represented as an imaginative replay of a historical text. If critical and poetic consciousness is 'poised at an … interface between history and textuality,' how can it avoid 'swerv[ing] from the very thing it appears to invoke and encounter'?

To my mind, the alternative to the literal ground of history or to the metaphor of surface and depth implicit in most attempts to disclose 'the painful rifts of difference creative of culture' (Liu 173) might lie not merely in the equally irreducible claim that the scene of history is always already symptomatic, but in the fragile hope that the reified appearance of empirical reality might nevertheless be provoked to tell the 'truth.' If traces and ruins of a decomposing figure are all we have, they are nevertheless decipherable, and the processes of condensation and displacement which render surfaces deceptive and depths impossible to retrieve contribute to the concreteness of history even if they militate against the latter's phenomenality.

If one must discern the place or function of the Romantic within the contemporary, such situating will no doubt rely on the Romantic revisioning of the virtues of contrariety. I have deferred consideration of David Clark's essay on Blake until now because I hoped to make it serve the cause of restoring the links between the epistemological and the ethico-political. The Introduction raises the possibility of deploying the Romantic text to expose the blind spots of post-structuralist appropriations of the Romantic legacy, an issue I hope to address briefly here.

The Romantic text's ability to 'contain' multitudes in the act of self-division acquires disturbing dimensions, to some of which I have already alluded. Clark explicitly locates the value of Blake's displacement of the stark opposition between being and becoming in Blake's searing awareness that 'meta-physical thinking is … always also a form of social practice.' The post-structuralist deconstruction of metaphysics in favour of difference, relation, and contrariety acquires substance when that deconstruction determines how 'onto-theological oppression [becomes] the alibi or origin of social oppression.' De Man's preoccupation with the nothingness of human matters eschews the dynamism of historical becoming for the stasis of aporia (itself a form of the stasis of 'being,' I would suggest). Clark notes the shift in Blake's work from metaphors of substance and identity to those of difference and displacement; however, the emancipatory dimension of Blake's work, its emphasis on 'the arduous and continually recreated faith in what could be,' would not be efficacious without the oppositional and dialectical power of contraries. In this sense, Blake's notion of contraries complicates the values of difference and displacement; that is, even though he does not posit difference on ontological grounds and acknowledges that antinomies imply and implicate each other, he wants to retain their historically produced antagonism, their status, precisely, as *contraries*, in the interests of revolution. In order, then, to make 'the object of vision ... not what was forgotten but what can be imagined,' I want to rewrite, in Clark's words, 'truth ... as a text suspended in and intersected by a context.' It is for this reason that I endorse Liu's en-gendering of the possibility of a self that responds to its situation or resists its determinations, that operates (to borrow Gayatri Spivak's phrase) as a graph or map of knowing. This conception of self makes it possible to resist the confusion of meaningful language with constative statements or propositions and reconstitutes significance in terms of the material consequences of discursive practices.

In other words, readable signs become interpretable events, and the emphasis on the performative dimension of language, as Balfour suggests, ensures that the abrogation of the intentional or willing self does not lapse into an abandonment of responsibility or accountability. This collection's methodological implications, therefore, must not be ignored. If the practice of contemporary criticism entails the performance of close readings that are never close enough, the revelation of the non-coincidence between intention and execution and the insistence on the singularity of event or the recalcitrance of reality must occur in the interests of critical negation which affirms political intervention. If a certain poststructuralist practice has appropriated the problematics of Romanticism in the service of a politics of displacement, this volume, I believe, has raised the possibility of a politics, precisely, of opposition. The link between theory and practice that I envisage, therefore, seeks to restore the frail links between insight and agency in order to produce discourses that disrupt the coercions of both systems of knowledge and structures of reality.

NOTES

1 David Clark, letter to the author, 1 February 1992
2 See also Karen Newman, 'Directing Traffic: Subjects, Objects, and the Politics of Exchange.'
3 See also Julian Henriques et al., *Changing the Subject: Psychology, Social Regulation and Subjectivity.*

WORKS CITED

de Man, Paul. *Blindness and Insight: Essays in the Rhetoric of Contemporary Criticism.* Introduction by Wlad Godzich. 2d ed., revised. Theory and History of Literature 7. 1971. Minneapolis: U of Minnesota P, 1983.
Derrida, Jacques. *Writing and Difference.* Trans. Alan Bass. Chicago: U of Chicago P, 1978.
Foucault, Michel. *Madness and Civilization: A History of Insanity in the Age of Reason.* Trans. Richard Howard. 1965. New York: Vintage Books, 1973.
Greenblatt, Stephen, and Giles Gunn, eds. *Redrawing the Boundaries: The Transformation of English and American Literary Studies.* New York: MLA, 1992.
Henriques, Julian, et al. *Changing the Subject: Psychology, Social Regulation and Subjectivity.* London and New York: Methuen, 1984.
Jameson, Fredric. *The Political Unconscious: Narrative as a Socially Symbolic Act.* Ithaca: Cornell UP, 1981.
Liu, Alan. Review of *Wordsworth's Historical Imagination: The Poetry of Displacement*, by David Simpson. *The Wordsworth Circle* 19.4 (Autumn 1988): 172–82.
Newman, Karen. 'Directing Traffic: Subjects, Objects, and the Politics of Exchange.' *Differences* 2.2 (1990): 41–54.
Radhakrishnan, R. 'The Changing Subject and the Politics of Theory.' *Differences* 2.2 (1990): 126–52.
Rajan, Tilottama. 'The Future of Deconstruction in Romantic Studies.' *Nineteenth-Century Contexts* 11.2 (Fall 1987): 131–53.
Spivak, Gayatri Chakravorty. *In Other Worlds: Essays in Cultural Politics.* 1987. New York and London: Routledge, 1988.

Notes on Contributors

Ian Balfour, Assistant Professor of English at York University and a member of York's Graduate Programme in Social and Political Thought, is the author of *Northrop Frye* (G.K. Hall, 1988) and of numerous essays on Romanticism, critical theory, and popular culture in such journals as *Modern Language Notes, camera obscura,* and *Essays on Canadian Writing.* In addition to guest-editing, with Cynthia Chase, a special issue of *diacritics* [22 (1992)], 'Commemorating Benjamin,' he has contributed essays to *Writing the Future* (Routledge, 1990) and *Responses: On Paul de Man's Wartime Journalism* (U of Nebraska P, 1989). He has a forthcoming book from Stanford UP entitled *The Rhetoric of Romantic Prophecy.*

Alan Bewell is Associate Professor of English at the University of Toronto and editor of the *University of Toronto Quarterly.* He has published *Wordsworth and the Enlightenment: Nature, Man, and Society in the Experimental Poetry* (Yale UP, 1989) and articles on Romanticism in *The Wordsworth Circle,* the *Yale Journal of Criticism, ELH,* and *Studies in Romanticism.* He was co-editor of a special issue of *Studies in Romanticism* on Wordsworth's *The Borderers,* and is currently writing a book entitled *English Romantic Geographies.*

David L. Clark, Associate Professor of English at McMaster University, is the author of articles on Blake, critical theory, and postmodernism in *Studies in Romanticism, Studies in Canadian Literature, The Wordsworth Circle,* and *Canadian Poetry: Studies, Documents, Reviews.* He has contributed essays to *The Mind in Creation: Essays on Romantic Literature in Honour of Ross G. Woodman,* ed. J. Douglas Kneale (McGill-Queen's UP, 1992), and to *Negation: Critical Theory and Postmodernism,* ed. Daniel Fischlin (Kluwer, 1994). He is co-editing, with Tilottama Rajan, *Intersections: Nineteenth-Century Philosophy and Contemporary Theory* (SUNY P, 1994).

Donald C. Goellnicht, Associate Professor of English at McMaster University, has published on Keats and on Asian-American and African-American literature. He is the author of *The Poet-Physician: Keats and Medical Science* (U of Pittsburgh P, 1984), and of articles in *Mosaic, JEGP, Tulsa Studies in Women's Literature,* and *English Studies in Canada.* He has contributed essays to *Critical Essays on John Keats* (G.K. Hall, 1990), *Approaches to Teaching the Poetry of Keats* (MLA, 1991), *Redefining Autobiography in Twentieth-Century Women's Fiction* (Garland, 1991), and *Reading the Literatures of Asian America* (Temple UP, 1992).

J. Douglas Kneale is Associate Professor in the Department of English at the University of Western Ontario. He has published *Monumental Writing: Aspects of Rhetoric in Wordsworth's Poetry* (U of Nebraska P, 1988), and articles on Wordsworth and Romanticism in such journals as *ELH, PMLA, English Studies in Canada,* and *Ariel.* He has also edited *The Mind in Creation: Essays on English Romantic Literature in Honour of Ross G. Woodman* (McGill-Queen's UP, 1992).

Tilottama Rajan is Professor in the Department of English and the Centre for the Study of Theory and Criticism at the University of Western Ontario. She is the author of *Dark Interpreter: The Discourse of Romanticism* (Cornell UP, 1980) and *The Supplement of Reading: Figures of Understanding in Romantic Theory and Practice* (Cornell UP, 1990), as well as numerous articles on Romanticism and critical theory in such journals as *Studies in Romanticism, ELH, New Literary History, Studies in the Novel,* and *Nineteenth-Century Contexts.* She has contributed essays to *Lyric Poetry: Beyond New Criticism* (Cornell UP, 1985), *The New Shelley: Later Twentieth-Century Views* (St Martin's P, 1992), and *Romantic Revolutions: Criticism and Theory* (Indiana UP, 1990). She is currently working on two books: *Romantic Narrative* (of which the present essay forms a part) and *Deconstruction Before and After Post-Structuralism.*

Asha Varadharajan was Webster Fellow in the Humanities at Queen's University and is now Assistant Professor of English at the University of Minnesota. She has published articles in and contributed reviews to *Papers/Cahiers, Recherches sémiotiques / Semiotic Inquiry, Ariel, Canadian Literature,* and the *CSH Bulletin.* She has forthcoming articles on the gendered subaltern and on postcolonial discourse in collections on 'Critical Theory in Canada' and on 'Gender and Colonialism,' and is completing a book entitled *Exotic Parodies: Subjectivity and Postcoloniality* (forthcoming from Minnesota UP, 1995).

Shelley Wall is a doctoral student in the Department of English at McMaster University. She is writing a dissertation on embedded narratives – especially dream visions and 'case histories' – in Romantic works.

Jean Wilson is Assistant Professor of German and Comparative Literature at McMaster University. She is the author of *The Challenge of Belatedness: Goethe, Kleist, Hofmannsthal* (UP of America, 1991), and of contributions on Lessing, Goethe, Schiller, Schlegel, and Kleist to *Sources of Dramatic Theory*, vol. 2 (Cambridge UP, 1994).

Index

Aarsleff, Hans, 247n22
Abelard, 62
Abrams, M.H., 6–7, 15, 20–1n 4, 216n26, 278
adolescence, 124–5, 129n23
Adorno, Theodor W., 31
Aeolian harps, 31
Agamben, Giorgio: *The Coming Community*, 212n22
Allen, David Elliston, 73, 97n6; *The Victorian Fern Craze*, 73
alter ego, 32, 43–4
alterity, 60, 62, 64. *See also* madness
Altick, Richard D., 105, 114, 128n18, 161n24
Altizer, Thomas: *The New Apocalypse*, 176
androgyny, 282
anti-historical critics, 146
Anz, Thomas, 262
apocalypse, 106, 171, 175, 189
Aries, Philippe, 124, 129n23
Aristotle, 179, 231–2
Armstrong, Nancy, 248n24
art: as agent for social change, 110, 127n10; as agent of reform in material culture, 111

Asche, Susanne, 258–9
Augustan couplet, 110
Augustine, Saint, 182
Ault, Donald, 216n26
Austen, Jane, 241
Austin, J.L., 18, 20, 229, 231, 236, 241, 246n16; *How to Do Things with Words*, 241, 246n16, 249n32. *See also* speech-act theory

Bachelard, Gaston: *The Psychoanalysis of Fire*, 135
Bailey, Benjamin, 119
Bakhtin, Mikhail, 254
Balfour, Ian, 10, 17–20, 276, 279
Barber, Lynn, 73, 97n7
Barnard, John, 83, 98n27
Barthes, Roland, 20, 48, 145
Bate, Walter Jackson, 102, 105, 122
Baudrillard, Jean, 12, 217n31
Bayley, John, 102, 126n3
Beauvoir, Simone de, 266
Beckett, Samuel, 54, 60
Belgardt, Raimund, 267n13
Bender, John, 248n26
Bennington, Geoffrey, 206

Bentham, Jeremy, 195–6, 198, 228, 246n12, 248n26. *See also* panopticon
Bewell, Alan, 12–14, 21n9, 105, 279, 281–2
Beyle, Marie Henri (pseud. Stendhal), 266
Biermann, Wolf, 262
Black Act, 228, 246n11
Blackwell, Basil, 102
Blackwood's Edinburgh Magazine, 107, 110, 115, 118–19, 121
Blair, Hugh, 214n26
Blake, William, 15–16, 81, 160n21, 164–206, 208–10, 212–13, 215–17, 285–6; *The Ancient of Days*, 172, 174; *Europe*, 172; *First Book of Urizen*, 182–3; *The Four Zoas*, 165, 168, 171–2, 174, 180, 190; *Glad Day*, 166; *Jerusalem*, 165–6, 168, 172, 176–9, 182, 185–90, 200, 203, 208, 217n33; *The Marriage of Heaven and Hell*, 168, 170, 172, 177, 180, 195, 211n9; *Songs of Innocence*, 197; *A Vision of the Last Judgment*, 183; *When the Morning Stars Sang Together*, 190, 193, 200
Blank, Kim G., 49n1
Bloom, Harold, 158n16, 211n9
Blunden, Edmund, 104, 115, 128n19
Boehme, Jacob, 212n15, 215n26
Boileau, Nicolas, 109
book-reviewing: politics and ideology of, 104, 107, 280. *See also* Keats, John
botany: and sex, 80, 86, 91; in Victorian culture, 13, 73, 90, 96; as women's language, 90. *See also* Keats, John
Brandes, Ute, 262

Brawne, Fanny, 98–9n30
Brewer, William D., 54, 57, 66n6
Briggs, Harold E., 104
Bromwich, David, 104, 128n15
Brooks, Peter, 137, 159n20
Brown, Charles, 72
Browne, Janet, 75, 97n11
Burke, Edmund, 225–7, 230, 235, 244n1, 245nn3, 7, 248n24; *Reflections on the Revolution in France*, 225, 244n1, 245nn3, 5
Bush, Douglas, 102
Butler, Judith, 210n3
Butler, Marilyn, 8, 99n31, 102, 245n7, 248n25, 260
Butlin, Martin, 196
Byron, George Gordon, Lord, 53, 72, 90–1, 101–2, 108, 118, 124. *See also* homosexuality

Cameron, Sharon, 31
Campbell, Thomas, 108
Caputo, John D., 178–80, 210, 212n16
Castle, Terry, 242, 249n31, 250nn34, 35
Cervantes, Miguel de, 252; *Don Quixote*, 251
Chambers, D.D.C., 97n12
Champion, 107–8
Chase, Cynthia, 144
Chodorow, Nancy, 185
Cixous, Hélène, 49n5
Clare, John, 73, 115
Clark, David L., 15, 21n11, 179, 182, 210n6, 216n26, 275, 279, 281, 285–6, 287n1
Clarke, Charles Cowden, 73, 115; *Adam, the Gardener*, 73
Cobbett, William: *Political Register*, 128n17

Coburn, Kathleen, 5
Cockney rhymes, 110–11
Cockney school of poetry, 77–8, 107, 112–13, 115–16, 118–19, 121, 127n10. *See also* Lockhart, John Gibson
Cockney slang, 114
Coleridge, Samuel T., 4–6, 89, 108, 117, 146, 157n9, 158n16, 182; *Biographia Literaria*, 146, 158n16; 'This Lime-Tree Bower My Prison,' 89
Columbus, Ferdinand: *Life and Actions of Christopher Columbus*, 154
Conder, Josiah, 107, 111
Cook, Capt. James, 75
Copernicus, Nicolaus, 171, 174
Corneille, Pierre, 109
Corngold, Stanley, 49n3
Cowper, William: *The Task*, 76
creativity, 259–60, 268n20
Croker, John Wilson, 98n20
Crompton, Louis, 100n31
cross-dressing, stylistic, 13, 89, 91, 282. *See also* Keats, John
cummings, e.e., 160n24
Curtius, Ernst Robert 158n17

Daemmrich, Horst, 267n14
Damon, S. Foster, 217n28
Dampier, William: *A New Voyage round the World*, 154
Damrosch, Leopold, 180, 186
Dante, 71, 171, 175, 251–2; *The Divine Comedy*, 171, 175; *Inferno*, 251
Darwin, Erasmus, 74–5, 81, 85–7, 99n31; *Botanic Garden*, 85; *The Loves of the Plants*, 74–5, 85
de Certeau, Michel, 137, 139, 155n1; *The Writing of History*, 138–9

deconstruction: deconstructive criticism, 21, 276, 280; deconstructive epistemology, 283; phenomenological deconstruction, 17, 276–7, 284. *See also* post-structuralism
de Man, Paul, 5–7, 9–10, 18, 20, 135, 143–4, 150, 157n11, 158n16, 210, 216n26, 217n34, 244, 246n17, 275–8, 280, 286; *Allegories of Reading*, 18; 'Intentional Structure of the Romantic Image,' 6; 'Shelley Disfigured,' 144, 150, 157n11
Derrida, Jacques, 19–20, 33, 145, 158n16, 162, 169, 184, 200, 203–8, 211n7, 212, 214n26, 216n26, 217–18n36, 228, 246n13, 247nn19, 22, 282; 'Cogito and the History of Madness,' 282; 'How to Avoid Speaking: Denials,' 200; 'Living On/BORDER LINES,' 205; *Memoires for Paul de Man*, 228, 246n13; *Of Grammatology*, 184, 203; 'Violence and Metaphysics,' 184
desire, 43, 46, 79–80, 82, 86, 95–6, 168, 257, 260, 275, 281, 283
dialogism, 16, 165, 181–2, 281
Dickstein, Morris, 104
Diderot, Denis, 231
Dietrich, Linda, 263, 269nn35, 43
discipline, 197–8; police, 62, 67n10, 170. *See also* Foucault, Michel
domestication, 62–3
Dowling, William C., 156n5
Drayton, Michael, 77
Dryden, John, 91, 156n8
Duval, Marguerite, 97n11

Eagleton, Terry, 102, 279
Eclectic Review, 107, 111

296 Index

Edinburgh Magazine, 107, 111, 119
Edinburgh Monthly Magazine, 111
Edinburgh Review, 107, 114–15
Edwards, Gavin, 247n20
effeminacy, 112, 116–17. *See also* lower orders
Egyptianism, 177–8, 180, 209. *See also* Nietzsche, Friedrich
Eichner, Hans, 5
Eliot, T.S., 5
Ellis, John M., 267n15
epic, 28
epic simile, 147, 159n17
epitaph, 153
Erdman, David V., 210n1
Esch, Deborah, 246n15
Essick, Robert N., 213n25
European Magazine, 107, 111, 113
Everest, Kelvin, 65, 66nn6, 8, 67n13, 247n20
Examiner, 106–7, 109, 114–15, 127n6, 128n17

female body, 37, 46; and disease, 117; and representation, 36
feminine position, 12, 53, 56, 62–3, 65, 92, 117–18, 125, 129n23, 185–7, 254, 279, 283
feminism, 10–11, 53
Ferguson, Frances, 8, 18n1, 277–80
Fetterley, Judith, 252
Fichte, Johann Gottlieb, 203, 217nn33, 37
Fish, Stanley, 137, 140, 156n4
Fliess, Wilhelm, 155n2
floral imagery, 12, 71–2, 78–9, 83, 90, 93, 96, 282; and women's writing, 87, 89, 96, 282. *See also* Keats, John
Fontana, Alessandro, 210n4

Foucault, Michel, 8, 15–16, 21nn5, 6, 64, 166, 168, 181, 190, 195–7, 199, 210n4, 211n10, 217n30, 280, 282; *The Archaeology of Knowledge*, 21n5; *Discipline and Punish*, 15, 168, 170, 181, 190, 195–6, 199, 217n30. *See also* panopticon; repressive hypothesis
Frank, Manfred, 16, 169, 179, 218n37
French Revolution, 4, 103, 106, 110, 145, 158n15, 186, 227, 245n7, 249n28, 278
French school of criticism, 109–10
French school of poetry, 110
Freud, Sigmund, 14–15, 135–7, 139–42, 146–7, 149, 152–3, 155nn1–2, 156nn3, 8, 158nn14–15, 159n20, 161n24, 258, 267n11; 'The Aetiology of Hysteria,' 135–6, 156n3; *Beyond the Pleasure Principle*, 149; *The Interpretation of Dreams*, 156n3; 'Recollecting, Repeating, and Working Through,' 159n20; 'Three Essays on the Theory of Sexuality,' 156n3
Fries, Marilyn, 263
Fry, Paul, 104–5
Frye, Northrop, 4–5, 30, 260
Furst, Lilian, 267n16

Gasché, Rodolphe, 207, 215n26, 217n35
Genesis, 199, 206
genre, 28–9. *See also* epic; lyric; narrative; pastoral; Petrarchan sonnet; quest-narrative; sentimental novel
Gilbert, Sir Humphrey, 154
Gilligan, Carol, 187

Girard, René, 193, 217n29
Gittings, Robert, 129n21
Gnostics, 170, 198, 211n9
Godwin, William, 18–20, 22n1, 108, 111, 225–39, 243–9; *Caleb Williams*, 19, 228, 230–1, 234–7, 239–40, 246n14, 247–9; *Enquiry Concerning Political Justice*, 225–6, 229–31, 235–9, 244, 245n4
Godzich, Wlad, 276
Goellnicht, Donald C., 13–14, 73, 83, 97nn5, 8, 98n28, 127n4, 279–81
Goethe, Johann Wolfgang, 10, 252–4, 261, 264; *Faust*, 253–5, 258; *The Sorrows of Young Werther*, 10, 252–3, 261, 264
Grandville, Albert: *Les Fleurs Animées*, 82, 98n23
Great Chain of Being, 164, 175, 181, 184, 193, 197
Great Tradition, 126nn1, 3, 101, 280
Greenblatt, Stephen, 14, 145–6; *Renaissance Self-Fashioning*, 14
Greene, Robert, 158n16
Günderrode, Karoline von, 262–6

Hakluyt, Richard, 154
Hamlin, Cyrus, 5
Handelman, Susan, 184
Hardy, Thomas, 144
Harpham, Geoffrey Galt, 47
Hartman, Geoffrey, 77, 97n16, 152, 155, 278
Harvard Keatsians, 102, 126nn2–3
Hayden, John O., 104, 110, 127; *The Romantic Reviewers*, 107
Haydon, Benjamin Robert, 106–7, 125
Hayes, Charles, 267n13

Hazlitt, W. Carew, 87, 99n33, 107, 111, 128nn17–18
Hegel, Georg W.F., 16, 21n11, 33, 43, 164, 166, 210n3, 216n27, 248n26; *Aesthetics*, 16
Heidegger, Martin, 6, 16, 169, 201, 211nn12, 14; *Being and Time*, 169
Heinzelman, Kurt, 105, 158n14
Henrich, Dieter, 217n33
Henriques, Julian, 287n3
Herder, Johann Gottfried, 231
Herminghouse, Patricia, 262
Herrick, Robert, 80
Hertz, Neil, 159n19, 258
Hill, James L., 66nn5–6
Hilton, Nelson, 216n26
Hirsch, Bernard A., 66nn6, 8
Hoagwood, Terence Allan, 105, 127n6
Hoffman, E.T.A., 10, 255; 'The Sandman,' 10, 255–9
Hogle, Jerrold, 214n26
Holcroft, Thomas: *Anna St. Ives*, 249n28
Hölderlin, Friedrich: 'The Root of All Evil,' 165
Homans, Margaret, 98n29, 252, 267n18
homosexuality, 90–1, 186
Hopkins, G.M., 128n15
Huang, Tsokan, 104
Hume, David: 'Of the Original Contract,' 225, 244n1
Hunt, Leigh, 73, 77, 80–1, 91, 106–22, 125, 127nn6, 14; *Autobiography*, 114; *The Story of Rimini*, 110, 116
Hunt, Lynn, 157n13
Hunter, Kathryn Montgomery:

298 Index

Doctors' Stories: The Narrative Structure of Medical Knowledge, 138
Hutcheon, Linda, 264, 269n39
hysteria, 138, 156n3

imperialism, 61, 284
Inchbald, Elizabeth, 18–19, 239–42, 249–50; *A Simple Story*, 18–19, 242–4, 246n17, 249–50
infantile seduction, 140
instrumental thinking, 262, 268n33
interpretive communities, 14

Jack, Ian, 81, 98n22
Jacobin: fiction and philosophy, 20, 239, 243–4, 250n35
Jacobus, Mary, 257–8, 268
James, Henry, 246n15
James, William, 190, 216n27
Jameson, Fredric, 6, 156n5, 285
Jardine, Alice, 62
Jauss, Hans Robert, 104
Job, Book of, 15, 165, 175, 190–3, 195–204, 208–9
Johnson, Mary Lynn, 172
Johnston, Kenneth, 157n12

Kamuf, Peggy, 245n6
Kant, Immanuel, 3, 169
Kaplan, E. Ann, 66n2
Kauffman, Linda S., 62
Keach, William, 104, 110, 127n4
Keane, J. Douglas, 158n17
Keats, George, 115, 119
Keats, Georgiana, 115
Keats, John, 6, 12–14, 62, 71–99, 101–15, 118–29, 189, 213n24, 280, 282; 'La Belle Dame Sans Merci,' 62, 93–4; *Endymion*, 71–3, 80, 86, 92, 98nn20, 30, 107, 110, 112, 114–15, 120–1, 123–5, 127n12, 128n18; *The Eve of St. Agnes*, 71, 77, 93; *The Fall of Hyperion*, 72, 93, 98–9n30; 'Great spirits …,' 106; *Hyperion*, 71; 'I stood tip-toe upon a little hill,' 78–9, 81–2, 85–6, 89–90, 112; *Isabella*, 92; *Lamia*, 72, 80, 94; 'Ode on Melancholy,' 93, 99n30; 'Ode to a Nightingale,' 72, 92; 'Ode to Psyche,' 71, 74–5, 86, 92; 'On Fame,' 95; 'On Receiving a Curious Shell, and a Copy of Verses, from the Same Ladies,' 89; *Poems* (1817), 13, 71–2, 89, 91–2, 107, 109, 113–14, 122, 128n18; 'Sleep and Poetry,' 71, 77, 80–1, 84, 110; 'To a Friend Who Sent Me Some Roses,' 89; 'To Autumn,' 72, 93, 99n30; 'To George Felton Mathew,' 86; 'To Kosciusko,' 106; 'To Leigh Hunt, Esq.,' 106; 'To My Brother George,' 106, 112, 120; 'To Some Ladies,' 89; 'Written on the Day That Mr. Leigh Hunt Left Prison,' 105–6. *See also* floral imagery
Keenan, Thomas, 246n10
Kelley, Theresa M., 105
Kelly, Gary, 249n28, 256, 261, 268n31
Kent, Elizabeth, 73, 76; *Flora Domestica; or, The Portable Flower Garden*, 73–6; *Sylvan; or, A Companion to the Park and Shrubbery*, 73
Kiely, Robert, 259, 267n18
Kierkegaard, Sören, 178–81, 209, 212nn16–17; *Repetition*, 178–81
Kilfeather, Siobhan, 249n29
King, James, 186

Klancher, Jon, 128n17
Kleist, Heinrich von, 262–5
Kneale, J. Douglas, 10, 14–15, 279, 284–5
Knight, Richard Payne, 99n31
Kristeva, Julia, 32, 36, 49nn5–6, 67n12; *Desire in Language*, 49nn5–6; *Revolution in Poetic Language*, 49n6
Kuhn, Anna K., 262–3, 269
Künstlernovelle, 257–8

La Belle, Jenijoy, 198
Lacan, Jacques, 32, 49n5, 155n1, 160n22. *See also* desire
landscape poetry, 143
Langan, Janine, 217n29
Leavis, F.R., 5, 28
Lehmann, Hans-Thies, 267n9
Lennox, Sara, 269n37
Lévi-Strauss, Claude, 204
Levinas, Emmanuel, 184, 210–11n7, 212nn19–20
Levinson, Marjorie, 8, 20n2, 98n19, 101–3, 105, 116, 126nn1–3, 145, 157n12; *Keats's Life of Allegory*, 101
literary tradition. *See* Great Tradition
Liu, Alan, 8, 14–15, 20n4, 21n6, 136, 141–6, 154–5, 156nn5–7, 157nn9–10, 12, 158nn14–15, 159n17, 280, 285–6; *Wordsworth and the Sense of History*, 14, 141–6
Locke, John, 225, 227, 232–3, 248n26, 250n35. *See also* social contract
Lockhart, John Gibson, 77–8, 91, 98n18, 113, 115. *See also* Cockney school of poetry
Loudon, John Claudius, 97n14
Lovejoy, Arthur O., 3–5, 7, 9, 20n1, 277

lower orders, 114, 116–18, 128n16. *See also* effeminacy
Lukács, Georg, 29, 49n2, 262
lyric, 16–17, 28–32, 34–5, 37–8, 45, 47, 60, 277, 283–4

MacLeod, Dawn, 97n13
madness, 11–12, 58, 61, 64–5, 282. *See also* reason
Mahony, Patrick, 137
Malthus, Thomas, 113–14, 128n16; *Essay on Population*, 113
mannerism, 80–1, 85
Marsh, G.L., 104
Marston, John: *The Fawn*, 121–2
Marvell, Andrew, 80
Marx, Karl, 166
Marxism, 101, 156n5, 279
masculinity, 117, 185–8, 279, 283; and hysteria, 113; as subject position, 53, 65, 66n2, 67n12, 80
masquerade, 242
mastery, 236; as scopic, 12, 53. *See also* voyeurism
masturbation, 112–13
materialism, 157n12, 278
Mathew, George Felton, 107, 113
Mathew, Mary Strange: *The Garland*, 97n8
Matthews, Ann and Caroline, 89
Matthews, Charles Skinner, 90–1
Matthews, G.M., 65, 66nn1, 6, 8, 67nn9–10, 104
Mazzeo, Joseph, 182
McGann, Jerome, 8–10, 20n1, 105, 278
medical semiotics, 138
Mellor, Anne K., 10
metaphysics, 10, 165–6, 169, 174, 176–7, 179–80, 182, 184, 188, 190, 201, 285

Miller, Hillis, 41
Milton, John, 71, 77, 85, 91, 98n30, 159n18, 170–2, 178, 183–4, 189–90, 208, 212–13n23, 218nn8–9; *Paradise Lost*, 158n16, 159n18, 160n24, 170–2, 177–8, 181, 183, 189
misogyny, 116. See also Keats, John
monologism, 281
Monthly Magazine, 107, 110, 119
Montolieu, Mrs, 87, 99n34; *The Enchanted Plants*, 87; 'Scandal; or the Painted Lady Sweet-Pea,' 87–9
Moore, Thomas, 108

Napoleon, 106, 145, 155, 161n24
Napoleonic Wars, 118
narcissism. See desire; Freud, Sigmund; masculinity
narrative, 16–17, 28–9, 30–2, 34–5, 43, 45–7, 60, 256, 282–4. See also desire
neoclassicism, 109–11, 113; French, 110
New Criticism, 4, 104
new historicism, 8, 20n4, 21n6, 145, 157n13
Newey, Vincent, 66n6
Newman, Beth, 66n2
Newman, Karen, 287n2
Nietzsche, Friedrich, 8, 16, 30, 36, 41, 165, 169–72, 174, 177, 180, 197, 209, 210n2, 211nn11, 13, 212n21; *The Birth of Tragedy*, 49n3; *Daybreak*, 10; *The Gay Science*, 170, 174; *Twilight of the Idols*, 177; *The Will To Power*, 3, 49n6

Oakeshott, Michael: *On Human Conduct*, 164
oaths, 238–9. See also Godwin, William; promise

Ogden, C.K., 246n12
Ollier, Charles and James, 66n7, 119–20, 128n18, 129n21
'On the Cockney School of Poetry.' See Cockney school of poetry
orientalism, 283–4
Orwell, George: *1984*, 199
Otto, Peter, 216n26
overdetermination, 139, 153, 284
Ovid, 62, 81, 86–7, 160n24; *Heroides*, 62
Owen, W.J.B., 5

Paley, William, 89
palimpsest, 139–40, 143, 149
panopticon, 195–6, 198, 207. See also Bentham, Jeremy; Foucault, Michel
Parens, David, 213n23
Park, Mungo: *Travels in the Interior of Africa*, 154
Parker, Patricia, 249n27, 268n21
parody, 264
Partridge, Eric: *Dictionary of Slang and Unconventional English*, 93
Pasquino, Pasquale, 210n4
pastoral, 12, 71, 96, 143, 251
Paulson, Ronald, 249n28
Peacock, Thomas Love, 99n31
Periodical Press of Great Britain and Ireland, 103
Perkins, David, 102
Perry, James: *Mimosa; or, The Sensitive Plant*, 86
Petrarchan sonnet, 106
phenomenology, 34, 43. See also deconstruction
Plato, 175, 178, 205, 208–9
Poe, Edgar Allen, 61
police discipline. See discipline, police

Poovey, Mary, 99n35, 260–1, 268nn25–26, 28, 32
Pope, Alexander, 110
population, 113–14, 128n16. *See also* Malthus, Thomas
Porter, Roy, 129n20
postmodernism, 11, 169
post-post-structuralism, 7, 9
post-structuralism, 5–6, 285–6. *See also* deconstruction
Poussin, Nicolas: *The Realm of Flora*, 81
power, 168, 187, 198, 208
Prawer, S.S., 267n11
Priestley, F.E.L., 245n4
Prometheus, 60, 67n9
promise, structure of, 18–20, 228, 230, 233, 236–7, 240, 243. *See also* supplement
psychoanalysis. *See* Freud, Sigmund; Lacan, Jacques

Quarterly Review, 107, 110, 114
quest-narrative, 28, 43

racism, 118
Radhakrishnan, R., 275, 277
Ragland-Sullivan, Ellie, 155n1
Rajan, Balachandra, 171, 213n23
Rajan, Tilottama, 4, 16–17, 20n2, 21n11, 28, 46, 212n21, 214n26, 216n26, 247n20, 276–7, 279, 283–4. *See also* deconstruction, phenomenological
reader-response theory, 52
reason, 11–12, 20, 58, 61, 64–5, 180, 233, 252–9, 262, 282–3. *See also* madness
Redpath, Theodore, 103–4, 127nn9, 11, 13

Reed, Thomas A., 105
reification, 279
Reiman, Donald, 104, 127nn9, 11, 13
repression, 140, 154
repressive hypothesis, 166, 168–9, 207, 210n4
resistance, 169, 280–1, 283
ressentiment, 166, 177, 197
revolution, 106, 114, 166, 168, 286
Reynolds, John Hamilton, 72, 84, 90, 96n2, 107–9, 113, 119–20, 122–3, 127n14, 129n22
Rich, Adrienne, 263
Richards, I.A., 120, 147
Richardson, Alan, 117, 185, 266n2
Ricks, Christopher, 98n19, 102, 126n3
Ricoeur, Paul, 47
Riley, Robert B., 97n10
Rogers, Samuel, 108
Rooke, Barbara, 5
Ross, Marlon B., 100n38
Rothstein, Eric, 247n20
Rousseau, Jean-Jacques, 18, 81, 109, 225, 231, 234, 243–4, 245n6, 246n17, 247n22, 248n23, 261, 268n29; *Reveries of the Solitary Walker*, 268
Rowden, Frances Arabella: *Poetical Introduction to the Study of Botany*, 87
Ryan, Judith, 265

Sade, Marquis de, 227–8, 245nn9–10
Sartre, Jean-Paul, 6
Sauer, Lieselotte, 267n13
scene, 135–8, 141, 158n16; and symptom, 139–41, 151
Schelling, Friedrich, 21n11, 169, 177, 211n14, 211–12n15, 215–16n26; *Of Human Freedom*, 211n15, 215n26

Schiller, Friedrich, 161n24; *Naïve and Sentimental Poetry*, 16
Schleiermacher, Friedrich, 215n26
Schmidt, Jochen, 258, 267n17
Schopenhauer, Arthur, 30, 49n3
Schwartz, Lewis M., 104
Scots Magazine, 107
semiotics, medical, 138
sentimental novel, 260
sexuality, 11, 118, 125, 128n16, 129n20: and disease, 113, 117
Shakespeare, William, 63, 71, 91, 147, 158n16, 159n18; *Macbeth*, 240; *Measure for Measure*, 159n18; *Much Ado about Nothing*, 159n18; 'Sonnet 116,' 159n18; *The Winter's Tale*, 153
Shelley, Mary, 255, 259–60, 268n24; *Frankenstein*, 11, 256, 259–60
Shelley, Percy Bysshe, 5–6, 12, 16–17, 27–9, 31, 36–8, 40–1, 46, 48, 49n1, 52–4, 56–7, 59, 62, 64–7, 80, 99n31, 107, 119–20, 124, 128n17, 144, 157n11, 214n26, 283; *Adonais*, 28; *Alastor*, 16–17, 28–32, 35, 44–5, 48, 49n1, 284; *A Defence of Poetry*, 33–4, 67; *Julian and Maddalo*, 11–12, 17, 52–67, 282; *Prometheus Unbound*, 27, 46; *The Revolt of Islam*, 27, 35; 'The Sensitive Plant,' 91; *The Triumph of Life*, 38, 157n11
Showalter, Elaine, 12
Shteir, Anne B., 97n5, 99n32
Simpson, David, 8–9
Siskin, Clifford, 105, 117–18, 124–5
slavery, 168, 236
Smith, Charlotte: *Beachy Head*, 89
sociability, 169–70, 177, 187
social contract, 19, 225–8, 233, 244, 246n17, 248n48. *See also* Burke, Edmund; Godwin, William; Locke, John; Rousseau, Jean-Jacques
speech-act theory, 18, 241
Spenser, Edmund, 71, 77, 91, 98n30
Sperry, Stuart M., 97n4
Spivak, Gayatri Chakravorty, 204, 286
Stendhal. *See* Beyle, Marie Henri
Stern, Robert, 215n26
Sterne, Laurence, 233
Stibbs, Edward, 128n18
subjection, 166, 168
supplement, 20, 38, 206, 229, 243
surveillance, 195, 198, 209
Swift, Jonathan, 161n24
symptom, 135–8, 142, 152, 155n1, 156n5. *See also* scene

Tatchell, Molly, 97n5
Taylor, Charles, 168
Taylor, J., 201
Taylor, John, 115, 125, 128n19; and Hessey, 73, 120, 122, 128n18
Taylor, Mark C., 217n36
temporality, 30–2, 35, 179–80
Tetrault, Ronald, 66n6
Thelwall, John, 108
Thomas, D.M.: *The White Hotel*, 138
Thompson, E.P., 248n11
Thornton, Robert, 82–3, 98nn24, 28; *The Temple of Flora*, 82
Thorslev, Peter, 21n8
Tighe, Mary: *Psyche*, 89
Towers, John: *The Domestic Gardener's Manual*, 73
trace, 31, 37, 48, 201
travel books, 154
Trilling, Lionel, 137

Urmson, J.O., 249n32

Vendler, Helen, 102
Virgil, 143, 150, 156n8, 157n10; *Georgics*, 143, 157n10
voyeurism, 61, 63. See also mastery, scopic

Wagner, Richard, 37
Wall, Shelley, 11–12, 17, 279, 282–3
Walley, George, 5
Walzer, Michael, 210n5
Ward, W.S., 104
Wardle, Ralph, 260, 268n28
Ware, Tracy, 66n6, 67n8
Wasserman, Earl R., 6, 66n6, 102
Watkins, Daniel P., 105
Wawrzyn, Leinhard, 267n15
Weiskel, Thomas, 49n7
Wellek, René, 4, 20n1
Wilkie, Brian, 172
Wilson, Jean, 10–11, 17, 279
Wilson, John, 115
Wilson, Milton, 5
Wittreich, Joseph Anthony, 212–13n23
Wolf, Christa, 11, 262–6, 268n33, 269nn36, 38, 42; *Kassandra*, 269n36; *No Place on Earth*, 11, 262–6
Wolfson, Susan, 105, 116, 127n4

Wollstonecraft, Mary, 234, 239, 247n20, 260–2, 268n27; *A Vindication of the Rights of Woman*, 250n35, 260–1; *The Wrongs of Woman; or, Maria*, 260–2
woman, veiled. See Shelley, Percy Bysshe
women: as object of exchange, 281; in Romanticism, 114, 117, 187, 251–66
Woodhouse, Richard, 92, 115
Woodman, Ross, 5
Wordsworth, Jonathan, 152
Wordsworth, William, 5, 9, 14–16, 28–30, 72, 74–7, 80, 84, 101, 106, 113, 117–18, 141–55, 157nn9–10, 12, 158n15, 160n24, 217n34; 'The Boy of Winander,' 30; *The Excursion*, 153; Lucy poems, 16, 29–30, 45, 49nn1, 4; *Michael*, 74; 'Nutting,' 146; *The Prelude*, 15, 136, 142, 146–55, 159n18, 217n34; *The Recluse*, 159n21; 'Revolution and Independence,' 152; 'There Was a Boy,' 146, 158n16

Yeats, William Butler, 126n1
Yeazell, Ruth Bernard, 98n25

Zizek, Slavoj, 158n14, 245n10